CELEBRITY/CULTURE

Over the past few decades, the public obsession with celebrity has exploded. There has also been a huge growth in the number of college and university courses and degrees on celebrity studies and celebrity journalism. Ellis Cashmore's *Celebrity/Culture* was among the first books to address this fascination, and remains the most comprehensive work of its kind. It explored the intriguing issue of celebrity culture: its origins, its meaning, and its global influence.

This fully updated and rewritten second edition investigates issues in celebrity culture from the paparazzi to politics, from voyeurism to self-perfection. Cashmore presents engaging case studies to analyze how social media has changed the nature of celebrity culture, and explores how we consume celebrity in today's society. His argument is driven by research, rather than invective. With pullout quotes and chapter summaries for ease of comprehension and teaching, this new edition is also available both as an eBook, and online in electronic format with abundant links and tooltips.

Cashmore considers in detail the evolution, development, and impact of celebrity culture in the public eye. This book will appeal to a wide undergraduate audience throughout the social sciences and humanities, in sociology, history, psychology, and media studies.

Ellis Cashmore is Professor of Culture, Media and Sport at Staffordshire University, UK. His recent books include *Beckham* (Polity, 2002), *Martin Scorsese's America* (Polity, 2009), *Making Sense of Sports* (fifth edition, Routledge, 2010), and *Beyond Black* (Bloomsbury Academic, 2012).

CELEBRITY/CULTURE

Second edition

ELLIS CASHMORE

Routledge
Taylor & Francis Group

NEW YORK AND LONDON

First published 2014
by Routledge
2 Park Square, Milton Park, Abingdon, Oxon OX14 4RN

and by Routledge
711 Third Avenue, New York, NY 10017

Routledge is an imprint of the Taylor & Francis Group, an informa business

If you want to access the enhanced edition of this title online but do not
have an access code, or have trouble accessing the enhanced edition with
the code provided, please contact AcademiceBooksSupport@informa.com
with proof of purchase to obtain a code and instructions on its use.

British Library Cataloguing-in-Publication Data
A catalogue record for this book is available from the British Library

Library of Congress Cataloguing-in-Publication Data
  Celebrity culture / Ellis Cashmore. — Second edition.
    pages cm
  Includes bibliographical references and index.
  1. Mass media and culture. 2. Celebrities. I. Title.
  P94.6.C376   2013
  306.4—dc23   2013010911

ISBN: 978-0-415-63109-9 (hbk)
ISBN: 978-0-415-63111-2 (pbk)
ISBN: 978-0-203-09713-7 (ebk)

Typeset in StoneSerif
by Apex CoVantage, LLC

Printed and bound by CPI Group (UK) Ltd, Croydon, CR0 4YY

CONTENTS

IMAGINATION

|SOME PEOPLE LIKE ME . . .
SOME DON'T

Victoria Beckham could have been forgiven for gloating. Reviled for years as the unsmiling one in a mediocrely talented yet universally acclaimed girl band, taunted for marrying a football player-cum-model-cum-global-icon, and ridiculed for her failure as a solo artist, reality tv star, and practically every other endeavor she tried, Victoria struggled to find a purpose in life outside that of an all-purpose celebrity.

So, when she decided to swap wearing designer clothes for designing the clothes herself, another grandiloquent failure was confidently expected by all. Victoria, friend of Domenico Dolce, Donatella Versace, Marc Jacobs, and everybody else who's anybody in the world of fashion, was a 24-inch-waist clotheshorse with whopping shades, not the creative director of

CHAPTER HIGHLIGHTS

- Celebrities are not people: they are what we imagine people are like
- There is a close link between celebrity culture and consumer society
- Consumers aren't drawn to celebrities by what they do, but by who they are
- The global media's focus on entertainment and sport had radical effects
- Before Madonna, entertainers avoided scandal; after her, they pursued it
- Several scholars suggest celebrities exist in a "pseudoenvironment" in our minds

a fashion house. It was like a sci-fi film fan deciding he wanted to direct a prequel to *2001: A space odyssey*. "You have no experience of directing; in fact you've never acted, nor stood behind a camera," someone might issue a reminder, only to be rebuked: "So what? I have money."

There were omens. Celebrity fashion lines rarely succeed, not even when the celebrity is at the height of her powers. JLo, for example, got her comeuppance when she tried to launch her own Sweetface label. Undeterred, Victoria planned a *prêt à porter* line with aspirations to compete with the elite in New York, London, and Paris. It sounded like another Victoria catastrophe in waiting.

The timing of the launch wasn't especially auspicious either. Victoria's debut as a designer was at New York fashion week in September 2008. In the same month, the investment bank Lehman Brothers collapsed, precipitating a global financial meltdown and the worst recession since the 1930s. But there was a surprise: reviewers were impressed by her catwalk shows, prestigious department stores competed for the right to sell her clothes, and customers, in turn, paid serious money to wear Victoria Beckham frocks and, later, accessories like bags and sunglasses. Turnover grew 120 percent in each of the three years after the launch and Victoria won the Designer Brand Award at the 2012 British Fashion Awards. The barely believable success of Victoria's label, both critical and commercial, took not just the fashion industry, but everybody, by surprise.

So, by September 2010, when she announced a new line called "Victoria," the artist formerly known as Posh probably felt herself changing from a fledgling waterfowl with a broad blunt bill and a waddling gait to an elegant bird of grace with all-white plumage – though, to many, she would always be just an ugly duckling lucky enough to lay golden eggs. As Victoria told the *Financial Times*' fashion editor Vanessa Friedman: "I'm a very polarizing figure: some people like me and some people really don't" (December 9, 2011).

Being loathed, detested, or abhorred never damaged a celebrity's career.

Being loathed, detested, or abhorred never damaged a celebrity's career: as long as the figure can elicit strong emotions from a wide constituency of consumers, he or she remains in business. Indifference is the reaction every celebrity or aspiring celebrity needs to avoid. Victoria must have become aware of that during her years with the Spice Girls (1994–98 and 2007–08), a band that sold 75 million cds (and counting). She also seems to have learned that a white lie dropped into an otherwise truthful narrative never hurts: "From the beginning I didn't want people to confuse Victoria Beckham the brand with the surname Beckham." As if.

With no formal design training or background in the fashion trade, did she really believe that her creations would stand any chance of success if she'd launched them incognito or in the name of, say, her sister Louise Adams? Contrary to her declaration, the whole rationale of a clothes range bearing her name was to invite a confusion of the brand with the surname. "Beckham" has been used to sell cars, cologne, razors, underwear, engine oil, felt-tipped pens, and enough commodities to keep eBay busy for years. Maybe the attempt to sell high-end habiliments was audacious, given Victoria's track record; but anything, literally *anything*, bearing the imprimatur Beckham was bound to get the world's attention.

Why? Not, we might guess, because of a belief in the innate talent of Victoria or that of her husband, a prodigious athlete in his day but in the sleepy autumn of his sports career at the time of the launch. Nor because Victoria was vested with any great values or principles that would distinguish her as, to use a clichéd term, role model. She was regularly lambasted as a living advertisement for anorexia nervosa and c-section births. The answer is not nearly so simple or glib, nor as implausible as these. It will take me the rest of this book to spell it out.

The story of how we – and I mean the world's population – came to be entranced by celebrities is, depending on your perspective, fantastic, inspired, repugnant, shameful, cataclysmic, or catastrophic. It is the story of a culture, again depending on perspective, driven by commercial interests, impelled by religious desiderata, designed, engineered, delivered by the media, and, this time regardless of perspective, perpetuated by you, me, and every other person who has ever watched tv, read a magazine, shopped online, or in some other way consumed commodities.

What we'll discover is that, when we discuss celebrities, we are not actually discussing people, at least not in the flesh-and-blood sense of the word. We're discussing people as we imagine them. Of course, there is a human being named Victoria Beckham who heads and whose name adorns a fashion label. There is also a Victoria Beckham who exists independently of time and space and who resides in our imaginations. In other words, the Victoria we imagine her to be. Loved and hated, probably in equal measures, Victoria's pre-eminent ability is not in her singing or designing. She is able to fascinate us. And by fascinate I mean draw our attention and interest to the point where we feel unable to resist.

STIMULATING DESIRE |

"Illiteracy, innumeracy, attention deficits, close-mindedness, civic ignorance, junk science, celebrity worship, anti-rationalism, and outright disdain for intellectualism." Wendy Kaminer lists some of the lamentable features of modern life (2008: 91). (Year of publication followed, where appropriate, by page numbers will be given in brackets throughout the text, with a full bibliography at the end of the book.) Notice how celebrity worship is right in there with illiteracy, close-mindedness, and the other afflictions. For some, our fascination with the lives of other people is apocalyptic, a sure sign that we are well and truly into an age of unreason. This is not a view I share. We certainly have a puzzling fascination with others, but, while illiteracy and the other features of modern life are unequivocally unwelcome, celebrity worship has an uncertain status, and one worth deeper investigation.

We've been incited, of course. In the early 1980s, we wouldn't instantly and greedily gobble up stories about the so-called private lives of the rich and famous. Our appetites have been whetted, our tastes cultivated. How, when, why, by whom, and with what consequences? There are answers to all these and more questions, most of them involving destruction – the destruction of unquestioned beliefs, and suppositions we have about celebs.

For example, you could argue that the most interesting things about celebrity culture are the least important – the celebrities, that is the actual real-life people who are the objects of our fascination. Less interesting but much more important is *our* preoccupation with famous persons whose lives never intersect with our own and whose fortunes make no material difference to us. Also interesting is the reason for the extravagant value we attach to the lives of public figures whose actual accomplishments may be limited, but whose visibility is extensive. Then there is the global industrial apparatus geared to producing talent-free entertainers, or even "ordinary people" who crave fleeting renown. Or consumer society and the relentless drive to convert everything and everyone into commodities that can be sold like items on a supermarket shelf. These all seem worthy of our attention.

You can't understand anything without context: the circumstances surrounding something, the conditions under which it comes into being, and the situations that precede and follow it. Celebrity culture is no exception. It didn't pop out of a vacuum: there were conditions, triggering episodes, and deep causes. The conditions include the proliferation of media in the 1980s and the loss in confidence in established forms of leadership and authority that happened around the same time. I'll deal with these in chapters to come. By triggers, I mean specific events and the people involved in them: like the scandalous picture of Elizabeth Taylor and Richard Burton, the emergence and death of Diana, and, most importantly, Madonna. Again, all these will be covered. The cause of celebrity culture insinuates us in a larger story, that of consumer society, and, in a sense, this story runs throughout the book, though I'll expand a little before we go on. (I also lay out these and other key features in a timeline toward the end of the book.)

The cast of characters that make up today's generation of celebrities couldn't be more saleable if they had barcodes. You don't need to be a cynic to realize that the instant someone scales the heights of public visibility and makes it into the headlines or onto television and becomes tweet-able subject matter, they start selling. If they're not directly selling dvds, movies, cds, concert tours, or books, they're indirectly selling cosmetics, cars, household appliances, and every other imaginable piece of merchandise.

Some might argue: that's what they're for – to sell. For instance, in their book on sports celebrities, David L. Andrews and Steven J. Jackson define their object of study as "a product of commercial culture, imbued with symbolic values, which seek to stimulate desire and identification among the consuming populace" (2001: 9).

All celebrities, not just sports stars, are simultaneously producers and products of a culture in which people as well as articles can be bought and sold in the marketplace; this is what Andrews and Jackson mean by a commercial culture. Celebrities are imbued with, or drenched in, feelings, qualities, or, as the authors point out, values that induce us to desire things, particularly the things we associate with them. If we identify with celebrities – by which I presume Andrews and Jackson mean relate to or feel we share characteristics or thinking with – we are likely to buy the kind of commodities we link with them.

This sounds an almost callous interpretation of celebrities. Are they really just devices produced to part us from our hard-earned money? Not "just," though they certainly have that effect. When you think about it, everything we consumers do in relation to celebrities involves spending money. Whether it's buying magazines, books, downloads, dvds, cinema or concert tickets, subscriptions to television channels, or the gazillions of products available in shops or online, we are involved in the kind of commercial activity, Andrews and Jackson have in mind.

This probably strikes you as a one-dimensional assessment; but it has merit. After all, entertainers and sports stars have, for years, sold tickets to cinemas or sports events on their name value. They've also operated sidelines in endorsements, allowing their names and images to be linked with products they might never have used, in exchange for hard cash. Contemporary celebrity culture brought with it a significant change.

> *Celebrities have become articles of trade that can be bought and sold in a marketplace.*

Other writers, whose work I review in later chapters, argue that today's celebrity culture is an extension of a collective preoccupation with the famous. It has longstanding historical antecedents. I think differently: there is something distinct about today's celebrity culture. Instead of being devices for marketing films, music, or the consumer products they endorsed, the celebrities became products themselves. They are now commodities in the sense that they've become articles of trade that can be bought and sold in a marketplace. Obviously, you can't buy *them*; but you can buy their representations, their sounds, and the products with which they're associated. Consumers pay for that presence.

You'd have to be a conspiracy theorist to leave it there, though. The image of a cabal of capitalist supremos huddled around a table plotting the next phase of consumer society and contriving the idea of changing famous people from moving advertisements to actual commodities is a delectable one. But it doesn't really play. We need a more detailed investigation into the changes that led us – the consumers, the fans, the audience – to embrace the celebs and, significantly, spend money in the process.

FAME WITHOUT EFFORT |

Celebrity culture became a feature of social life, especially in the developed world, during the late 1980s/early 1990s, and extended into the twenty-first century, assisted by a global media, which promoted, lauded, sometimes abominated, and occasionally annihilated figures, principally from entertainment and sports.

We became progressively preoccupied with famous persons in whom we endowed great meaning, though without really reflecting on why. Their public visibility, or profile, seemed to be more crucial than what they said or did. Only rarely did we ask: "Why do I want to know about this person?" or "Why did this person become famous in the first place?" The phrase "famous for being famous" was once a tautological joke. It eventually became a reasonable explanation of why someone or other was fêted.

By the end of the 1990s, the bar had been lowered: in previous decades, famous figures, or "personalities" as they were often called, had to work harder to achieve fame or notoriety. The Rolling Stones had to trash countless hotel rooms and get busted for drugs. The Sex Pistols had to remain determinedly obnoxious even on their days off. Even Elizabeth Taylor, who reigned empress-like in the 1960s, intrigued her global audience with extra-marital improprieties. And they had to produce music and films too. (More on Taylor in the next chapter.)

Now, their essays in sleaze and scandal seem unacceptably devoid of depravity. We demand something different of today's celebrities. What's more, we don't want to wait for it to be discovered: celebs must surrender themselves to life in a kind of virtual Panopticon – the ideal prison where the cells are arranged around a central watchtower in which concealed authority figures can inspect without being inspected. We, the fans, are in the watchtower and the celebs are open to our inspection. The moment they withdraw or become reticent, we lose interest and start peering at others. Just as we vote wannabe celebs out of the *Big Brother* house, we can send celebs to oblivion. And we know it.

> *We're not hapless chumps who just luxuriate in whatever is dropped on us.*

Skilled in the art of celeb-making and celeb-breaking, we consumers have more power collectively than at any time in history. Contrary to how we're often depicted, we're not hapless chumps who just luxuriate in whatever is dropped on us. We're educated in the arts of celeb-production by the very channels that present them. Put another way, we didn't just look at the pictures: we've become able readers. In fact, we do most of the work. This is Joshua Gamson's argument and one I find completely persuasive. His 1994 study portrays fans as knowing and savvy participants in the celebrity production process: "The position audiences embrace includes the roles of simultaneous voyeurs of and performers in commercial culture" (1994: 137).

All the entertainers did was make themselves available. Madonna (b. 1958) might have been the first to render her manufacture completely transparent, but everyone who followed was almost forced to do likewise. Even if celebs were bashful about revealing to their fans evidence of the elaborate and monstrously expensive publicity and marketing that went into videos, cds, stage acts, movies, and, indeed, themselves, fans were aware enough to figure it out for themselves. The pleasure in being in celebrity culture is that the consumer observes, secure in the knowledge that he or she is actually not just an observer, but a player too.

Consumers know that the accomplishments of many of the people they follow are insubstantial and that their effects on society are inconsequential. They know that so-and-so became famous because she slept (and told) with someone who was vaguely a "someone." And that a former reality show contestant earns several million a year in spite of a self-acknowledged absence of intellect, taste, knowledge, skill, or anything worthy of merit. We know these things: we just choose not to dwell on them for long or see them as reasons to stop following them. It's more enjoyable to participate in the joys of celebrity culture.

And, crucially, we are prepared to keep dealing: we pay and the celebrities supply us with . . . what exactly? They don't exactly sell their labor, or expertise, so much as their presence. In other words, they just appear. As Moya Luckett puts it: "Celebrity feeds on exposure without work . . . fame without effort" (2010: 40).

Luckett contrasts this with the state of being a famous or exceptionally gifted performer in the world of entertainment or sports: "At some level stardom depends on work," she writes. "The star's work defines an on- and off-screen (or record, or video) self, cleaving his or her image into public and private" (2010: 40).

So, Luckett distinguishes between celebrities and stars, the latter, she argues, being the possessors of valuable skills, which they peddle. They also cleave, or split apart, their image into public and private aspects. But are we fascinated by, say, Tom

Cruise because of his dramatic performances, or because of his weird affiliation with Scientology, his stern repudiation of the suggestion that he is gay, his serial marriages, and his extraordinary behavior on *Oprah* on May 23, 2005? Cruise's private life never seemed especially private, if by private we mean not to be shared with or revealed to others. "The celebrity tends to connote a primary emphasis on the star's private life, rather than his or her professional roles," writes Sarah Sinwell, indicating how Luckett's distinction between stars and celebrities is far from clear-cut (2010: 126).

Consumers aren't drawn to stars by their "work," by which Luckett presumably means the activities that involve efforts to entertain, whether in films, on stage, on the catwalk, and other public places where they exhibit their skills. The celebrity's talent has no necessary relationship to his or her celebrity status. Contestants on a reality television show have no conspicuous talent, yet they often get status, if only for a short period. Once they're in the celebrity labor market, they can start dispensing the same resource that makes Hollywood actors and global rock stars celebrities: not talent, but presence. People like Kim Kardashian and Amy Childs have no official work, anyway: they rose to prominence in the reality tv show *Keeping Up with the Kardashians* and the dramality *The Only Way Is Essex* respectively. In these shows, their lack of anything resembling what used to pass for talent and their sheer ordinariness were paramount. They were both, if the reader will excuse the word, *celebrified*: I'll define celebrify as "to invest common persons with great importance." As long as consumers maintain an interest in them, they remain the beneficiaries of what Ronald Bishop calls "the high-intensity version of fame" (2011).

Like it or loathe it, celebrity culture is with us: it surrounds us and even invades us. It shapes our thought and conduct, style and manner. It affects, and is affected by, not just hardcore fans but by entire populations whose lives have been changed by the shift from manufacturing to service societies and the corresponding shift from plain consumer to aspirational consumer – a change we'll focus on shortly.

"The mass media with their cult of celebrity and their attempt to surround it with glamour and excitement have made Americans a nation of fans and moviegoers," wrote Christopher Lasch in 1979. Reflecting on what he called *The Culture of Narcissism*, Lasch added: "The media give substance to and thus intensify narcissistic dreams of fame and glory, encourage the common man to identify himself with the stars and to hate the 'herd' and make it more and more difficult for him to accept the banality of everyday existence" (1980: 21).

We survive by dreaming narcissistic dreams.

Since then, we've been further encouraged to identify with the stars. But, far from making it more difficult for us to accept the "banality of everyday existence," celebrity culture seems to have had the opposite effect: it enables us to accommodate it. True, we might secretly harbor and perhaps quite explicitly express dissatisfaction with our lives, but the invisible attachment to the glitzy world of the celebs functions as a lifeline. We survive by dreaming those "narcissistic dreams" Lasch thought to be so damaging. Maybe they are. That's an issue we will need to consider toward the end of the book rather than at the start. For now, let's take Lasch's point about the media (we tend not to use "mass" nowadays).

A peculiarity of celebrity culture is the shift of emphasis from achievement-based fame to media-driven renown. We still talk about stars and, to a lesser degree, stardom, but, as Luckett's slightly misguided point indicated, stars are no longer famous for their official work.

In 2000, David Giles argued that: "The ultimate modern celebrity is the member of the public who becomes famous solely through media involvement" (2000: 25). While the "ultimate" celebrity's rise might be attributable "solely" to the media, celebrities typically perform some deed, however modest, to attract initial attention. That deed might involve an appearance on a television quiz show, a criminal action, or an inept showing at a major sports event. In other words, conduct that would hardly be regarded as commendable and deserving of recognition in earlier eras, perhaps as recently as the 1980s.

During the late 1980s and early 1990s, however, our concept of merit changed. Figures who traditionally earned distinction and drew praise for their efforts vied with characters whose achievements were often uncertain. Literally worthless individuals, it seemed, began cropping up. What's more, they commanded interest for nothing in particular. In fact, they were not completely worthless, worth being an equivalent value of merit conferred on someone or something by a population. Whether the neophyte celebs actually deserved reverence is not a question I'm going to answer in this book. But I'll give the reasons why so many others believed they deserved it. All sorts of characters who, in another age, might be viewed as unworthy of attention ascended from obscurity to public visibility and, in some cases, global fame without seeming to do anything at all.

What they *did* do was appear; their images were relayed to millions via television and internet sites; newspapers recorded their exploits; magazines recounted their thoughts. "Media involvement," to repeat Giles' term, was the key: celebrities engaged the media. And we were delighted: at least, the response to the new generation of celebs suggested this. The world was being persuaded that people with no talent, no obvious gifts, nor any characteristic worthy of distinction were deserving of our serious attention just because they were in the media. It worked.

There are reasons why the media changed its focus and with such dramatic effect. The first is in the iconoclastic tendencies of photographers that became known collectively as the paparazzi. Fatigued, perhaps bored and certainly inured to the anodyne output of the Hollywood film industry, fans eagerly devoured the work of journalists who ignored the unwritten rules about the boundaries between private and public life. The entertainment industry had previously controlled the release of information on stars' private lives. The paparazzi discovered that fans had an appetite for another version; the one in which famous faces were caught in embarrassing moments, doing things they weren't supposed to and looking like they shouldn't.

So, by the time of the extraterrestrial changes in broadcasting, consumers had become quite habituated to peering into the hitherto well-protected private lives of movie and music stars. Few could have predicted how the time-space compression introduced by media technology would have affected their ability not just to peer but to examine and scrutinize in forensic detail. The globalization of the media introduced the capacity to transmit large volumes of information around the world, not just quickly, but instantly. By information, I mean news, entertainment, and, perhaps most crucially, advertising.

Satellites, or transponders, were the instruments of the media's global expansion. By wrapping the world in an invisible network of communications, satellite broadcasters were able to bounce information off satellites and send them literally anywhere. Satellite television companies recognized no national boundaries. This effectively meant that virtually everyone on earth was part of one huge market. It also meant that the size and power of corporations grew, leading to increasing control over economic and institutional resources and, much more importantly, an enhanced capacity to shape popular attitudes, beliefs, and values.

Rupert Murdoch, perhaps more than any other media figure, exploited the opportunities offered by the satellite technology pioneered in the 1960s, and the deregulation and privatization of the television industry in the 1980s and early 1990s. In February 1989, Murdoch's European satellite started beaming programs via satellite through his Sky network. A decade later, his various channels reached 66 percent of the world's population.

The problem with having so many channels was content: what do you fill them with? MTV supplied a clue. To keep so much of the world riveted to the screen, television networks needed a formula. Televised programming detached itself from fixed content and began firing off in the direction of entertainment, for which we should read *amusement* – something that occupies us agreeably, diverting our minds from matters that might prompt introspection, analysis, or reflection. This is not to suggest that drama that provokes contemplation or critical examination can't be entertaining too, nor even that the narratives of soaps or cartoons are not open to critical reading. And it certainly doesn't underestimate the viewers' speedy acquisition of skills for screening and skimming information. But, for the most part, entertainment doesn't prompt us to modify ourselves in any substantive way.

Light entertainment, to use a more indicative term, became a staple of a formula that demanded only a modest level of attention from viewers. Music+movies+sport. Asked to respond to this in the 1990s, an informed person might have said: people will soon get sick of it; they will feel as if they're suffocating under a superabundance of froth. This didn't prove to be the case. Of course, the communications revolution didn't end with television, and the proliferation of multimedia brought a further layer of information conduits, notably the internet.

These changes in the media's orientation had an impact on the relationships between performers and the newly emergent media. Even before it was called showbusiness, the entertainment industry provided individual artists who drew acclaim and were used as selling points. From nineteenth-century minstrel shows, through ragtime, the British music halls, silent film, radio, and, of course, theater, popular entertainment forms invariably provided a showcase for figures who distinguished themselves from their contemporaries. The Hollywood star system, beginning in the 1940s, was able to exploit this as no other industry ever had, operating a smooth-functioning, factory-like production line in which "stars" were treated much as commodities. Their use value was in generating box-office sales.

> *After her fourth album in 1989, Madonna appears to have seen the future.*

While the concept of producing stars rather than waiting for them to emerge stayed largely intact until the mid-1980s, the newly prolific media both offered different opportunities and demanded a different kind of engagement with artists. Madonna, more than any other entertainer, realized this. After the success of her fourth album, *Like a Prayer*, in 1989, Madonna appears to have seen the future: the days when people got to be famous and stayed that way through just making movies, having hit records, or writing bestsellers were approaching an end. The most important feature of the coming age was visibility: doing was less important than just being in the public gaze. With so many channels of communication being filled up with all manner of entertainment, there was bound to be an overflow of entertainers, most of whom would make little impression on the public consciousness. The ones who did were those who would not just make themselves visible, but transparent – there was no contradiction.

Madonna not only epitomized this, but also helped it materialize. She seems to have struck a bargain with the media. It was something like: "I will tell you more, show you more about me than any other rock or movie star in history; I will disclose my personal secrets, share my fears, joys, sorrows, what makes me happy or sad, angry or gratified; I will be more candid and unrestricted in my interviews than any other entertainer. In other words, I'll be completely see-through. In return, I want coverage like no other: I want to be omnipresent, ubiquitous, and pervasive – I want to be everywhere, all the time." It was a captivating *quid pro quo*. As the 1980s turned into the 1990s, Madonna was, as she wanted to be, everywhere.

Madonna's dressing room on the Blonde Ambition tour of 1991 must have been like an echo chamber for celebrity culture: massed media workers would cram in to probe for information and would probably not leave disappointed. Fourteen years after the Blonde Ambition tour, which was diarized in the movie *Truth or Dare*, or *In Bed with Madonna* as it was called in Britain, Gwen Stefani griped about the media, but shrugged: "I understand how the game works" (quoted by Duerden 2005: 12). The rules of that game were drafted in the late 1980s and Madonna played no small part in their formulation. You almost wonder whether Madonna set out to reinvigorate popular culture by continually breaking rules and getting rewarded for her misbehavior. Probably not. But, encouraged by her early successes, she seems to have used them as guides. I won't reveal my argument yet. Let's just say it produced what Gabler hails the "art form of the 21st century" (2009).

|IN OUR HEADS

"Celebrities exist because people have the capacity to fantasize," writes Andrew Houston. He goes on: "Fantasy is usually conceived as a scenario wherein a person's desire is realized" (2010: 94). Houston, a drama scholar, believes celebrity culture functions as a kind of drama we stage in our own minds. Our *dramatis personae* are the actors we see in the popular media and we write our own scripts, according to our own wishes. As Houston concludes: "Our attraction to celebrities is a lesson in how to desire." Celebrity culture, in this conception, becomes a theatre of the senses.

> *Celebrities exist because people have the capacity to fantasize.*
>
> **ANDREW HOUSTON, 2010**

Neal Gabler, a cultural historian and film critic, seems to agree. "Celebrity really isn't a person. Celebrity is more like a vast, multicharacter show," he suggests. "Celebrity is narrative, even though we understandably conflate the protagonist of the narrative with the narrative itself and use the terms interchangeably" (2009).

While he doesn't define exactly what he means by narrative, I presume he refers to an unbroken account, consisting of incidents and people that connect to form an overall story. The story may be a chronicle, a history, or a record of events, and it may incorporate elements of a fable in the sense that it conveys a moral or lesson.

Anthony J. Ferri, a professor of journalism, invokes a term used by Walter Lippman in 1922, to link the imagined celebrities to the actual characters we read and gossip about. There is, he reckons, "a distinction between their real environment or the objectified world, and the 'pseudoenvironment' made up of the images in our heads of the world outside" (2010: 407).

None of these helps us understand why we have become so drawn to celebrities in recent years, though Ferri offers the view: "Celebrities, whether they are acting out a role in a particular medium or behaving badly in everyday life, help us purge our frustrations." I'll return to this, but for now merely want to record the thoughts of three writers, all from different intellectual backgrounds, but all agreed that, when we talk or think about celebrities, we are not referring to actual people, but rather to ideas, thoughts, concepts, or mental impressions of those people. What Daniel Harris calls mirages: "Our contact with celebrities is so limited that we view them as mirages" (2008b: 619).

"Fantasies? Images? Mirages? What kind of nonsense is this? Surely celebrities are real people," readers might respond. Clearly, there are such physical beings as Kim, Amy, Madonna, and the innumerable other celebrities who populate not just our mental landscape but also the cultural landscape. They're not just physical people though, claims Nigel Thrift: "The glamorous celebrity is neither person nor thing but something in between, an unobtainable reality, an imaginary friend, and an accessory" (2008: 19).

The "unobtainable" person only becomes obtainable when we are actively involved. So, when we come to examining celebrity culture, our focus should be "less on celebrity than on the mass public's ability to create the celebrity, the ways in which the public can confer and deny, circulate and consume fame," to steal a phrase from English professor Stacey Margolis (2009: 714).

What does she mean? *Confer*: grant or bestow. *Deny*: refuse to give. *Circulate*: move continuously and freely. *Consume*: ingest; buy; use; preoccupy; completely destroy. Margolis uses these terms to describe how we can both award or take away, communicate and engage with fame. We make people famous; and we also make them obscure. Consumers are the final arbiters: they – that is, *we* – serve out the plaudits and the condemnations. And to people we don't actually know.

We shouldn't underestimate the colossal power of interest groups in promoting and sustaining celebrity culture. Barry King remarks: "All kinds of performers – rock stars, sports stars, literary stars, actors, politicians – circulate through the media via appearances in diverse media forms and formats" (2010: 9).

King doesn't mean they literally circulate: he is describing how representations, images, or even sounds move continuously through media, which is also continuously moving, changing shape and size. The media are our confederates, as are the corporations that stand to gain, or lose, from the fortunes of people who vie for our attentions.

A confederate is an accomplice, a collaborator, an ally; something or someone that is in league with us, and not manipulating, taking advantage of, or just playing us. There are costs involved in being part of a culture in which we attach value to the kind of people and objects that would not rate a moment's thought as recently as 15 years ago. Today, celebrities contribute to daily life at practically every level, from the institutional to the personal; and they're factors in how we create and attach meanings to all manner of events that affect us. It could be argued that celebrities help us think about ourselves and, as such, incite us to refashion our self-identities. There are many more claims, several of which will appear in the pages to come.

The problem with many accounts of celebrity culture is that they strain to be coherent. There's nothing wrong with an argument that's clear, logical, and consistent, but social life usually resists being squeezed into unity. My intention is not to provide an uncluttered, well-ordered theory: it is to open readers' eyes to the unruly complexity of celebrity culture, replete with loose ends and insoluble puzzles. I make no apology for this. Learning always implicates you in realizing not so much how much you know, but how much you don't: the brighter the light, the darker the shadows.

HISTORY

CHAMPIONS, POETS, AND WARRIORS, 63 BC–AD 1700

"A celebrity, like Tinkerbell, is the creation of the beholder's gaze and the symbolic expression of their needs," writes Aviad Kleinberg, a history professor, who thinks celebrities have been around for centuries (2011: 397). Why "like Tinkerbell"? The Hollywoodized fairy from J. M. Barrie's 1904 play *Peter Pan*, who sprinkled the pixie dust that made humans fly, became a fabulous icon for Walt Disney, and did, of course, spring from Barrie's imagination. But, once you accept the premise of a boy with magical powers who never matured and his villainous adversary, a pirate with a hook instead of a right hand, a fairy is not such a leap: in Barrie's world, all the characters are real. So what is the status of celebrities in Kleinberg's world?

The comparison with Tinkerbell confuses what is otherwise a clear argument: Kleinberg believes celebrities, far from being recent arrivals, have been around for centuries. He claims: "Successful charioteers, gladiators, Olympic champions, Bedouin poets, Balkan warriors could all be celebrities," though not because of their resemblance to today's celebrities. For Kleinberg, the similarities of actual people are less important than their reception. "Why does one community celebrate lawmen and another outlaws?" he asks, his point being that, throughout history, there have been people who have "powers attributed to them."

At various stages, military leaders, artists, musicians, and so on have been attributed, or credited with, extraordinary powers of some kind. Kleinberg thinks these characters qualify as celebrities. In other words, there have, for long, been individuals who are not in themselves special, but have been assigned a special status by their "communities." This leads Kleinberg to the conclusion that celebrities and the cultures that conjure them up have been around since antiquity.

Kleinberg is one of several scholars, especially historians, who insist there is little if anything novel or unprecedented about celebrity culture. It appears fresh and without parallel in history; but close inspection suggests there have been formative versions of celebrity at earlier periods in history. Scholars convey a panorama of 1,600 years, in which politicians, warriors, and a miscellany of others have been immortalized in the popular mind.

The condition of being well known is immemorial: dramatists and philosophers earned reputations for their wisdom, and political and military leaders for notable achievements after the growth of city-states in the Aegean from 900 BC. Homer, Pythagoras, and Plato remain canonical figures. Alexander the Great commemorated victories over the Persian Empire by naming cities in his honor: the Egyptian port Alexandria was founded in 332 BC. Alexander has been identified by Leo Braudy as the first figure to foment his own fame (1997).

Augustus (63 BC–AD 14), the first Roman emperor, who gained supreme power in 31 BC, is Robert Garland's archetypal celebrity: "He knew full well how to turn the fascination of the Roman public with his superstar status to his distinct political advantage . . . he would easily have outdone even his adoptive father Julius Caesar" (2010: 485).

Tom Payne finds evidence of celebrity culture in Homeric tales of the eighth century BC, in the myth of the sixteenth-century German necromancer Dr Faustus, and in the Renaissance and Romantic Period ("the age of the individual genius") of the seventeenth century. Its content is variable, though its presence is universal. He hears echoes of Euripides' Electra when he tells the tale of Britney Spears. Our legends, fables, and folk tales reveal celebrity narratives. "We make patterns out of them, and make tales of the famous fit the structures of fables," writes Payne (2009: 239).

Certainly, famous people appear throughout history; indeed, the way we study history is principally through the decisions and deeds of the famous. But celebrities index a particular type of historical context, one in which fame and accomplishments are decoupled. In other words, famous figures are famous for *something*: their achievements are recognized by others as worthy, so their fame is a byproduct. For Braudy and Payne, celebrity is just a synonym for the state of being widely recognized: it is a pre-modern mode of renown. This is too much of a stretch for other scholars, who prefer to see celebrity as a product of modernity.

The scientific revolution of the seventeenth century, the Enlightenment of the eighteenth, and the Industrial Revolution of the late eighteenth and early nineteenth centuries instigated changes that brought an age in which modern values predominated. Modernity was characterized by a confidence in scientific knowledge and the explanatory power of theories (such as those of Darwin, Freud, and Einstein), a decline in the social importance of religion and the emergence of a more secular culture (i.e. more worldly than sacred), and a striving toward more universal standards, absolute principles, and uniformity. So, when scholars such as Tena L. Helton assert, "Celebrity is not a modern phenomenon," we should appreciate that modernity brought with it a new kind of fame (2010: 500).

STARS OF MASS CULTURE, 1700–1901

"In the first half of the eighteenth century a process occurred by which a nascent culture of celebrity began to form side by side with an existing culture of fame," writes Stella Tillyard (2005: 22). She identifies three specific sets of circumstances in England, all of which combined to produce a particular type of culture: a weak English monarchy with limited moral authority, the lapsing of legislation controlling the numbers of printing presses and, to some extent, printing itself, "and a public interested in new ways of thinking about other people and themselves." The new thinking involved "speculation and gossip far freer, more direct, personal and scurrilous than we have today."

Shearer West partly agrees but remains mindful of the scale of this embryonic celebrity culture: "The circulation and consumption of print media and theatre in the smallish world of eighteenth century London would have generated a different kind of social dynamic than the multimedia exploitation of celebrities today." As an example: "An eighteenth century Londoner would have been likely to meet [David] Garrick [an actor-manager, 1717–79] on the street; in the twenty-first century Madonna is only glimpsed through the telephoto lens of the voyeuristic paparazzi" (2004: 611).

West's mention of print media is worth amplifying: Johannes Gutenberg (1400–68) had used movable type and a press to produce his famous Gutenberg Bible in the mid-fifteenth century. His technology hastened the scientific revolution by permitting the circulation of evidence of experiments and theories. It also made possible the proliferation of periodicals that eventually became the mass media (mass, in this instance, meaning a large number of consumers). Is fame in the sense we understand it today possible without even a print, let alone electronic, media? Those who argue fame is immemorial don't consider whether the absence of mass media complicates their analysis.

Newspapers and journals had been around since the early 1800s. In the absence of radio and television, fame was disseminated via these publications. The invention of the rotary press in the 1840s and the construction of news wire services both quickened the rate at which reports could be made available and broadened the scope of circulations. News was what happened yesterday, not the week before. Nor was news necessarily reportage of people and events that directly concerned the reader. Newspapers covered items of interest, that is, information that appealed to "novelty, interest and curiosity," as Neil Postman puts it (1985: 65).

Rising literacy rates, when combined with technological innovations and improvements in transportation, resulted in a 400 percent rise in the circulation of daily newspapers between 1870 and the end of the century. Some publications, such as *McClure's*, chronicled the feats of admirable and heroic figures, not just military leaders, but also inventors and heads of business corporations. There was also another type of curiosity: entertainers intrigued people. In her "Media and the rise of celebrity culture," Amy Henderson quotes an American newspaper story written in the 1880s: "It is remarkable how much attention the stage and things pertaining to it are receiving nowadays from the magazines . . . it has become a topic of conversation among all classes, furnishing an endless gossip to the trivial, and intellectual interest to the serious" (1992: 2).

I'll return to gossip and entertainers in a while, but, for a moment, I want to note the interconnectedness of fame and mass society "characterized by urbanization, consumer capitalism, political democracy, mass literacy and the growth of mass media," as Simon Morgan encapsulates it (2011: 95). Morgan offers the thought that "the 'construction' of fame . . . began with the emergence of a cheap mass-circulation press around the middle of the nineteenth century" (2011: 98).

Lenard R. Berlanstein also identifies the mid-nineteenth century as the time when celebrity culture "'trickled down' to the masses from media," and "in this sense, celebrity was an interest that united rather than divided the upper classes and the masses" (2004: 82). Berlanstein is primarily interested in the ways in which flamboyant European women became what he considers "the first celebrities"; he offers the interesting view that "ostentatious display, frivolity, and glamour" were more important than achievement. The journals of the day made this visible to the masses through words and illustrations.

Remember, photography had not yet been perfected. Louis Daguerre (1789–1851) invented the first practical photographic process, known as the daguerreotype, but the reproduction of images in various tones of gray, i.e. halftone, was not commercially available until the 1880s. This prompts Heather McPherson to ask: "How was celebrity constructed and disseminated before photography in the age of Garrick and [Sarah] Siddons [a noted English Shakespearean actor, 1755–1831]?" (2000: 281). Portraits, miniatures, and plates are the answer, according to McPherson. Illustrations were vital transmitters.

Charles Dickens (1812–70) built a literary reputation with his chronicles of poverty, corruption, and the inefficiencies of the English legal system. His novels have been the source of many films, among them *Oliver Twist* (first published 1837–38), *A Christmas Carol* (1843), and *Great Expectations* (1860–61). "Many years before the apparently unprecedented global fame of modern celebrities like Elvis and the Beatles, Dickens experienced the euphoria and then the claustrophobia of his own fame," reckons Juliet John. "He was the first self-made media star of the age of mass culture" (2007: 178).

> **Dickens experienced the euphoria and then the claustrophobia of his own fame.**
> **JULIET JOHN, 2007**

Dickens became a print-borne celebrity, according to John; though, unlike the majority of contemporary celebrities, he grew uncomfortable with "his acute sense of himself as a commodity to be exploited." During a promotional visit to America, he realized that "he was a pawn in the larger dynamics of a mass culture that he could not control" (2007: 180).

What distinguishes John's analysis from many other arguments about notable historical figures who approximate to what we today call celebrities is that she examines Dickens' responses to his rise in prominence. He discerned how he had inadvertently surrendered control over much of his professional and private life. Nowadays, literary figures, no less than showbusiness and sports stars, understand that public renown involves this kind of sacrifice. In the 1840s, with the mass media facilitating international fame in a way previously unknown, Dickens experienced "a sense of violation."

John's claim that Dickens was the first star of mass culture is a bold one and shouldn't pass without question. Figures who were prominent at a time when the media's size and influence were modest were known, though not subject to anything like the same kind of scrutiny either enjoyed or endured by today's celebrities. John's more potent argument concerns Dickens' perception that he was treated as a fungible commodity and his presence in America an exchangeable resource. Dickens may have complained about being treated as a commodity; later, celebrities welcomed the process.

The glare of publicity was discomfiting for Dickens in 1842, but he would have found it unbearable after the Victorian era

(1837–1901). Victorian attitudes and values were characterized by a stifling and prudish moral earnestness. "Fame rested on social distance, deference, and adoration," writes Robert W. Snyder (2003: 440).

When a media fortified with printing presses and embellished with halftones turned its attentions to deserving individuals, the social distance closed up. Charles L. Ponce de Leon (2002) argues that the journalism of the early twentieth century emphasized individual achievement and success: it profiled personalities, their public affairs, and, crucially, the more personal aspects of their lives. Journalists' attentions swung toward what Ponce de Leon calls "the subject's real self." The period about which he is writing, 1890–1940, witnessed other cultural changes, the rise of a consumer culture being one of them. This, perhaps more than any other aspect of social change, was responsible for further narrowing of the distance between the famous and their audience.

SCREEN SELVES, 1902–29 |

Recall Henderson's observation that, from the 1880s, figures of interest and gossip came from "the stage and things," by which she means entertainment, or what became known as showbusiness. The print media, aided from the 1920s by radio, elevated diverse figures to visibility. Some of the famous figures at the turn of the century were showmen, such as Blondin (1824–97), the highwire performer who crossed Niagara Falls several times, William F. Cody (1846–1917), or "Buffalo Bill," who toured the world with his Wild West Show, and Harry Houdini (1874–1926), the great escapologist. All achieved even greater fame later in the century, when they became subjects of Hollywood films, Cody several times over, Houdini in George Marshall's 1953 *Houdini*. In fact, the lives of practically all the heroes and antiheroes of that time were later turned into biopics: *Dempsey* (1983), *Lindbergh* (1990), *The Babe* (1991), and *Dillinger* (1973) included.

Arguably more interesting and revealing were the people who went to great lengths to avoid being famous, yet were not so much publicized as mythicized by the media. "As early as 1927, actress Clara Bow, filmdom's preeminent 'It girl,' distanced herself from the ebullient character that made her famous," writes Kirk Curnutt, who quotes her: "The person you see on the screen is not my true self at all; it's my screen self" (1999: 294).

Howard Hughes and Greta Garbo were recluses, but their lives were turned into public property almost independently of them. Both sought obscurity, at least ostensibly – in Garbo's case, her trademark plea "I want to be alone" became an effective marketing tool. The myths surrounding them grew immeasurably larger than the people themselves, suggesting a new role for print and wireless radio media in creating public interest rather than merely publishing and broadcasting in response to public interest. (Hughes, the eccentric movie producer, plane maker, and hotelier, was the focus of a 2004 movie, *The Aviator*.)

Stories of artists behaving badly had become almost a subfield of journalism. Decorum was preserved by presenting these as having genuine "human interest," a euphemism for voyeuristic appeal. Few entertainers actually seemed set on scandalizing themselves. Most tried to accommodate the demand for information on them by releasing it in controlled bursts.

The mission to illuminate and expose the "real self" behind the screen or stage façade, meanwhile, galvanized journalists. Ponce de Leon argues that one of the effects of the ever-more intrusive media's reportage of the private lives of the famous was that of "promoting the notion that success, happiness and self-fulfillment had little to do with material goods or social status – a comforting thought for people to embrace in a society increasingly characterized by stark inequalities of wealth and power" (2002: 108).

With the Victorian era consigned to history, twentieth-century modernity brought with it different aspirations, goals, and ambitions, as well as opportunities for achieving them amid the inequalities germane to industrial society and the market economy on which it was based. Entertainers were conspicuously achieving individuals and, in this sense, became models of success. As the haves' half of a haves/have-nots division, stars had responsibilities. "Fame was not free of obligation," writes Curnutt (1999: 292). "Regardless of métier, the 1930s media personality was required to prove herself a natural talent and not a manufactured phenomenon."

People of limited means could read and hear about their efforts and, in the process, identify with them without actually thinking they were like them. While they took voyeuristic pleasure from peering surreptitiously through peepholes or eavesdropping on putative private conversations, there was also comfort from the reassurance that the talented, rich, and famous had home lives just like everyone else.

Richard deCordova (1990) offers the thought that audiences were fascinated by the secrets of the stars, especially salacious secrets. Virginia L. Blum adds: "Early on [in the twentieth century] we find audiences interested in undermining the very equivalence between real and 'reel' lives" (2003: 149).

The rules of the game, as we called them in the previous chapter, were being rendered inoperative, with journalists eager to venture into hitherto occluded aspects of entertainers' lives and entertainers eager to allow them, but only so far. If the private self complemented the public self, then there was harmony. Discord was another thing entirely. So it was important to grant the media access, but offer them only cosmetic fidelity. The most famous casualty of the failure to harmonize was Roscoe "Fatty" Arbuckle (1887–1933), a silent screen comic, who became the first actor to earn a million dollars a year. At the height of his powers, his crushing personal unhappiness became known: an alcoholic and smackhead, he was framed for both rape and murder. His ruination served as a valuable caution that, in a part of the world known for its earthquakes, reputations were as precarious as matchstick models. (More about Arbuckle in Chapter 6.)

The response was effective. As Snyder puts it: "Image managers learned how to calibrate the balance of public exposure [and] journalists were caught – knowingly and sometimes with their own connivance – in struggles for interview time with celebrities that compromised their own independence" (2003: 441).

Publicists, agents, managers, and the gamut of other personnel exploiting, working for, or attending to the needs of the entertainers became self-taught guardians of images. Far from being interrogators, the journalists, whose livelihood depended on access to those entertainers, either accepted the stories that came out of the dream factory's publicity departments or conspired with them to produce anemic stories. It was a cozy alliance designed to protect the famous, most of them from the "flickers," as the silent films of the early twentieth century were called, or vaudeville, the variety music hall entertainment. It relieved the entertainers of pestering journalists, while satisfying those journalists by providing them with good "human interest" copy.

Perhaps the event that presaged the appearance of the media not only as conveyors but also as creators of information was the faked car accident and supposed death in 1910 of "The Biograph Girl," as Florence Lawrence was called (after the Biograph Studio to which she was contracted). Previously, screen actors had performed anonymously. Carl Laemmle (1867–1939), the pioneer mogul and founder of Universal Pictures, signed Lawrence from Biograph and contrived his ingenious if deceptive way of getting her name into lights. It worked and, in so doing, alerted the industry to the value of managing public images. In this sense, it inaugurated a new era in the film industry.

By the time "talkies" replaced silent movies in the late 1920s, there was an embryonic public relations industry. The

P. T. Barnum-style "no publicity is bad publicity" canon looked manifestly untrue: pr was predicated on producing news, not just any news, but news that enhanced or complemented a particular image. Press releases, press conferences, press accreditation: these were all parts of an apparatus assembled in the first decades of the century. They helped establish the industrial unit known as the film industry, the star system, or the Hollywood machine.

The machine cranked into action by the Lawrence hoax proved an efficient and reliable way of turning base ore into precious metal – box-office gold. The studio chiefs might secretly have known that there was no such thing as god-given star quality, but they were not about to admit it; not while movie fans seemed enchanted by the notion. The big studios perpetrated and perpetuated the concept of a Hollywood cosmos that was populated by luminous celestial bodies who were remote and untouchable, quite unlike the rest of us.

The studios never actually perfected the machine. After all, for every Rudolph Valentino, Cary Grant, or Greta Garbo, there was a John Gilbert (a silent screen star who vanished with the talkies), Jennifer Jones, whom David O. Selznick tried to turn into a star, or Anna Sten, Samuel Goldwyn's would-be successor to Garbo. But, for the most part, it was the machinery that produced stars and, in this sense, it was an early version of vertical integration: actors were the studios' primary materials; they were contracted to appear in films that were produced, marketed, and distributed by those same studios. It was an "economic system," according to Douglas Gomery (2005).

"The first decades of the twentieth century witnessed the advent of a luxuriously developed consumer and mass culture – the emergence of modern advertising firms, the apotheosis of the department store, the wide ownership of the automobile, and the increasingly glamorous vision of Hollywood celebrity," reflects Michael Newbury (2011: 126). On the surface, these might have looked like separate developments; but they were separate only in the same way that engine, wheels, chassis, and body are separate parts of a car.

In 1932, the Frank Borzage film of *A Farewell to Arms* brought its source book's author Ernest Hemingway international praise and recognition. According to Leonard Leff, this initiated a struggle between Hemingway, the authentic man and author with serious aesthetic ambitions, and "Hemingway," the macho persona lauded by the media for his non-literary pursuits. Leff's 1997 book *Hemingway and his Conspirators* is a study of "the making of American culture" and details how Hemingway's publishers, agents, and the film industry that turned his novels into blockbusters – *For Whom the Bell Tolls* (1943) and *To Have and Have Not* (1945) were among the others – collectively created a public character with which the writer was never comfortable. Leff suggests that there was something fraudulent about the onstage "Hemingway": he uses inverted commas to distinguish this media creation from the authentic artist.

The public representation was a construction of a developing apparatus of production. Hemingway, while anguished, colluded with the film industry, not only by making changes to style and content, but also in perpetuating the image of a venturesome, testosterone-pumped man's man who was as happy in a bar or a bullring as sitting behind his typewriter. Suzanne Del Gizzo argues that eventually, "he [Hemingway] found it difficult to counter his well-known and familiar image publicly, in part because to do so would involve deeply personal revelations, but perhaps also because such revelations would have undermined the popular image he had worked so hard to create" (2010: 25).

This interpretation of the two Hemingways chimes with Daniel Boorstin's "guide to pseudo-events," which records the predominance of the image and, by implication, suggests that authentically "real" people lay behind the premeditated performances and designed personalities on offer to consumers (1992).

"Key to understanding the attraction of celebrity," writes Morgan, "is the fan's ability to develop an imagined intimacy with the celebrity subject" (2011: 99). One actor, perhaps more than any other, espied the emergent interest of the media in entertainers as individuals with personalities, rather than just as the occupants of screen or stage roles. Taking advantage of the shift in journalistic priorities, Errol Flynn (1909–59) conducted his private life in a way that mirrored his onscreen persona and adventures. A modest actor with little training, the English-educated Tasmanian made his mark in Hollywood with swashbuckling performances in the title roles of *Captain Blood* (1935), *The Adventures of Robin Hood* (1938), and *Gentleman Jim* (Corbett, the prize fighter) (1942). His offscreen affrays suggested a symmetry between the personal and the professional, though it was his amatory performances that launched gossip of mythic dimensions. "He seemed to wish to elevate the artistic self to the mythical status of his fictional creations," states his entry in the Biography Resource Center (2004). By the time he took on another title role in *The Adventures of Don Juan* in 1948, aged nearly 40, Flynn's reputation had grown to the point where there was an almost perfect congruence.

Heroic deeds were the traditional route to great renown, but the Hollywood assembly line was beginning to churn out figures of what we might call faux greatness: actors who played characters, fictional or real, who performed heroic deeds. Errol Flynn was one such actor, of course, though the archetypal faux hero was to arrive in 1939 with the release of John Ford's seminal western *Stagecoach*, in which John Wayne played the Ringo Kid, an outlaw seeking revenge for the murder of his father and brother. Although he'd appeared in earlier films, *Stagecoach* launched Wayne on a career of – and this time, the cliché is apt – epic proportions. As James T. Campbell writes in his review " 'Print the legend': John Wayne and postwar American culture," he became "not only one of the most recognized figures in the world but one of the most influential, the seeming quintessence of American manhood" (2000: 466).

How was this possible? After all, Wayne never saw real military action. Despite this, he was regarded as an all-purpose hero. "Reality and representation," as Campbell points out, were becoming "so interwoven as to be inextricable" (2000: 465). Wayne's screen exploits saw him as Davy Crockett at *The Alamo* (1960), on *The Sands of Iwo Jima* (1949) in the Second World War, and leading *The Green Berets* (1968) in Vietnam. It was hard to think of Wayne as separate from these roles.

> *Like John Wayne and Errol Flynn, James Cagney became indistinguishable from the fictional characters he played.*

In a similar way, it was difficult to imagine James Cagney the actor as distinct from the two-fisted tough guy who shot fast and talked even faster. Four Warner Bros gangster classics from *The Public Enemy* (1931) to *White Heat* (1949) created an imperishable image of Cagney as a scowling, pugnacious mobster whose natural environment was the mean streets of inter-war America. Like Wayne and, before him, Flynn, Cagney became indistinguishable from the fictional characters he played. The melding was achieved, in large part, through careful selection of film roles, of course. But there was also precision in the way other kinds of images were presented. Gamson argues that the development of sound and film realism in the 1930s signaled the end of entertainers as "popularly 'elected' gods and goddesses" and the start of stars as ordinary mortals with whom audiences could feel "a sense of connection and intimacy."

"Crucial to this process was the ubiquitous narrative principle of the 'inside' journey into the 'real lives' of celebrities," writes Gamson (1992: 8). Fans were treated to larger and larger amounts of information about the stars' so-called private lives. So, it was imperative that all the information dispensed complemented rather than contradicted screen representations. Flynn's career would have been jeopardized if the "revelation" that he was bisexual published in 1980 by Charles Higham had been released during his heyday in the 1930s and 1940s. As interest in the "real lives" of entertainers grew, the film industry was forced to exercise greater control over material in popular publications, such as *American Magazine* and *Photoplay.*

Managing publicity became a smoothly functioning machine-like practice. The trick, according to Gamson, was to preserve the notion of natural talent, so that the stars appeared as ordinary people, in one sense, but ordinary people who were gifted with a little something extra: charisma, magic, *je ne sais quoi* – an indefinable quality that made them stars. The publicity machine's job was to highlight or amplify the natural qualities of its subjects. Unlike their predecessors, they weren't inclined to fabricate stories or stage stunts.

On Gamson's account, the success of the manufacturing process depended on its ability to obscure its own rationale. If it had presented its subjects not as real people but as studio artifice – which is what they were – the entire narrative would have collapsed. It would have been like the conmen who made *The Emperor's New Clothes* letting the crowd in on their hoax before they let the naked monarch go strutting among his public. Not that cineastes were totally gullible. While most magazines enjoyed a snug relationship with the major studios' pr machines in the 1930s, some were staking out a critical distance from them in the 1940s. The idea that fame was manufactured rather than the result of some natural divine gift became popular and this caused the occasional contretemps. "But the skepticism heightened by increasingly visible publicity activities was contained more commonly by being acknowledged," Gamson remarks (1992: 12).

The same author elaborates this point in his book *Claims to Fame: Celebrity in contemporary America*, where he writes of the irony that became more pronounced from the 1940s, when studios "luxuriated" in stories of artificial production. Far from trying to conceal their aims, they prided themselves on their machinations. On Gamson's account this visibility was later to become a key feature of a celebrity production process in which fans were "simultaneous voyeurs of and performers in commercial culture" (1994: 137).

While Gamson doesn't mention it, an event in 1950 effected a modification to the production process. James Stewart, who, like other Hollywood actors, was under studio contract, negotiated a different kind of contract for the Anthony Mann film *Winchester '73*. In taking a share of the profits as well as a flat studio rate, he paved the way for others to assert their independence from the studios.

Obviously, without an audience, no one can be famous. Fans genuinely make certain people famous. The publicity machine's conceit was in telling audiences exactly that: "You are the ones who deserve the credit for making so-and-so famous. And the reason you've made them famous is because you recognize their abundant talent!"

This message was perfectly consistent with what Ponce de Leon, as we noted earlier, called "the spread of the market economy and the rise of democratic, individualistic values." Ponce de Leon argues that the growth of fame in the way we understand it today was accompanied by the development of a definition of achievement that fitted neatly with the consumer culture that was emerging in the first decades of the twentieth century.

Let me illustrate this with a classic study from the 1930s. Robert Merton concluded that our ultimate goal was material success, which we wanted to display, and display conspicuously. Good clothes, cars, electrical appliances: these were all commodities that were relatively recent arrivals in the marketplace and ones that people wanted, perhaps craved. People valued their ability to consume and they were encouraged through various media, such as schools and particularly advertising, to maximize this ability – within certain boundaries. Merton's view was that the boundaries defined the legitimate means through which people could achieve their goals. There are right ways and wrong ways to achieve them. When people strove for material goods but lacked the means to get them, they often opted for the wrong ways. In other words, they stole the goods that the advertising hoarding and the radio commercials were telling them they should have. The "non-conforming" conduct, as Merton called it, was a response to this condition.

The study underscored the point that the market was turning us all into avid buyers of consumable products – consumers. Merton was writing at the cusp: at a time when consumable goods were more available, but before we had fully arrived at the view that happiness, satisfaction, and fulfillment could actually be bought and sold. That became more visible in the 1950s and 1960s. In the 1930s and 1940s, the pursuit of modest success became possible through purchasing. Commodities gave people a means of defining success.

They also provided an important, if restricted, autonomy: people could choose what they wanted to buy. This may seem a minor privilege, but it hastened a sense of individualism. In exercising choice in the way they spent their hard-earned cash, people were offered the chance to see themselves as shapers of their own limited destinies.

The period saw the growth of status consciousness, as newly affluent workers began to entertain the possibility of social mobility, of rising through a hierarchy in which the central criterion was not so much wealth or income as possessions, specifically the kind of possessions that brought kudos, cachet, prestige – status.

People began to display their status through their transportation, accommodation, and attire. So cars were no longer a means of traveling from A to B, but moving advertisements of relative success. Homes were powerful signifiers of standing, their location becoming more important than their number of rooms. While the term designer label didn't come into popular usage until 1977 – when Warren Hirsh, of Murjani, persuaded American socialite Gloria Vanderbilt to lend her name to denim jeans – the concept of advertising success through clothes is much older; in the 1940s, clothes began to acquire new potential. Looking successful became a precondition of actually being successful.

If earlier generations had understood their social position as relatively changeless, as if fixed by immutable forces, the postwar cohort understood it quite differently. Position, rank, or station were temporary. This was underlined in a series of studies. In many ways an exemplary product of its time, *The Affluent Worker* research of the early 1960s showed British industrial workers motivated by a desire for self-improvement, especially through the acquisition of material possessions (Goldthorpe *et al.* 1968). In the USA, there were several studies, many of them synthesized by the widely read scholar Vance Packard (1914–96), who, in 1959, published his argument that personal fulfillment and social recognition were twinned in the minds of newly aspirational Americans who were striving for consumer symbols of success. They were, as the title of Packard's book suggested, *The Status Seekers*.

| CONSUMPTION AS A WAY OF LIFE, 1960–2000

When Packard was compiling his data, television was still in its infancy; by the time his book was published, the tube had found its way into nine in ten American households; the ratio was similar in Britain. Consumers were ambushed by television. It was as if advertisers had been lying in wait, biding their time while waiting for the arrival of the medium that would transform the entire industry, not to mention the lifestyles of the population of the USA and, eventually, everywhere else. In Britain, commercial television didn't arrive until the mid-1950s when the BBC lost its monopoly. But, in the USA, advertising drove television from the outset. Commercial "messages," as advertisements were called, punctuated every program, stealthily refining their approach so as to target precise demographic sectors.

Advertising quickened the change to a consumer society. In a sense, we've always been consumers. From the mid-1950s, we became aspirational consumers, buying not just to subsist, but to make statements about our progress in the world. The commercials we saw on tv provided a kind of blueprint. They didn't just show merchandise; they revealed its hidden properties. For example, shampoo was ostensibly to clean hair, but it provided shine, silkiness, and radiance. Cars were to be experienced rather than driven. Packard turned his attention to advertising in his *The Hidden Persuaders*, first published in 1957. In the 1950s, advertising was relatively primitive. Today, every advertisement tries to sell something other than the actual product: a lifestyle, an image, or a solution to a problem with which it has no obvious association. As Christopher Lasch pointed out in his book *The Culture of Narcissism*: "Advertising serves not so much to advertise products as to promote consumption as a way of life" (1980: 72).

Part of Lasch's thesis, which we'll examine in more detail later in the book, is that, once the economies of the USA and, we might add, most of what we now call Old Europe had reached the point where technology was capable of satisfying basic material needs, they started to rely on the creation of new consumer demands – "on convincing people to buy goods for which they are unaware of any need until the 'need' is forcibly brought to their attention by the mass media" (1980: 72).

What is luxury? Costly homes, clothes, furniture, food? Expensive vacations? Anything that we desire for comfort or enjoyment but that isn't indispensable? In other words, what we could actually do without. Microwaves, cell phones and personal computers, for example? Cars, air conditioning, central heating, television? Most people would call these necessities rather than luxuries. It wasn't always so. During the second half of the twentieth century, there was a redefinition of luxuries as essentials. Items that were once seen as either fantastic toys or the exclusive property of the seriously rich were incorporated into a culture of consumption. From where we're now standing, there seems no end in sight for the incorporation: it just goes on and on. This is a global process too: commodities that would have once been seen as extravagances now circulate around the world as fluidly as the images and messages that advertise them.

Packard's study of *The Waste Makers* (1960), who designed and built commodities so that they would become obsolete in a few years, combined with his other work to portray a society in which traditional values, such as abstinence, prudence, and frugality, were replaced by the ethic of wellbeing. The narcissistic impulse to pay close attention to one's own physical self was complemented by an endless supply of commodities that would, in some way, enhance, enrich, or just improve experience.

The advertising industry was central to the transition to a consumer culture. It governed the depiction of reality in which material goods became constituent parts of a good life "conceived as endless novelty, change and excitement, as the titillation of the senses by every available stimulant," according to Lasch in *The True and Only Heaven* (1991: 520).

Advertising became ubiquitous: not just on the hoardings, on television, or at the movies, but in every aspect of a media that, by the 1960s, had become the dominant source of information. The media of the consumer culture inverted the idea that success, happiness, and self-fulfillment had little to do with material goods or social status – which, as we should recall, Ponce de Leon argued was promoted by the media in the early years of the century (2002: 108). It proved an intoxicating prospect: success, happiness, self-fulfillment – the good life – could be bought.

Through the 1960s and 1970s, the media, especially advertising and television, became increasingly interested in, or, if Lasch is to be believed, obsessed by, youth, glamour, sex, money, violence, and celebrity. The media implicitly promoted the conception of a good life; the one lived by the affluent consumer with a cornucopia of material goods. Hollywood stars fitted the bill.

In a sense, movie stars were exemplars, though, by the 1960s, musicians, particularly rock musicians, were jostling for a place among the elite. Frank Sinatra had reaped the benefits of a career-transforming role in 1953's *From Here to Eternity* and became a prototype for many other singers, most notably Elvis Presley. In this period, success in the music industry was never enough: film was still the *sine qua non* – the ultimate qualification. The big band leader Glenn Miller didn't make the transition himself, though he was so ably portrayed by James Stewart in *The Glenn Miller Story* (1953) nine years after his death in 1944 that his reputation grew posthumously as a result.

The expansion of demand for consumer goods and the continual revision of the criteria for luxury and necessity were products of a market economy and a culture in which the ethic of individualism prevailed. People were consumers, aspirational consumers at that. And they were sovereign decision-makers: they made the choices about what to buy. The ethic is stronger now than ever.

> *A change in the way we visualize ourselves was vital to what was later to become celebrity culture . . . We saw ourselves not so much as parts of a design but as designers.*

A change in the way we visualize ourselves was vital to what was later to become celebrity culture: as masters of our fortune and deciders of our own fate, we had the means to distinguish ourselves from others. We saw ourselves not so much as parts of a design but as designers ourselves. Some writers on America, such as Warren Susman, believe that this change in orientation is as recent as the 1930s, when the concept of divine providence began to weaken (1984). We were no longer creatures who enjoyed the protection of god: we were out there fending for ourselves. As such, we wanted to make the best we possibly could out of ourselves and, when successful, display this to others. Advertising provided us with ways of defining and exhibiting ourselves. The stars were its accomplices.

|HUMAN COMMODITIES, THE 21ST CENTURY

"Beginning in the 1950s," writes Gamson, "celebrity began to be commonly represented not only as *useful to* selling and business, but as business itself, *created by selling*" (1992: 14). He means that, while Hollywood stars and other figures of renown had been used to declare their approval of commodities – endorsers, in other words – they began to be treated as commodities in their own right.

Both functions fitted hand-in-glove with the emergent consumer society. If you wanted someone to give a product credibility, who better than a well-known and possibly respected figure from the media? It would have been reassuring for consumers to see figures they knew, liked, and in whom they had confidence giving their support to a product – even if they suspected they'd been paid to do so. The unexpected bonus arrived when, as Gamson suggests, the figures themselves became products that could be bought and sold on the marketplace just like any other piece of merchandise.

The process through which any person or thing can be converted into a saleable object is known as commodification. The stars became raw material that needed refining, developing, and packaging before they could be turned into marketable wares to be displayed in films, theater, and, later, on television. But, once they were commercially viable, they were like property.

This was and is a key process in celebrity culture: making people tradeable commodities, objects for consumption.

Remember: the publicity machinery was already running. No one needed reminding of the importance of creating and maintaining an image, or a fabricated, popular representation that could be widely circulated and accepted by consumers. Commodification effectively doubled the ways through which those images could be manipulated and consumed.

The consumers were anything but passive. If Gamson is to be believed, they were empowered by the development, recognizing their roles in making and shaping careers, as well as ending them. Elisabeth Bronfen, in her essay "Celebrating catastrophe," points out "how the intensity of our gaze upon celebrity not only transforms the famous into commodities, but usually ends up destroying them" (2002: 181). Once our voyeurism reached a certain pitch, there was no other way to satisfy us other than ruining the very celebrity careers we had helped make. After consuming them, audiences consigned them to what Bronfen calls "the shadowy limbo of oblivion." We discarded them just like the commodities they resembled.

The trend continued, so that, by the mid-1990s, Jill Neimark was able to sum up: "Celebrities are borne aloft on images marketed, sold, and disseminated with a rapidity and cunning unimagined by the heroes of old, and then just as quickly cast aside" (1995: 56).

But, in the 1960s, the star-as-commodity idea was still in its infancy. It was a protracted infancy, according to Gamson, who reckons even early Hollywood "greats" such as Clark Gable and Myrna Loy in the 1930s were conscious that they were property owned by both the studios and, in a sense, the public (1994: 34–5). Yet this is not quite the same as being a commodity that can be produced, traded, and marketed. As Graeme Turner expresses it: "In this context, the celebrity's primary function is commercial and promotional . . . the celebrity is defined instrumentally, in terms of the role they play within the operation of the mass media, promotion and publicity industries" (2004: 9).

This is the "primary function" of contemporary celebrities, as far as Turner is concerned. It isn't their only one: in other words, they don't exist exclusively to assist in marketing operations. But, from the 1960s, marketing did become a bigger part of any star's remit. The very mention of their name could trigger an image powerful enough to change market behavior. Whether consumers bought a movie theater ticket, an LP (the forerunner of cds and downloads), a magazine, or any of the other countless items associated with the star, there was a money transaction. And, cumulatively, transactions drove consumer culture.

There is, as Michael Newbury puts it, "more to the well known than well-knowness" (2000: 272). "Fixing celebrity's origins requires the examination of something more than individual figures, though concentrating on such individuals may usefully make larger cultural processes concrete."

Over the past two chapters, we have examined several individual figures, always staying mindful of the distinct circumstances in which they emerged and, crucially, in which they were consumed. Popularity, fame, and reputations are not constant qualities: they change over time and the only way to make sense of celebrity today is to, as Newbury recommends, "document a change in the cultural comprehension of renown" (2000: 273).

The way we understand fame and celebrity today is particular and unique. A celebrity emerging from a reality tv show in the twenty-first century is just not known in the same way as Buffalo Bill was at the turn of the twentieth century, or Errol Flynn in the 1930s, Elizabeth Taylor in the 1960s, or even Madonna in the 1990s. They all, in a way, surrendered parts of their selves to an apparatus of promotion that became progressively elaborated through the twentieth century. And they could all lay fair claim to international fame. But the cultural contexts in which they came into view were as different from each other as they are different from today's context.

Celebrity, at least in the sense we recognize it, has origins in the late nineteenth century, when the circulation of newspapers featuring halftone photographs climbed and news was redefined as something that happened days rather than weeks before. Subsequent developments in the media, at first magazines and radio, then film, opened new horizons, while setting new limits. The free flow of both news and entertainment entitled populations to share in new sources of information; yet it also initiated something of a dependency. We not only relied on the media for information: we trusted and had confidence in them. The consequences of this are all around us: from where else do we get our information, if not the papers, radio, tv, or the net? What would we do if we had to do without all these, if only for a day or so? For right or wrong, the media became the machinery of addiction.

> *We became aspirational shoppers in a marketplace where public figures could be bought and sold as readily as breakfast cereal or washing machines.*

The "period of industrialization" was when the serial production of public images began in earnest in the 1930s, as motion pictures ascended to their paramount position in popular culture. Fraudulent as many public images were – Rock Hudson, who was gay, was projected as a rakishly handsome ladies' man, for example – they were emblems of a culture in transition. Consumerism and the market economy that encouraged individualism, freedom of choice, and unvarying demand for commodities effectively modernized populations into customers. We became aspirational shoppers in a marketplace where public figures could be bought and sold as readily as breakfast cereal or washing machines (themselves symbols of consumer society).

Looking at celebrity culture in this way is like taking off the back of a watch to expose its mechanism. You can see the cogs, springs, and levers moving synchronously, but you won't be able to tell the time till you glance at the dial. As the twentieth century unwound, the visible drama, the narrative, and the personalities were all open for public inspection and consumption. The overwhelming success of the entertainment industry throughout the twentieth century was testimony both to the reach and influence of the media and its elasticity in responding to changing tastes. The united power of the print and electronic media was irresistible. But, while remaining respectful of the stars, particularly those products of Hollywood, the media were also adaptive and, as tastes meandered away from the straight and narrow, the media too deviated.

When audiences gawped with relish at "candid" pictures of the famous, which began appearing with rapidity in the 1960s, they might just as well have called time on the unwritten code that had protected the stars' private lives. If, as some suspected, "authentic" people operated separately from the fabricated personae that appeared on screens and in print, then they were under siege. The paparazzi of the early 1960s wanted the image behind the image. This is why the shot of Elizabeth Taylor's indiscretion with Richard Burton was such a harbinger: it foreshadowed a change between the media and the stars. It declared a kind of open season. It was a genuinely iconic shot and I will examine it in the next chapter.

Publications that traded in amazing tales and gore exchanged gore for gossip and became unofficial organs of the rich and famous. The *National Enquirer* was the *primus inter pares*, introducing a new education in the indecencies of Hollywood life. Sales figures, as we noted, reflected a lively interest in the racy aspects of life at the top. Fidelity was not an issue.

If any single figure validated the power of the media in the 1980s and 1990s, it was Diana. She was virtually hijacked by paparazzi every time she appeared in public. Even when she didn't, there were enough quisling confidants to guarantee supplies of insider accounts. Diana's near-divine status wasn't solely the creation of media manipulation. Diana "was a ce-lebrity," as Lewis Lapham confirmed, "and celebrities are con-sumer products meant to be consumed" (1997: 11).

In a way, the entertainment industry had always treated its stars as consumer products, though it adjusted to meet the changing requirements in the 1980s. The multiplicity of tele-vision channels specializing in light entertainment opened up new opportunities, but it also set a new question for aspiring showbiz types: are you going to resist the brazen, usually disre-spectful, often insidious, and always inquisitive media; or meet them halfway when they come snooping into your private af-fairs? Put another way: you are a consumer product; are you going to be like a Lamborghini Murciélago, at around $330,000 with a waiting list of up to 18 months, or a Hyundai coupe?

Madonna didn't singlehandedly start celebrity culture as we know it. What she did was realize that Hyundais are accessible, affordable, and move out of showrooms in greater numbers than Lamborghinis. Abandoning any vestige of the old public vs. private domains, Madonna made her whole self available for commodification. She became the complete product. The dawning of her era saw the stars' music taking second place to what they looked like, whom they were dating, which diet they currently favored, and where they last did rehab.

After Madonna's seemingly inexorable rise, the rules of the game changed so fundamentally that no entertainer could sur-vive without extensive concessions to the media. Even then, the prospect was not scary enough to deter the legions of wan-nabes who couldn't wait to bare all in their efforts to become famous, albeit momentarily.

There are several levels to celebrity culture. The consumer-oriented market economy lies beneath a change in popular consciousness with freedom of choice and individual prefer-ence becoming primary values. An attendant technology-driven enlargement of the media had implications for the way we receive and consume not only information but also the products conveyed by that information. This, in turn, fueled consumer culture. In this way, consumers were both creators and creations. We – consumers – created celebrity culture with our voracious desire for new figures. We were also creations of an industrial process that fed us like rats in a maze, but which went wrong once we tasted the more scrumptious fare served up by voyeuristic journalism. It was at this point that celebrity culture, in the particular way we understand it today, began to take shape. Being a consumer no longer meant standing on the outside: it meant being an active player – a creator as well as consumer of celebrities.

MEDIA

ELIZABETH TAYLOR AND THE RISE OF THE PAPS

A million. It was unheard of. She might have topped the *Motion Picture Herald*'s "top ten box office" draws. But no female actor, or actress as it was in the 1950s, could seriously demand one million dollars for a single movie.

In September 1960, Elizabeth Taylor (1932–2011) arrived in London to begin work on *Cleopatra*. Twentieth Century Fox agreed to her unprecedented and, in those days, preposterous fee. Then again, this was the world's foremost screen goddess, a sparkling extravagance that mesmerized the world, not just with her acting, but with her turbulent private life. Famous enough to adorn the cover of *Time* magazine in 1949 when aged only 17, Taylor transformed from child star to superstar, commanding the attention of the planet.

In the course of her rise, Taylor had made a habit of getting involved in relationships that, while not scandalous, were out of the ordinary. She had been either involved with or married to men who had turned out to be abusive, alcoholic, or philandering. She'd also been attracted to the gay actor Montgomery Clift and married to Michael Wilding, who was 19 years her senior.

When she started shooting *Cleopatra*, she was married to Eddie Fisher, who happened to have been her ex-husband Mike Todd's best man at her wedding with Todd. Fisher himself had left his wife Debbie for Taylor. Ensconced at London's Dorchester hotel, Taylor's entourage, which included three children, several dogs and cats, and a large staff, lived up to expectations, having food specially brought in from around the world and embarking on shopping trips that would have shamed Mariah Carey. The movie script was in such dire need of rewriting that no actual filming was done before Taylor became dangerously ill and flew back to California to recuperate.

By summer 1961, the film was already beginning to look doomed. Members of its original cast dropped out and its director Rouben Mamoulian was replaced by Joseph L. Mankiewicz. When shooting resumed in September, the location was switched from London to Rome. All the time, the production costs were mounting. *Cleopatra* would eventually become the most expensive film to date, at an estimated $44 million.

Among the several personnel changes was the substitution of Richard Burton for Stephen Boyd in the role of Mark Antony. Burton landed the part after appearing as King Arthur in the Broadway production of *Camelot*. Having established himself in theater rather than film, Burton had distinguished himself playing many of the major Shakespearean roles. He had also received an Oscar nomination in 1952 for his part in the screen adaptation of Daphne du Maurier's *My Cousin Rachel*, in which he played opposite Olivia de Havilland.

While he was a respected actor, in terms of global fame, Burton wasn't in the same league as Taylor. And yet, together, with the enthusiastic assistance of a newly rapacious media, they were to figure prominently and collectively in one of the most dramatic changes in popular culture of the twentieth century.

Prior to *Cleopatra*, neither Taylor nor Burton had been tormented by the invasive photojournalists who had been memorably parodied in Federico Fellini's 1960 *La Dolce Vita*, a prophetic film in which one of the characters, named "Paparazzo," is a photographer who resorts to often manic means to secure his shots. Like other great fictional characters, such as Lothario, Romeo, and Pangloss, Paparazzo contributed his name to the popular vocabulary. In Italy, photographers were zealous chroniclers of the lives of those deemed worthy of public interest. Anita Ekberg, who had been in the Fellini film herself, had famously taken a bow-and-arrow to an especially inquisitive photographer and had unwittingly contributed to what was to become a genre – that of the paparazzi.

The 1950s and early 1960s defined a kind of golden age of glamour. Hollywood stars, in particular, were parts of a pantheon: like deities, they seemed to exist at a level above that of other mortals. They lived lives of such opulence, such splendor, such sublime beauty that they seemed unapproachable. And, in a genuine sense, they were. They secured themselves away and dripfed their fans with occasional personal appearances and carefully controlled silvery images. Even stepping off a plane was a procedure so meticulously rehearsed that ensuing photographs looked like portraits. This was an age when cameras were fitted with flash attachments and the pop of a bulb was an announcement that a star had arrived. Every picture evoked a wonderworld, one that was at once remote yet touchable, distant yet close.

Some photographers, however, were experimenting with a new piece of technology: the zoom lens. One of them was Marcello Geppetti (1933–98). Maybe he suspected that there was something going on between Taylor and Burton, or maybe he was just reconnoitering the exclusive sector of Rome's Mediterranean coast where the privileged moored their elegant crafts. Whatever his motives, Geppetti must have felt his pulse race as an image of Taylor and Burton came into his sight. Not just any old image either. Taylor lay on the deck of the yacht serene in the comfortable knowledge that she was away from prying eyes. Burton was craned across her body in an embrace that was unmistakably that of lovers. Geppetti snapped as his subjects kissed.

As an illustration of theories about the unpredictability of distant events, the closing of the lens shutter is not comparable with the flutter of a butterfly's wings somewhere over tropical Africa. But its unintended influence on subsequent events could hardly have been predicted. And, if there was a chaos theory of cultural change, this might qualify as evidence.

Geppetti's shot depicted Taylor and Burton, two married adults, a mother and a father, in the capital of a Catholic

The picture that launched celebrity culture? Elizabeth Taylor embraces Richard Burton, unaware of the presence of photographer Marcello Geppetti © Willi Schneider/Rex Features

country, indeed in the spiritual center of the Catholic world. Remember: this was 1962. The image signified an adulterous relationship. The product of Geppetti's initiative encircled the world, with newspapers and magazines featuring the picture alongside stories of an affair that started secretly but was now the most famous liaison in the world. Even the Vatican was moved to condemn the relationship. The US State Department was urged to revoke Burton's entry visa on the grounds that he was "detrimental to the morals of the youth of our nation."

Taylor's status as one of the world's most accredited beauties and, of course, the foremost female movie star ensured that the story would travel. Burton, a handsome thespian, with a solid track record of amorous affairs, made a great foil. But it was the fact that they were both married with children that elevated this above the level of an ordinary scandal. The outrage it prompted also signaled a new age was beginning.

Once, it was possible for Hollywood stars to divide themselves, presenting a public persona to their adoring audience while reserving a space for their private selves. The parts of their lives they preferred not to reveal were warily kept from the fans. The industry was geared up for this kind of dualism: after all, it thrived on images. The stories of the screen were complemented by the stories of the lives of those who inhabited the screen. Even compellingly newsworthy figures like Taylor were able to keep their distance. There might have been curiosity about her private life. But her audience knew only as much as she, or her advisers, thought appropriate. There was a respectful relationship between the media and objects of their attention. All that was about to be mixed up.

It wasn't just the Taylor–Burton image that changed the relationship. But there was a sense in which it signaled the change. As the dog days of summer succumb to the freshening fall, so the stars' days of peace and quiet gave way to an open season. They were now fair game.

> **Not even Taylor could prevent the intrusively ingenious Italian media spoiling a privacy that had never before been infringed.**

Not even Taylor, perhaps especially not Taylor, could prevent the intrusively ingenious Italian media spoiling her privacy, a privacy that had never before been seriously infringed. In Rome, the media weren't nearly as respectful, or as obedient, as they were in the USA. And, armed with a telephoto lens, they had the hardware to challenge most attempts to cordon off the private lives of stars.

A new era was beginning. Actually, it had been taking shape in continental Europe for some years before 1961. *La Dolce Vita* was a riotous, yet not entirely false, rendition of the Italian media. Its central character secures his exclusives by gatecrashing parties thrown by the rich and famous, whom he sometimes seduces and who then become scandalized by his stories. He gets caught up with a news item that could easily have jumped off this week's front page of the *National Enquirer*: CHILD SPOTS THE VIRGIN MARY.

Swedish actor Anita Ekberg (b. 1931), who was in the film, was involved in a life-imitates-art altercation with annoying cameramen (they were all male) outside her villa in Rome. Along with Brigitte Bardot, whom Geppetti caught lying sans bikini top in St Tropez, Gina Lollobrigida, and Sophia Loren, Ekberg was among an elite of women whom European photographers pursued.

Whether by accident or on purpose, photographers discovered that these and lesser stars were more interesting when provoked to anger than when allowed to present themselves in peace. As Tazio Secchiaroli, a contemporary of Geppetti and a probable model for the "Paparazzo" character in Fellini's film, reflected: "We found that, with small events created on purpose, we could earn 200,000 lira [about $1,100 today], while before we got 3,000" (quoted in Richards 1997: E.01).

Nowadays, off-guard shots of celebrities are more common than poses: we're used to seeing celebs shielding themselves, caught by surprise, fleeing, or gesticulating irritably, as if stung by having their personal space invaded. In the 1960s, the stars were used to being photographed in the way they, not the photographer, desired. They wanted to be seen as majestic, dignified, graceful, pleasing to the eye. The kind of way *Vogue* would portray them on its front cover. Photographers who specialized in catching them bleary-eyed during a night on the tiles, their mascara smudged, hair tousled, bra straps showing, were unwelcome.

If photographers could earn almost 70 times as much for these kinds of shots as they could for straightforward poses, then there must have been a market for them. Audiences might initially have been shocked to glimpse their favorite stars in unusual circumstances, with their dignity compromised yet looking uncannily like themselves. But they clearly got used to it and, eventually, came to expect it. Stylized shots must have seemed bland by comparison.

The Taylor–Burton shot was one of the triggers of celebrity culture: it sort of liberated not just photojournalists but the rest of the media, releasing them in new directions; but it also set off a chain reaction among the stars and, perhaps most importantly, the fans. They were the ones whose attention and money were needed, not just by the film industry that helped both develop and make use of the stars, but by the entire media surrounding that industry. After all, they all lived in a symbiotic world, in which the existence of each party benefited the others. Even the fans, whose cash kept the wheels of the industry turning, profited; they wouldn't watch, read about, and follow the exploits of the famous if they didn't get something from it. Their tastes were changing.

The fans were not like passive alien abductees whisked away and reprogrammed by the marauding media, then sent back with new appetites for humiliating pictures and salacious gossip. Yet there was a sense in which tastes changed to accommodate the variation in images. Compared to the output of the new generation of photojournalists, the designed shots seemed antiseptic, tame, bland, colorless, even disingenuous, and, worst of all, downright dull. After glimpsing the stars in the raw, so to speak, audiences would never be satisfied with lush, dreamy portraits that had been such staples of showbusiness.

The images and words that accompanied them might have piqued a routine curiosity in the stars. But never much more. The major Hollywood studios employed in-house photographers who, as Amy Henderson puts it in her essay "Media and the rise of celebrity culture," "created a style of portraiture that crystallized stardom" (1992: 5). The representations offered by the paparazzi had the opposite effect: the stars deliquesced like ice crystals on a radiator.

Scarcely credible as it was, onlookers watched the hitherto untouchable stars dissolve into characters who bore a remarkable resemblance to themselves. Did this make them any less fascinating? No: if anything, interest in them grew. Fans might previously have been served up answers to questions they never really cared about. Now, they were asking different questions, the answers to which had to be sought outside the official studio sources.

| MARILYN'S DEATH, A DEMOCRATIC EPIPHANY

Elizabeth Taylor's affair with Burton had awakened consumers to the guilty pleasures of scandal: they were yammering about the indiscretion and generating publicity for *Cleopatra*, which was to be released in 1963. The studio might have trembled when it heard how much Taylor wanted for her services, but her dalliance had brought an unexpected bounty. So it seemed like sour grapes when Marilyn Monroe whined: "Fox should start paying as much attention to me as they are paying to Elizabeth Taylor."

Marilyn, then 35, was getting $100,000 for her next film *Something's Got to Give* (1962). "Larry," she addressed photographer Lawrence Schiller when they were discussing a photoshoot in 1960, "if I do come out of the pool with nothing on, I want your guarantee that when your pictures appear on the covers of magazines, Elizabeth Taylor is not anywhere in the same issue." Schiller relates the story in his memoir *Marilyn & Me* (2012). Clearly vexed by the global attention – and money – Taylor had attracted, Marilyn was prepared to fight scandal with scandal. She duly stripped, plunged into the pool, and emerged naked, before sliding into a blue terry-cloth bathrobe. Schiller recalls how he took the shots and instantly and excitedly called the picture editor of *Paris Match*, assuring him he had "the first nudes of Marilyn in over ten years. The pictures are going to blow your mind!"

Marilyn remains the most alive dead person in history, rivaled only by Princess Diana.

The collection may not have become as iconic as the Geppetti image, but it confirmed Marilyn's position as the most shamelessly intemperate Hollywood star of the time. Yet Marilyn's torment continued when she was fired by Fox, in part because of the enormous budget overrun of Taylor's film. Marilyn's poor health caused several delays to *Something's Got to Give*'s production and, even though Fox relented, and rehired her, the movie was never completed. Marilyn died on August 5, 1962. The following year, Marilyn's close friend, President John F. Kennedy, was assassinated. In both cases, the loss of life was immediately followed by regeneration.

"Our contact with celebrities is so limited that we view them as mirages until the one event that restores them their real physical presence, their deaths, the moment of our greatest intimacy with them," writes Daniel Harris in his "Celebrity deaths" (2008b: 619). Harris's argument is that the death of celebrities is "the ultimate democratic epiphany" in that, in a sudden moment of revelation, their demise reminds us that, despite their status, they are "as liable to physical misfortunes as the best of us."

Barron H. Lerner has a similar view of sick celebrities whose illnesses are documented in the media for consumers' delectation (2006). Lerner examines how the rules of the game, as we called them, have changed over time. Steve McQueen's diagnosis of cancer, for instance, was first reported in 1980 by the *National Enquirer*, which based the report on a hospital nurse's aide's leak. Prior to this, the media respected the privacy of famous patients; after McQueen (1930–80), the media had no compunction about investigating the suffering of anybody, regardless of their public prominence.

The emotional reaction of consumers to sickness has become a factor in a kind of democratization of disease. The reaction to death is stronger: it serves to reinforce what Harris calls solidarity, by which I presume he means a unity or harmony that endures long after. Posthumous exposés may lay bare aspects of a celebrity's life that may change consumers' evaluations, but a dead person can't actually do anything to alter a bond forged by death. Marilyn may have set a deplorable example of ostentation and promiscuity in the 1950s, but on her death she was beatified. Indeed, later revelations made her seem more a victim than she ever did in life. Elton John and Bernie Taupin memorably used T.H. White's 1958 phrase "Candle in the wind" to capture her fragility in their 1973 song; they modified the lyrics in 1997 to eulogize Princess Diana, who was also worshiped more in death than in life.

Norma Jeane Mortenson may have died, but Marilyn lived on, making hers the first death to lead to a renewal and, for this reason, the first celebrity death. James Dean died earlier, in 1955, aged 24, and his image was borne on countless tee-shirts and posters. But his life was never probed and exhibited, and he was revered more for the postwar rebellious spirit of youth he personified than for himself.

Wheeler Winston Dixon (1999) observes how images of dead celebrities become frozen in time, surrounded with manufactured fantasies, immune from aging. The everlasting image of Marilyn, who was 36 when she died, is of a lucent-eyed, smolderingly vivacious, and affectingly shallow blonde. Her depths were plumbed only after her death. Hers was a death that guaranteed immortality. And there were others. Jimi Hendrix (1942–70), Elvis Presley (1935–77), John Lennon (1940–80), and Tupac Shakur (1971–96) were all sanctified in a secular sense. "Any negativity [about their lives] has long been digested by the popular culture – and they've stood the test of time," writes Robert Klara (2011: 10).

Helping them stand the test were corporations with interests in resurrecting them via music, film and merchandise. Digital technologies facilitated their appearance in advertising and, in the cases of Frank Sinatra (1915–98), on stage – in the form of a moving holographic image. All have been subjects of biopics, in Marilyn's case several times over. Her death started a cycle of renewal as writers, filmmakers, and corporations revived not just her image, but her existence in any exploitable form. Ross D. Petty and Denver D'Rozario have produced a cold-hearted analysis of the bonuses offered by the departed: "Living celebrities are both expensive and risky . . . Deceased celebrities have the advantage of being both less expensive and less likely to suddenly lose popularity" (2009: 37).

It's too trite to say Marilyn left a legacy: a cultural benefaction would be nearer. Her death changed the way consumers related to the death of a star: with sympathy at first, but later with a kind of intimacy suggested by Harris. Fans, even those who can remember Marilyn as a 24-year-old in *The Asphalt Jungle*

(1950), don't miss or mourn for her: she remained as much a celebrity presence as she ever had in her life.

Despite drawing acclaim for her roles in movies such as *The Seven Year Itch* (1955), *Bus Stop* (1956), and *Some Like It Hot* (1959), the myth of Marilyn grew larger, immeasurably larger, than the person or the body of work she left behind. She remains perhaps the most alive dead person in history, rivaled only by Princess Diana, to whom I will turn shortly.

| JUST AS WRETCHED AS YOU

In 1968, Generoso Pope moved the editorial headquarters of one of his magazines from New York to Lantana, Florida. There, beneath the cerulean skies, among the oleanders and palmettos, amid the cicadas and flamingos, the magazine grew just like hibiscus. Its circulation went from one million to three million.

Pope had bought the *National Enquirer* 14 years earlier and changed what used to be a horseracing guide into a weekly catalog of incredible and gruesome stories with headlines like I CUT OUT HER HEART AND STOMPED ON IT and I ATE MY BABY! The only news items consisted of stories about the excesses of Hollywood stars. Judy Garland (1922–69), in particular, was a munificent source of news: her drunken binges, overdoses, and serial marriages were stock items. When she died in 1969, the *National Enquirer* might have faced a crisis. But it adapted quite efficiently, specializing in stories about the Hollywood set's miscreant behavior.

In the 1960s, stars were much more circumspect about their lives; so the stories had to be pursued with vigilance. The Taylor–Burton story was like a hardy annual, popping up at regular intervals over several years. Its power to move magazine off newsstands was undeniable, though in the early 1970s the *National Enquirer* hit the equivalent of pay dirt when Sonny Bono (1935–98) and Cher Lapeer emerged as television show hosts, as well as the recording artists they had been in the 1960s. When the too-good-to-be-true couple started heading for their 1974 breakup, the magazine featured them consistently, taking a keen interest in either one's indiscretions. Warning shots about the end of their private lives had been fired in the 1960s. Sonny and Cher's marital collapse happened in full view of the world. The *National Enquirer* was selling five million copies per week by the mid-1970s.

Cher was developing into a kind of prototype contemporary celebrity. When she appeared with apple cheeks and blue jeans in 1965, she looked like she might have walked in straight from a trailer park. Then it was like Mountain Dew turning to Cristal champagne. But, unlike today's celebs, she was stung by tales of her extravagances. Billy Ingram, in his "A short history of the *National Enquirer*," recounts how, in 1976, Cher reacted gruffly to a report in the British newspaper the *Observer*, which, on her account, described her: "This woman lives in a two million-dollar house, spends 500 bucks a week on manicures, drives one of her three Ferraris, when she's not using her Rolls-Royce or Mercedes, has 600 pairs of shoes, and 1,000 beaded dresses, and she's not happy" (no date: 6). Nowadays, celebrities might be embarrassed by such frugality.

Cher became a staple with not only the *National Enquirer*, but also the other comparable publications that were launched in the mid-1970s. These included the Rupert Murdoch-owned *National Star*, *People*, and *US Weekly,* all appearing in 1974 and all specializing in the same mix of gossip and muckraking. Her relationships or alleged relationships were legion. Journalists covering her exploits had a simple remit, according to Ingram: "Just throw in a few other bizarre details, true or not, it didn't matter – because it's perfectly legal to print just about anything you like about a celebrity" (no date: 7).

It wasn't quite "perfectly legal," but the comment summarizes the thrust of tabloids as competition intensified in the late 1970s. Pictures of celebrities became the currency of choice and the pushy approach pioneered by Italian paparazzi came to the fore. When Elvis Presley died in 1977, the *National Enquirer* featured a picture of him lying embalmed in his coffin and was rewarded with sales of seven million. Celebrity deaths proved to be dependable boosts to circulation, as strong sales following the deaths of Bing Crosby and John Lennon indicated.

The shrieking headlines that told of sightings of Elvis in the most unlikely places years after his death made the *National Enquirer* internationally famous. It didn't just capture the spirit of the 1970s and 1980s: it caged it and taught it to do tricks. But, as those times changed, the *National Enquirer* wasn't so quick to adjust as some of its rivals, and the sightings, the accounts of alien abductions, and the gory reports seemed dated alongside the celebrity muckraking of its rivals like the *Globe* and the *Star*, both cheap newsprint tabloids that sold off the stands near the supermarket checkouts. *People*'s recipe was the most congruent with the times. Its "focus was entirely on the active personalities of our time" (Neimark 1995: 86).

In the 1990s, Bill Clinton's affair with Monica Lewinsky (of which more in Chapter 11) and Jesse Jackson's "love child" were the kind of stories that sold magazines more effectively than LOCH NESS MONSTER ATE MY HUSBAND. The O.J. Simpson trial in 1994 was a major event for the media: its focus was a celebrated ex-athlete and popular entertainer who was arrested, accused of murdering his wife and her male companion, but acquitted after probably the highest-profile trial in history.

Tabloid attention switched from the ordinary to the celebrated sectors of society, and the emphasis changed from the extraordinary to the ordinary. The success of magazines such as *People* and, in Britain, *Heat* and *Hello!* indicated that people preferred to read about everyday events in the lives of fantastic people rather than fantastic events in the lives of everyday people. There's also evidence that this preference was reflected in traditional news media. "From 1977–1997, the amount of 'soft news' (celebrity, scandal, gossip and other human interest stories) in the American news media increased from 15 percent to 43 percent," according to Kathy Koch (1998: 5).

The fortunes of the *National Enquirer* fluctuated as the traditional newspapers softened and tabloid rivals adapted more flexibly. The *Star*, for example, in 2004 reinvented itself as a glossy mag, which, as the *Economist* of July 8, 2004 reported, "treats celebrities as people to envy (better clothes, better dates, better sex and, inevitably, better body parts) but also, if captured from a slightly different angle, as people who are just as wretched as you."

By the time of the *Star's* new beginning, our preoccupation with celebrities – in the sense we use the term today – was in full evidence. In particular, interest in the foibles and fallibilities of celebrities seemed to issue a personal demand to magazines such as the *National Enquirer*: "Show us how cosmetic surgery can go grotesquely wrong. How age corrodes the most sublime beauties. How marriages made in heaven can descend to Stygian depths."

Our national passions, cultural watersheds, sexual mores, gender and racial battles, and political climate are viewed through the ever-shifting kaleidoscope of stories about people.

JILL NEIMARK

It was as if an entire culture had been redefined in personal terms, as seen through the eyes of celebrities. As Jill Neimark wrote in her "The culture of celebrity": "Our national passions, cultural watersheds, sexual mores, gender and racial battles, and political climate are viewed through the ever-shifting kaleidoscope of stories about people" (1995: 84).

In its own bizarre way, the *National Enquirer* has been a cultural heart rate monitor, providing a visible display of changes without revealing their sources. The magazine, which remains the mother of all tabloids, did more than record changes: it contributed to them, providing the basic elements of rumor and fanciful stories that fermented into soft news. One of the challenges in this book is to apportion causal priority to the chicken of the media or the egg of public taste. Which came first? Did the softening of the news media with its focus on personalities and their trivial pursuits change us? Or did we demand insights into the glitzy world of entertainers, confessions of their personal failings, and prurient details of their private lives?

| DIANA, THE INDESTRUCTIBLE PRINCESS

"Like the making of sausage or violin strings, the minting of celebrity is not a pretty business," observes Lewis H. Lapham. Both the chow that makes such a tasty breakfast and the twine that produces the mellifluous sound are prepared from the intestines of pigs, sheep, or horses.

Writing for *Harper's* in the months following the death of Diana, Princess of Wales, Lapham detected a Faustian bargain offered by a media that confers "temporary divinity" on individuals and all but guarantees "the gifts of wealth and applause" in return for "remnants of his or her humanity" that are made available to "the ritual of the public feast" (1997: 13).

Diana always gave the appearance of "having been granted every wish in Aladdin's cave – youth, beauty, pretty dresses, a prince for a husband, and Elton John for a pet." Her fans, who came from all quarters, cherished her for her neediness, which was, on Lapham's account, "as desperate and as formless as their own" (1997: 13).

Interest in the royal family had been largely reverential. Onlookers were exactly that: detached observers, watching as subjects rather than participants. Only Queen Elizabeth's sister, Princess Margaret, induced a more involved curiosity, her trysting occupying the paparazzi, though without sending them into the kind of frenzy that Diana did. As celebrities go, Diana was *ne plus ultra*: the highest form of such a being. No woman or man has ever commanded such reverence, respect, and collective love from such a wide constituency – in her case, the world. Even the most sober account of her life and death seems like a fairy-tale that got out of hand. It has the staples of love and death, as well as liberation, deliverance, and tragedy. Like other great fairytales, its motif was transformation. As raggedy servants are transformed into glass-slippered belles of the ball, and sleeping beauties are awakened by the kiss of handsome princes, Diana was changed from ingénue kindergarten teacher in a London school to the nearest the twentieth century had to a goddess.

Unlike other fairy stories, Diana's transformation was no magical affair. It was, as Lapham suggests, a more prosaic business, akin to that of the sausage-maker or the manufacturer of violin strings. In other words, a production in which raw materials are refined into items of taste and grace. Not that Diana herself was without her own immanent elegance. She was one of those "individuals who are defined in the first place as possessing some kind of ineffable 'essence' – an aura that sets them apart from ordinary mortals," as Giselle Bastin captures it (2009: 36).

Born in 1961 at Park House, the home that her parents rented on Queen Elizabeth II's Sandringham estate, she was the third child of Edward John Spencer, Viscount Althorp, heir to the 7th Earl Spencer, and his first wife Frances Ruth Burke Roche, daughter of the 4th Baron of Fermoy. So, her aristocratic credentials were sound. She became Lady Diana Spencer in 1975, when her father became an earl. Returning to England after attending finishing school in Switzerland, Diana grew close to Prince Charles. They announced their engagement in February 1981 and married later in that year. The wedding ceremony was televised globally. Their first child, William, was born in 1982 and their second, Henry, or Harry as he was to become known, in 1984.

Over the next eight years, interest in Diana spiraled upward. Already the most admired and, perhaps, accepted member of the royal family, she contrived to remain imperious, while developing a common touch. Time and again, people would testify that "she touched me" even though they might never have met her, or even seen her in the flesh. There was a tangible quality, not so much in her presence but in her sheer image. And this was made possible by exhaustive media coverage that occasionally, in fact once too often, became dangerously invasive.

The image was a cross between Cinderella and Rapunzel: a beautiful, yet lonely princess imprisoned in a loveless marriage with a prince whose suspected infidelity with an older and less attractive woman was the talk of the court. Trapped and with no apparent escape route, she seemed defenseless against a powerful and uncaring royal family. Diana made an enchanting victim, a vision of sacrificial womanhood. She kept her mask of motherly serenity, smiling beatifically to her millions of followers. And, as Scott Wilson writes, there were developments: "Diana's beauty remained indestructible and even blossomed when she became not only the most celebrated 'female victim of a brutal world,' but the patron of victims everywhere" (1997: para 6).

Her popularity seemed to grow in inverse proportion to that of her husband. Diana threw herself into charitable work and aligned herself with great causes, visiting people living with AIDS, children in hospitals, and other groups, all of whom responded empathically, as Jane Caputi reflects: "Those who participated in this flow of identification included people with AIDS, the young urban homeless, the injured, the socially marginalised, the poor, the imprisoned, the depressed, and the unloved" (1999: 108).

> *The flow of identification became tidal as people, especially women, from everywhere were drawn to someone, who, in her silence, seemed to speak for everyone.*

The "flow of identification" became tidal as people, especially women, from everywhere were drawn to someone, who, in her silence, seemed to speak for everyone. Diane Rubenstein highlights her absence of preconceived ideas or predetermined ambitions as factors in her magnetism; she was "a blank-screen on which women could not resist projecting their fantasies and fears" (1997: para.2).

WATCHING THEIR OWN SUFFERING |

The separation was one of those worst-kept secrets. When it was finally announced in 1992, both Diana and Charles continued to carry out their royal duties. They jointly participated in raising the two children. Diana continued with her charitable endeavors, attracting battalions of photojournalists wherever she went. If there was a high point during this period, it came in January 1997, when, as an International Red Cross VIP volunteer, she visited Angola to talk to landmine survivors. Pictures of Diana in helmet and flak jacket were among the most dramatic images of the late twentieth century. In August of that year, she traveled to Bosnia, again to visit survivors of landmine explosions. From there she went to see her companion, Dodi Al-Fayed, in France.

Late in the evening of August 30, 1997, Diana and Al-Fayed, their driver and bodyguard left the Ritz hotel in the Place Vendôme, Paris and drove along the north bank of the Seine. Ever vigilant, the media were soon alerted and pursued the Mercedes in which the party was traveling. Remember: by 1997, Diana's every movement was closely monitored. Interest in every aspect of her life was genuinely global. Not only was she fêted the world over, she was inspected too. The appetite for news – any kind of news, however insignificant – was devoured. "Diana," remarked Lapham, "was a celebrity of the most vulnerable and therefore the most nourishing type, a victim for all seasons."

At twenty-five minutes past midnight, nine vehicles carrying the media and a single motorcycle followed Diana and Al-Fayed into an underpass below the Place de l'Alma. As the

Mercedes sped away from the pursuant pack, it clipped a wall and veered to the left, colliding with a supporting pillar before spinning to a halt. There followed a few moments while the chasing photographers paused to consider their options. Inside the wrecked Mercedes were four motionless bodies, including that of the world's most famous, most esteemed, most adored, most treasured, and most celebrated woman. Photos of the wreckage would be hard currency. But to delay helping her and her fellow travelers might jeopardize their chances of survival. The paparazzi took their shots.

Diana was still alive when she was freed and rushed by ambulance to a nearby hospital. Attempts to save her life were futile and, at 4.00am, doctors pronounced her dead. Of the Mercedes passengers, only Trevor Rees-Jones, Al-Fayed's body-guard, survived. None of the others was wearing a seatbelt. It was later revealed that the chauffeur, Henri Paul, had been drinking earlier in the evening. The media people were cleared.

There followed the most extraordinary expression of public grief ever. This is unarguable: the scale, scope, and intensity of the response to her death distinguished it from any compara-ble manifestation of sorrow, even those mentioned earlier. The response to Diana's death defined an emblematic moment, one of transferred emotion. In the days leading to her funeral on September 6, over a million people flocked to pay their last re-spects, many leaving bouquets at her London home at Kensing-ton Palace. Her funeral attracted three million mourners, who cast flowers along the entire length of the journey. A global television audience of 26 million watched the day's events.

Diana's friend Elton John sang and later released a rewrit-ten version of his Marilyn tribute, "Candle in the Wind," in allusion to Diana's Aeolian frailties. While John's venture was not born out of commercial greed, there were plenty of exploitable byproducts to follow. A foretaste of the celebrity value of Diana came when the first issue of *Time* magazine fol-lowing her death sold 750,000 more copies than usual. Sales of a commemorative issue exceeded 1.2 million. The *National Enquirer*, in a somewhat hypocritical gesture, refused to publish pictures of Diana's death scene, despite having headlined a story the week before DI GOES SEX MAD.

Then came the merchandise. A planned comic book featuring Diana risen from the dead and invested with superpowers and entitled (following the Bond movie) *Di Another Day* was ditched by Marvel Comics amid protest. But less offensive products, such as statuettes, decorative plates and "Sindy"-like dolls began to appear on the shelves within months of the tragedy.

The near-inevitable conspiracy theories surrounding the death were equal to those of the moon landing, the JFK assassination, or 9/11. More rational attributions of blame centered on the chasing pack of paparazzi. Diana's brother, the Earl of Spencer, offered this view: "I always believed the press would kill her in the end," quoted by Jacqueline Sharkey in her 1997 article "The Diana aftermath." "Every proprietor and editor of every publication that has paid for intrusive and exploitative photographs of her, encouraging greedy and ruthless individuals to risk everything in pursuit of Diana's image, has blood on his hands" (1997: 18).

If they hadn't been so manic about getting their photographs, they wouldn't have pursued her car so heedlessly. Sharkey reflects on how "the public and some members of the press denounced the photographers – and journalists in general – as 'barracuda,' 'jackals,' piranha' and 'vultures' feeding off celebrities" (1997: 18).

So went the argument. Few wanted to extend that same argument further. If they had, they would have concluded that the paparazzi were motivated by money offered by media corporations that could sell publications in their millions to consumers whose thirst for pictures and stories of Diana seemed unquenchable. In the event, the photographers were cleared of any wrongdoing by a French court in 1999. The fact remains: all parties, from the paparazzi to the fans, were connected as if by invisible thread.

And then something interesting happened. As Donna Cox puts it in her *"Diana: Her true story*: post-modern transgressions in identity"*: "We became voyeurs to our own displays of 'suffering', playing 'Diana' to ourselves through blinking television monitors" (1999: 330).

The audience not only watched the Diana fairytale reach its denouement, but saw themselves as bit-part players in that same fairytale. This narrative transformation was both revealing and concealing. The media's part in the death of Diana might have been laid bare, but consumers' complicity, though recognized, was left unexamined, at least not in a deep or critical sense. While audiences might have agreed with the Earl of Spencer and condemned the media, they rewarded them with high sales and record viewing figures.

Perhaps transformation overstates the change. Anyone who was aware of Diana – and it's difficult to imagine anyone who wasn't – was forced to inspect the way in which news values had been subverted by entertainment values. After all, Diana's greatest triumph was not so much in ushering in world peace, or saving the planet, but in offering so much pleasure to so many people.

Yet the inspection was momentary. It didn't bring to an end the gathering interest in figures, who, like Diana, offered pleasure while presenting absolutely nothing that would materially alter their lives or the lives of any other living thing. The interest in recognizable people was probably interrupted by Diana's death. Then, after a spell of earnest introspection and critical evaluation of the media, the interest resumed.

The scandal precipitated by Taylor's affair was the single most important episode in the transition to a culture in which almost everything we knew arrived via the media and everything we did was designed to take us closer to a life of endless novelty, pleasure, and the commodities.

THE MONSTER SHE HELPED UNLEASH|

During the 36 years that separated the Taylor–Burton scandal and the death of Diana, the word "paparazzi" was introduced into the popular vocabulary, as were "tabloid" and "celebs." "Reality tv" would arrive soon after. Diana had become the paragon of celebrity. Taylor might have been the most famous, perhaps most revered woman of the 1960s, but, by the time of Diana's emergence in the 1980s, the simmering pot of interest in the rich and famous had been brought to the boil. In 1992, when her separation from Charles became official, the pot boiled over. Diana herself was news: not just what she was doing or saying or even wearing. People seemed to gasp in wonder at the very mention of her name.

In the 1960s, the most adventurous clairvoyant would have been hard pressed to predict the tumult of interest in Diana. Something happened. Not to Diana, but to *us*. We, the living human beings who attributed to her so much celestial power, were the ones who changed. And, after her death, we would go on changing.

Following the death of Diana and Al-Fayed, *Time* magazine writer Margaret Carlson observed: "By the time of the couple's dinner at Paris' Ritz Hotel, the rules of engagement sometimes observed between the photo hounds and the princess had gone completely by the board, as the street value of a grainy shot of Diana with al Fayed reached six figures" (1997: 46).

In previous chapters, I've used rule of the *game* rather than *engagement*. Carlson's phrase carries connotations of the principles that bind the actions of parties involved in some sort of conflict or competition. That wasn't the case here, though the circumstances of Diana's death certainly had the elements of opposition. Carlson's point is that "the run-ins between celebrities and those who take pictures of them are growing increasingly ugly."

The likes of Geppetti and Secchiaroli weren't exactly welcomed by the stars of the 1960s, but they became parties to an initially uneasy accommodation, which later became symbiotic, benefiting both. A renowned exception was photo-journalist Ron Galella's near-obsessional pursuit of Jacqueline Kennedy Onassis. Incensed by the ceaseless attention, Onassis secured a court order that prevented Galella encroaching on what she considered her private space. In this case, the rules of engagement were enshrined in law – and the well-documented run-ins were truly ugly.

The media weren't going to let their subjects appear as if they'd come straight from a makeover. Nor were they going to run anemic copy like: "Her favorite recreation is motoring and she is never so happy as when spinning along a country road, the fresh air blowing in her face" (this is actually plucked from the fan magazine *Film Weekly* by Matthew Sweet in his 2005 book *Shepperton Babylon*). The picture agency Big Pictures was set up in 1992 by Darryn Lyons and soon became the world's largest agency, specializing in celebrity shots. In many ways, the agency symbolized the releasing of the media.

In September 1997, shortly after Diana's death, The *New Republic*'s Jean Bethke Elshtain wrote: "Diana was no doubt tormented by the monster she herself had helped to unleash. That the celebrity machine will now give her children no peace, even to mourn her passing, is the cruelest of ironies" (1997: 25).

The "monster" may have tormented Diana, but her children, William and Harry, far from being tormented, learned to live with it, both in their different ways, responding to an environment populated by an expanding number of new species of the paparazzi genus.

There were other evolutionary diversifications. For example, The *National Enquirer* and other tabloids with their relentless focus on the exploits of famous personalities were, as Neimark put it, reducing the scope of world events to individuals (1995: 84). We, in turn, became habituated to a softening of news in which entertainment – and I use this in its widest sense: anything that amuses or occupies us agreeably – became an increasingly large staple in our intellectual diets. Our interest in politics took on a personal focus, as we were drawn to politicians as much as, if not more than, their politics – we will examine this in Chapter 11.

We started to understand the world through people rather than events, processes, or actions. Interest that, in the 1960s and perhaps 1970s, would have been seen as unwholesome or downright salacious became much more commonplace. The scandal precipitated by Taylor's affair may not have started this, but it was the single most important episode in the transition to a culture in which almost everything we knew arrived via the media and everything we did was designed to take us closer to a life of endless novelty, pleasure, and the commodities.

INTIMACY

| PARANORMAL FAMILIARITY

"The reasons for being interested in celebrities are luminously obvious," declared Blake Brooker in 2010. "They are figures who are distinguished from others. Looks, talent, power, luck, wealth, appetite, intelligence, drive, or opportunity blend in various combinations to create this separation" (quoted in McCutcheon *et al.* 2010: 9).

CHAPTER HIGHLIGHTS

- Television and radio didn't just change the way we spend time: they changed us
- MTV played a pivotal role in the development of celebrity culture
- By making her private life public, Madonna changed the "way the game works"
- Before Madonna, entertainers avoided scandal; after her, they pursued it
- Entertainers' relationships with the media changed drastically after the 1980s
- Celebrities have replaced political, church, and military leaders as moral authorities

The artistic director of a Canadian theater company, he would have been right – once: there was a time when famous figures had the full package and we didn't so much admire as idolize and fawn over them. Yet today he is about as wrong as it's possible to be: the reason we are interested in celebrities is that they are *not* separated from us; they are like us – we make sure of that. As for the list of qualities Brooker proposes: consumers were once awestruck by celebrities' abundant talent and wondrous looks, but not today. They've certainly had luck and opportunity, and those have led to their power and wealth. But I repeat: Brooker would have been right at one time in history. Let me explain.

There were two periods in the twentieth century when social change and technological change converged dramatically; and both have a bearing on our understanding of celebrity culture. One started in 1950, but the first followed the end of the First World War (1914–18). For all its destruction, the war had widened the horizons of the allied forces, particularly the notoriously insular Americans, two million of whom had glimpsed European cities, their culture, and their liberal sexual morality. Women, having played a vigorous role in the war, had challenged the illusion of the female as a delicate creature in need of men's protection. A vocal and effective suffragette movement was prying open new areas in politics and education. The sense of emancipation was enhanced by the consumer goods that became available after the war: the radio, the affordable car, and the talking movie. These didn't just change the way we spent our leisure time: they changed our entire social experience.

People were brought together as never before: they could have the same feelings at the same time, despite being thousands of miles apart. The power of the media was stunningly revealed during the 1927 boxing match between Gene Tunney and Jack Dempsey, when five radio listeners supposedly died from heart attacks. The car was equal in its impact: as ownership rose, so social and physical liberation came together. Places that were once remote became accessible (by 1930, 23 million Americans and 2.3 million British people owned cars). New towns, new counties, even new states were within reach. Conceptions of physical space concertinaed, collapsing and compressing distances that once seemed unimaginably great. This complemented the sense of immediacy introduced by radio and, later, modified by the cinema and, more importantly, television. The rise of tv started in 1950, and this is where the second key period begins.

Television, bringing famous faces and sounds into our homes, has created different kinds of celebrity.
DAVID GILES

Those who purloin the gifts of science and technology are often punished, though in less spectacular ways than the demigod Prometheus, who stole fire from Olympus and taught humans to use it, but was later chained to a rock and preyed on by an eagle. Television is like fire: it illuminates, ignites, and affects us in ways we rarely dwell on. Most of us could hardly bear thinking about life without television. As essentials of contemporary culture go, it has no challengers. Yet, it's been held responsible for, among other things, shortening our attention spans, precipitating violent behavior, and reducing local cultures to insignificance.

During the second half of the twentieth century, television transformed the way we thought and behaved. It affected the way we relaxed, the way we learned, the way we communicated. The complete cultural landscape was transfigured by television, to the point where we can't recognize its presence. So much of what we know about the world is gleaned from tv that we find it tough to think where else we find out about some event or other. The internet has, of course, emerged as an alternative.

It barely needs stating that celebrity culture wouldn't have been possible without television. Prior to its acceptance as a domestic appliance in the 1950s, we knew about prominent figures mainly by their names or artist's impressions, still photographs, or newsreels shown at the movies. "Television, bringing famous faces and sounds into our homes, has created different kinds of celebrity," writes David Giles (2000: 32).

Television brought with it intimacy: we were able to see moving images and hear voices – in our own homes. It also brought replication: those images and sounds were not just one-offs: they could be repeated time and again, exposing us to the famous in a way that stirred us to new interest. We saw people who were previously remote and perhaps unknowable as ordinary humans with the same kinds of mannerisms, faults, and maybe foibles as the rest of us.

Giles argues that the proliferation of media, specifically television, in the late twentieth century expanded the opportunities for people to become famous. In material terms, there were more tv screens on which they could appear and become known. Viewers could not only see and hear a new array of people: they could almost reach out and touch them. In a way, they could almost swear they knew them. The more they felt they knew them, the more they became entranced.

Giles invokes a term from a 1956 article in the journal *Psychiatry* to capture the emerging relationship between tv figures and viewers: "parasocial interaction" (Horton and Wohl coined the term in 1956). The 1950s was the decade of growth for television: at the start, few households had a tv; by the end, over 90 percent of households in the USA and 70 percent in the UK had at least one set. Viewers were forming unusual attachments. They were developing "friendships" with television characters, some fictional and others real (like announcers or weather forecasters). They also "hated" some of them. Familiarity led to a sense of intimacy. Viewers actually thought they knew the figures they saw on their screens. They interacted with them parasocially. The relationships were, and still are, strictly one-way.

It's called parasocial because *para* means beyond, as in paranormal. The attachment might only have been as strong as a beam of light from a cathode ray tube. Yet it was experienced as strong and meaningful. Consumers actually felt they knew people they had never met, probably never seen in the flesh, and who knew nothing of their existence. So, there is no actual "interaction" (*inter* means "between"): it's one-way. This doesn't stop the consumer feeling like there's a genuine interaction. In this sense, it's an interesting term that captures the way we think and feel about people we don't know and who don't know us, but who sometimes unwittingly and unknowingly move us to act, occasionally in erratic and irrational ways.

As Prometheus can confirm, anything can go awry when trying to snatch wisdom. In his case, human fallibility was exposed by the gods. In the case of tv, it was the impressionability of viewers. Television might have started with the best of intentions. In Britain, the BBC ostentatiously promised a theater of the airwaves. And, although it was funded by advertising revenue and had to remain audience-friendly, US television harbored similar aspirations in the 1950s.

Television used wire transmission: sending electrical signals over various types of wire, including coaxial cable. In 1962, Telstar, the first of a series of active communications satellites, was launched by the USA. Satellite systems allowed the exchange of television or telephone signals by means of microwaves, which are very short electromagnetic waves – the same things that heat your food. Signals were bounced off them while they orbited the earth so that telephone conversations and live television transmissions were made through space. In 1964, coverage of the summer Olympics in Tokyo was sent around the world via the Syncom 3 satellite. In 1969, the Apollo 11 satellite beamed images from the moon's surface into people's living rooms.

Technological developments over the next few years made it possible for some stations to use satellite delivery for all their programs. HBO, for example, began its service in 1975, transmitting from the Philippines the heavyweight title fight between Muhammad Ali and Joe Frazier known as the "Thrilla in Manila." HBO offered something different from the usual television menu: films, concerts, and sports events. Other channels to use satellite broadcasts included the Star movie channel, WTBS, Ted Turner's "superstation," as he called it, and The Christian Broadcasting Network, later to become the Family Channel, all breaking away from the traditional varied makeup of programming and opting for just one type of program.

The cable tv industry, which had started in 1948 as a primitive solution to the reception problems experienced by those in mountainous areas, quickly followed the early examples, Turner's CNN specialized in news, Nickelodeon in children's programs, and ESPN in sports only. But most influential in the development of celebrity culture was Warner's MTV station.

Imagine this: two tv execs leave a movie theater in 1977 after seeing John Badham's *Saturday Night Fever*. With a perfunctory plot and almost ceaseless disco music and dancing, the film sounds irritating beyond belief, but became a huge global success and launched the career of John Travolta. Impressed by the music that throbbed throughout the film and the nifty footwork of Travolta *et al.*, one exec suggests to the other that they start a tv channel on which they show nothing but the kind of material they've just witnessed. The other scoffs: "Look, that was 118 minutes and it was held together by a plot, even if it was a pretty thin one. Why would anyone want to watch music clips nonstop without even a story to sustain their interest?"

Four years later, in 1981, MTV began transmitting. Fanciful as the *Saturday Night Fever* scenario seems, it actually isn't too far from the truth: MTV was started by John Lack, who worked for Warner Cable, Robert W. Pittman, an NBC radio programmer, and Les Garland; together they dreamed up the idea, having taken note of a similar set-up in New Zealand, which showed pop videos and, in turn, promoted record sales. In fact, the distinction between promotional material and entertainment was smudged, if not erased, by MTV, which showed only music clips, including concert footage, interspersed with chat from video jockeys, or vjs.

The program content came from record companies, which were eager to grab what was effectively free advertising from the new cable outlet, owned by Warner Amex (i.e. Warner Communications and American Express). Pop music was not then at the point where every commercial single was augmented by a video, but it was moving in that direction, especially in the British recording industry. MTV's income came from advertising revenue, which went up in proportion to their viewing figures, and its share of cable subscriptions. So all parties benefited from each other.

While it seems a perfectly brilliant concept today, in the late 1970s, it must have seemed preposterous. In fact, it must have seemed that way in the first year of operation too: fewer than one million viewers subscribed to the channel. Now, there are about 350 million viewers, mostly 18–25 with no dependents and disposable income, the kind of demographic that advertisers yearn for. MTV's global venture started in 1987 with MTV Europe and continued with such stations as MTV Mandarin, MTV Japan, and MTV Africa. It has more imitators than the iPad: other channels have hijacked the all-music idea, leaving MTV to mutate into a reality tv station. Record companies still crave the inclusion of their videos on MTV's playlists and advertisers love the demographics the station serves up.

Have you ever thought what's happening when you watch videos? Are you being entertained, or held captive in front of a three-minute commercial? You could ask a similar question of sports: Does enjoying the competition implicate you in witnessing advertisements for cars, razor blades, beer, and all the other kinds of products aimed at the sports fan market? Does it really matter? After all, television keeps us engrossed, absorbed, and amused. We usually have little inclination to analyze whether the hidden persuaders are surreptitiously bending our shopping preferences to their own requirements. Advertisers and tv companies figured this out long ago. MTV was, in its own way, a prototype. As its imitators proliferated, blurring the difference between entertainment and marketing became passé: making the two one and the same thing was the task. The band Dire Straits satirized the tightening relationship between pop music, television, and consumerism in their 1985 track "Money for nothing," in which they boast of getting to "play the guitar on the MTV," while acknowledging their unwritten responsibility: "We gotta install microwave ovens/custom kitchen deliveries/ we gotta move these refrigerators/we gotta move these color tvs."

DEVOURING MADONNA |

"We have far too much information about celebrities these days," according to Jill Neimark. Writing in *Psychology Today*, she lists some of the superfluities as "their love affairs, their private conversations on cellular phones, the color of their underwear, how many nose jobs they've had, how many intestinal polyps" (1995: 57).

Too much perhaps for Neimark, but the whole point about celebrities is that there can never be too much information. There might not have been too much interest in Elizabeth Taylor's underwear, or, if there was, in the 1960s, it would have been regarded as prurient. But there was certainly major interest in her love affairs, especially the association with Burton. Today, no detail of a celebrity's private life is privileged: to be a celebrity means to be willing to go public with the minutiae of what, at another time in history, might be known as a private life. No one recognized this as clearly as Madonna Louise Veronica Ciccone.

Around the time of the release of her album *Like a Prayer* in 1989 Madonna (b. 1958) seems to have had one of those "Eureka!" moments. Or maybe it was more like a peek at a crystal ball. She seems to have arrived at the conclusion that a new age was upon us, one in which celebrities would rule the earth.

"I have seen the future," she might have declared, "and it is one in which the fans will demand more and receive more; and those who are prepared to give them what they want – or even more – will prevail." Over the next five years, she did precisely this. "Madonna would later comment that this entire period of her life was designed to give the world every single morsel of what they (sic) seemed to be demanding in their invasion of her private life" (according to World4Madonna.com).

The world didn't so much "demand" details of or "invade" her private life: it was inescapably, unavoidably, obligatorily surrounded by her life, which might have been "private" in one sense, but was opened up for full public inspection. Before her, stars had tried to section off parts of their lives. After her, they either gave up trying, or gave up trying to be a star.

From 1989, Madonna jumped repeatedly out of the frying pan into the fire, then back into the frying pan.

The organizing themes of Madonna's career 1989–94 were classic celebrity: finely judged scandal, continuous media exposure, a cycle of dramatic makeovers, and sex. Its momentum was such that it carried her through over three decades as a leading showbusiness performer. She sold more records than any other female in history (300 million and counting) and amassed a personal wealth of $650 million, according to *Forbes*. Even in her fifties, she sold out world tours and still managed to stir controversy. Madonna earned paeans, prizes, and plaudits and drew censure, condemnation, and jeers.

Her first album *Madonna* was released in 1983 and produced three successful singles, all of them heavily featured on MTV, then in its ascendancy. The music channel could legitimately be credited with making many artists – Duran Duran included – and stymieing the progress of others: numerous African American artists had their videos turned down by MTV, and it took pressure from CBS to ensure a place for Michael Jackson's "Billie

Jean" on the playlist in 1983. Madonna, however, was perfectly congruent with MTV's preferred profile: white, twentysome-thing, tons of junk jewelry, and a wardrobe that might have been put together from a flea market. Anyone could look like Madonna; millions actually did.

Then she assumed a new image: a manquée bottle-blonde Marilyn Monroe dripping with Harry Winston diamonds for her "Like a virgin" video, Madonna kept changing, keeping her fans guessing as to what she would look like. Two movies, an appearance in a Broadway play, a tempestuous marriage, the publication of nude photospreads (against her wishes; the shots were taken in the early 1980s), and multimillion record sales had turned Madonna into a major performer. She could have opted to stick with the formula: more albums, more chameleon-like changes of image and occasional ventures into drama; in which case, she would have been remembered in the same way as her contemporaries, like Mariah Carey or Pat Benatar.

In the golden age of Hollywood, adultery, underage sex, abortion, alcoholism, venereal disease, and suicide were rife. But journalists in the main refrained from gossiping about the hedonistic excesses of the stars. Controversy and scandal were unwelcome detours on the professional highway for movie and music stars. Often they were roads to oblivion. The me-dia respected this and limited their criticisms to onscreen per-formances. In 1989, Madonna deviated with what might have been suicidal recklessness. For the next seven years, she all but dared the media not to get involved as she jumped repeatedly out of the frying pan into the fire, then back into the frying pan.

1989. In the video for the title track of the *Like a Prayer* al-bum, Madonna appeared with long raven hair, portraying a prostitute who witnesses a rape and murder. After a black man is falsely accused and jailed, Madonna goes to church, where a status of St Martin de Porres resembling the accused comes to life and kisses her passionately. The video, which also featured burning crosses, was denounced by the Vatican (echoes of Elizabeth Taylor) for its "blasphemous" eroticism and Catholic symbolism. Pepsi Cola pulled out of a $5 million endorsement deal with Madonna. The furor placed Madonna at the center of an international news story and helped turn the album into a global success: three more hit singles were taken from the album. (Pepsi was also embarrassed by endorsers Michael Jackson and Britney Spears, the latter photographed while drinking Coca-Cola.)

1990. MTV banned "Justify my love," a single with sexually explicitly lyrics ("You put this in me . . ."), and an erotic video with gay and lesbian scenes to match. Being banned by the very medium that had been key to her initial success was a delicious paradox and the media devoured it. Over a million copies of the cd were moved. The visual style of the "Vogue" video bore gay influences.

1991. For the feature documentary *Truth or Dare*, or *In Bed with Madonna,* as it was entitled in Britain, Madonna allowed cameras access to areas of her private life. What audiences remembered was her bitchiness and self-regarding wit, but also her sensitive visit to her mother's grave and her softer, reflective side. Even talking bitchily behind the scenes of her Blonde Ambition tour, she came over as an ordinary mortal. It's difficult to imagine any other performer inviting cameras to examine them close-up in this way. But, as Joshua Rich reflects in *Entertainment Weekly*: "A warts-and-all movie confessional – rare from a diva of her stature – made total, perverse sense" (2002: 84). By coincidence or perhaps synchronicity, during the 1991 Persian Gulf War, millions of viewers turned to CNN to watch the war occurring in real time. The cable tv channel offered viewers a novel and unique way of viewing a real event "unplugged," so to speak.

1992. No book published in the same year received as much publicity. Inside the sheet metal covers of *Sex*, Madonna could be seen in poses that suggested lesbianism, anal sex, and sadomasochism. The book sold in a vacuum-sealed cover at $50. Its publication coincided with the release of *Erotica,* an album that complemented the book thematically. The accompanying video featured Madonna, then 33, dressed androgynously. This was a star at or approaching the peak of her popularity, fabulously rich, with several hugely successful albums and a presence in movies, baring herself and playing out sexual fantasies to anyone who cared to look. For what? Mischief? Outrage and media exposure were umbilically linked. Her intuitive brilliance in both brought rewards in the form of a seven-year $60 million deal with Time-Warner. Around this time, softish porn material from her background began to emerge, so her stylized bawdiness functioned as a distraction from this.

1993. Even in failure, Madonna created news. Playing opposite Willem Dafoe in the execrable *Body of Evidence,* she was mercilessly maligned and lampooned (*The New York Times* called the film "a sluggish courtroom melodrama relieved only by unintentional laughter"). She weighed in as a dominatrix who introduces her defense attorney to the delights of having hot candle wax dripped onto his genitals. Masturbation, sodomy, and bondage fill the holes in the plot. Her much-discussed friendship with cross-dressing basketball player Dennis Rodman, then at the height of his celebrity rating, was one of those singer/athlete affairs that were to become popular in the years ahead (cf. Posh and Becks).

1994. The subject of the single "Secret" was a love affair between a straight man and a transsexual, though the infamous episode of Madonna's year was reserved for *The Late Show with David Letterman* on which she let loose with 15 repetitions of the word "fuck," all bleeped. From one perspective, it was a coarse, undignified, unnecessarily offensive display from a woman who could lay claim to being the world's leading female singer. From another, it was another example of Madonna's capacity to turn the unlikeliest event into a showcase for herself. In the same year, the trial of O.J. Simpson for the murders of his ex-wife and her friend generated unprecedented global media coverage. Even before the internet had taken grip of the world, the Simpson trial disclosed a human verity: we are fascinated by scandal.

1996. Madonna found herself in court testifying that Robert Hoskins had scaled the fence of her home and stalked her. We'll return to this case in the next chapter.

But then there were signs of, for want of a better word, mundanity. Madonna's appearance in a 2003 television commercial for Gap may not have surprised many, but those who had followed her career over the long term would have divined a symbolic meaning. This was a fashionista of the first order swapping her Gaultier conical bras and Versace gowns for sensible tee-shirts and khakis: "The onetime mistress of reinvention once negotiated her celebrity like a game of chess – precisely by not catering to the masses," writes Danielle Sacks in her article "Who's that girl?". "She sought out controversy. She sought to offend." But: "You can't be a pop icon and a spiritualistic writer and sing about the flaws of American consumerism and make out with same-sex pop stars half your age and be the face of one of the most generic brands in America all at once" (2003: 32).

Over the next decade, Madonna transformed from *grande amoureuse* to *grande dame*. She wrote and directed her own movie *W/E* in 2011 (presumably emboldened by winning a Golden Globe award for *Evita* in 1996). She had converted to the Judaic sect known as the Kabbalah (changing her name to Esther in the process), written children's books, had children, moved to London, married, and divorced. "I have earned a reputation for being many things," Madonna reflected in 2008, when interviewed by Steve Klein. "For being a provocateur, for never taking no for an answer, for endlessly reinventing myself, for being a cult member, a kidnapper, for being ambitious, outrageous, irreverent, and for never settling for second best."

In 2006, the taboo-breaker extraordinaire discovered a new cultural prohibition to ignore when she applied to adopt the one-year-old David Banda. "I think it's still considered taboo," Madonna, then 48, answered critics who dismissed her adoption of a Malawi child as a pr stunt. She later adopted a second Malawi child and embarked on a school-building program in Malawi. As ever, it was a controversial move, not entirely welcomed by the Malawi government.

It seemed she relished and luxuriated in the notoriety she created for herself, making her decision to sue the British newspaper the *Mail on Sunday* in 2009 seem paradoxical. Madonna claimed successfully that the publication had breached her privacy and copyright by publishing photos of her 2000 wedding to Guy Ritchie. Breaching Madonna's privacy must have been close to a contradiction in terms. By this time, the couple had divorced – and Madonna had agreed to a £76 million ($93m) settlement with Ritchie. Ritchie declined and took just £10 million ($15.14m).

In 2012, Madonna, then 53, exposed her breast during a concert in Istanbul, watched by 55,000. It came nine years after she had kissed Britney Spears in full view of a concert audience. Her capacity to upstage practically anyone seemed undiminished. When interviewed by Cynthia McFadden of ABC News, she proudly stated: "I've spent my life pushing the envelope. I'm not gonna stop just because I've got children." But the transition was complete and the breast flash was a tiny reminder of Madonna's once-mighty potential to shock rather than a return to old values.

This might read like a criticism, though it's no more than a complimentary observation: it doesn't lessen the overall impact she made on popular culture. Commemorating two decades of her influence, *Harper's Bazaar*, in September 2003, held that "the ultimate pop-culture icon['s] . . . influence is endless" (issue 3502: 303). Even allowing for exaggeration, the point is that Madonna changed "how the game works," as Gwen Stefani later put it: the principles that bind the actions of parties involved either cooperatively or competitively with the media.

"I'm going to provoke, surprise, aggravate, and generally upset as many people as I can, and I'm going to let you watch me do it," Madonna might have promised the media. "In the process, I will disclose more of myself than any pop or movie star in history. My body, my sexuality, my erotic fantasies: nothing is out of bounds."

> *Madonna, more than anyone else, effected a change in style and the manner with which stars engaged with the media.*

The *quid pro quo* was simple: Madonna wanted – and got – more saturation media coverage than anyone, present and past. She was operating in an age of global media, when entertainment was becoming the hard currency of tv and when having a video vetoed by the likes of MTV made international news. Compellingly newsworthy in everything she did or said, Madonna was ubiquitous for at least the first half of the 1990s. Thereafter, her presence might have faded, but her influence remained. After her, no one could aspire to becoming a celebrity if they wanted anything resembling a private life. The boundary-blurring that had started in Rome in 1962 was completely obliterated during Madonna's rise, or, as some might have it, diabolically masterminded descent.

Writing for *Rolling Stone*, Britney Spears offers the view: "Madonna was the first female pop star to take control of every aspect of her career and to take responsibility for creating her image, no matter how much flak she might get" (2004: 124). It's a common observation, though one that misses the more important point that, in taking control of her own career, she needed the assistance of a media that had, by the end of the 1980s, become potent makers and breakers of careers. Hers could have finished prematurely in a comic shambles if her 1986 tale of a teen pregnancy "Papa don't preach" had been dismissed as a contrived attempt to inflame conservative moralists and prompt further outrage. Instead, it was hailed by the media as a daring and inventive attempt to break away from the insubstantialities of pop music.

She did risk the flak, as Spears points out, but, as with all Madonna's gambles, it was a carefully calculated one. Emboldened by her success, she deepened her liaisons with the media until confident she had won them over. She provided great copy; they provided great coverage. The rules changed.

From the vantage point of the twenty-first century, Madonna is a middle-aged diva who reigned long and who made good music. Some might suspect that I exaggerate the extent of her influence. I'm not arguing that she singlehandedly introduced celebrity culture. But she, more than anyone else, effected a change in style and the manner with which stars engaged with the media. And, in this sense, she both epitomized and helped usher in an age in which the epithets "shocking," "disgusting," or "filthy" didn't presage the end of a career. On the contrary: when treated appropriately by the media, they occasioned the popping of champagne corks in celebration.

Almost every requirement of celebrity culture was met by the time of Madonna's fusillade of expletives on Letterman's show in 1994: a prying, ravenous media hungry for every "morsel" and a proliferation of global television networks with little else to fill their channels apart from entertainment; a breakdown in the traditional public vs. private domains; and a class of figures of world renown who had been changed as if by sorcery into what we now call icons – the word actually deriving from the Greek *eikon*, meaning a statue of a revered person, sometimes thought to be sacred itself. There is still something missing: us.

PEOPLE WHO PLAY PEOPLE WHO DO GREAT THINGS |

There was a time when we admired, respected, and followed the exploits of heroes. These included statesmen, scientists, explorers, and military figures, people – usually, though not always, men – who distinguished themselves by their accomplishments. Whether on the battlefield, in the laboratory, or atop mountains, heroes were great achievers. They were known for their deeds rather than their "well-knownness," a term coined by Daniel Boorstin in 1961 in *The Image* (republished in 1992); he intended it ironically, though there seems no irony in it now.

We've changed. At least according to Len Sherman, who writes: "We have forsaken our traditional heroes and replaced them with actors and athletes . . . where we once admired people who do great things, now we admire people who play people who do great things" (1992: 26).

Sherman means actors who play great historical characters, such as Alexander the Great, or athletes who talk about winning a football game as if they've conquered Everest, or pop stars who believe their status entitles them to make pronouncements on how to save the planet, solve Third World debt, or bring peace on earth. For Sherman, celebrities have replaced heroes, but without having to inherit the responsibilities attendant on heroic status. He means by this that heroes "embodied the best of their people's convictions and hopes. They consciously aspired to live in such a manner so as to serve as examples for the rest of society" (1992: 26).

By contrast, today's replacements make a point of operating "outside the morals and ethics and rules by which the rest of populace lives." We might go so far as to say that maintaining a celebrity status is contingent on breaking a few rules here and there, just to demonstrate a disregard of the norms that govern or guide the conduct of the rest of society. Madonna's contrived transgressions served notice that she could violate as many rules as she wanted with impunity.

While Sherman is specifically interested in the ways in which athletes were, and are, able to flout social conventions in a way that attracts publicity and so reinforces their status, his point is worth extending. Perhaps we have changed to the point where we've "forsaken" (itself a revealingly quaint word) or given up on traditional leaders and shifted our allegiance instead to people who don't actually do much, but appear everywhere. While Sherman doesn't refer to them, the Watergate affair and the anti-Vietnam War movement increased cynicism about not only government, but the media too.

> **We are transferring moral authority to the only public servants that remain: pop singers, Hollywood stars, and the casts of our favorite sitcoms.**
>
> ### DANIEL HARRIS

When Sherman was writing in the early 1990s, there was less evidence about than there is today. His claim seems more solid now than then: we lack respect and hold in contempt many of our political leaders and regard men of the Church as out of sync with contemporary values; we might be aware of the quests of mountaineers and pathbreaking scientists, but we're unlikely to be able to name them, let alone know much more about them.

Why? The spread of the market economy and the rise of democratic, individualistic values. That's the view of Charles Ponce de Leon. These have "steadily eroded all sources of authority," argues Ponce de Leon (2002: 4). Our faith was being shaken by the start of the twentieth century; by the start of the Second World War, we thought about public figures in a less reverential way, questioning their wisdom and credentials for making pronouncements. These, we might note, are signs of progress: a healthy mistrust, a constructive skepticism, and a privileging of corroboration over faith are surely signs of a ripening modern democracy. They inclined us toward other non-traditional sources of authority, as Daniel Harris intimates: "We are transferring moral authority to the only public servants that remain: pop singers, Hollywood stars, and the casts of our favorite sitcoms" (2008a: 139).

In times of crisis, we have little alternative but to look to established leaders. We want and need them to make the decisions; our wellbeing depends on it. Political, military, and religious leaders are burdened with the expectations of many. Whether they make the right or wrong choices, people's lives are affected. This becomes particularly acute when security at home is under threat. At times like these, leaders seem to have intrinsic, inviolable value. We have no choice but to trust them. Names like Roosevelt, Churchill, MacArthur, and Montgomery ring out through history. Their status has an imperishable quality that time can't erode. Their reputations were founded on actions rather than . . . well, reputations.

Pioneers were also venerated, not because of what people believed about them, but because of what they pioneered, whether, like Albert Einstein, new scientific boundaries, or, like Edmund Hillary, natural limits. Religious and spiritual leaders were respected by virtue of their position, but were also obliged to dispense wisdom of practical utility in guiding their followers, especially in troubled times. They too earned their status, rather than having it dropped on them.

Only excessive and unjustified respect could produce a world at once so meek and so fickle that its heroes are configured in a loop of images. That, in effect, is the argument put forward by Boorstin, whose work is still resonant over five decades after its original publication in 1961 (with the different subtitle of "or what happened to the American dream"). The image has become more important than the substance. Celebrities are "fabricated," according to Boorstin, and what passed for their achievements were no more than artificial contrivances, what he called "pseudo-events." He saw American culture in the throes of change, entertainers replacing genuine heroes, their public "personalities" eclipsing what they stood for, did, or said. Boorstin might have been interested in the 1977 film *MacArthur: The rebel general*, in which the archetypal American Second World War hero was portrayed by Gregory Peck, himself venerated, though, in his case, for "being one of those people who play people who do great things."

The fragile simulation of Peck would have been no match for the real thing in the 1940s in Southeast Asia, but, in the 1970s, with Vietnam appearing as an avoidable rather than inevitable conflict, the dark handsomeness of Peck would have won out.

You could plot a graph of the rise and fall of faith in established leaders, the horizontal axis ordered chronologically, the vertical measuring collective confidence. The spikes would appear in times of crisis, particularly when domestic security is under threat. In Britain, trust in political leaders has probably receded since the 1970s, after the IRA bombings grew less and less frequent. Following the Pearl Harbor attack, the USA's boundaries were not breached until September 11, 2001, by which time celebrity culture had taken root even in politics. So we can understand the waning reliance on the great statesmen and church leaders in terms of our not actually needing to trust, have confidence, or, less still, have faith in them.

It's also possible to explain our gradual abandonment of inventors and explorers as the result of a combination of world-weariness and cynicism. After electricity, the internal combustion engine, television, the cure for tuberculosis, and gene therapy, what's left to discover? And, with Everest and the lesser mountains conquered, the world circumnavigated several dozen times by boat, and the Amazon charted, adventurers now have to devise their own challenges rather than rely on nature. The end of the Cold War and the emergence of panic induced by the specter of an all-pervasive, ever-present yet invisible enemy, against which political figures seem ineffective, served to undermine established authority even further.

There wasn't an automatic transfer of moral authority, though consumers became less interested in or concerned about leaders, and less deferential about their opinions. They also became progressively engrossed with celebrities who, by the mid-1990s, were "worthy of our slavish devotion, attention and respect," as Mark Harris of *Entertainment Today* put it (quoted in Neimark, 1995: 90).

But, if our lack of conviction in more traditional leaders is comprehensible, our sometimes preposterous, diverting interest in celebrities, or, as Boorstin might say, their images, needs more explanation. Before moving to an explanation, let's keep in mind the constituents of celebrity culture, or at least those we've covered so far. Think in terms of a DNA double helix except with three strands coiling inside each other like some Philippe Starck-inspired spiral staircase. One strand represents a predatory, persistent, and progressively omnipresent corps of photojournalists who showed none of the respect or well-mannered deference of their predecessors in their search for new prey. Emerging as a force in the late 1960s, the paparazzi dissolved the previous demarcation lines between the public and private spheres. Their presence signaled a kind of open season.

New rules of engagement weren't far off. If it hadn't been Madonna who rewrote them, it would have been some other starlet with savvy enough to cut a different type of deal with the media: "I show all and you tell all." Media coverage would never be the same. This is a second strand and it wove together perfectly with the newfound value attributed to entertainment in the late 1980s, a time when television channels were multiplying like tribbles (those prolifically reproductive creatures from the classic *Star Trek* episode).

The sudden multiplication is the third strand. "As the number of shows and Web sites increased, so did competition for audiences and ad dollars," writes Howard Altman of *CQ Researcher.* "In turn, that raised the demand for more cheap content, such as the latest celebrity gossip, to fill the burgeoning amounts of broadcast airtime" (2005: 2).

Entertainers found themselves on display like never before. More outlets, more time, and more viewers. Light entertainment was like hard currency on the international televisual exchange. You didn't have to be a Hollywood star to be an entertainer: tv was the medium of choice and it gave rise to a new class of celebrity. Members of this class, or, more accurately, images of and gossip about them, accessed resources of power not from any hitherto untapped natural resources, but from us. Our change from hero-worshipers to idolaters of images was all that was needed to complete the transition to celebrity culture.

Too neat? Absolutely. There had to be a process as industrial as the kind of process that produces household products, except designed to manufacture celebrities. "Celebrity as the fleeting product of a vacuum cleaner/sausage maker," is how Joshua Gamson describes this process (1992: 1). We'll consider it in more detail in the next chapter.

VOYEURISM

Fame is . . . it's such a strange thing, isn't it? You never quite get used to being public property, really. Take our conversation now. You have just walked into this room and started telling me shit about myself and that's, like, weird, it's crazy, because we are strangers.

(Gwen Stefani, interviewed by Nick Duerden, August 2005)

CHAPTER HIGHLIGHTS

- Fans have used digital technologies to transform the "dynamics of power"
- There is a "worship scale" of fans, from agnostics to extreme worshipers
- Fans' relationships with celebs help define themselves
- Gossip is what one writer calls the "social elixir," a magical potion
- Stalkers with obsessions may not be so different from other fans
- Fans gain a sense of power, often over the lives of others

"One of the driving forces driving voyeurism comes from our expectations and changing conception of what information should remain closed and private and what information should become available to the public," argue Lea C. Hellmueller and Nina Aeschbacher (2010: 11). A voyeur is someone who gains pleasure, usually sexual pleasure, from watching others, particularly when they are buck naked or engaged in sex, or possibly in pain; it derives from *voir*, the French for "see."

Hellmueller and Aeschbacher are using voyeurism more loosely to describe the habits of consumers who pry into the private affairs of others. Their point is that conceptions of what is or isn't private are in flux and "journalists develop routines based on assumptions or institutional presuppositions about the consuming audience" (2010: 11).

After the rise of Madonna in the 1980s, anyone who aspired to be famous had to stay mindful of the sacrifice she made. She may not have slaughtered an animal or child as an offering to god, but she gave up something that had been regarded as important to previous entertainers: her privacy. Had social media been around, she would have had no choice. But, in the days when traditional media were dominant, she opted to start a process that would eventually turn privacy inside out. Eventually, fans, instead of relying on what the media provided, asserted themselves. But they needed assistance. As Mark Poster points out: "The shift from analog to digital technology alters the basic features of the production, storage, reproduction, and dissemination of culture" (2008: 690).

> *The relationship between celebrities and fans became progressively more fluid, involving a collaboration and exchange of ideas between celeb and audience.*

Today, underwater cables, communications satellites, and the internet have made it possible for consumers all over the world to create, send, and circulate texts, images, and sounds via different platforms, systems, and applications, all of which are interconnected. Consumers have no need to depend on traditional media for information on celebrities' lives: they can access it for themselves; and, if they can't do that, they will make it up. Either way, it satisfies the voyeuristic impulse.

Actually, voyeurism doesn't quite catch it: it sounds too one-directional, as if one group is peeping at another through a keyhole; celebrities supply raw material to eager followers.

Madonna certainly delivered a product in the 1980s, but she was forced to change. In the 1990s, widespread access to digital technology, according to Rosemary J. Coombe and Andrew Herman, "transformed the dynamics of power . . . [and provided] unprecedented opportunities for new and dynamic dialogues between producers of products and imagery and those who consume them" (2001: 921). Fans, or consumers, became producers and permitted corporate producers to engage with them: "They are making mass culture into popular culture." Coombe and Herman were writing in 2001, after the early days of networking, electronic bulletin boards, and blogging, but before the rise of Facebook, YouTube, and Twitter; these appeared from 2004, 2005 and 2006 respectively.

The relationship between celebrities and fans became progressively more fluid, involving a collaboration and exchange of ideas between celeb and audience (reaching an unedifying point in 2012 when Justin Bieber's fans elected via Twitter to name his penis "Jerry"). It's difficult to imagine unapproachable, unreachable, untouchable stars, such as Elizabeth Taylor, Marilyn Monroe, and their contemporaries in the 1950s and 1960s, tweeting. But, if they were around in times of 360-degree connectivity, they would be obliged to do exactly that (though probably not sharing the nomenclature of their genitalia).

Stars once earned their names: like celestial bodies, they were remote, far removed from the lives of the people who either idolized, followed, or perhaps just knew about them. And how did they know about them? Through movies, advertisements, magazines, and newspapers – all parts of a mass media that proffered well-edited information. In the twenty-first century, celebrities have more work to do.

Lady Gaga, rated by *Forbes* as the most powerful female entertainer in the world (more influential than Oprah, the executive editor of the *New York Times*, and the Head of Homeland Security), has over 27 million followers on Twitter. "Gaga proclaims the paradox of human life," philosophizes Frederick Turner, "that each of us contains the full human genome, and each of us is radically individual" (2011: 497).

Turner's point is that even the biggest popstar in the world can't afford to switch to autopilot, even with earnings of $52 million per year: she acknowledges her reliance on the people she calls her "little monsters" through daily debriefings and updates, involving them in her world rather than distancing herself from theirs as the Hollywood stars once did. "Gaga projects confidence that her 'little monsters' are meaningfully connecting with her aesthetic," writes Victor P. Corona (2011: 16). If, by "her aesthetic," Corona means the principles underlying and guiding Lady Gaga's artistic work, then he raises a small, but interesting question: do fans, or "little monsters," connect more meaningfully than fans of stars of previous eras? Or just differently?

AGNOSTICS AND WORSHIPERS |

Charlie Parker, John Coltrane, Miles Davis. These were leading lights among a firmament of jazz musicians appearing in the 1950s. They were the epitome of cool – then meaning a sense, style, attitude, and approach to music that signified an indifference to audiences and which stuck a defiant swivel-on-it finger up to mainstream society. "These musicians were less secular stars than quasi-religious figures and their fans often referred to them with godly reverence," wrote Nelson George in his *The Death of Rhythm and Blues* (1988: 25).

There's nothing unique, nor indeed unusual, about bestowing divine status on mere mortals. History is full of characters who actually encouraged their followers to do so (the Caesars, Aztec leaders, Pharaohs) and, in the modern world, millennial cults are typically led by charismatic figures claiming messianic powers. Even musicians who have scorned such attributions, such as Bob Marley or Bob Dylan, have been endowed with deistic eminence by fans. Marley had an oracular presence and his songs were infused with Rastafarian prophecy. Dylan perplexed one generation, while inspiring another with his sour condemnations of war and prejudice. Their influence makes their veneration comprehensible.

So far, we've examined the changing social conditions under which celebrities came to occupy positions not just of prominence but exaltation – and I use this word carefully, indicating the way in which celebs today are praised, dignified, and often ennobled by rapturous fans. There are still figures of today whom we regard with great respect: Nelson Mandela (1918–) and Muhammad Ali (1942–) for sure, Queen Elizabeth II and Bill Gates maybe, possibly Oprah and Roger Federer. Consumers tend to stand back and treat all of them with the kind of reverence they had for Mother Teresa of Calcutta (1910–97) – as we saw previously, death does not necessarily interrupt meaningful associations. They wouldn't want to probe too deeply into their private lives, preferring to regard them as off-limits, taboo celebrities, customs prohibiting too close an association with them.

More usually, fans seek out information on celebrities; that is part of the fun of being a fan: searching, finding, sharing, and, of course, gossiping. Integral to celebrity culture is the involvement in the lives of figures who have, for some reason, become well known. This much is obvious. Often, the objects of the fans' interest and, perhaps, praise seem to have done nothing to justify such fascination. Such is the peculiarity of celebrity culture: ostensibly undeserving people are richly rewarded as much for being as doing. They offer themselves for acclaim rather than actually accomplishing something that might merit it. This may sound like a cynic's evaluation, but it's intended as a prompt. Why do fans involve themselves with celebrities who just don't appear to warrant or deserve it?

First, we should clarify what we mean by "fan." There are two versions of the source of the word. One traces it to the adjective "fanatic," from the Latin *fanaticus*, meaning "of a temple"; so the fan is someone who is excessively enthusiastic or filled with the kind of zeal usually associated with religious fervor. The term crept into baseball in the late 1880s, but as a replacement for the more pejorative "crank," according to Tom Sullivan, writing for the *Sporting Life* of November 23, 1887. The alternative is even older: the "fancy" was the collective name given to patrons of prizefighting in the early nineteenth century. There are references in Pierce Egan's 1812 classic *Boxiana*. Whatever its etymology, "fan" lost its religious and patrician connotations and became a description of followers, devotees, or admirers of virtually anybody or anything in popular culture.

The origins are less important than the relationships today's fans have with celebrities. In a sense, we're all fans of varying degrees. Even those who are disenchanted by, or even despise, celebrity culture's meretricious excesses would be hard pressed to avoid watching and listening to celebs. Just reading a newspaper, watching tv, or going to the movies implicates someone in celebrity culture and thus turns them into a fan of some order. For reasons that will soon become clear, we'll call this group of hard-bitten yet celebrity-aware fans "agnostics," as distinct from what Lynn McCutcheon and her research colleagues call low-worship fans, who just watch and read about celebrities (2002). Other types of fans are: those for whom following celebrities more keenly has a more "entertainment-social character"; those who manifest more "intense-personal feelings" with celebrities; and those "extreme" worshipers who "over-identify" with celebrities and who behave compulsively and obsessively toward them in a "borderline pathological" manner (Maltby *et al.* 2004).

A parasocial interaction, as we've seen, describes the relationship fans have with figures they have never met, nor probably ever will meet. Although it's one-way interaction, this doesn't lessen its impact on the fan, who might experience the relationship as genuine and just as valid as other kinds of social interaction. Every type of fan, even the ostensibly uninterested, has this kind of interaction with celebs, if only because it's unavoidable. Even if we wanted to insulate ourselves for a while, we couldn't escape overhearing chats, glancing at newspaper or magazine covers, or resisting switching on the tv, even if only for the news. The cumulative effect is what the psychologists Horton and Wohl, who introduced "parasocial interaction" in the 1950s, called "intimacy at a distance" (1956).

Like it or not, we do get the feeling that we "know" celebrities. Think about anyone from any point along the alphabetical scale that defines how prestigious a celebrity is. The probability is that you will either like or dislike someone from the A-list and feel progressively indifferent to those further along the scale. But what do you actually know about any of them? What you've gleaned from the media, which act as effective filters on information, and perhaps a few supplementary fragments sourced from sundry gossip. In other words, not really enough on which to make a judgment. We do the rest ourselves: we decide on how to interpret what is, after all, limited information about celebrities rather as we might choose how to watch a DVD of a film: we can change the sequence of the scenes, view one part repeatedly, slow down or freeze passages, explore how the special fx were achieved, or just watch outtakes. In other words, celebrities aren't just *there*: we create them out of the two-dimensional material presented on the screen. In the process, they become so real to us that we feel we know something about them – or, in the case of the intense-personal or the borderline pathological fans, they feel they actually know them and have feelings that are reciprocated.

ORDINARY PEOPLE WITH EXTRAORDINARY FRIENDS

In a revealing study published in 1991, Neil Alperstein wrote about "Imaginary social relationships with celebrities appearing in television commercials." The "artificial involvement," as Alperstein calls it, in the lives of people viewers have never met paradoxically helps them "make sense of reality." The other paradox of intimacy at a distance features in the research – viewers expressing feelings of closeness, loyalty, or perhaps detestation about performers they know via their tv screens. In fact, they *know* them as they know a painting or a book: they have discerned, fathomed, read, and, in other ways, made intelligible the figures they have only seen on television.

The screen might flatten the characters, but the fans "inflate that image – adding dimensions to the interaction – as evidenced in the descriptions of their attraction to celebrities" (1991). One viewer disclosed how she regarded Joan Lunden, who used to host the *Good Morning America* show, as "a trusted friend": "When she happens to be sick or on vacation, I miss her."

Another viewer described how Orson Welles, or, more accurately, his perception of Welles, had shaped his entire life: his "maverick attitude," "his emphasis on quality at the expense of acclaim," the "grudging respect" frequently accorded him. These helped the subject shape himself. So, it came as a shock to discover Welles endorsing wine in a tv commercial. "Seriously disillusioning . . . It was not a happy experience," said the fan.

Alperstein describes what he calls "a give-and-take with a multitude of media figures," with fans incorporating celebrities into their "imaginary social worlds." Far from dismissing his subjects as obsessive or even disillusioned, Alperstein credits them with intelligence, wit, and even skepticism. They enjoy "the confluence of information, gossip, and experiences" so much that they can suspend the last of these qualities whenever it suits them. Alperstein's study uncovers viewers entangled in a "complex web they weave through entertainment programming, news, sports and advertising," so that the complete experience is intricately satisfying. They're willing participants in the creation of "multiple realities"; so their lives are not constantly upset and their everyday routines disrupted. Their relationships with celebrities are seamlessly integrated into their daily lives, so that they remain a rewarding and, on this account, even enriching addition.

A later piece of research by Benson Fraser and William Brown yielded similar conclusions, though this time about one celebrity in particular. In their "Media, celebrities, and social influence: identification with Elvis Presley," Fraser and Brown wrote: "Fans develop self-defining relationships with celebrities and seek to adopt their perceived attributes, resulting in powerful forms of personal and social transformation" (2002: 196).

Like the Welles fan, the followers of Elvis in this study entered into a cognitive and emotional relationship that led to a "selective integration" of what they considered to be Elvis' key qualities into their own lives. As a result, they "changed substantially." Presley died in 1977. The fans in the study didn't take the *National Enquirer*-style approach and insist he was still living on a remote Pacific island or somewhere even weirder. As one fan testified: "I can feel him in my heart. I can see him in my dreams. I can see him on my wall in my posters, that's the stuff that's the real Elvis" (2002: 196). The *real* Elvis.

Fraser and Brown argued that the concept of parasocial relationship couldn't adequately cope with the bilateral, or two-way, character of this kind of fan–celebrity interaction: it precipitates affective and behavioral changes in the fan. Nor do they find the idea that fans model themselves on celebrities convincing "because it does not address the relationship between media consumers and media personae." They introduce a third possibility: *identification*, by which they mean that fans "reconstruct their own attitudes, values, or behaviors in response to the images of people they admire, real and imagined, both through personal and mediated relationships" (2002:187).

The study's conclusions embrace all three possibilities. (1) "Ordinary people develop extraordinary psychological relationships with celebrities, whether living or dead"; (2) fans regard celebrities as role models; (3) fans adopt what they see as the celebrity's attributes, including his or her values and behavior. While it could be argued that Elvis was and, on the output of this study, is a singular celebrity, the fans' response appears to be representative in that they derived what they considered to be relevant to their own lives from mediated images. "The fabric of their self-identity is intricately interwoven with their image of Elvis, not only as an entertainer, but also as a friend, lover, husband, father, patriot and citizen," write Fraser and Brown (2002: 197). "The image of a celebrity can be more tightly held and more powerful than the real person on which it is based."

Both studies took place amid celebrity culture and both conveyed plausibly the manner in which contemporary fans immerse themselves in relationships that are both imaginary, yet tangible, in their consequences for the behavior and attitudes of fans. Any notions of the fan as a gullible dupe suckered by the wiles of artful celebrity-manipulators are blown away. Instead, we view the fan as attentive and fully aware. Far from being a pointless and meaningless pursuit, following celebrities turns out to be a gratifying and significant activity that can and, according to these accounts, often does, prompt changes. But it's not Elvis or Lady Gaga, or even Nelson Mandela that's exerting the influence: it's the fans' interpretations of what those celebs are like, regardless of whether or not they're accurate assessments. What matters is that they are credible assessments.

A third study confirmed that celebrities influence attitudes and personal values, including work ethic and ethical stances. Susan Boon and Christine Lomore were interested in the peculiar attachments fans have to celebrities. Part of the research required participants to list celebrities, or idols, they felt affected their lives (2001). Apart from Elvis, several other influential figures were long gone, Jim Morrison (1943–71), Albert Einstein (1879–1955), and John Wayne (1907–79) included.

Consumers use media creatively: they turn inert materials into narratives that become meaningful to them and their peers and make imagined relationships as real as actual ones.

Again, the image of the fan as a hapless victim is exposed as flawed: the subjects interviewed were wide awake to the influences of celebrities and accepted that many celebrities had been inspirational in a positive way. They expressed strong feelings, which suggested that they had thought about what they believe some celebrities embodied, stood for, or exemplified. Boon and Lomore concluded that "as changing social and demographic patterns continue to weaken and fragment social networks," attachments are likely to become stronger. Perhaps so. This could mean more people retreating into the solace of parasocial relationships with posters, DVDs, or other kinds of merchandise bearing celebrity images, like the character Jess in Gurinder Chadha's film *Bend It Like Beckham*. Unable to confide in her parents or close friends, Jess has her feelings stirred every night by a poster of David Beckham on her bedroom ceiling and spends time confessing her deepest desires to the inert image.

The fictional Jess may have a lot in common with countless other worshipful fans of one of the world's leading celebrity athletes of the early 2000s. For her and maybe them, Beckham became a lifeline connecting them to resources that, at least in their eyes, weren't available to dilettantes or outsiders. Only they truly had access. To them, their relationships were singular, personal, and exclusive. Posters don't respect fans any more than dolls, or any other kind of celebrity merchandise. They simply exist.

The fourth piece of research of interest to us is a social media era study of 11–18-year-olds in Singapore. Authors Stella C. Chia and Yip Ling Poo take "involvement with celebrities" to mean "the degree to which an individual actively participates in decoding a media message . . . that regards media consumers as active seekers" (2009: 24). Fans, in other words, convert whatever texts they discover in digital or traditional media into intelligible language, i.e. a pattern of communication that's structured in a way that's meaningful to them. As their involvement deepens, they experience the same kind of intimacy with the abstract celebrities – and, remember, they *are* abstract: they don't have a physical existence, but exist in the minds of the fan – as they do with their friends: "Relation-ships with celebrities are similar to actual interpersonal rela-tionships in that the relationship between adolescents and ce-lebrities can indeed grow even though the interaction between them is vicarious and non-reciprocal" (2009: 34). "Vicarious" means experienced in the imagination through the actions of another; "non-reciprocal" indicates there is no give-and-take.

The Singapore study suggests there is a kind of self-perpetuating motion: as the feelings of intimacy develop, so fans consume more media material, translate it into their own grammar, and experience "intense-personal feelings," which is effec-tively the same as parasocial relationships. The study shows how consumers use media creatively: they turn inert materi-als into narratives that become meaningful to them and their peers, and, it appears, make imagined relationships as real as actual ones.

Taken together, these studies provide a different picture of fans and their relationship to celebrities. The attachments are not the result of desperate innocence, but of involvement, sometimes morphing into enthrallment. Not a sign of intellec-tual bankruptcy, but of emotional liquidity. The fans actually form the relationship, inflating the significance of the celebrity, perhaps, but with a well-meaning intensity that stimulates and inspires. The research cited here makes us realize that there's an invention that's often mistaken for inanity in the fans' rela-tionship. It also reminds us that, while some fans develop per-sonal, perhaps clandestine, and, in their own eyes, privileged relationships, others just itch to share their enthusiasm with like-minded members of their cohort.

GOSSIP, THE SOCIAL ELIXIR

Simply by talking about celebrities, "we collectively define who we are and what we value as a culture." And, in case you think that grandiose claim came from some pompous professor of cultural studies, think again. It comes from the pages of that trusted purveyor of knowledge, wisdom, and facts, *USA Today* (September 14, 2004: News section, p. 21a). In a short, yet illuminating article "What celebrity worship says about us," Carol Brooks (herself the editor of celeb mag *First for Women*) commented on the research of Lynn McCutcheon and her colleagues – which we touched on earlier in this chapter.

The original research paper, "Conceptualization and measurement of celebrity worship," established that "parasocial interactions are part of the normal identity-development" (2002: 68). Those who are either "mild" celebrity worshipers, including introverts and those who are intuitively drawn to a celebrity without thinking about it too deeply, reported "fewer and less intimate relationships than they did before becoming a fan." So the *Bend It Like Beckham* scenario rings true.

Brooks pulled out what she took to be an underlying proposition in the research: "Pointless conversation is one powerfully healthy social elixir." While the academics weren't explicit about this, Brooks detects that being a fan might involve more than worshipfully talking to posters. "Just by gabbing in the right way [about celebrities] you can expand your social circle, deepen your existing relationships, consolidate your sense of self and feel dramatically less stressed" (2004: 21a).

Even if the academic study was more circumspect in its conclusions, it provided the raw material for such an extrapolation. One of the joys of following the exploits of celebrities was, and, of course, is, being able to confer about them, what Brooks calls "using other people's triumphs and tragedies as fodder for discussion." But maybe there are other purposes that even Brooks, or the scholars she quoted, didn't spot. First, let me define gossip: casual or unconstrained conversations about other people that are based on rumor, hearsay, whispers, tittle-tattle, or downright lies. Gossip typically involves discussion about others' private lives. We started gossiping long before celebrities emerged and a short historical segue should help us recognize its lasting importance.

Modernity started in the 1500s, picking up pace with the scientific revolution of the seventeenth century, the Enlightenment of the eighteenth century, and the Industrial Revolution of the late eighteenth and early nineteenth centuries. One of its effects was the breakup of old-style communities in which the bonds people had with each other were organic, in the sense that they formed and grew like living phenomena. Industrialization, urbanization, and the multiple transformations they introduced didn't exactly destroy communities, but they changed their character. One of the consequences was atomization: we lost contact with each other and became individualistic, like the fine particles that spray from those cologne atomizers, each headed in a different direction.

Several writers have pondered the effects of the end of old-style communities and the rise of habits of independence and self-reliance. The French nobleman Alexis de Tocqueville (1805–59) toured North America in the 1830s, reflecting on the individualism he saw developing around him and how religion and the family might act as counterweights to this tendency. In 1887, the German scholar Ferdinand Tönnies (1855–1936) wrote about the replacement of *Gemeinschaft*, or community, with *Gesellschaft*, that is, modern society, and the indifference to others brought about by the latter.

One of the most influential statements on the subject in the mid-twentieth century included the concept of the "other directed" person. According to David Riesman (1909–2002) and his collaborators, the people who de Tocqueville had observed in the nineteenth century were inner-directed by religious or spiritual principles, and therefore determined individualists. The typical American of the 1950s, by contrast, had become "other-directed" and wanted to be loved rather than esteemed. His or her mission was not necessarily to control others but to relate to them. Other-directed people need assurance that they are emotionally in tune with people around them. *The Lonely Crowd* (1950) described a society composed of individuals who interacted with each other but who had had no meaningful ties or obligations other than those arising from self-interests.

So, while Brooks doesn't mention them, she draws on a rich scholarly tradition when she observes: "Throughout our history, humans have generally lived in small communities in which the topic of 'social grooming' couldn't be more obvious – stories involving one's friends and neighbors." She goes on: "But in our current fragmented, fast-paced society, we all have multiple 'villages': where we live, where we work, where we vacation, where we're from, even what chat rooms we log on to."

We're constantly shuttling from one "village" to another, striking up relationships – some fleeting, some enduring – with others with whom we share conversation. These aren't villages in the established sense, but portable or even cyber communities in which people can remain transient, yet still interact habitually, perhaps even changing identities as they shuttle between them. To do so, they need a "universal cultural currency" that extends across all villages. For Brooks, that currency is "celebrity chatter." Wherever we happen to be, we can always strike up a conversation about celebs. Try it next time you are, well, practically anywhere and with anyone: checking a book out of the library, standing at the supermarket checkout, getting served at a bar. "Far from being victimized by information about celebrities, we're using it for our own positive social ends," concludes Brooks (2004: 21a).

This is a persuasive argument and augments rather than contradicts reports of celebrity worship. Being worshipful carries no connotation of passivity, according to the original research. True, the researchers describe an "enthralled" population, which "reveres" celebrities. But Brooks stresses the activity of reaching out to people with whom we have little in common apart from an interest in celebrities, sharing information with them, and, in the process, strengthening a network of people we know, if only through a shared fascination with other people we don't know but with whom we still feel intimate. But, as anyone with even the most superficial acquaintance with fandom knows, the pleasure of being a fan is not just interrogating and sharing.

David Beer and Ruth Penfold-Mounce maintain that celebrity gossip "often tells of the mundane lives of celebrities in spectacular and moralizing tones" (2009). Gossips delight not simply in discussing the personal lives of others, but in dramatizing them in a way that lends itself to evaluation, especially moral evaluation – the rightness or wrongness of someone's actions. So, from where does the gossip originate? A little-known character in Sherlock Holmes' adventures is Langton Pike, who appears in Sir Arthur Conan Doyle's "The adventure of the Three Gables," first published in 1926:

> This strange, languid creature spent his waking hours in the bow window of a St. James's Street club and was the receiving-station as well as the transmitter for all the gossip of the metropolis. He made, it was said, a four-figure income by the paragraphs which he contributed every week to the garbage papers which cater to an inquisitive public.
>
> (1981: 1028)

When the great detective enquires discreetly into a "celebrated beauty" betrothed to an English nobleman, he is obliged to consult this "human book of reference upon all matters of social scandal." Today, Pike would probably be writing for *People* magazine and have a 5 million Twitter following. But would he still be one of the instigators of widespread gossip?

Julie A. Wilson thinks he probably would, but with a difference: "Today's celebrity gossip peddlers glamorize the Hollywood lifestyle while probing the personal lives of stars, but, like tabloid gossip they interpellate readers as jurists" (2010: 29). By "interpellate", Wilson means to bring into being, or to insert into, which is actually *interpolate*: strictly speaking, interpellate means to interrupt, though the confusion of the two words is commonplace. Beer and Penfold-Mounce contend the consumer has a more proactive role in affecting the content of the media and, in times when there are about 3,000 tweets every second, this seems plausible: consumers are often *prosumers*, the *pro* standing for "producer" or "proactive," depending on which definition you choose.

Wherever we locate the prime cause, it's a strong argument. Fans are interested voyeurs, as we know, but they are voyeurs with a reason: they want to monitor celebrities, but they also want to make judgements on them. It's as if consumers preside over their own courts, weighing up evidence, drawing on precedents, and delivering verdicts. Gossip is morality in action.

Whether condemnatory, approving, or moot, gossip makes celebrities seem simultaneously more dramatic and more ordinary, as Erin Meyers explains in her analysis of gossip about Britney Spears. The fact that the "truth" about someone can never be known is immaterial: "Celebrating or deriding . . . helps audiences make sense of her [Britney's] image." Meyers proposes a crucial feedback loop: "Celebrity gossip stories 'bounce off and add to the established image' of a star" (2009: 899).

Anthony J. Ferri suspects gossip has a further purpose: "Celebrities, whether they are acting out a role in a particular medium or behaving badly in everyday life, help us purge our frustrations within our own lives" (2010: 407). Ferri is at pains to point out that he is using "the Aristotelian concept of purgation" and, while he doesn't explain, I take it he means as a "release" or catharsis through drama (from Aristotle's *Poetics, c*.335 BC), rather than the more contemporary meaning: venting our aggression.

Gossip, from this perspective, is not just talk about a celebrity: it *is* the celebrity. The celebrity exists in what Ferri calls a pseudoenvironment "made up of images in our heads . . . the product of others' interpretations, or 'opinions' of events" (2010: 407). This type of approach to fandom, as the collectivity of fans has become known, accentuates the positive. Celebrities have been the inspiration behind many social benefits, including a new propensity to connect with each other and the recreation of cyber communities.

Fans chattering about so-and-so's new hairdo, wondering out loud about whether whatshisname is having an affair with you-know-who, and deploring or applauding her ladyship's adoption of so many children all seems innocently wholesome. Yet there is a darker side to being a fan and one that Brooks and the other writers who point out the cohesive functions of celebrity gossip neglect.

IN MY HEART, IN MY DREAMS, IN THE CROSSHAIRS OF MY GUN |

In 1949, baseball player Eddie Waitkus ensured himself a dubious place in history when a female fan shot him. The incident provided the raw material for at least two films featuring passionate and vengeful baseball fans: *The Fan*, in which salesman Robert De Niro, who gets his spiritual nourishment only by following baseball, turns viciously against his team's recently signed superstar after discovering the player is motivated only by money; and *The Natural*, based on Bernard Malamud's novel, in which player Robert Redford is shot by an admiring *femme fatale*.

Celebrity athletes and musical celebs are worshiped more intensely than other kinds of celebrities, according to McCutcheon *et al*. Their fans sometimes evince "a mixture of empathy with the celebrity's successes and failures, over-identification with the celebrity, compulsive behaviours, as well as obsession with details of the celebrity's life" (2002: 67).

Although they're labeled "borderline-pathological," these fans are not necessarily dangerous to either themselves or to the objects of their adoration, although, as Waitkus and many other celebrities have discovered, they can be. In "A cognitive profile of individuals who tend to worship celebrities," Mc-Cutcheon *et al.* describe a typical borderline-pathological as someone who might spend several thousand dollars on a napkin or a plate used by a celebrity (2003). And yet, there is a point at which collecting, gossiping, reading, or other forms of pursuit from a safe distance fail to satisfy some fans. They seek a more active engagement in the lives of their idols.

While McCutcheon and her colleagues don't cite them, there are several standout cases that illustrate that the borderline is occasionally crossed. Günther Parche, an unemployed lathe operator from Germany, was obsessed with the tennis player Steffi Graf. He followed her career with precisely the mixture of empathy and over-identification reported by McCutcheon *et al.* At his home, he built an altar in her honor so that he could worship the object of his commitment. When Monica Seles replaced Graf as the world's leading female player, Parche was stung into devising a way of restoring his idol to her rightful place. When Graf met her rival in the German Open of 1993, Parche ran onto the court and stabbed Seles, putting her out of action. During her inactivity, Graf resumed her place as the world's number one. Seles eventually came back, but without ever capturing her irresistible form. Parche ended up in prison, but he accomplished his mission. Graf took the number-one spot.

McCutcheon *et al.*'s research indicated that "extreme" celebrity worshippers who inflict harm or pursue rapaciously might qualify for membership of a pathological fan club. Yet the study concluded that: "The distinction between pathological and nonpathological celebrity worship is somewhat tenuous." Broken into its component parts, celebrity worship involves, as we've seen, such practices as watching, hearing and talking about celebrities, empathizing, perhaps even over-identifying with them, and compulsively collecting items, such as pictures, souvenirs, or other artifacts. All celebrity worshipers do one or more of these, but "as celebrity worship increases, these behaviours increasingly occur together."

While the researchers urge caution, this is an interesting finding: fans often labeled obsessive-compulsives, stalkers, or even full-on headcases do not, according to this account, do anything that other fans don't typically do. Nor do they register any different items on the "celebrity worship scale." At lower levels of the scale, fans tend to worship alone, while, at higher levels, they reach out and connect to form what Brooks calls villages, and, at the highest level, they revert to more solitary worship. Conceptually, they are all on the one scale.

What happens at the most extreme level is called *absorption*, which involves a total commitment of all available "perceptual, motoric, imaginative and ideational resources to a unified representation of the attention object" ("motoric" refers to movement; "ideational" refers to the capacity to form ideas). The fan might be motivated to learn more and more about their chosen celebrity, perhaps seeking out obscure sources of information that are not available to most fans. Harry Veltman was one such fan: he became fixated with the skater Katarina Witt, found out her home address, and bombarded her with mail, some of which included nude pictures of himself. He then managed to discover her telephone number and called to profess his love.

At some point during his parasocial involvement with Witt, Veltman had presumably grown dissatisfied and sought to develop a two-way relationship, which, in an odd way, he did. In McCutcheon *et al.*'s terms, his need or capacity for absorption was so high that he wanted access to parts of Witt's life that other fans were denied. Crucially, he cultivated the deluded belief that he had a special relationship with Witt: he became convinced that they were married.

Erotomania describes a condition in which someone believes that another, usually of higher social status (sometimes older), is in love with him or her. Such beliefs, when held by absorbed fans, are resistant to extinction. Fans often actively create conditions under which they appear "true": they rationalize them, making them seem perfectly reasonable. In this sense, obsessive fans control their own destinies, though only with the unwilling cooperation of celebrities. Facing one such fan, Robert Hoskins, across a California courtroom in 1996, Madonna said of his trial: "I feel it made his fantasies come true. I'm sitting in front of him and that's what he wants" (quoted in Meloy 1997: 177). Hoskins had made three approaches onto Madonna's property and was shot twice by a security guard. (Celebrities are not the only recipients of erotomanic attention: research indicates that over one in six US females and one in nineteen men receive unwelcome attention from "stalkers." See Wood and Wood 2002; Home Office 2003. The Stalking Resource Center has further details.)

Sometimes, fans remain engrossed for years. Mark Bailey broke into the home of Brooke Shields in 1985, seven years after her film début as a 12-year-old nymphet in *Pretty Baby*. He was put on five years' probation, before surfacing again in 1992, when he made threats to Shields. Seven months' imprisonment did little to stifle him. A legal order in 1998 prohibited him from ever contacting Shields, though he continued to write to her, which prompted his arrest in 2000. He was carrying a three-page letter for Shields, a greeting card and a .25-caliber automatic. It's probable that this absorption will endure into its third decade.

Occasionally, fans threaten partners. Catherine Zeta-Jones, wife of Michael Douglas, was threatened by a fan who became convinced she stood between herself and Douglas. Dawnette Knight claimed she met Douglas at a party in Miami in 1999 and had a two-year relationship with him. In one of her letters to Douglas, she referred to Zeta-Jones: "We are going to slice her up like meat on a bone and feed her to the dogs." She was jailed for three years in 2005. Zeta-Jones herself had been the object of a fan who professed his undying love for her and harassed her with a stream of unwelcome email messages.

Anyone still thinking that being a fan is sweetness and light should learn about Ricardo Lopez, who, in 1996, sent the singer Björk a package that, if opened, would have exploded with sulfuric acid and who videotaped himself committing suicide in a perverse supplication. The grim and tragic episode dispensed a reminder that celebrity-worshiping fandom has its dangers. While Lopez's motives can't be interrogated, it was thought he became upset on learning Björk was seeing the British artist Goldie.

Even when there is no delusion of romantic reciprocation, a fan can still sustain the belief in a relationship – up to a point. This is why empathy turns to obsession: the delusion of the special relationship becomes harder and harder to preserve. This is the theme of Martin Scorsese's 1982 movie *The King of Comedy*. In it, another De Niro character, Rupert Pupkin, obsesses over getting his own tv show, creating his own mock studio, complete with cutout guests, at his apartment. Not only does he follow the stars: he uses them as his own, imagining he's with them, that he has what they have, that he can do what they do. It's a triumph of fantasy. He deludes himself into believing he has a close amicable relationship with a real talk show host, whom he buttonholes and later visits at his home, arriving unannounced and introducing himself to the maid as a personal friend.

The film finds an academic confederate in the research of Rense Lange and James Houran who report the existence of a "positive (self-reinforcing) feedback loop" among subjects who believe they have had paranormal experiences (1999). While far from exact, the parallels are there to see: fans who crave a special relationship with celebrities can tolerate ambiguous experiences or interpret events to buttress their personally held beliefs. Potentially damaging episodes can be neutralized, setting in motion a kind of irrefutable, self-perpetuating cycle.

This seems to have been the case with William Lepeska, who, in 2005, tracked 1990s tennis star Anna Kournikova to within three doors of her Miami Beach residence and settled down naked at a poolside to wait for her. When police apprehended him, he implored the tennis pro-turned-model "Anna, save me!" and later explained: "I had all kinds of delusional assumptions about Anna's feelings toward me."

> **The difference between the devoted admirer and the dangerous 'stalker' may be alarmingly narrow.**
> **DAVID GILES**

Previously, Lepeska had written copious letters and posted messages on her webpage and, though his communication was unanswered, Kournikova, like most other globally known celebrities, made herself or, at least, her representations widely accessible. Once her sports career was over, Kournikova busied herself with fashion engagements, which guaranteed her visibility. Any internet search engine will still generate about a million results for Kournikova. Lepeska selectively screened the superabundant information about Kournikova and decoded it in a way that supported his own interpretation. Improbably, Lepeska was allowed to cross-question Kournikova when he defended himself during a hearing.

One wonders how many Kournikova fantasists were (maybe still are) out there, all with human fallibilities, all harboring forlorn yet expectant beliefs about her, all somehow expressing their allegiance to her, mostly in ways that escape public attention. Inadvertently perhaps, celebs supply sustenance: their sheer appearance is enough to keep some fans' faith alive. This went on for so long in the case of Dave Gahan, who grew uncomfortable with a male fan who kept an all-night vigil outside the Depeche Mode singer's Hollywood home that Gahan ended up headbutting the fan, who then sued, claiming brain damage. The fan ended up with $40,000 but, we presume, lost his faith (Dalton 2005: 22).

As I noted before, some fans develop a tolerance to behavior that at one stage satisfied their need for absorption and need to go one step further. Compulsive behavior and obsessional tendencies characterize addicted celebrity worshipers. The point to bear in mind is that there might be much more psychological resemblance between this type of fan and those who enthuse over celebs but without expressing any thoughts or behavior that might be considered inappropriate.

Clearly, there are momentous exceptions. Recent history has thrown up the likes of Mark Chapman and John Hinckley Jr, both of whom believed they were acting as proxies for others when they embarked on their missions to kill John Lennon and wound President Ronald Reagan respectively. Chapman said he received instructions through J.D. Salinger's novel *Catcher in the Rye*, while Hinckley was motivated by his erotomaniacal fixation with Jodie Foster. Yet even in these two extreme cases we can discern qualities common to most other kinds of fans, albeit taken to extremes.

Hinckley, in particular, shares much with the absorbed fans of Björk, Graf, Witt, and Kournikova, in both their spurious romantic attributions and in their delusion that they were responding to the caprice of others. "The obsessive fan who camps on the star's doorstep has the potential to become either a murderer or a marriage partner," David Giles reminds us. "The difference between the devoted admirer and the dangerous 'stalker' may be alarmingly narrow" (2000: 146).

Giles was writing before social media connected low worship with borderline-pathological and every other type of fan in an electronic global network. Armed with the force of digitized communications, fans who are vengeful, unwittingly fearsome, or perhaps just plain creepy have found a conduit for their words and images. The practice of communicating deliberately hurtful and malicious messages through social media became known as "trolling," and the perpetrators, "trolls"; though, as Giles's point makes clear, the difference between deliberately harmful trolls and sycophantic devotees may be narrow. Fans are blissfully aware that they share a pseudoenvironment – in this case, in cyberspace – with others, some of whom will be more virtuous, others more nefarious, than themselves. Their judgments are directed at those who either are or purport to be celebrities, not each other.

| POWER OVER THE LIVES OF OTHERS

None of the obsessive fans we've dealt with in this chapter just woke up one morning as predators or trolls. They all, in some way, progressed, often via circuitous routes, to a recognition that what they were doing was insufficient and they needed to ramp up. Anything, literally anything, could prompt such recognition. As Charles B. Strozier writes: "The slightest hint of injury, as the disdain of a lifted eyebrow, can cause great emotional suffering among the socially disempowered" (2002: 290).

Disempowered: what does this mean? People and groups that have little or no authority, low self-confidence, not much status, and not enough money to enjoy the kind of lifestyle they crave. They have no power to enable them to make things happen at a personal, let alone a political, level. Their feelings of impotence drag them to the conclusion that they should try something different, if only to see what happens. If it enables them to do something or make something happen, especially in controlling their own or others' lives, then it might be empowering. It might give them an authority, or a power to enforce obedience, however perverse that may seem. Consider this: a female fan of the multiple-times world snooker champion Stephen Hendry wrote him a series of letters that became progressively more abusive and included a threat to shoot him. She claimed that her threat afforded her "power over people's lives . . . to know that you can cause such harm to people by doing something as simple as writing a letter" (quoted in *The Sunday Times*, September 29, 1996).

Whether this is understood as an addictive craving for satia-
tion or an attempt to neutralize feelings of helplessness, the
feelings of power are undeniable – to the perpetrator. The fan
can change the life of a celebrity in the same way as he or she
might highlight a piece of text and hit the "delete" key on the
computer. Such influence over the life of another, especially
someone they worship, carries its own terrifying power.

Most fans didn't fit into popular stereotypes, such as the
"obsessive loner" who personifies the isolation and atomization of mass culture, or members of a "hysterical crowd," all
of them victims of mass persuasion. Fans have been around
as long as there have been famous figures to admire, respect,
and mimic, and the weight of evidence suggests most of them
are toward the agnostic end of McCutcheon *et al.*'s scale. They
may avoid the pernicious methods of Hendry's poison-pen
fan, but, in their own way, they too might be questing for empowerment.

*Fans' influence may be limited to buying or not buy-
ing downloads, but it might include committing suicide,
sending parcel bombs, or shooting to kill.*

Cheryl Harris thinks so: introducing her 1998 volume *Theorizing Fandom: Fans, subculture and identity* (co-edited with
Alison Alexander), she argues that fans "find empowerment
in their consumption of popular culture." Yet there is a paradox: "At the same time, it is impossible to ignore the extent to
which media industries may be said to engage in an attempt to
economically *disempower* fans by encouraging heavy spending
on artifacts and merchandise" (1998: 43).

Harris's reference to the corporate media apparatus alerts us
to the pitfalls of trying to make sense of fans by analyzing them
as if they were compressed into their own autonomous clusters.
They operate in a culture of consumption and, as such, are not
joyless victims of commodification, but cheerful contributors

to the process. The central insight of Harris and her collab-orators is that being a fan leads to a sense of influence and control "in the face of a monolithic industry." In other words, it's empowering. Fandom is "a phenomenon in which mem-bers of subordinated groups try to align themselves with mean-ings embodied in stars or other texts that best express their own sense of social identity" (1998: 49–50).

This is consistent with the approaches of Gamson (covered in Chapter 3) and Brooks (earlier in this chapter) and helps broaden the analysis offered by McCutcheon and her psycholo-gist colleagues. Following the exploits of others and perhaps displacing their own perceived inadequacies in the process, fans can negate their feelings of powerlessness and replace them with a sense of influence. This influence may be limited to buying or not buying downloads, whispering to posters on bedroom ceilings, or sending admiring letters. It might include committing suicide, sending parcel bombs. or shooting to kill. Seen in this way, the acts are all parts of one "spectrum of fan activities," as Harris calls it: "The ultimate payoff for fans has less to do with whether or not they get the ostensible goals they have articulated and more to do with the activity of being a fan" (1998: 52).

On this account, just doing the things fans do confers feel-ings of power onto people who are objectively quite powerless. It might sound like a rudimentary observation, but it helps explain the behavior of the "extreme worshipers," including obsessive and compulsive devotees, without marginalizing them to a path-ological fringe. I can anticipate the challenge: how else do we comprehend the likes of the Goth fans who armed themselves to the teeth and killed 12 of their peers and a teacher at Colum-bine High in April 1999? Or the besotted fan of actor Rebecca Schaeffer who shot her dead with a .357 Magnum and explained: "I have an obsession with the unattainable. I have to eliminate what I cannot attain" (quoted in Hooper 1995: 18)? These seem a universe away from the breezy enthusiasts who chat and collect.

But they are in the same spectrum; just at different parts. Schaeffer's killer, Robert Bardo, had written to her many times and watched her endlessly in *My Sister Sam*, which he taped. Her role in the CBS tv show was all nice and virtuous. Bardo was upset when he saw her play a much juicier role in the sex-comedy movie *Scenes from the Class Struggle in Beverly Hills*. Days later, he got the gun. In custody, he insisted that Schaeffer had his name and number in her address book; she hadn't (Merschman 2001).

You can laugh at the suggestion that the killers are motivated by the same concerns as the Twitterati and other social media enthusiasts who follow the likes of Lady Gaga (27m+), Justin Bieber (25m+), and Rihanna (23m+). Yet they are all engaged in the attempt "to align themselves with meanings embodied in stars," to repeat Harris. Giving support, being closer, and in some way affiliating themselves with someone they admire, respect, like, or even hate confer a sensation of power that is felt across the whole spectrum of fandom.

INFAMY

Imagine you are the managing editor of *The Vigilance*, a hypothetical regional newspaper in a medium-sized city. One afternoon, a colleague bursts into your office, holds out her smartphone, and exclaims: "Watch this video! It's got Sky Roquette dead bang." Roquette is a premier football player who is black, known for his extravagant rock 'n' roll lifestyle, and his all-night parties have frequently

CHAPTER HIGHLIGHTS

- Stars once hushed up potential scandals, but now they use them to their advantage
- Public attitudes toward sex scandals changed after the Rob Lowe affair of 1989
- Michael Jackson's life was a tableau of transgressive behavior – as was his death
- Race is a factor in the response to scandal: it impacts black and white celebrities differently
- Perceptions of victims affect the manner in which fans respond to celebrities' wrongdoing
- Some celebrities recover by adopting new personae, while others slide into oblivion
- Apologies via the media are the equivalent of wearing sackcloth, and have similar effects

upset his neighbors in the affluent and exclusive part of town where he lives. He's the part owner of an independent record label specializing in hip-hop music.

"Slow down," you tell her. "First, where did you get this from?" All she says is that she obtained it legally. It's a known fact that Roquette recently had a big fire at his place, and so many people, including firefighters, police officers, and insurance investigators, must have had access to his private belongings. Equally, it could have been hacked.

She plays the video and, sure enough, there is someone who looks a lot like Roquette, together with someone who is almost surely his wife Bombôn, a well-known photographic model, and an unidentified female who looks as if she's about 14. They are having sex. "This is going to be uploaded onto YouTube in three days," she tells you. "Shall we run the story?"

Scandal is like novocaine: the more of it we have, the less sensitive we become.

You tell her she must get more facts before it becomes a legitimate story, so she sets about the task. Two days later, she has nothing to add. Roquette is out of the country and not contactable. Bombôn agrees to a conference call in the presence of her agent and divulges that she and her husband occasionally record their sexual activities. But, beyond that, she refuses to comment. The video has still not appeared online.

"OK, what do we have?" you wonder out loud. "A recording of what seems to be a three-way sex situation. There's a guy who looks and sounds a lot like, and might even be, Roquette and someone else who is a dead ringer for Bombôn. And then there's this young girl; and she really does look like no more than a girl and could be under age. We just don't have enough to run with this. I know you don't want to disclose your sources, but, off the record, where did you get this?" She prevaricates, and then tells you: "A police officer."

You call a staff meeting. "Is there a backstory here?" enquires the newspaper's features editor. "I don't see this as a page-one news story, but an investigative piece that asks how a cop came into possession of the video in the first place and why that officer has been unusually cooperative in giving it to us."

Your colleague reminds you that: "Roquette has a giant-sized rep. Remember that time he boasted that he spends more on a bottle of champagne than a police officer's weekly take-home pay? His record label has artists who rail against the police in their music. And let's not forget he's black."

In media circles, it's rumored that Roquette has taken out a court injunction to prevent the publication of something he prefers not to be out in the open. By definition, the injunction prohibits the media from even reporting that it exists. Knowing Roquette, he would be bound to sue for millions if anybody leaked.

Another colleague chips in: "He and Bombôn have a pretty explosive relationship too. She's told some of the tabloids that he's slapped her about on more than one occasion. Perhaps she's trying to get back at him by releasing the video."

"I don't think the video itself is the story," another colleague responds. "But the events surrounding it are. Think of the context in which everything after has happened, like his status and the status of his wife and the well-documented tension between them. Would we be in possession of this video if the principal subject was a white non-celebrity, or even a white celebrity athlete without Roquette's reputation, or even a white celebrity athlete with the same kind of reputation?"

Time is against you. The recording could appear on the net at any time, or perhaps not at all. You might have the scoop of the year in your grasp, or you might fall prey to the hoax of the decade. You could end up in court. What's your call?

While the newspaper is fictitious, the narrative is pastiche – made up from fragments of actual events rather than entirely invented. Whatever happens to Roquette and Bombôn, one thing is for sure: their fame will grow if either the paper publishes the story, or the recording goes online. Such is the nature of celebrity culture: whether the social response is one of outrage or admiration, condemnation or compassion, repugnance or approval, the subject or subjects typically loom large in the public imagination. Scandal is like novocaine: the more of it we have, the less sensitive we become. Nowadays, the numbing effect of so many moral outrages has left us almost insensible, so any aspiring or established celebrity who intends to scandalize consumers will have to come up with something special. Take note: to *scandalize* means to shock by a real or imagined violation of propriety or morality, so consumers' responses are decisive.

Often a celebrity in need of more visibility will use scandal as a get-out-of-jail card. Or, in the case of Lindsay Lohan, a get-into-jail card: in 2007, the prodigious transgressor was sentenced to four days, though she served only one, after reaching a plea deal on drunken driving and cocaine charges. The case elicited renewed interest in the former child star, whose career had dipped in the previous two years. Her last major box-office movie had been *Herbie: Fully Loaded*, in 2005; and her albums were selling poorly. Now, she is known primarily for her generously documented struggles with drink, drugs, and eating disorders; her parole conditions and sexual preferences are of more interest than her albums.

Entertainers, politicians, military leaders, and all manner of other figures who occupied the public's attention in the twentieth century were wary of malicious gossip or the outcry occasioned by scandal. They carefully tiptoed around any action or event that might be regarded as morally or legally untoward. Contrast Lohan's spell in jail with that of Robert Mitchum (1917–97): toward the start of what became a shimmering Hollywood career, he was convicted of using marijuana. Biographer Lee Server relates how the incident was tactfully hushed up and Mitchum, then 31, was able to resume acting with little or no collateral damage. That was 1948.

In 2011, when stories of alcoholism, drug use, and domestic violence surfaced, Charlie Sheen (b. 1965) had no need of a hush job. By this time, the media was more watchful and encompassing, anyway; so it wouldn't have been possible. The stories didn't derail his career: he was fired by CBS and then resumed his career in an FX sitcom without breaking stride.

Celebrity history is full of such contrasts, all of which remind us that scandal is like an improvised explosive device, or IED: to some, a valuable, but extremely volatile resource. It can blow a nondescript figure to the stratosphere of fame in an instant, or it can wreak destruction. Some celebrities come crashing to earth; others contrive a way back; still others remain serenely airborne.

O.J. Simpson crashed: the athlete-turned-actor was well known in the USA but not much beyond before 1994. His generously covered murder trial ensured that his renown became global. Presumably fearing his presence in a film would be a box-office curse, studio chiefs disregarded him and he was forced to auction his estate for less than $4 million in order to pay debts. In 2008, desperate for money, Simpson was sentenced to 15 years in prison for a botched attempt to recover sports memorabilia.

Mike Tyson, on the other hand, was able to resume his boxing career after three years' imprisonment for rape. For his first fight after his release in 1995, he earned $10 million and went on fighting for another ten years. His earning capacity (ranging between $4 million and $17 million per fight) reflected public fascination with him, not in spite of, but because of, his notoriety. Either boxing promoters are more inveterate risk takers than film producers or they are more used to offending sensibilities in their quest for material rewards. Probably the latter. Whatever the reason, there is at least inferential evidence that suggests Simpson could, given an opportunistic studio, have prolonged his film career if his trial had taken place ten years later. Simpson, in case readers forget, was found *not* guilty.

So was Roscoe "Fatty" Arbuckle (1887–1933), though, again, he was condemned anyway. One of the pre-eminent silent film stars of his day, Arbuckle was arrested in 1921 for the sexual assault and manslaughter of a female actor at a party in San Francisco. His films were withdrawn and Paramount canceled his contract. Even though he was acquitted at his third trial, the media had already ensured that a stigma was burned into him. Studios ignored him, while creditors pursued him. He turned to drink and died destitute, aged 46, in 1933. His fate served as a warning to any popular entertainer. There was no uncertainty about the effect of scandal, especially sex-related scandal, on a showbusiness career. The famous violated or were seen to violate the law or social mores at their peril. After all, Arbuckle was cleared: his innocence mattered far less than the media's evaluation and subsequent treatment of him.

As the media's influence grew, so did their ability to shape, make, and break popular entertainers' careers. Even at a time when the Hollywood industry had a close and cozy relationship with the media, it was possible for someone to get swept to an untimely doom by a media wave. Mary Astor, who had played the duplicitous siren Brigid O'Shaughnessy in John Huston's 1941 version of *The Maltese Falcon*, was viewed as scandalous as a result of three divorces, alcoholism, and an attempted suicide. She appeared in only five minor roles during the whole of the 1950s, underlining how important it was to maintain a wholesome image.

Errol Flynn (1909–59) was not known for his assiduous discretion when it came to women: a lothario of the first order, he was applauded or at least admired for his priapic carousing. So, in 1942, when he walked free from a Los Angeles courtroom after being cleared of the statutory rape of a 17-year-old woman, his career was far from ruined and he resumed his film career. It was not the only sex charge Flynn was forced to deny, but, in a sense, his name was difficult to besmirch: he was known as a sexually dangerous character. The various charges seemed trumped up, anyway. Had any of them stuck, even Flynn would have been shunned by Hollywood – as he was in the 1950s when his age precluded him from playing the womanizing roles.

Today, we credit celebrities with inadvertent ingenuity for becoming involved in a moral indiscretion that manages to outrage and delight in such proportions that it creates rather than destroys their careers. Media indignation serves only to spur us into taking more notice. Take Paris Hilton's *succès de scandale*.

| SEX ON THE TABLE

The great granddaughter of hotel-chain founder Conrad Hilton (1897–1979) and heiress to a fortune, Paris claimed no talent apart from possible photogenicity: walk-on parts in minor movies seemed the limit of her dramatic prowess. Still, her party-going and A-list connections kept her in the gossip columns and generated enough buzz for Fox to feature her in *The Simple Life*, a reality tv show shot on an Arkansas farm. Days before her début in 2003, *Us*, the celeb magazine, was shown excerpts from a video featuring Hilton having sex in a hotel room three years earlier. Marvad Corp., a porn company, planned to sell the full version over the net. The *New York Times* reported that an anonymous source was offering samples to media outlets.

In spite of Hilton's parents' threat to sue anyone who helped make the tape public, excerpts appeared on the net and tabloids reported on it, often in explicit detail. Hilton became a cover story. Then, the story migrated to other media. As Cynthia Cotts of the *Village Voice* wrote: "Serious new outlets were scrutinizing a celebrity who had done nothing to merit their attention . . . two points emerged: Why do we care, and how exactly has the tape hurt this girl's reputation?" (2003: 32).

The answer to the first question is implicit in Cotts' own article: because media of every variety afforded it coverage; this helped draw 13 million viewers to their screens for the first episode of *The Simple Life*. The second question is invalid because, far from damaging her reputation, it actually made it. Hilton went from a rich-kid socialite to the "must-have" celebrity of the season. The Fox show was a hit, her memoirs were published as *Confessions of an Heiress*, and film roles beckoned. Every reader of this book has probably heard of Paris Hilton, though how many can name her film roles? Between the 2003 scandal and 2012, she appeared in 11 movies, including *House of Wax*, *Pledge This!*, and *Repo! The Genetic Opera,* and several tv series. She also produced and executive-produced several films, as well as writing books and making albums.

> *Like a rebranding exercise, an indiscretion that might have ended a career in earlier times offered the chance to adjust the public image and renew fortunes.*

When did sex scandals lose their destructive character and acquire a screaming potential to turn unremarkable people into luminaries? Obviously, there isn't an exact date, though one case catches the changing mood. In 1989, the year in which Madonna's *Like a Prayer* was released, Rob Lowe, then 25, underwent a transformation. Having established his credentials in films like *About Last Night* and *St. Elmo's Fire*, Lowe became a reluctant star of a porn video. In an episode comparable to Paris Hilton's, Lowe had engaged in hotel-room sex in front of a videocam. Bootleg duplicates of the video began circulating; if the net had been up and running then, it would surely have gone online. The allegations of exploitation and extortion, and the court case that followed, were incidental to the main action: the media had been animated by the scandal of a young star – a princely one – and videoed sex.

The media lined up to kick the corpse of Lowe's once-promising career. Today, critics might even have dismissed it as a vulgar and transparently obvious publicity stunt. Lowe's next film was *Bad Influence*, in which he played a manipulative Beelzebub-like character who films his impressionable friend's sexual encounters. But the movie, though opportune, did poorly at the box office and Lowe found himself yanked off the front covers of magazines, such as *Teen*, which immediately spared its four million readers' blushes by spiking a feature on him.

One of the more honest pronouncements came from Jeanne Wolf of *Entertainment Tonight*, who seemed less concerned about the act itself and more about the self-inflicted career harm it occasioned: "The [Hollywood] community looks down on Rob's bad judgment for doing something that would put his career in jeopardy" (quoted in *USA Today*, June 26, 1989: 1D). It was a conclusion that seemed to chime with the dictum of early science fiction author H. G. Wells (1866–1946): "Moral outrage is jealousy with a halo."

Viewers of *The West Wing* will know what happened next. A chastened Lowe traipsed forth into the celebrity wilderness, cropping up in unlikely places, like *Wayne's World* in 1992, and in *Mulholland Falls* in 1996 (an uncredited role). His appearance at the White House, albeit television's version, was providential. By the time the multi-Emmy-winning and globally watched tv series premiered in 1999, Lowe's misdemeanors seemed not exactly harmless, but nowhere as shocking as they had looked ten years before. So, when Hilton's contribution to the video-sex genre came into view, there was prurient interest, displeasure with its poor taste, but no widespread condemnation.

When Lowe was given his own tv show, *The Lyon's Den,* in 2003, the moral censure that had followed his sex tapes had long since abated. In the interim, Madonna, who had been breaking sexual taboos as a career-advancing tactic since the late 1980s, had helped redraw the lines of decency. Sexual mores too had changed in a way that not only permitted the famous to be riskier, edgier, and altogether more venturesome, but often rewarded them for doing so.

Hugh Grant, for example, was fined and put on two years' probation after pleading no contest to charges of lewd behavior with prostitute Divine Brown on Hollywood's Sunset Strip in 1995. Over the next ten years, Grant made 15 films, including blockbusters like *Bridget Jones's Diary* and *Love Actually*. His notoriety, though short-lived, enabled him to exchange his image as a Cary Grant epigone and suitor of Estée Lauder's golden girl for that of a rakish libertine. Like a rebranding exercise, an indiscretion that might have ended a career in earlier times offered the chance to adjust the public image and renew fortunes.

Occasionally, there was a kind of defiance, as in the case of r&b artist R. Kelly. Again, sex tapes were the source of a scandal, though Kelly's alleged appearance with an underage female complicated the affair. After a series of lawsuits and dropped charges, Kelly faced 14 counts of child pornography. Kelly kept producing cds, including a series of five singles linked by a narrative about his waking up with a woman and having to hide from her husband, who then discovers them and later reveals himself as a pastor who is also having a relationship, in his case with a man! The whole suite was called "Trapped in the closet." More self-consciously and resourcefully than any other celeb, Kelly exploited his sexual imbroglio by creating his own opus.

George Michael also turned a potentially embarrassing and maybe ruinous incident into an opportunity following his arrest for lewd behavior in a public lavatory in 1998. Fined and ordered to do community service, Michael was virtually forced into coming out and declaring that he was gay. The video accompanying his next single following the arrest, "Outside," featured kitsch s&m scenes with characters dressed in burlesque police uniforms. As if this didn't generate enough publicity for the single, the arresting officer later tried to sue Michael for causing him humiliation and emotional distress by "mocking" him in the video. (In 2005, Michael suggested he was retiring from being famous because "the business of media and celebrity" was "unbearable." At the time, he was worth £65 million ($110.5m), according to *The Sunday Times* "Rich list". By 2012, his wealth was up to £90 million ($136m).)

For historical contrast, consider the experience of Shakespearean actor John Gielgud (1904–2000), who was arrested in 1953 for a similar offence in a public convenience in London, to which he pled guilty and was fined. At that point in his career, he was predominantly a stage actor, though he'd just finished making *Julius Caesar.* He had appeared in only the occasional film, such as *The Prime Minister* in 1941 (he would later appear in Laurence Olivier's acclaimed 1955 *Richard III*). One wonders, had Gielgud been part of the protective Hollywood system, whether his dalliance would have ever been publicly known. Only later did Gielgud embrace Hollywood: he won an Oscar for his supporting role as the waspish butler in the original version of *Arthur* in 1981.

His fellow thespian Alec Guinness (1914–2000) improvised with his own evasive technique when he was caught soliciting for sex in a public toilet in 1948: he gave the name Herbert Pocket, the Dickens character he had recently played in David Lean's *Great Expectations*. It's doubtful whether such a ruse would have worked in the 1970s, by which time Guinness was featuring in Hollywood films. How many police officers would believe a suspect named Ben Obi-Wan Kenobi? (Britain didn't decriminalize homosexual acts between consenting adults until 1967; the USA began repealing its sodomy laws in 1971.)

"The rules are changing because of a whole new cultural climate created by the media," according to Maer Roshan, an editor at *New York* magazine, who suggests that the protections once afforded celebrities have vanished: "As with everything else, their sexuality is now on the table" (quoted in Kirby 2001: 56).

| MICHAEL JACKSON: THE PSYCHODRAMA

If Michael Jackson's life was a biopic, this is how the plot might unfold: it is late 2002 and the world's premier male popstar of the late twentieth century reclines on his laurels and enjoys his personal fortune in the privacy of his own ranch in California, reflecting on his lustrous career. We then go to flashback: we see a conspicuously gifted child star mature to a young man in his twenties with a global following and a succession of tours, albums, and videos. He begins to attract interest more for what his fans don't know about him than what they do; his stage presence is interesting, but the really interesting aspects of him were the ones outsiders couldn't see. Questions about his apparently oddball habits circulate: why did he keep having plastic surgery, or collect the skeletons of people, or sleep in an oxygen tent? As the media's glare becomes more incessant, Jackson seems to recoil, hiding away and becoming protective about his private life. Nothing whets the media's appetite more than a reclusive celebrity who either doesn't want or pretends not to want their attention.

The more rumors circulate, the more Jackson seems to insulate himself from the world outside his 3,000-acre Neverland home, which he appears to have turned into his own gigantic playground where children could visit and stay and share the same bedroom as Jackson. His personal life becomes a kind of self-replenishing fountain of whispered secrets, hearsay, and innuendo. In 1994, Jackson agrees to pay Jordy Chandler, then 14, an undisclosed sum, thought to be over $25 million, to stop a sex abuse lawsuit ever reaching court. Jackson was never put under oath for a civil deposition that could be used in a criminal trial. Despite two marriages, stories of his companionship with young boys circulate.

Back to 2002, where we see Jackson pondering what to do to quash the stories that are now troubling him. His albums no longer sell in their dozens of millions, but, combined with his back catalog, royalties provide him with a prolific income. All the same, his manner suggests he may have money problems.

For reasons the biopic leaves uncertain, Jackson agrees to an interview, which airs on February 6, 2003 on ABC's *20/20*. Jackson discusses sharing his bed with children. After the telecast,

Jackson moans that his interviewer, Britain's Martin Bashir, has betrayed him and files complaints with British media watchdog groups. Then, he helps produce a rebuttal entitled *The Michael Jackson Interview: The footage you were never meant to see*, which is shown on Fox two weeks later. Meanwhile, rumors that Jackson has money troubles are supported by the multiple lawsuits filed against him. Several suits remain unresolved. Jackson's former financial adviser sues him for $12 million in unpaid fees and services; he countersues and the matter is settled out of court for an undisclosed sum.

A German concert promoter sues him for dropping out of concerts and is awarded $5.3 million; both sides appeal. A design firm claims that Jackson didn't pay for $78,000 of work on a proposed theme park, Neverland Estates: the case is settled on undisclosed terms. But worse is to come: in November, Jackson is arrested for allegedly molesting a 12-year-old boy, who was at the time undergoing treatment for lymphoma. Jackson contracts an illness that attorney Brian Oxman calls a "reaction to lawsuits."

> **What happens when a celebrity whose genius has been acknowledged as both genuine and unique appears to have become unwholesome and possibly harmful?**

In June 2004, after a trial that dominates headlines for four months, Jackson is cleared of the charges and walks from court a free man. Within a month, his record company Sony/ BMG – presumably subscribing to the R Kelly/G Michael scandal→sales theory of causation – releases *The Essential Michael Jackson* compilation double cd. It works: interest in Jackson rises sharply, though the singer's stage appearances become fewer. In 2006, he disappoints fans in his first appearance since being cleared, by singing just a few lines of "We are the world" at the World Music Awards in London. There are suspicions that Jackson has acquired a dependency on prescription drugs.

In 2008, Jackson attempts to reprise his career as the King of Pop: it is announced that he will play at London's O2 Arena, the concert intended to coincide with the 25th anniversary of the release of *Thriller*. It does not materialize; though, in March 2009, more definite plans surface when promoters confidently publicize a ten-concert residency at the same 20,000-seat arena, scheduled to start in July. Jackson's motivation for undertaking such a punishing schedule is unclear, though the running costs of Neverland, which amount to $3 million (£2.1m) per year, are possibly a factor. It is reported by the BBC that Jackson will earn $400 million (£283m) for the concerts, which sell out in minutes.

Imagine that's a rough cut of the biopic so far. What's required now is a denouement that will make this a psychodrama of the highest order, packed with mystery, weirdness, and forbidden sex. The central character is a man who had matured from child virtuoso to the world's greatest pop singer and then became an inscrutable, color-changing recluse with uncertain predilections and money problems.

The album *Diana Ross Presents the Jackson 5* was released in December 1969. MICHAEL JACKSON DIES AT 50 was the front-page headline of innumerable newspapers on June 26, 2009. Jackson's longevity as a world-class celeb was due to his mutability: he changed from a prodigy to the pop monarch who ruled the MTV age, before becoming an engaging eccentric and then a man-child with unwholesome interests. Maybe news of his death didn't define the end of Jackson so much as the start of another transition. Jackson could have died a broken man, his finances in a mess and his career finished; at the time of his death, his estate was $500 million (£320m) in the red.

But celebrity culture, as we've seen, alchemizes success from scandal. Three years later, the Jackson estate reported profits of $475 million thank to postmortem earnings such as a $60 million (£38.26m) upfront payment for the concert film *This Is It*, a seven-year, ten-project record deal with Sony for $250 million (£160m), a joint venture with Cirque du Soleil called *Michael Jackson: The Immortal World Tour*, which grossed over $2 million per show, and royalties from album sales – 20–30 million sold in the six months after he died alone. For the three years following his death, he was second highest-earning pop music act, dead or alive. He, or rather his estate, earned $170 million from one year alone.

What happens when a celebrity whose genius has been acknowledged as both genuine and unique appears to have become unwholesome and possibly harmful? When the whiff of sexual wrongdoing becomes an odor too pungent to ignore? When the mysteries surrounding him become so impenetrably deep that no one can properly claim to have known anything about him for certain? What happens when he unexpectedly dies? The answer we take from Jackson's experience is that the celebrity becomes both exalted and vilified, and acquires a status that guarantees him a place among celebrities, like Marilyn, who died, taking with them sex secrets that fans will forever puzzle over.

Jackson was, of course, a singular character: he didn't need to do a thing; the rumor stuck with him like an ice cream wrapper on the sole of his sebago loafer. He could never dispose of it. Practically everything he did occasioned talk about possible impropriety. Even his death generated high-voltage controversy: was he murdered, as many suspected? Or did the numbing pressure of having his every movement monitored by the media eventually get to him?

One theory is that a desperate Jackson, fearing that his comeback concerts could be canceled unless he was able to sleep, administered himself propofol, a drug that promotes relaxation and sleep. Conrad Murray, his personal physician, was trying to wean him off. Jackson may also have swallowed eight lorazepam tablets (typically prescribed to treat anxiety disorders) while Murray was not watching. The official verdict was that

Murray had complied with Jackson's demands for anesthetics to help him sleep. In 2011, Murray was convicted of involuntary manslaughter and sentenced to four years' imprisonment.

Jackson's celebrity afterlife continued in 2012, when the Jackson family members started squabbling with lawyers over control of the estate. Michael's sister Janet and four of her siblings accused the people who controlled the estate of fraud and of abusing their mother.

WINDS OF CHANGE

Reactions to scandal, especially sex scandal, form four main categories: condemnation; indifference; resentment; and approval. Whichever of these dominates depends more on the context than the outcome. As we've seen, for most of the twentieth century prior to the arrival of what we regard as celebrity culture, unsparing efforts were made to suppress news of Hollywood transgressions. The fear – and a well-founded fear – was that they would be damaging. Widespread condemnation, disapproval, and censure could ruin careers. Elizabeth Taylor's indiscretion, as we saw earlier, was the most publicized and, therefore, "biggest" scandal to date. Far from ruining either Taylor or Burton's reputations, the notoriety produced by their affair intensified interest in both of them. In an arch piece of casting, Lindsay Lohan was chosen to play Taylor in the 2012 film *Liz and Dick*, which told of the tempestuous affair.

Swirling forces of conflict were gathering in the early 1960s: civil rights protests, the decolonization of Africa, and the rebellious rhythms of rock music added to the growing sense of emancipation. It was as if entire nations were involved in collective rule breaking. Despite the furor in conservative Catholic Italy, Taylor's deviance hardly qualified for moral turpitude elsewhere. In a way, it seemed in accord with the times. Swinging-age liberation had arrived and, while some might have found her action imprudent, others would have admired and perhaps longed for her ability to disobey convention.

The dawn of the celebrity age in the late 1980s opened new vistas for both the media and the aspirant celebrities. As we saw in Chapter 4, Madonna refined rule breaking into a method of career advancement. While the 1989 film *sex, lies and video-tape* wasn't actually about videoed sex (the videotapes feature women *talking* about their sexual experiences), the title's link-age was tantalizing. So, Rob Lowe's VCR exploits in the year of the film's release occasioned questions about whether it was such an awful wrongdoing and if it would finish his career. The fact that Lowe emerged – eventually – unscathed and, 16 years later, was commanding a leading role in London's West End indicates that he had been swept safely by the winds of change.

> *Being a celebrity had distinct advantages for white de-fendants, whereas for Black defendants, being a celeb-rity was a liability.*
>
> JENNIFER KNIGHT et al.

The first big sex scandal of the 1990s involved William Kennedy Smith, the nephew of Senator Edward Kennedy and member of the illustrious extended family. He was acquitted of rape, the thrust of a successful defense being that his accuser wasn't credible, having had abortions and been abused as a child. There was also the matter of the skimpy black underwear she favored; this was interpreted by the defense to signify in-tention. Kennedy Smith was white and of what might be called "good stock."

Mike Tyson was black, a product of a dysfunctional family in the Brownsville slum district of New York. He wasn't the first black athlete to have made the headlines for off-field offenses. Darryl Strawberry rarely seemed out of trouble in the early 1990s. Nor the last: Jamal Lewis was sentenced to four months following a drugs case.

Again, context was all-important. In a sense, Tyson's guilt or innocence of the myriad violations of which he was accused at some point or other was less relevant than times, places, and personnel. America in the 1990s was a time when celebrity subsumed culpability. And yet his case, like that of Simpson and, later, Jackson, dramatized the relative values of celebrity.

In their study "Famous or infamous? The influence of celebrity status and race on perceptions of responsibility for rape," Jennifer Knight and her co-researchers discovered that "being a celebrity had distinct advantages for white defendants, whereas for Black defendants, being a celebrity was a liability" (2001: 183).

While they were concerned mainly with rape cases, the psychologists broadened their conclusions to include other types of cases in which sex had been involved. "Social attractiveness" describes a quality attributed to celebrities, particularly by jurors who adjudge sex violations as "out of character" for high-status defendants. In other words, celebrities can often receive a lenient verdict simply because of the esteem they enjoy.

But not all celebrities. According to Knight *et al.*: "Aversive racism theory proposes that although most people today are not openly racist, a subtle form of prejudice emerges when people feel safe to express themselves" (2001: 184). This kind of racism thrives in the courtroom, leading to the study's conclusion: "Black celebrities were perceived more negatively than were Black noncelebrities, whereas White celebrities were viewed more positively than were White noncelebrities" (2001: 187).

This is plausible, especially when set against the cases of Winona Ryder, Christian Slater, Martha Stewart, and Robert Downey Jr., and the previously mentioned Charlie Sheen, Kennedy Smith, and Rob Lowe. It could be argued that where sex is absent from the offense – Ryder was caught shoplifting, for example – forgiveness is easier to come by. Supporters of Tyson, who included Jesse Jackson, Al Sharpton, Spike Lee, and Don King, speculated how the trial might have gone differently had a prominent white athlete been in the dock.

The picture is further complicated by polls collected during both the Simpson and Tyson trials. The majority of African Americans believed Simpson and Tyson to be innocent, while the majority of whites thought they were guilty. In their *Contemporary Controversies and the American Divide* (2000), Robert Smith and Richard Seltzer explain the differences in terms of distinct historical and social experiences, and the disparity in economic circumstances between blacks and whites. And, as if to confuse matters even more, we should remind ourselves that "negative perceptions" don't necessarily impair a celebrity career. Tyson continued to sell out arenas and move pay-per-view buys for ten years after his release. Sales of Michael Jackson cds spiked for the first time in years after his acquittal.

Throughout this book, I've argued that, while the media's influence is great, it's far from total. We, the consumers, aren't like children who can be persuaded into believing in magic by a few conjuror's tricks. At the height of the Simpson trial, LexisNexis, the online news service, asked the question: "Which sports figure is the undisputed champ in generating the most negative media coverage for off-the-field incidents?" After surveying print and broadcast media, the research showed that, up to August 1994, the media had reported 9,906 stories about Tyson, comfortably more than the widely disparaged Simpson (6,754) and Ben Johnson (6,688), whose use of steroids in 1988 earned him universal opprobrium (*Business Wire*, August 29, 1994). Yet, we remained absorbed by Tyson. Had comparable research been done during early 2005 with all celebrities included, would Jackson have headed the list? And, if so, would it have made much difference to his status?

The findings so far appear as fragmentary and possibly contradictory. Scandals that once killed careers now boost them. Unless the celebrity is black, in which case their status doesn't enhance perceptions of them in the same way as it does for whites. That is, until the asymmetry between blacks and whites is taken into consideration: then black celebrities involved in scandal are perceived more positively by black people, while whites see them in a negative light. But, even then, black celebrities often have a kind of post-scandal renascence, suggesting that actual popularity isn't a necessary prerequisite for celebrity. Interest in them is. Two final cases will help us see the arterial connections between these and enable us to understand why and how some celebs have risen, while others have fallen in the aftermath of scandals.

UNABLE TO SEE STRAIGHT |

Celebrity culture is prismatic: it enables us to see something, but its refractive surface ensures that what we see depends on the angle from which we look. One of the least surprising survey results was that of a *CNN/USA Today*/Gallup poll conducted in July and August 2003. About 63 percent of black people felt sympathetic to Kobe Bryant, at that time facing charges of sexual assault, compared to 40 percent of whites. The consistency with similar polls taken at the time of the Simpson and Tyson cases is striking yet predictable. Whereas 68 percent of blacks believed the charges against Bryant were false, only 41 percent of whites saw it that way.

Bryant, the Los Angeles Lakers' guard, was found not guilty of sexual assault. He had been accused by a white woman of raping her when she was 19 and, if convicted, faced four years to life in prison. His widely reported reply was: "I didn't force her to do anything against her will." The case against him collapsed in 2004 when she refused to testify against him the day before the criminal case was due to start. Bryant later settled a civil lawsuit with the woman, though the terms were never disclosed.

Bryant was, in many ways, the antithesis of the stereotype black sportsman. Raised in Italy and in the suburbs of Philadelphia, he progressed through basketball without any of the histrionics that typically accompany a black athlete's ascent. No fights, drugs, wild parties, or any of the usual revelry associated with top-flight athletes. If anyone could take over the mantle of Michael Jordan, it was Bryant. His clean-cut image made him a favorite with advertisers: he had contracts with adidas, McDonald's, and Sprite. But the accusation left grubby fingerprints and, while Bryant continued to play for the Lakers, his image was soiled. His Sprite ads were pulled by Coca-Cola and McDonald's announced that it would not be renewing its contract with him. As with Arbuckle and Simpson, being cleared of all charges proved of less significance than the initial smear.

While Bryant's destiny unspooled, a remorseful Martha Stewart was serving 12 months behind bars. British readers may not be familiar with Stewart; so think of Delia Smith crossed with Dame Judi Dench, but with the kind of affection typically reserved for Mother Teresa. Then imagine what might happen if such a figure were found guilty of illegal dealing in stocks and shares. By the time she left prison (complete with electronic tag) in her private jet in March 2005, her company's share price had trebled, taking her personal stake's value to $1 billion (£575m). Two tv shows awaited her, including *The Apprentice*, for which she was paid $100,000 per episode. Her prison memoirs were likely to earn her another $5 million. And she continued to draw her $900,000 per year salary. The then 63-year-old convicted felon emerged considerably richer and more fascinating than when she went into prison.

NBC Universal's CEO Robert Wright, when explaining his decision to sign her to *The Apprentice*, likened Stewart's rise, fall, and redemption to a drama: "Americans are waiting for the next act. They want to see a happy ending" (quoted in *The Independent on Sunday*: BusinessWeek, February 27, 2005, p. 8). There may be some truth to this, but there wasn't too much curiosity about how Simpson fared and, while Bryant continued to play basketball, he lost much of his celebrity luster. Of course, Stewart's sin was monetary, rather than sexual or homicidal. But she was, after all, found guilty, prompting the thought that her whiteness and perhaps her gender had some bearing on the response to her.

Recall the injunction of our fictional journalist at the start of this chapter: "Think of the context." The circumstances surrounding an event, the conditions under which it happens, and the situations that precede and follow it fix its meaning. As we've seen, scandals that once damned the famous have become opportunities for revitalizing a celebrity career. Our relationship with celebrities becomes judgmental only when certain criteria are met. The most important of these is that the victim or casualty or party injured by a violation of some sort must be valid. Another is that the wrongdoing is indisputable. The wrongdoing in this sense is not necessarily the offense for which the suspect is charged, but the less visible, though no less real, transgression as interpreted by a wide constituency of consumers.

Who was Stewart's victim? Of course, there were victims; thousands of stockholders whose fortunes were adversely affected by her trading activities. But the stock exchange is an anonymous abstraction without a human face. Who got hurt by Lowe's misadventures, or Hilton's injudicious conduct? Was Saks Fifth Avenue in Beverly Hills going to miss the few thousand dollars' worth of merchandise lifted by Ryder in 2001? Where there is no tangible victim, the offense becomes an embarrassment rather than a catastrophe. Forgiveness isn't even needed.

In any scandal, consumers focus on the actual offense itself. Simpson was cleared, so was Bryant. They both negotiated civil suits, though these were, in a way, postscripts to the main narratives. The widespread assumption following the Simpson verdict was that he remained "guilty" in the eyes of many, and he was condemned accordingly. Many didn't share the reasonable doubt discerned by the jury. The question is: was the murder of his wife and her friend in 1994 Simpson's real offense? Nicole Simpson was a white woman. As was the woman who had sex with Bryant.

Earlier, I offered the metaphor of celebrity culture as a prism through which we look at the world, the angle from which we look affecting the image we see. Race works as another refracting lens, according to Alton H. Maddox. "Whites are naturally unable to see straight about Black male/white female sex," he wrote in the *New York Amsterdam News*. "Black wealth has no chance against white power" (2003: 12).

Maddox likened Bryant's predicament to those of Emmett Till and the Scottsboro Boys, who were punished for their purported behavior toward white women (2003). Maddox might have added Dick "Diamond" Rowland, whose alleged misconduct started a riot in Tulsa in 1921. It was a challenging argument and it implied that, even today, a taboo hangs over relationships between black men and white women. The days when black men were lynched, as Till was, because of a casual remark to a white woman, have passed. Yet there is still discomfort occasioned by the notion of a black man getting together with a white woman.

> *Even in an age when dishonor and outrage bring their own rewards, a black male can expect indignity at best and oblivion at worst if the "offense" – as popularly perceived – involves a white female as "victim."*

In 2004, 199 years after Emancipation and 40 years after civil rights, Bryant was cleared of rape, but remained culpable of one of the most culturally sensitive and perhaps unpardonable improprieties. Tyson became a wretched totem of a people linked unendingly to a natural primitivism. Would he have been so easily absolved and applauded in his futile pursuit of redemption had he raped a white woman instead of Desiree Washington, the black beauty pageant contestant? We can only surmise, though, on Maddox's account, it is unlikely. The aversive racism found by Knight *et al*. and the negative perceptions it encourages add weight to this.

Back to Jackson: a black male whose alarmingly variable appearance gave many the impression he was trying to divest himself of his blackness, Jackson was Wacko Jacko to detractors and the King of Pop to admirers. He married white women and, in the absence of evidence to the contrary, consummated his relationships. It could be argued that the taint of an unhealthy interest in children is colorfast – no amount of washing would remove it. But Jackson simply doesn't fit into any coherent pattern. Of course, he was an African American, but was he perceived as black? Perhaps not in the same way as the other black male celebrities we have discussed in this chapter. He was what Nederveen Pieterse (1992) would call a symbolic eunuch: someone who is valuable, though not threatening. The penchant for children, harmless or not, functioned as proof of this. Married to a white woman, he seemed more joyful in the company of children. This, I stress, was a *perception*; but perceptions are part of the context.

From the time of his appearance as an artist, Jackson had magicked innocence from what might otherwise be seen as certifiable weirdness. He could do this because of his disinclination or perhaps inability to fit into established categories. Instead, he appeared at the thresholds between several, a borderline or liminal figure. He was a black person with white skin, an adult with childlike characteristics, a man with feminine mannerisms. His near-treble voice and naive giggling helped make it possible to believe a reclusive millionaire's inviting children into his personal wonderland was not as unwholesome as it might have been had anyone else been the millionaire.

Like other celebrities who have resurfaced after being submerged by the media deluge that accompanies a scandal, Jackson found his fans attentive, many of them still worshipful. What might at another time have been a nightmare finale was, in fact, a happy ending. It is the anomalous nature of Jackson's scandal that alerts us to how the very categories he avoided dictate the kind of fall-out from all other celebrity scandals. Even in an age when dishonor and outrage bring their own rewards, a black male can expect indignity at best and oblivion at worst if the "offense" – as popularly perceived – involves a white female as "victim." We doom innocent parties to cultural bankruptcy, leaving them stripped of their most basic asset – interest – while granting malefactors new leases on their celebrity lives.

| AND FOR MY NEXT OUTRAGE . . .

"Celebrities and other achievers face continual pressure to match or beat their previous accomplishments," observe K. Bryant Smalley and William D. McIntosh. "The very public nature of their performance leads them to constantly push themselves" (2011: 387).

Figures who enter the social imagination like a lightning bolt either want to return to obscurity as quickly as they can, or else face the prospect of maintaining their position. Smalley and McIntosh are interested in what they call the "death of fame." What happens when a figure who has been carried to prominence by the media is dispatched to oblivion? Put another way, what happens in the second part of the Rise and Fall of . . . stories? There are – as there always are in studies such as this – generalizations, though there are also conclusions that are integral to subjects of scandal. Smalley and McIntosh's theory is that celebrities go through a kind of cycle of fame or notoriety, reaching a peak, what they call an "ultimate performance," which is when both their public visibility and their self-awareness are heightened. The ultimate performance can be practically anything, though a scandal, such as those covered earlier in the chapter, qualifies.

Smalley and McIntosh are both psychologists and are interested in how, at this peak, there is a separation of a celebrity's private and public selves, the former of which "begins to atrophy," or deteriorate, leaving the figure "with a simple, self-aggrandized, mythologized public self" (2011: 387).

"Self-aggrandized" suggests that, at this stage, the celebrity has promoted his or her own importance or power.

Susan Hubert would probably agree with this: in her analysis of Princess Diana's struggles with the media, Hubert offers the view that: "Diana's attempts to control her public image and limit media access to her private life were 'bizarre' and a sign of emotional instability" (1999: 131). Impressions of her instability were self-fulfilling: every effort to protect her atrophying private self was processed and presented by the media as a sign of fickleness or unreliability. Diana's status was not the product of a single, shocking incident, though her estrangement and separation from Prince Charles, starting in 1991 (ten years after their marriage), implicated her in a royal scandal of heroic proportions. Charles later admitted his infidelity. For figures who have reached our consciousness via a scandal and nothing much apart from a scandal, we wait in breathless anticipation, or more probably in hope that there will be a return to nondescriptness. Often there is. But, for others, there beckons a kind of zombie-esque life in which, as Smalley and McIntosh put it, "a celebrity's core self has been replaced by a public persona." What happens when the public is no longer there? (Just for clarity: a *persona* is the aspect of someone's character that is either presented to, or perceived by, others; it is usually contrasted with *anima*, the part of the psyche that's directed inward.)

Tyson supplies one answer: revive the public persona. On his release from prison in 1995, Tyson was worse than broke: he owed back taxes. He was also ring-rusty, not having had a competitive fight since 1991. He did, however, have a valuable resource: his persona. No one seriously thought the brutal, primeval character "Iron Mike," had been rehabilitated. If anything, the interlude in prison had added an air of secrecy to the Tyson myth: what had happened to him during his incarceration? Had he been emasculated? Had he grown wilder? Is it another *Psycho*?

Actually, no one asked the final question, at least not before now. *Psycho* was the classic Alfred Hitchcock movie from 1960, in which Anthony Perkins played the creepy, mother-loving, cross-dressing serial killer Norman Bates. Perkins had enjoyed modest film and theatre success in the 1950s, but, according to Smalley and McIntosh, "his public persona was forever changed" by the film. In consumers' minds, he became synonymous with Bates and was never able to dissociate himself from the role. "The distance between his core and public selves was vast, and his core self gradually began to relent under the insistence of his public image" (2011: 389).

Tyson also relented, though "accepted" is probably a more appropriate description of his actions: realizing that the scowling menace that had excited a generation of fans still had his uses, Tyson revived him. He threatened to eat opponents' babies, created mayhem at press conferences, and badmouthed anyone in listening range. It was reassuring that jailtime had, if anything, made Tyson wilder. Whether Tyson was more monster than monstered, we'll never know. To monster someone is to abominate or severely criticize them. But he certainly played the role to perfection. Only after he'd retired from boxing in 2005 did anyone glimpse an alternative Tyson. It was like watching a snarling tiger in a zoo, then, after 20 years, unlocking its cage only to discover the snarling, while initially genuine, was now just an act to excite spectators. The tiger had long since been tamed.

"Commodification is especially relevant to celebrities" caught in this quandary, write Smalley and McIntosh. They mean that someone's public persona can be turned into a saleable product. They give various examples of celebrities who find it impossible to escape popular images and so exploit them to their own advantage. One of their examples is Tiffany, a one-hit wonder from 1987 who was tormented by the clean-cut, girl-next-door persona and hit the drugs and booze, cropped her hair, pierced her body, had breast augmentation, and posed nude for *Playboy* in 2002 – as did Lindsay Lohan in the January/February 2012 edition. It was a shameless attempt to draw attention, but it didn't prompt as much controversy as she had probably anticipated. Smalley and McIntosh argue that commercial success eluded Tiffany and she eventually reverted to a kind of mature version of her earlier public self, "readopting the image of that commodity," in an effort to recapture her fame. Tiffany's strategy was bizarrely like Tyson's. While Smalley and McIntosh don't mention it, she is still performing and recording.

Smalley and McIntosh call this strategy *clinging,* and it's one of four possible reactions to losing fame. *Reinventing* is another way celebrities attempt to contrive a way back into the consumers' consciousness. Paris Hilton, as we saw earlier, has changed herself into an actor, singer, author, and DJ, though, even in her thirties, her most tradable commodity was the persona she had striven to dump – the well-heeled heiress to a fortune with connections in fashionable circles and a well-documented penchant for parties and ancillary forms of recreation. Rob Lowe, also mentioned earlier, engaged in a kind of reinvention: his career threatened by scandal, he lowered his profile for a modest period, before re-emerging in thoughtful film roles that tended to give him more gravitas.

Downward-spiraling is the best-known and most common response, when the celebrity's desperate groping to remain visible leads to a corkscrew-like descent into some form of dependency, mental illness, or even suicide. Arbuckle was a tragic, harrowing prototype. Gig Young (1913–78) was 56 when he won an Oscar for his role in the 1969 film *They Shoot Horses Don't They?*. "For Young, the Oscar was literally the kiss of death," writes Anthony Holden (1993: 275). He drank heavily, becoming too unreliable for Hollywood. The parts dried up hastening the slide down the spiral. In 1978, he was found dead in his New York apartment. It's believed he killed his wife and then himself. While Young's death came at a low point in his career, many suicides are committed by figures at or near their peak, of course. Ernest Hemingway (1899–1961), Kurt Cobain (1967–94), and Alexander McQueen (1969–2010) were among the many lamentable losses of this kind.

According to Smalley and McIntosh, "instant celebrities," as they call them – by which they presumably mean reality tv stars or characters propelled to fame by a scandal – are much less likely to experience the downward spiral and will resort either to clinging to a tried-and-tested persona, or reinventing themselves in a new guise.

| PULLING ON THE SACKCLOTH

Let me add to Smalley and McIntosh's a fourth category: *wearing sackcloth*. I allude to the wearing of sackcloth and having ashes sprinkled on the head as a sign of penitence. Public demonstrations of regret can be surprisingly effective. "Kate Moss's grovelling apology to her friends, family and business associates, appears to have saved her from losing a lucrative contract with Coty Beauty's Rimmel London brand after admitting she has 'various personal issues'," *BrandRepublic*'s Julia Pearlman speculated in September 2005. The supermodel had been captured on camera apparently snorting cocaine. By December, she had been in rehab and returned with an estimated £12 million ($20m) of work lined up. Longchamps, Roberto Cavalli, and Calvin Klein seemed unembarrassed about being associated with her (or her temporary sackcloth). She played out a similar moral fable to Martha Stewart and returned to the fray damaged, but not irreparably.

Woods became another African American whose catastrophe was not so much a product of his own compulsions, as nature asserting its advantage over nurture, as it tends to do in the lives of black men.

"I take full responsibility for my actions," Stewart affirmed in a repentant, but ritualistic confession that had echoes in Tiger Woods's "I am the only person to blame." Woods pulled on the sackcloth in 2010 in an attempt to defuse the explosive potential of what he called his "transgressions." As every reader will know, Woods' persona was so well established that he was practically an archetype of the clean-living family man. Like Moss, he had his spell in rehab (in his case for sex addiction) and, after a period of remorse, returned to the fray, though in his case not fully restored to his former glory. Woods lost several advertising contracts, but retained enough to ensure he kept his annual income around the $60 million (£45m) mark. Whether the scandal had any effect on his golfing or whether, in his late thirties, he just began to lose his edge, we can't know. But, though he resumed his athletic activities, he never dominated as he once had.

Recall Knight *et al.*'s remark about a "subtle form of prejudice" emerging "when people feel safe to express themselves," as they were able when Woods was exposed. Here was a black man, stupendously rich, admired universally, and whose persona was utterly at odds with traditional stereotypes. In so many ways, he was the antithesis of Tyson. Until November 2009; then he became another African American whose catastrophe was not so much a product of his own compulsions, as nature asserting its advantage over nurture, as it tends to do in the lives of black men.

Historically, notoriety has offered a shortcut to oblivion. As such, it was studiously avoided. Then, scandal became a resource, as either an entrée to a showbiz career, a route to martyrdom, or a means of securing the abhorrence of society. The same kinds of misdemeanors or suspected misdemeanors that once brought an abrupt halt to careers can now be occasions for rejuvenation. While infamy was once the bane of the famous, the Lowe case in 1989 heralded a change. "It's almost quaint to think about now, because now people do sex tapes to HELP their careers," Lowe himself mused in 2011. But do they still work? Even sex videos have lost their potency today; as have dependencies, gambling problems, and drug use. Even affairs are diurnal events. Consumers have been overscandalized: it takes something special to shock, appall, outrage, horrify, disgust, or sicken us; and when it comes to being offended, our immune system is fully functional.

For today's celebs, the most terrible, vile, awful experience, and the experience they strive continuously to avoid, is being overlooked. Once the media fail to notice a celeb's presence, their status as a celeb disintegrates. A scandal, by definition, fires up interest. There is no chance of being disregarded. The media attention might be for the wrong reasons; but, there again, the precise reasons are of secondary importance. Of primary importance is the attention itself.

APPEARANCE

SHORT CUT TO HAPPINESS?|

CHAPTER HIGHLIGHTS

- More people undergo plastic surgery than at any time in history
- The culture of narcissism emerged in the 1970s and changed the way we look at ourselves
- Jane Fonda was a key figure in a movement that hailed fitness, wellbeing, and beauty as the way to happiness
- Conceptions of beauty and ugliness are influenced by images of celebrities
- Today, we realize that, physically, celebrities are just as imperfect as ordinary people
- Celebrities can age with consumers' consent

Your name is Paul Newman and it's 1962. You're about as hot as any actor in the world. You've already triumphed in Somebody Up There Likes Me *(1956) and* Long Hot Summer *(1958), but your pièce de résistance is Oscar-nominated* The Hustler, *in which you play the cocksure young pool player "Fast Eddie" Felson. The character is years younger than you, but you always look as if you've come straight from a cosmetic makeover session. Are you really 37? Your skin is flawless, you have a full head of sleek hair, succulent lips, and eyes like an unclouded vault of heaven. You could pass for 25 and a smolderingly sexy 25 at that.*

Just one thing. A tiny thing, but, on close inspection, one or two frown lines are appearing on your forehead, probably because you have a low brow and tend to raise your eyes. Studio chiefs have doubtless assured you that they're nothing to worry about and, in fact, might add a little character to your otherwise wrinkle-free visage. On the other hand, those furrows will deepen with age and might spoil your otherwise exquisite looks.

Botox wasn't around in 1962. If it had been, might Newman (1925–2008), a man of Apollonian handsomeness, have succumbed to a shot or two, just to smooth out the incipient brow lines? Its application is simple, practically as easy as waxing your chest, and less hassle than having your teeth bleached. Newman might have opted for the latter to remove the stains left by smoking cigarettes. But Botox? Probably not. In the 1960s, being gorgeous was a valuable advantage, not a bounden duty of every Hollywood star. Now, as serial cosmetic surgery recipient Joan Rivers puts it: "We're in a business where it counts" (quoted in the *Independent*, May 11, 2005, p. 36). Actually, we all are.

Of the many dubious gifts brought to us by celebrity culture, perfection is simultaneously the most innocuous and pernicious. What's wrong with trying to improve your physical appearance? It's a fair question and deserves a straightforward answer. It's this: nothing – unless the search for perfection becomes a dizzyingly compulsive fixation that translates into an intolerance for anything slightly less than faultless. It becomes additionally damaging if the inevitable consequences of age must be denied or rejected by whatever surgical means available. In other words, like most other human predilections, the quest for beauty can become an endless and fruitless pursuit that leads to discontent rather than satisfaction. Then again, as in most quests, the pursuit is probably more fulfilling than the accomplishment of the prescribed task.

In 2002, *People* writer Michelle Green wrote, "Those lips, that face . . . ," which reported on a number of fans who had undergone cosmetic surgery in order to look like their favorite celebrity. In the spirit of the MTV show *I Want a Famous Face*, Green interviewed a devotee of Keanu Reeves who had paid $9,000

(£5,800) for two rhinoplasties (nose jobs) and an implant to fill out his chin. "It's cured my vanity problem," the fan confirmed, presumably meaning it had indulged his conceit (2002: 127).

Of the other fans interviewed, one had undergone gluteal augmentation to give her buttocks the JLo/KK look. Another had breast implants that took her from a B- to a C-cup; not huge, but closer to Britney Spears's bosom. And, perhaps surprisingly, one had a gastric bypass that left her with loose skin, and then needed 12 pounds of that skin removed before her body could resemble what she described as the "curvy and voluptuous" Kate Winslet. Green catalogs several other patients, or, perhaps more properly, clients, who had submitted themselves to surgical remodeling so that they could look like celebrities.

While Green records the usual caveats about "unrealistic expectations" and the "shortcut to happiness" cosmetic surgery offers but rarely delivers, there is conspicuous ethical neutrality about her tone. In the 1960s, before cosmetic surgery was as accessible as it is today, a story such as hers would have carried dire warnings about how invasive and potentially traumatic the surgery can be (duly noted by Green), but there would also have been disapproval. To have one's face or other body parts reconstructed just to look like a famous person, however admirable that person might be, would have been regarded as plain sick. In a sense, maybe mimicking celebrities still is. Cosmetic surgery in itself obviously isn't.

Since 2000, there has been an 87 percent increase in the number of people opting for a nip, tuck, or enhancement of some order. In the USA, 14 million clients have "work" done every year, spending $10.1 billion (£6.5bn) in the process – on collagen and Botox injections, breast implants, buttock lifts, and nose jobs. Men opt for breast reduction (+8 percent on 2010), rhinoplasty, and blepharoplasty (eyelid modification). Two percent of the total procedures involved teenagers.

People are increasingly unhappy, frustrated, or in some way discontented with their own bodies.

While the British are not at US levels, a total of 43,069 procedures (total UK population: 62.6 million) were completed, mostly for women (90 percent), in 2011, a rise of 5.8 percent since 2008. Perhaps more interestingly, research indicates that 72 percent of British women wanted cosmetic surgery and 49 percent were actually planning to have work done.

They're not all trying to look like celebs, though an unknown number of them would have what Virginia Blum calls "delusional identification." She means that consumers rarely study close up the people whom they wish to emulate. "It is the stars' 'image,' the very dimension in which they appear to their fans, that ordinary people long to emulate," reasons Blum, reminding that most of our impressions of celebrities are based on two-dimensional representations (2007: 53). I'll elaborate on Blum's arguments later in the chapter.

Looked at another way, everyone who elects for cosmetic procedures, however minor, has been influenced by the predominance of celebrities in contemporary culture. "Plastic surgery," as Brenda R. Weber maintains, is "a form of conspicuous consumption meriting attention, display, and (hoped-for) praise" (2009a: 293). I will return to Weber's research later.

In the 1960s, and perhaps until the 1980s, cosmetic surgery was a luxury reserved mostly for stars and elite white women. Now there is much more access. The surgery is still expensive, but many more people are prepared to pay whatever it costs to effect the modification. The reason for this is simultaneously simple and complex. People are increasingly unhappy, frustrated, or in some way discontented with their own bodies. Why otherwise would they want them changed? That's the simple part. What isn't so clear is whether they have become more – or less – dissatisfied in recent years and why they are opting for what can be discomforting procedures, which are usually followed by a painful post-op period.

UNDER THE SPELL OF NARCISSUS |

James Ellroy's crime thrillers are fictional narratives punctuated by chunks of fact and biography. His *LA Confidential* (1990) is set in the 1940s and 1950s and tracks the lives of three Los Angeles police officers as they investigate a multiple killing at a café. One of the cops has a relationship with a prostitute who closely resembles Veronica Lake, the alluring 1940s star. She works at a high-end brothel where the employees have undergone cosmetic surgery to look like Hollywood stars. Kim Basinger plays the Veronica Lake (1922–73) look-alike in the 1997 movie based on the book.

The brothel has featured in other fictional accounts and has something of an iconic presence in Southern California folklore. Its premise is a powerful one: men who couldn't actually have sex with the stars could pay to have the next best thing – sex with someone who was a dead ringer for whomever they desired. Even in the 1950s, plastic surgery, as it was then called, was sophisticated enough to transfigure prostitutes into facsimiles of the stars.

The Culture of Narcissism is the title of Christopher Lasch's book on the changes that began in the 1970s. It describes "the apotheosis of individualism," in which self-centered feeling or conduct reached its highest state of development. The book was originally published in 1979 and reflected on the turbulent 1960s, in which young people all over the world challenged and subverted traditional ideals, values, and norms. People saw the same problems – war, nuclear proliferation, structured inequality, persistent racism, political corruption, and ideological divergence. Their rebellious efforts changed hearts and minds, but not the material facts. So, they "retreated to purely personal preoccupations," according to Lasch, "getting in touch with their feelings, eating health food, taking lessons in ballet or belly-dancing, immersing themselves in the wisdom of the East, jogging, learning how to 'relate,' overcoming the 'fear of pleasure'" (1980: 4).

Lasch saw no harm in any of these pursuits in themselves, but he rued the break with history, the turning away from collective activity, and the switch from trying to change society to changing oneself. Personal wellbeing, health, and psychic security became the motivating goals for the generation that had earlier wanted to change the world.

Narcissus was the Greek mythological character who fell in love with his reflection in water. His name is used to describe the tendency to self-worship and develop an excessive interest in one's own personal features. Like Narcissus, we looked for our reflection and became absorbed by it. But this wasn't enough. What counted is what others saw. "The narcissist depends on others to validate his self-esteem," observed Lasch. "He cannot live without an admiring audience . . . For the narcissist, the world is a mirror" (1980: 10).

There were two dimensions to the culture of narcissism: on the one hand, swathes of people abandoned their collective endeavors and contented themselves with individual quests for satisfaction and happiness; yet, on the other, they depended on each other for confirmation that they were looking and feeling good. The cultural and moral climate became one of "self-absorption," and a generation progressively insulated itself from the very features of society that it once opposed, including military conflict, poverty, and injustice.

One of the most pronounced tendencies to emerge from this climate was "the therapeutic outlook," in which, as Lasch put it, "the individual endlessly examines himself for signs of aging and ill health, for tell-tale symptoms of psychic stress, for blemishes and flaws that might diminish his attractiveness" (1980: 49). (It will be obvious by now that, writing in the 1970s, Lasch used the masculine pronoun for both sexes.)

The harvest of this culture became evident in the 1980s. Health clubs and gyms, countless diets, a profusion of anti-wrinkle aids, and any number of therapies, including colonic irrigation, acupuncture, hypnosis, and aromatherapy; all of them designed in some way to palliate the "stressful" consequences of self-absorption and delay the diminution of "attractiveness." And what diminishes attractiveness more than just about anything apart from disfigurement? Age.

"People cling to the illusion of youth until it can no longer be maintained, at which point they must either accept their superfluous status or sink into dull despair," wrote Lasch in the 1970s (1980: 212). Actually, there were ways in which that illusion of youth could be maintained. It was just that they were available only to the few privileged enough to afford them. Twenty years after Lasch's observation, there had been democratization: cosmetic surgery was not only available but also accessible to a wider distribution of people.

At some stage, probably in the late 1970s, the line between surgery to correct or ameliorate ailments or disorders and surgery for purely cosmetic purposes became less distinct. The word cosmetic is from the Greek *kosmetikos*, meaning "adorn" or "beautify," and its current meaning is faithful to its source. But a related meaning is: "to restore normal appearance." Surgery to remove stigmas or other kinds of natural marks or scars on the skin, or to eradicate disfigurements, was always cosmetic in the sense that it was designed to improve appearance without necessarily changing bodily functions.

Disfiguring injuries suffered by servicemen in the First World War (1914–18) occasioned restorative surgery. Techniques continued to improve in the interwar years, giving rise to the possibility of utilizing surgery for other purposes. Plastic surgery, as it was called, was completely synthetic and had no ostensible purpose besides altering appearance. Rhinoplasty might have improved breathing in patients who had broken their noses, but its principal purpose was to change the shape of the nose. A primitive, unsuccessful method of disguising wrinkles involved injecting paraffin into facial skin, the idea being that the odorless, oily substance would plump up the epidermal layer. The problem was that, after a while, the paraffin turned to waxy lumps, creating an uneven surface on the skin.

Fanny Brice (1891–1951), the showgirl who was played by Barbra Streisand in the movies *Funny Girl* and *Funny Lady*, had surgery to reshape her nose in the 1920s. She became famous in the lavish Ziegfeld revues. Later, Hollywood stars such as Hedy Lamaar and Merle Oberon opted for surgical enhancement. Samantha Barbas believes the attention to women's appearances had even earlier origins: "Though historical developments of the 1920s (in particular, the aggressive development of the visual mass media) intensified both the cultural scrutiny of women's bodies and women's self-scrutiny, as early as the 1870s, women were acutely aware of their physical surveillance" (2004: 1118).

The rise of Hollywood brought male stars under surveillance too: Burt Lancaster and even hewn-of-granite John Wayne resorted to surgery to alter their appearances. Elvis Presley was rumored to have had bags under his eyes removed in 1975 when he was 40. In the 1970s, purely cosmetic surgery was still the preserve of the rich and conceited, or Hollywood stars. But changes were afoot: the therapeutic outlook imbued cosmetic change with new meanings.

Changing one's appearance became more than a superficial pursuit for people so conceited and full of themselves that they couldn't bear the prospect of ageing: it enabled people to feel better about themselves. The culture of narcissism elevated appearance in importance. Lasch reminds readers that advertising as far back as the 1920s encouraged women (not men) to be self-critical about their appearance. He quotes the strapline of an ad: "Your masterpiece – Yourself" (1980: 92).

The ad enjoined people to divide themselves into subjects and objects, so that they could be both their body and an admirer of that body; in this way, consumers would become acutely aware of themselves, examine themselves, and reflect on how they could change.

The message might have had a commercial function, but the possibilities it raised were to be realized over the next few decades. We started to subject ourselves to regimes that promised to make our bodies resemble cultural norms of good looks. Like all the priorities of consumer society, this one was determined by ourselves: we chose – and were not impelled – to embark on body regulation. Such is the beauty of consumerism: conveying the impression of choice, while obscuring the influence of the directive.

From the 1970s, men were also included in the imperative to "project an attractive image." It was a new perception: "Outward appearances, in this view, involuntarily expressed the inner man" (1980: 92). So, it became necessary to study one's own image, not out of vanity, but in a critical spirit, to spot flaws, signs of fatigue, or, worse still, ageing. In the process, we were encouraged to make objects of ourselves: treat our bodies, to repeat the early ad, as a masterpiece on which we should work, striving toward perfection.

It bears remembering that, if Lasch is to be accepted, this was part of a complete change in orientation. Turning in on oneself, becoming self-aware, self-absorbed, and self-reflexive (i.e. constantly examining and regulating ourselves) has counterparts in the way we understood the world and our place in that world. There wasn't what psychologists call a Gestalt switch, in which perceptions suddenly change completely: more of an accelerating tendency that had been around for decades, but that during the 1970s (and, we should add, 1980s) gathered even more momentum and left hardly anyone unaffected.

As the end of the twentieth century approached, baby boomers – the demographic group born in the period after the Second World War (1946–64) – began to hit 50. "They have long been obsessed with youth and vitality," observed Nora

Underwood in her *Maclean's* article "Body envy." So, it was a happy coincidence that "the prospects for a longer, healthier life were increasing all the time" (2000: 36).

Underwood wasn't just referring to the advances in medical science and health facilities that lengthened life expectancy: she meant the all-round broadening of awareness of how to adjust lifestyles in a way that promoted health and fitness. And good looks. There was an almost natural correspondence between them.

So the culture of narcissism was not the result of some fiendish connivance to destabilize people, render them insecure about their appearance, and send them scuttling to the nearest gym, whole foods store, or cosmetic surgeon. But nor was it a completely voluntary act of spontaneity done willingly and without prompting. Like everything else about celebrity culture, it emerged from a paradox: consumers are both active and passive, producers and products, controllers and the controlled.

│ZEN AND THE DEMOCRATIZATION OF NARCISSISM

No one can catch lightning in a bottle; but Jane Fonda (b. 1937) came close. The lightning, in this instance, was the fervor for fitness that seemed to have flashed in from nowhere; the bottle was a video – not a movie, a dvd, or a download, but one of those black plastic rectangular contrivances that brought consumers unprecedented flexibility in the way they viewed movies and tv programs. In 1982, Fonda, then a youthful-looking 45, had established her reputation in films such as Alan Pakula's *Klute* (1971) and Colin Higgins's *Nine to Five* (1980), though it was her earlier appearance in 1967 as *Barbarella* (director: Roger Vadim), the comic-strip character from the year 40,000, that defined her persona: a radiant, rebellious nymphet.

Fonda had identified herself as a feminist and campaigned for various social causes, including those of Native Americans and women's rights. Yet it was her 90-minute video, originally titled *Workout, starring Jane Fonda,* and later better known as *Jane Fonda's Workout* (released by Karl Video, 1982) that captured the zeitgeist if not the lightning.

The video was based on Fonda's own book *Jane Fonda's Workout Book,* which had been published in 1981, the year in which Diana married Charles, and MTV started transmission. While aerobics classes were filling up across the world, not everyone wanted to squeeze into clingy gear and cavort in the company of others. Fonda's video instructed beginners how to get fit without fear of embarrassment and without the expense of joining a gym: all you needed was a vcr and a room. Over the next several years, Fonda's original video sold 17 million copies – making it the best-selling video in history – and spawned 23 specialist tapes (exercise for pregnant women; working out with weights, etc.). As Jane Fonda the actor faded from view, Fonda the fitness guru shone like a beacon, guiding a generation toward regular workouts.

Fonda enjoyed a status as both a glamorous Hollywood star and a hellion – her willingness to join forces with political and social movements earned her a reputation as a troublemaker. In another era, this would have been disastrous for a mainstream actor. In the 1970s, with the US's unpopular involvement in the Vietnam War and civil rights legislation proving less effective than expected, a high-profile woman – and gender was a burning issue – who was prepared to engage publicly with these and other matters of wide concern was an exceptional being. She was believable. At least in the 1980s: in 2002, she was heckled during a trip to Jerusalem.

Maturity was also a factor: even on the cusp of middle age and, in Hollywood terms at least, a veteran – *Barbarella* had been 15 years before the video, remember – Fonda provided living evidence of the benefits of exercise for women, mature or adolescent.

Am I exaggerating Fonda's role in the culture of narcissism? Perhaps. After all, no single individual sets in motion a cultural change of such unprecedented productivity. She didn't single-handedly launch a culture preoccupied with lithe bodies, clear skin, and ageless good looks. If she hadn't done it, someone else would have emerged. In an era of big hair, rah-rah skirts, power shoulders, and *Like a Virgin* (1984), Fonda became the symbol of a new femininity: strong, able, fit, and still unambiguously female. The Victorian myth of women's physical frailty had long since been exposed, but, even so, exercise had still been seen as largely a man's domain.

If Fonda hadn't broken the link and created a new association, someone else would have. Someone like Jamie Lee Curtis, who played an aerobics instructor in the 1985 movie *Perfect* (director: James Bridges) or *Flashdance* star Jennifer Beals. Both would have made credible guarantors of the new culture. Incidentally, French dancer Marine Jahan, the uncredited body double for Beals, who performed the dance sequences in the film, released her own workout video series.

All these women, in their own way, testified to exercise's ability to make you not only feel good, but also *look* good. In this sense, it assisted what Steve Hall *et al.* call the "democratisation of narcissism and its assimilation of everyday individuals into conspicuous consumption and the competitive individualist ethos" (2008: 215).

While Hall and his colleagues believe this process started much earlier in the twentieth century, it underwent a kind of spurt in the early 1980s: any woman could potentially look as sexy as Jane Fonda. They could buy the products, do the workouts, and, later, with the greater accessibility of cosmetic surgery, change their appearance to meet the challenges of a competitive culture that valued both individual success and the *appearance* of success.

Narcissism, for many, sounds like a nightmarish culture based on hollowness and superficiality. The quest for the kind of perfect looks that Jane Fonda and, eventually, a fitness industry championed may be like the quest for El Dorado, the mythic city abounding with gold: futile. But the search had a Zen detour. "In a culture obsessed with images, alterations of the flesh can indeed change feelings and personalities," Barbas writes (2004: 1122). Physical changes can have profound transformative potential, as Barbas enigmatically suggests: "We end up on a kind of Möbius strip of desire, changing our behaviors and looks in the elusive pursuit of perfection." This is an interesting metaphor: a Möbius strip is a ribbon with its ends joined after it's been twisted 180° – you can then run a finger along the surface of both of its sides continuously. Presumably, Barbas means that a culture of narcissism has no depth, only one side, but possesses a remarkable property in that its surface is never-ending.

Back to Weber, specifically her *Makeover TV*. A makeover is, of course, a transformation or remodeling of something or, more usually, someone, though Weber uses the concept in a wider sense to capture a set of proposals, imperatives, programs, and routines offered to entire populations and which become integrated into popular attitudes and behavior. We're encouraged to think of our selves as in a kind of anterior, or preparatory, state. "One of makeover's critical premises is that it does not construct, it reveals," Weber explains (2009b: 7). "Makeover does not create selfhood but rather it salvages that which is already present, but weak."

The transformative potential of the makeover is in its capacity to release: consumers are enabled to escape the confinement of their imperfect selves. Weber's principal interest lies in the television genre that has its origins in the 1960s, but which proliferated as reality tv arrived in the 2000s. All makeover shows had transformation as their central theme: participants were provided with the resources to effect changes in their physical appearance by a variety of means, from losing weight, grooming more attentively, and restocking closets with new clothes to undergoing plastic surgery.

Makeover became a trope to explain how, by changing practices, we could instigate empowering changes in our inner selves. It was predicated on what Weber calls "an informed consumerism," in the sense that change was available to all, at a price, and consumer choice was paramount. Nobody forced anyone to discover their real selves: they could stay fat and ugly if they wished. It was also active; even placing yourself in the hands of a plastic surgeon was a conscious, deliberate decision.

The Zen was this: while the aim was ostensibly to release the "real you," Meredith Jones discerns: "The process of *becoming something better* is more important than achieving a static point of completion" (2008: 1).

As a concept, the makeover was both compatible with and an expansion of the narcissism that had its sources in the 1970s and was widened into fitness culture in the 1980s. Self-centered feeling and conduct were favored over collective or state action; the habit of being independent, self-reliant, and capable of instigating change became commonsense. "Becoming something better," as Jones puts it, became, if not an obligation, an expectation. Think of the expression "You owe it to yourself." It sounds illogical, but is actually self-reflexive and so consistent with the culture of narcissism.

| BEAUTY IN 2D

How long before you will be looking at a screen? If you lift your head and there's a computer on your desk, seconds. Later, you'll probably stare at the television screen. Maybe tonight you'll catch a movie. Screens have become major parts of our lives. We educate as well as entertain ourselves by gaping at flat luminous panels. We rely on photographic imagery of one kind or another. The reliance has become so great that the distinction between the human and the two-dimensional has narrowed or even become disrupted. At least that's the view of one scholar.

"The beauty of images symbolizes what is now experienced as their essential lure, and plastic surgery is the cultural allegory of transforming the body into an image," writes Virginia Blum. In her 2003 book *Flesh Wounds*, Blum presents one of the most challenging arguments about celebrity culture and one in which cosmetic surgery is central. The issue of cosmetic surgery is embedded in a culture that has become indebted to two-dimensional images, the ones we watch every single day, many of them digitally enhanced or created. According to Blum, we have become "infatuated" with 2D images to the point where we identify with them. By identifying not with living people but moving images, we have been drawn into an engagement with a kind of fantasy.

Images of beauty, both female and male, are ubiquitous. Even a visit to the supermarket implicates us in looking at the magazine covers at the checkout. It's impossible to watch tv for an hour before someone gorgeous appears, whether in a commercial or drama, or perhaps reading the news (even newsreaders have to look good nowadays). "It is no wonder that the identification with the image of beauty is so compelling," Blum remarks (2003: 19). But we're not identifying with actual human beings, but with mediated images of them. This finds qualified support in the research of Natalie King *et al.*, who discovered that, while we can't escape the images of celebrities, we don't all identify or even see them in the same way. Specifically, "women who are concerned about their own body shape view thin women in the media as being even thinner than they actually are, whereas women who are unconcerned about their body view them accurately" (2000: 345).

If we link this finding to Blum's general observation, we're drawn to the conclusion that the more we're dissatisfied with our own looks, the more we tend to idealize or exaggerate the beauty of celebrities – which would tend to heighten our dissatisfaction without reducing our identification. Those who are less satisfied with themselves and who see celebs in an excessively favorable way would, on this account, be the ones who would be inclined to take action.

There is a self-imposed regulating function to this: we form judgments about ourselves by comparing our bodies against cultural ideals that are held before us – again, in only two dimensions – and modify ourselves accordingly. No one, on Blum's account, can escape this. We assess the bodies of others as we assess our own. So, while Blum refers to the "relentless coercion of a youth-and-beauty-centered culture," we don't experience it as coercion at all. In fact, we voluntarily aspire to what is culturally desirable. The images help us make up our minds about what is and isn't.

Beauty might be in the eye of the beholder, but, unless that beholder has been raised as a feral child without human company, his or her evaluation will have been affected by the culture in which he or she operates. Obviously, culture is ultimately a human enterprise, yet we shouldn't underestimate the manner in which it provides everything that makes us human, including language. We learn to communicate from others. We also learn other uniquely human characteristics from others. Taste, for instance: this isn't something that spontaneously springs into our minds. We learn to discriminate, judge, and appraise. So, while there are those who rhapsodize about timeless beauty, there is no such thing. Standards and values change, often very quickly. Take a look at a copy of *Vogue* from 30 years ago and you see immediately that the models, who were paragons of classy good looks, now appear to be a little fuller-faced and a bit shorter. Go back even further to Rubens' seventeenth-century masterworks in which you'll find women who are plump by today's benchmark. We simply can't remain indifferent to cultural changes. There's nothing optional about it. Our conceptions of beauty and ugliness are shaped.

There's a scene in the Farrelly brothers' *Shallow Hal* (2001) where Jack Black's Hal haughtily reminds his critics which one of them is escorting a stunningly glamorous blonde: not them but him. The conceit of the film is that Hal, having undergone off-the-cuff hypnosis, is smitten by an ample, prosthetically enlarged Gwyneth Paltrow, though he can only see her as the normal-sized Paltrow. Others look on incredulously at love-struck Hal and the corpulent object of his affections. In other cultures, at different stages in history, Hal's tastes wouldn't have been questioned. And Paltrow in her "natural" state might be seen as too stick-like to be attractive. But today Paltrow is seen as much closer to the cultural norm of beauty than, say, Beth Ditto or Queen Latifa (either of whom could have posed for Rubens, by the way).

AS IF |

With the expanding presence of the media in the twentieth century came a new and unprecedented influence. It's difficult to imagine any single phenomenon with the kind of supreme power to influence not only behavior, but also thought and per-haps even feeling. Circulating with the endless supply of words was an endless supply of images, representations, or signs that indicated or suggested the direction of our taste. While the popular association between, for example, beauty and youth is seen as natural, there is really nothing natural about it. There's nothing immanently beautiful about leanness, white teeth, or the absence of wrinkles. These associations have been suggested so much that we take them for granted, as if they were exactly as they feel – natural.

> *The body is nothing until it's jolted into being by the image of something it could become.*
>
> **VICTORIA BLUM**

In many other cultures, it's quite probable that people were just not aware of their bodies in the way we are. Perhaps they simply didn't think about the body apart from when they were sick or if they lost some part, as the work of, among others, Michel Foucault reminds us. So the kind of narcissistic grooming and modifying we're all habituated to just wouldn't be contemplated. "The body is nothing until it's jolted into being by the image of something it could become," writes Blum, adding the kinds of images she has in mind: "a movie star, supermodel, a beautiful body" (2003: 54).

It becomes a body only once we start thinking about it in comparison with other bodies, specifically those of exemplary subjects. We can't genuinely talk in terms of what Blum calls a "premediated body": she means that we are only aware of our own bodies through the medium of others. In a narcissistic culture, we are all likely to be more vigilant about our bodies, and this means we're likely to be vigilant about other people's bodies too. These are made available for our close inspection courtesy of a media that has grown in importance in large part because of our interest in others.

From Hollywood in the 1930s came a new standard of beauty, one that drew near-unanimous agreement. As we've seen previously, an industry geared to promoting and marketing stars ensured the widespread availability of airbrushed images. Collectively, they defined a kind of gold standard of beauty. It's unlikely that there had ever been such a standardization of taste. Cinema and its analogous publications made this possible.

Consumers' fantasies, like those of children, are delicate invocations: we might imagine that we had a Beverly Hills home, multiple Ferraris, a body like Fonda, or eyes like Newman, but we realize that whimsy is no replacement for a life plan. Prior to the late 1980s, the Hollywood stars had an other-worldly quality. As we've seen, they were marketed in a way that perpetuated the idea that they were people with special talents that separated Them from the rest of Us. Blum observes: "Star culture, its beauty in particular, is dependent on a universal conviction of great beauty as special and privileged" (2003: 259).

The ensorcellment with the stars made us restless, yearning to be a little more like them yet never quite believing we could be. And then it changed. Celebrity culture brought with it an immediacy that was both enlightening and maddening. Enlightening because it showed that the celebrities were much more ordinary than previously thought. Maddening because the special privileges they enjoyed were probably less to do with talent and more to do with any number of other factors, including happenstance, or fluke, or tampering. "Once their beauty turns out to be surgical, something any of us can have for the purchase, then we are no longer in the thrall," writes Blum. "By ourselves entering the order of illusion, there is no longer any illusion as such, because there is no difference between them (the illusion of celebrity bodies) and us (real bodies)" (2003: 259).

It's as if we've internalized the two-dimensional images for so long, all the time believing that the celebrities lived on another plane, their conspicuously different status and lifestyles being the product of some sort of gift. The new celebrity culture brought with it an apparent openness and honesty. After the "rules of the game," as we've been calling them, changed, so did the relationship we had with famous movie stars and the other kinds of entertainers who had joined them on their special plateau.

Blum captures this relationship in her phrase "as if lives." She takes the phrase from the psychoanalyst Helene Deutsch (1918–82), who, in the 1940s, used "as if personality" to describe individuals whose "whole relationship to life" was lacking in genuineness and yet outwardly ran along "as if" it were complete (1986). In idealizing and modeling ourselves on celebrities, we are identifying with subjects whose very living depends on continuously shifting identities. While Blum doesn't elaborate, she must have in mind actors, who transfer from role to role, rock stars who change chameleon-like so that fans never get bored (Madonna being the supreme example, Lady

Gaga being another), and athletes who switch teams or essay new ventures. Identifying with fast-changing models means "our experience of identity is made not only insubstantial but also . . . transformational" (2003: 147).

Remember Blum's premise: our identification is not with people but with 2D images. She likens them collectively to an "ever-unfolding pageant," a spectacular procession of figures that never stops. And, like characters in pageants, celebrities have an allegorical purpose: "They represent for us both what we are and what (and where) we long to be" (2003: 147).

This close and forever incomplete identification with representations works as both the cause and effect of cosmetic surgery. While the distance between stars and fans was closing, cosmetic surgery became more accessible and affordable. Fans learned about how the fabulous looks of the stars they saw on-screen and in magazines were not as special or as god-given as they might have supposed. So their quest to identify with them took on what Blum calls an "aggressive" character. If stars could have themselves surgically changed to look beautiful, so could fans. Anyone could have good looks.

In the early 1980s, only seriously big stars would have used surgery to modify normal, functioning features. Now, anybody can do it. They might have to save for a while. But most things of value necessitate a little belt-tightening. "What would a consumer want more?" asks Blum rhetorically. "A new car? A sleek new jawline?" There are always choices; they give the consumer sovereignty. Weber weighs in with a similar point: "Rather than being passive in the hands of surgeons or a wider beauty culture, those who choose cosmetic options often do so with a sense of agency, thus contributing to their own self-making" (2009a: 9).

Plastic surgery is a perfect complement to a consumer culture predicated on the principle that anything can be bought in the market.

Another interpretation is that the clients, that is, the consumers, are the ones being bought and sold. And, if there is still a missing link between cosmetic surgery and celebrity culture, it is this: all problems have solutions that can be bought. Everything is potentially soluble, as long as the consumer has enough money. As we know, consumer society generates problems of a particular kind: the ones that have their sources in insecurities, anxieties, cravings, greed, and desires. Plastic surgery has become a buyable solution to a problem that starts in identifying with mediated images.

In Blum's vision, plastic surgery is no mere byproduct of a culture driven by vanity, but an experience that distills the raw materials of celebrity culture. It's as if the imperatives of consumerism, its narcissistic excesses, and its media-promoted visions of the good life were heated into vapor, condensed by cold air, then re-collected in the form of what Blum calls a "cult of the surface."

There is something both liberating and oppressive about this. Proponents might point to the boosts in self-esteem or confidence brought about by cosmetic surgery. Opponents might deplore an enterprise founded on superficiality and surface appearance. Someone sitting in a locked car in which the doors are jammed might turn the ignition and drive to wherever they want. Those standing outside the car might pity the poor soul trapped in the environmentally hostile metal conveyance.

One thing is for sure: plastic surgery is a perfect complement to a consumer culture predicated on the principle that anything – *anything* – can be bought in the market. Even good looks.

Every ingredient of what we've come to regard as the good life arrives at our senses through the media. Think about what would make you happy. It probably involves either having or appearing. Possessing cars, clothes, or homes, for example. Looking better than the most drop-dead celeb imaginable. We know things can be bought. Increasingly, so can looks. The urge to improve ourselves, again brought to us courtesy of the media, involves commodities – commodities without utility, apart from their image value. We desire things not so much for appropriation, but for presentation: to stimulate ourselves by projecting ourselves in a certain way.

Celebrity culture has brought with it new possibilities: the endless novelty of new commodities disguised as people with images that titillate and inspire emulation. Their distinctive manner of living, their enviable belongings, and, just as importantly, their attractive appearance make us restless. We want to be more like them. How can we resist figures with whom we identify so closely?

|LIKE THREE DIFFERENT WOMEN

Before closing this chapter, I need to consider two more questions: Why don't more celebs come out and admit they've had work done; and would it make any difference if they did? Joan Rivers insists: "Look at any actress over 60 who doesn't have jowls. They say they've done nothing, but they're lying" (in the above-cited *Independent* story). When it comes to cosmetic surgery, Rivers vaunts: "I go to my surgeon once every two years, like you service your car or repaint your house." She made fun of other celebrities who denied having work done. Eyebrows have been raised metaphorically at the manner in which other facial features have been literally raised. While Rivers and the other famed cosmetic surgery aficionada Cher talk as openly about their surgery as they might do about their clothes, the vast majority of celebs, young and old, treat their surgery like a dark secret. It's almost as if they're embarrassed to reveal that their looks are not entirely natural. Or that they live in fear that their professional careers are contingent on their physical looks and that a disintegration of one will lead to a disintegration of the other.

If their motive is to preserve their specialness, they should think again. Fans, as we have seen, are both participants and voyeurs: they are astute enough to see through the subterfuge of the celebrity industry. Anyway, on the account presented here, it wouldn't matter. The whole point about cosmetic surgery is that it is the highest development – or, to use one of Lasch's words, the apotheosis – of celebrity culture. So, when Melanie Griffith appears in three Revlon advertising campaigns between 1995 and 2001 and, as Blum puts it, "looks like three different women," it doesn't matter at all. The shifting, transitory character of celebs is central to their appeal. We might suspect that Griffith's age-defying transition is more attributable to surgery than moisturizer, but neither her status nor Revlon's suffered.

As nature abhors a vacuum, celebrity culture abhors stillness. Change, novelty, surprise are prerequisites. The enduring celebrities are transformational, changing appearance and identity in a way that keeps consumers stimulated and refreshed, though not always with comparable results. Contrast Clint Eastwood (b. 1930) and Burt Reynolds (b. 1936). Eastwood's early roles created for him two alter egos, "The Man with No Name" from the *A Fistful of Dollars* series and Harry Callahan from *Dirty Harry* and its sequels. Eastwood diversified into different roles in different genres, directing as well as acting, and, at one point, taking an elected mayoral position in Carmel, California. His appearance ripened as his professional personae expanded. In contrast, Reynolds seemed to strive painfully to retain the dark, mustachioed macho looks for which he became known in such movies as *Deliverance* and *Smokey and the Bandit* in the 1970s. As his looks matured, so the roles disappeared and his celebrity waned. His face seemed to reflect heroic efforts to make time stand still. In the 1990s, he reappeared in *Boogie Nights*, but in a role that seemed to either echo or parody his former self.

Celebs are allowed to age. What they're not allowed to do is stay the same. Even Britain's ever-youthful septuagenarian Cliff Richard, whose musical career spans five decades and whose looks seemed resistant to age, changed considerably in choice of music, as well as physical appearance. The secret of his longevity lay in his adaptability. Were he to opt for cosmetic surgery, his considerable fan base would suffer no damage at all. It would just be a further signal of his intention to keep changing.

The fans' pleasure is in possessing celebrities just like they possess all the other articles of expendable and obsolescing merchandise. Celebs who are prepared to keep changing present themselves just as possessions that can be upgraded. Obviously, there's a qualitative difference between being a devotee of someone and desiring a new Audi. There's also a similarity. If Audi produced the same models as it did in 1990, we would go off them and turn to a make of car that cycles in new models every few years. We want change. We want celebrities to change. How they change, with what methods, and with what results is of secondary importance.

CONSUMPTION

CHAPTER HIGHLIGHTS

- The millions advertisers pay celebrities only makes sense in a society in which commodities are prized so highly
- Research suggests only 10 percent of tv commercials make an impact on consumers
- How do celebrities justify the lavish amounts of money advertisers pay them?
- Some celebrities are credible, while others are *incredible*
- Today's consumers are discerning and judicious, and advertisers compete for their souls as well as their money
- When they buy commodities, consumers are shaping their identities as well as buying merchandise
- The line between advertising and entertainment is barely noticeable

COMMODITY HEDONISM |

Long before celebrity culture as we know it took grip, entertainers were lending their names and images to commercial products. In 1910, King Edward VII, son of Queen Victoria and Prince Albert, appeared in a print ad endorsing Angelus piano-players, according to the advertising history book *The Age of Persuasion*. Lillie Langtry (1853–1929) boosted sales of Pears soap, not for any financial gain, but, according to some, because she liked it. When radio and, later, television arrived in the twentieth century, classic broadcast stars such as Jack Benny and Bob Hope were associated with corporate sponsors like Jell-O pudding and Pepsodent toothpaste, and would namecheck their paymasters' products during the shows. In perhaps the most grimly ironic series of advertisements in the 1950s, John Wayne

(1907–79) endorsed Camel cigarettes, boasting that he'd been smoking them for 20 years. Wayne died of lung cancer.

Today, an advertising deal is a seal of approval for anyone with aspirations of being a celebrity. Being tracked by a stalker, possibly more than one, is also a recognized benchmark. And, of course, a spell in rehab is almost an industry standard. Anybody aiming to occupy a place in the popular imagination should have at least one, if not all, of these in his or her portfolio. But advertising merchandise is a *sine qua non*.

The act of giving explicit approval or support and recommending a product or service in advertising is endorsement, but it's only one of a number of ways famous figures have advertised products. Licensing is another: a famous figure permits the use of his or her name or image in association with a line of products. "The practice of licensed celebrity merchandise started in 1913 with Teddy Roosevelt [1858–1919] licensing his name to the Teddy Bear," write Ross D. Petty and Denver D'Rozario (2009: 37). The 26th president of the USA was an enthusiastic bear hunter. The child star of the 1930s Shirley Temple (b. 1928) authorized the sale of dolls in her image (still available on eBay).

A more recent trend has been for celebrities effectively to take up positions in a company. Black Eyed Peas frontman will.i.am, in 2011, became "Director of Creative Innovation" for computer chip maker Intel Corp. The artist's role was to collaborate with Intel on creative and technology endeavors across the "compute continuum." The same artist featured in a pullout vinyl ad for Budweiser that could actually be played on a turntable. However the corporations fashion the relationship with the celebrities, the impact is still to draw attention to a product or range of products in order to promote sales. Having the imprimatur or guarantee from a known source, it seems, helps.

> *Advertising has long worked to establish the ideal of a golden life that can only be achieved through the purchase of specific objects.*
>
> BRENDA R. WEBER

Next time you glance at some sort of advertisement, whether on a screen or on paper (or vinyl), possibly for beer, broadband, computers, or cars, you won't think to yourself, "I must buy that product . . . even if will.i.am helped design it." Advertisers can't force us to buy anything we don't already want; they don't bend our wills to their ends, or exert a direct influence on our consumer choices. Somehow they have to cajole us into wanting something. So who better to coax us than someone we know, or at least think we know, and who seems prepared to stake their reputation on the product?

This appears to be the reasoning employed by L'Oréal, Pepsi, and LG, among others, when they collectively helped Eva Longoria earn $13 million (£8.3m) from advertising in 2012 alone. And it seems to have been on Kmart's mind when the discount store chain paid Sofia Vergara a $7 million (£4.5m) advance for her licensed clothing line to be sold at their stores. When the likes of Sears and Midori liqueur contributed to Kim Kardashian's annual income of $18 million (£11.5m), they knew the ubiquitous reality tv star would be known to practically everyone. And, while Polaroid may not actually have needed Lady Gaga's input when it appointed her as a creative director, she did help design camera glasses – apparently.

Nowadays, advertisers are prepared to part with what seem ruinous sums of money just to have their products or services linked with celebrities. And, while entertainers, politicians, or other types of famous figures may once have prevaricated over whether they might be debasing themselves by putting themselves out for hire, they rarely hesitate nowadays. It's part of being a celebrity.

There is, however, a difference between the celebrity advertising of 20 years ago and that of today. "Advertising has long worked to establish the ideal of a golden life that can only be achieved through the purchase of specific objects," submits Brenda R. Weber (2009b: 59). Historically, celebrities have supported products. Now they are themselves advertisements, not just for the products they're paid to promote, but for the culture in which those products have value and the golden life those products yield. While it's often said that celebrities themselves are commodities, this betrays a misunderstanding of both the status and purpose of celebrities: their very presence advertises a conception of a life in which every available stimulant, toy, and accessory is readily at hand.

Think what celebrities do – sell. dvds, downloads, admission tickets, books, and magazines are just the start: every celebrity advertises products that can be bought and sold. So what happened to turn people who entertained us into people who sell us stuff? Charles Fairfield's answer is brief but emphatic. Since 1982, there has been a concentration of ownership of the media and a corresponding withdrawal of the media from serious discussion. We have arrived at the point where: "Society is imagined only as a market – segmented and regimented for the purpose of selling advertising" (1997: 26).

The advertising industry sustains, buttresses, and amplifies consumer culture. It doesn't keep dark secrets that enable it to turn us into dependents (I'll avoid using the near-obsolete term addict) so that we crave externally provided stimulation in ever-increasing doses. It simply brings those products to our attention, but in a way that beguiles, absorbs, and excites us. The result is what Christopher Lasch in 1991 called "a constant revision of material expectations, a never-ending redefinition of luxuries as necessities" (1991: 186).

The desired result is that we want things, specifically things we can buy. Advertising promotes an ethos of commodity hedonism, the belief that the pursuit of satisfaction through the acquisition of products is the proper aim of human life. Its purpose is to create new demands that can only be met by the consumption of commodities. And it does so by inducing dissatisfaction with our own lives; so we reflect on how much better our lives would be if we enhanced them with better clothes, cars, homes, drugs, and countless other products that are all within our grasp – as long as we have the means to pay for them. The kind of consumerist logic that guides advertising also governs our depiction of reality: the good life is one in which we're surrounded by commodities. Thrift, self-denial, deferred gratification? These are values from a different age. Celebrity culture emphasizes extravagance, impulse, and immediacy.

Once we were utilitarian shoppers: we bought products when we needed them, not because we craved them. Products had functions; we used them. But we were persuaded that products, whether the everyday ones we get from a supermarket or the luxuries we used to have to save for, were more than functional items: they were possessions that held the potential to change us and not just in a superficial way. "In today's society, consumers are constantly transporting symbolic properties out of products into their lives to construct their self. Consumers' possessions and consumption of certain products often reflect their individuality and help enhance their identity," write professors of advertising Sejung Marina Choi and Nora J. Rifon (2007: 307).

"Consumption is part of how people make their identities," confirms sociology professor Joshua Gamson, who adds that we live in times "in which consuming is central to social experience, where shopping, buying and getting commodities is central to social existence" (quoted in Hoopes and Heverin 2009: 38).

This is quite a claim: buying commodities helps us construct our individuality and shape our identity, as well as being part of our very existence. It's a strong, almost intoxicating point but one that makes the kinds of sums paid to Eva Longoria *et al.* more intelligible. The airwaves and cyberspace have been taken over by people promoting a vision of the good life that promises instant glamour and excitement. In a sense, celebrities are not just advertising products, or even brands: they are themselves living, breathing, moving advertisements for a particular kind of culture. A culture in which value is placed on novelty, change, excitement, and extravagance, all of which are available for purchase. Celebrities have become the standard-bearers, representatives, and living embodiments of this culture.

| 90 PERCENT WASTE

When Choi and Rifon inform us that a quarter of all television commercials feature celebrities, our response is probably: "Only a quarter?" We're accustomed to seeing celebrities as much in advertising of some sort as in their natural habitat, whether a soap, movies, or reality tv. A few years ago, some writers, such as Katy Guest of Britain's *Independent on Sunday*, speculated that this was leading to a kind of celebrity fatigue: the celebs had become so inescapable that we felt exhausted and would soon rebel against products advertised by celebs: "We have had enough. The automatic association between a famous face and a successful product is over" (February 20, 2005, p. 16). She didn't mean that we would all start poring over consumer guides like *Consumer Reports* or *Which?*, though our exhaustion was beginning to show: "Shoppers are bored with endorsements and actually finding fame a turn-off."

Guest cited market research conducted by Mintel, which discovered that 20 percent of shoppers were actually "celebrity-resistant," 60 percent were "bored with celebrities," and only 8 percent indicated that they would buy a celebrity-endorsed product and even then only if the celeb was someone they "admired or trusted." Paradoxically, in the same publication as

Guest's article, Steve Bloomfield analyzed the roles played by Kylie Minogue and Scarlett Johansson. Bloomfield used a sidebar quote from a 16-year-old woman: "Your mind doesn't look at the product being promoted but at the people promoting it. You don't consider whether it's meant for your skin. Celebrities have a lot of influence and we believe them when they say these products work."

Whom should *we* believe? The likes of Guest are skeptical about the effectiveness of celebrities in advertising, while Bloomfield and, presumably, a sizable portion of the advertising industry believe celebrities are good value, even at the prices charged by Vergara and co. I'll try to answer this question in the course of this chapter. An instructive case study will get us started.

The advertising agency Ogilvy & Mather in 2004 decided to dump celebrities: it got together with Dove's marketing team and came up with the idea for "The campaign for real beauty." Spurning the trend for featuring gorgeous, waiflike celebrities or even lesser-known models for the ad campaign, Dove used women who looked "ordinary": some had freckles, some were middle-aged, most had bodies that were more Adele than Shakira.

"I personally think it is risky," said Richard Kirshenbaum, of the ad agency Kirshenbaum Bond & Partners, to New York's *Daily News*. "I've often found using real people to be problematic" (July 31, 2005). Leaving aside the question of whether or not celebrities are "real people," the strategy was undeniably risky. But the gamble on "real" women, with abundant cellulite and cutaneous imperfections reaped rewards. In Britain, where the campaign was initiated, sales of Dove rose 9 percent in the year to £120 million ($76.5m), while sales of its firming lotion rose 700 percent. Unilever, which owns Dove (and spends over $3 billion a year on advertising), didn't release US sales figures, though there's no obvious reason to suppose the campaign didn't meet with a similar response.

Also in 2004, Gillette, which is owned by Procter & Gamble – a corporation that spends about $10 billion every year on advertising – signed David Beckham to an endorsement deal for its M3Power razor. The deal was thought to be worth $40 million (£25.5m) over three years. Sales of the M3Power surged by 13 percent in 2005. Encouraged by the results, in 2008, Gillette signed Tiger Woods, Thierry Henry, and Roger Federer to front a similar campaign for its Fusion Power razor. Incidentally, Federer, even in the autumn of his tennis career, earned $30 million (£19m) per year in advertising income thanks to Nike, Wilson, Rolex, Mercedes-Benz, as well as Gillette and others.

Advertisers must decide whether to use models who most resemble typical consumers or models who represent what most consumers want. "It is primarily the wealth or good looks of a celebrity that we wish to emulate, his or her purchasing power or ability to attract the opposite sex that we wish to enjoy," writes Roberta Newman (2003: 26).

This is a reductive appraisal: how about their ostentatiously attractive lifestyle, circle of glamorous friends and confidants, ability to grab the attention of the media, and the influence some celebrities are able to exert on politics and world events? These are qualities consumers not only admire and crave, but perhaps feel they can absorb, as if by osmosis. But it doesn't necessarily make them spend money.

Gillette, the leader in the men's grooming products market, would be interested in the research of Jib Fowles, who discovered that television advertising isn't as effective as many assume. In response to the question of how well tv commercials work, Fowles writes: "The answer is both *not very* and *quite a bit*, depending on how the situation is perceived" (1992: 209).

This isn't quite as useless an answer as it first appears. While his book *Why Viewers Watch: A reappraisal of television's effects* was published in 1992, some of its insights are timeless. Fowles rounds up the evidence to conclude: "Not only don't commercials make an impression on us, but as strange as it may seem, no experimental evidence exists that they get us to buy anything" (1992: 209).

Strange indeed; especially as companies like Unilever and General Motors regularly spend 10–12 percent of their annual sales receipts on the following year's advertising, with about 40 percent still on tv commercials. The size of the audience is, as Fowles puts it, the key. "All but about 10% of the money spent on television commercials is wasted," records Fowles (1992: 209). Only that percentage of tv viewers retains product knowledge after watching an ad. Even then, only 10 percent of that sub-group might actually go out and buy the product. But that percentage is from a total population of millions.

Some sports events, such as the Super Bowl, which draws about 200 million viewers, or the World Cup Final which gets 1.7 billion – that's a quarter of the world's population – are spectacularly huge and untypical. Britain's *The X Factor* became an advertising phenomenon in the 2000s, when it averaged 11 million viewers from a total population of 62.6 million; advertisers paid the ITV network £250,000 ($392,000) per 30-second spot. Finales of popular sitcoms are also great viewer magnets: 52.5 million US viewers were glued to the last episode of *Friends* (8.6 million Brits watched). Even a modest show can draw, say, 15 million in the USA, or 3 million in Britain. When a five-times-weekly soap like *Coronation Street* can bring nine or ten million viewers to their sets for every episode, then an advertiser might be swayed by the prospect of 110,000 potential buys.

Michael Schudson opens his book *Advertising, the Uneasy Persuasion* bluntly: "Advertising is much less powerful than advertisers and critics of advertising claim," but qualifies this with "advertising helps sell goods even if it never persuades a consumer of anything" (1993: xv). He argues that a self-fulfilling prophecy operates, with key personnel tending to believe advertising works. In other words, if retailers and sales staff think advertising works, they tend to push one product rather than another. For an ad to work, it must be seen to work.

> *A celebrity's approval might convince some consumers that they are buying something authentic, substantial, or even profound . . . they are buying a commodity, plain if not simple.*

So, if an advertiser can design some way of not just distinguishing a product, but distinguishing it in a way that enables both vendors to stock it and consumers to confer extra value on it, then they have something like the goose that laid the golden eggs. This is, of course, where celebrities come in. Advertisers are always on the lookout for a "face of" some product or another; that is, someone who personifies a product or a range of products, or perhaps even an entire brand. That someone might be the right match or fit for one type of product rather than another.

Elizabeth Hurley was the spokesperson for, and hence the face of, Estée Lauder for ten years up to 2005. Presumably, Lauder – which owns, among other lines, Bobbi Brown and Clinique – felt she radiated the kind of values it wanted associated with the brand. That is, until she hit 40, when Lauder replaced her with Gwyneth Paltrow, seven years her junior, for $15 million. Arizona Muse took over in 2012, the year of Paltrow's 40th birthday.

Castrol Motor Oil, Snickers bars, Coors Light, or thousands of other products would have found little use for Hurley, Paltrow, or Muse. Unless Coors Light decided to reposition its beer in the marketplace: for example, it might follow the example of Häagen-Dazs ice cream, which was marketed by its owner Pillsbury as seduction fuel rather than dessert or sugary junk food for children. This is an unlikely scenario: Coors Light knows its demographics, which is why the company often uses male artists, like Ice Cube, who are easily identifiable and embody the kind of values typically associated with an uncomplicated beer.

Whatever the pitch, the appeal, or the spiel, the consumer appears to get only one thing – merchandise. A celebrity's approval might convince some consumers that they are buying something authentic, substantial, or even profound. The product might be promoted as desirable and "real." And the consumer might walk away from the store feeling like they have acquired something of genuine value. They might even believe they have taken another step toward being the person they want to be. That doesn't alter the fact that they are buying a commodity, plain if not simple.

Value doesn't exist in any pure form: products are invested with value. Think of the countless items discarded by celebrities and endowed with great value when circulated on eBay or some other exchange system. An old toothbrush, a used tissue, or a worn sock become exceptional items. Most shoppers are aware that endorsed products are, essentially, the same as the generic ones: the majority of products are functionally indistinguishable. Advertising agencies are as aware of this as consumers; which is why they get paid to make those indistinguishable products distinguishable.

. . . BECAUSE THEY'RE WORTH IT? |

Selecting a celebrity to advertise a product is a science, like astrology or alchemy; in other words, a nebulous, imprecise, and uncertain one. The metrics are equivocal. Media visibility (exposure in print, television, radio, and online) is a key factor. Hence, film and television actors, tv personalities, models, sportsmen and women, authors, musicians, comics, and, of course, reality tv figures are obvious candidates. Their visibility is measurable in terms of appearances and namechecks. Beyond that, the science becomes, at best, art, and, at worst, guesswork.

Celebrities such as Taylor Swift, Beyoncé, and Tyler Perry offer continuity and consistency in the way they go about their business efficiently and reliably: the chances of a scandal erupting around them are slim and they are known to a wide spectrum of people. Not that a hint of indecorum is a bad thing.

Sales of Katie Holmes' high-end ready-to-wear fashion line, Holmes & Yang, increased in the wake of her unsavory divorce from Tom Cruise. "Unsurprisingly, the label has benefited from Holmes's increased visibility," confirmed Charlotte Cowles of *New York* magazine (July 30, 2012).

Jennifer Lopez, a prodigious endorser of, among other things, Kohl's clothing and lifestyle collection, was caught up in an 18-month on-off relationship with Ben Affleck in 2003 and 2004. The Latina singer-actor was one-half of "Bennifer," as the couple was known. The tumultuous relationship coincided with a career slump defined by box-office flops (*Gigli, Jersey Girl*) and disappointing cd sales (*Brave, Como Ama una Mujer*).

Becoming a judge on *American Idol* smacked of desperation, yet it turned out to be a career savior and, by 2012, at the age of 42, she was, according to *Forbes*, the most sought-after celebrity by advertisers. *Idol* regularly pulled 26 million viewers to their televisions (i.e. 9.8 percent of the total potential audience), most of them in the 18–49-year-old segment advertisers love. JLo used the series as a showcase to premiere music videos and perform singles. "On the floor" went multi-platinum, and the music video amassed over 530 million YouTube views. Mariah Carey must have been enthused by the prospect of emulating JLo when she accepted the offer to become a judge on *Idol*, though the $18 million (£11.6m) one-off fee was a further incentive. Mariah's advertising file included T-Mobile, *Mariah's . . .* fragrances, and Jenny Craig, for whom she directed a diet plan commercial.

JLo and Mariah are among an elite of celebrities whose name or image adds value to a brand and, in turn, makes products move off shelves. In this sense, they are in the same league as Michael Jordan once was. Jordan is still busy endorsing Nike products, of course, but, in the 1990s, he was without peer. In the June 1998 issue of *Fortune* magazine, Roy Johnson and Ann Harrington analyzed what they called "The Jordan effect," which described the celebrity athlete's impact on the overall economy of the USA. Nike developed the Air Jordan line of footwear and apparel and, over the 1990s, it was worth, in terms of sales, $5.2 billion (£3bn). Nike, which spends nearly $2.5 billion a year on advertising, still dominates the world market in sportswear, claiming 19.7 percent of all sales. After Jordan, there was Tiger Woods, whose first contract with Nike in 1996 earned him $40 million. His second was estimated at $125 million, the biggest endorsement contract to date. In return, Nike saw a $50 million revenue growth in golf balls and the overall golf line gross $250 million in annual sales.

Nike's market leadership encouraged rivals toward what seems profligacy. Reebok splashed out $100 million on Allen Iverson, but made such little impact on Nike's leadership that it was taken over by adidas in a $3.8 million deal in 2005. Earlier, Reebok had signed Shaq O'Neal for $15 million over five years, but passed on a renewal when the contract expired in 1998. Just signing a celebrity athlete is no guarantee of sales. Nike's judgment has been near faultless, while its rivals' has been hit-and-miss. So, when Nike closed arguably its most audacious endorsement deal in 2003, there was less surprise, but not shock: LeBron James was a high school basketball player, unproven either at college or NBA levels, when Nike signed him for a reported $90 million.

Such is the confidence of advertisers in the added value brought to a product by the imprimatur of a celebrity that Chanel No. 5, in 2004, bought the services of Nicole Kidman for just one television commercial. The commercial reunited Kidman with director Baz Luhrmann with whom she had worked on the movie *Moulin Rouge*. The one-off advertisement was estimated to have cost $32 million (£18m), Kidman's fee for four days' shooting being, at its lowest estimate, $3.6 million (£2m) (*Guardian*, November 19, 2004). No sales figures were released in the aftermath of the transmission, though Chanel have pursued a similar mini-movie structure approach to advertising since, in 2009 featuring Audrey Tatou in an Orient Express-themed commercial that lasted nearly two-and-a-half minutes. And, in 2012, it secured the services of Brad Pitt to front a campaign.

Advertising has moved away from the practical approach in which product information was at the forefront. Many global brands avoid even mentioning products in an attempt to create synonymy between their brand and the celebrity endorser. Of all the endorsers used by L'Oréal, Beyoncé is perhaps most closely associated with the brand and its signature tagline ". . . because I'm worth it" (a slogan dreamt up by Ilon Specht, of McCann Erickson, in 1973 and which is now recognized by 70 percent of consumers, according to Lewis and Bridger 2001: 39; L'Oréal spends over $1.3 billion per year on advertising to maintain this kind of brand recognition). Apart from a contretemps in 2008, when L'Oréal denied that it lightened Beyoncé's skin for an advertisement, which appeared in the magazine *Elle*, the relationship – which started in 2001 – has been as productive as any in advertising history.

| BELIEVE IT OR NOT

But seriously: Does anyone else in the world believe Kim Kardashian or any of the other celebrities are sincere when they advocate, recommend, or vouch for a cellphone? Sofia Vergara is hardly likely to shop at a discount department store chain, particularly after that same store chain paid her $7 million. Is anyone in the world unable to spell out the motive behind celebrities' behavior (clue: five letters beginning with "m")? Is anyone so absolutely, completely, and utterly gullible that they are prepared to accept the word of a well-paid mercenary when they part with their hard-earned cash? We'd probably like to say the answer to all these is an emphatic *no!* On inspection, though, we probably conclude that it's *no-ish*.

Fowles, in another of his instructive books *Advertising and Popular Culture*, quotes market research on the efficacy of the ad from 1991. At the time, the football player Joe Montana was probably the best-known athlete in the USA and beyond. Diet Pepsi never revealed how much it paid him to feature in a commercial shown in a break in the Super Bowl, but we can assume the then top-rated quarterback did not come cheap. Result: a healthy 70 percent of the television audience recalled that Montana had appeared in the commercial, but only 18 percent remembered the product he was endorsing (1996: 125). The celebrity rather than the product registered. Not all geese lay golden eggs.

If a person who is endorsing a product is believable, what he or she says is likely to be convincing; but the *fit* between the two is crucial. Both the statement and its source must be believable. When advertisers scan for likely endorsers, credibility is uppermost in their minds. If consumers regard the celebrity as credible, they're more likely to take notice of the message. If they don't, there opens up a credibility gap: a seeming difference between what's being said and what's seen as the truth.

Ford, for example, thought a credibility gap had opened up when Eminem released his single "Ass like that" in 2005. Encouraged by the way young people appeared to take notice of Eminem and afford him respect, Ford, which spends about $2.4 billion a year on advertising, was offered what seemed an ideal opportunity to shed its staid image when the rapper asked to feature one of its new models in his video. There seemed to be a good fit: Eminem, or Marshall Mathers, was born in Detroit, the home of the car manufacturer, and had a huge following among the demographically desirable young adults.

Earlier, the conservative American Family Association had urged consumers to boycott Ford on the grounds that it had a "pro-gay" agenda, having made cash donations to a gay and lesbian rights group, Gay and Lesbian Advocates and Defenders,

(Glad), based on the purchase of a Jaguar or Land Rover. (Pepsi had earlier felt the wrath of conservatism when Madonna, with whom it had a $5 million contract, released the "Like a prayer" video in 1989; as we saw in Chapter 4, a furor ensured.) Eminem could hardly be described as "pro-gay," of course. He was edgy, though, being white, not as threatening as many black rap artists.

All the same, there was a credibility problem: would potential Ford buyers consider Eminem believable? After all, the lyrics to the track in question included a plea to Gwen Stefani – "Will you pee-pee on me please?" – and his previous cds received as many criticisms as accolades. Ford might have done a cost-benefit calculation and decided that the possible harm done by association outweighed the advantages of attracting the attention of a young market, which would collectively ask itself: Would Eminem really drive a Ford?

Similar questions could be asked about any celebrity endorser. But the answers might be different. The legendary Brazilian footballer Pelé began promoting erectile dysfunction drug Viagra in 2005, but six years later said he had never had recourse to use the product. In 1983, Pepsi paid Michael Jackson a then record $5 million (£3m) to front a new campaign. But did Jackson actually drink Pepsi? An 8 percent rise in sales in the first year after he appeared in ads suggested consumers thought he did; in fact, he didn't. There was also an unusual sidebar: in 1984, while shooting a commercial for Pepsi, Jackson's hair caught fire. Jackson suffered second-degree burns and many trace his dependence on painkillers to the incident. Pepsi gave Jackson $1.5 million as a result.

The relationship has a coda: in 2012, three years after Michael Jackson's death, Pepsi announced a deal with Jackson's estate that would enable it to use his image for its new global marketing campaign that would include a tv commercial, special edition cans bearing the King of Pop's image (they produced a billion), and chances to download remixes of some of

Jackson's most famous tracks. At the time, PepsiCo was trying to capture markets outside the USA and a figure of Jackson's global renown was a perfect vehicle, even though he was dead. Remember Petty and D'Rozario's observation: "Deceased celebrities have the advantage of being both less expensive and less likely to suddenly lose popularity" (2009: 37).

But just appearing in an ad itself can cause a sudden loss of popularity. Consider Grammy-winning r&b singer Mary J. Blige, style icon and personification of cool: in 2012, she appeared in a Burger King commercial in which she stood on a restaurant table and sang about fried chicken. The advertisement was immediately condemned for perpetuating racist stereotypes about black people and was quickly pulled, leaving Blige with a hole in her credibility.

Rachel Weisz may have actually used L'Oréal's Revitalift Repair in the past and possibly still does; in fact, she looked *so* fabulous in the ads, she would be foolish not to. But, according to Britain's Advertising Standards Agency, the ads allegedly "misleadingly exaggerated" the antiwrinkle cream's performance by digitally enhancing Weisz's image, making her skin look smoother and more even-looking than it really was. All the same, it was perfectly feasible to assume Weisz would use the product.

And it's possible that the numerous endorsers of fragrances (JLo led the field with 19 at the time of writing) probably availed themselves of the products every so often. George Clooney probably drank Nespresso coffee, used an Android smartphone, and may even have had a bank account with Norway's DnB NOR, all of which he's advertised. And even the likes of Katy Perry and Justin Bieber are vulnerable to acne, and might resort to Proactive. Reese Witherspoon could favor the Avon cosmetics she advertises too. The last one might be a stretch. While consumers might be aware that endorsers are rewarded financially, there is still the issue of whether they see them as potential users.

| COMPETING FOR THE CONSUMER'S SOUL

In the age of celebrity, market researchers are forever trying to establish the exact properties that make some celebrities fit advertisements and others seem like videocassettes in a Bluray player. Source credibility sits at the top of a hierarchy of properties that affect whether consumers will take notice of the endorser. This is far from straightforward: credibility is, according to Rajan Nataraajan and Sudhir Chawla, a "multidimensional variable," the main dimensions being "expertise, trustworthiness, and attractiveness" (1997: 120). One of their conclusions was that "celebrity endorsed ads are perceived to be significantly more credible than ads endorsed by noncelebrities."

Fowles adds another dimension when he writes: "As the star's image cycles back into popular culture, it does so with the new accretions of inferences from the commercial detour" (1996: 131). The very fact of appearing in a campaign can add credibility, which then enhances a celebrity's popularity. Bill Cosby's "detour" with Jell-O in 1974 had this effect. Gary Lineker's lackluster image was given panache by his appearance in Walkers snacks commercials on British tv. So there is a kind a feedback loop in which credibility built in one medium transfers to another, which then transfers back and so on?

Michael Basil's research uncovered another factor. "Identification occurs when an individual adopts an attitude or behavior from another person when that attitude or behavior is associated with a satisfying self-defining relationship with that person" (1996: 479). In other words, buying something "being advocated by that celebrity can be seen as a way of 'hitching your wagon to the star'." We discussed identification when we saw how some fans develop "self-defining relationships with celebrities and seek to adopt their perceived attributes."

So, if consumers believe celebs are credible and they identify with them, then they are likely to be persuaded. This
still doesn't tell us exactly why. In their analysis of what they
call *The Soul of the New Consumer*, David Lewis and Darren
Bridger provide an answer: "New consumers are really seeking to discover themselves. Not the people they feel themselves to be at this moment, but the kind of men and women
they aspire to be and feel it within their power to become"
(2001: 28).

From the mid-1950s, we became aspirational consumers,
buying not just to subsist, but to make statements about our
progress in the world. The "new consumers" were shaped
by the social changes that ensued in the 1960s, particularly
the "exponential growth in power and wealth of corporations," which has mirrored the rise in consumer influence
and power. Previously, manufacturers and suppliers dictated
all major aspects of transactions with "old consumers." But,
as the balance of power shifted, so consumers were increasingly able to dictate not only what they wanted, but how,
where, and even how much they wanted to pay for products.
Schudson puts it plainly when he writes that commodities
are not "foisted unwillingly upon defenseless consumers"
(1993: 16).

Many might respond that this so-called power of the
consumer is largely illusory and the more tangible power of
corporations is ultimately decisive. Lewis and Bridger, by contrast, suggest that the new consumer is armed to the teeth
with more accessible information than at any point in history and uses that information, if necessary, to undermine
corporations. They give the example of copyright-defying file
sharing. The boycott of Nestlé products would also support
their argument: Nestlé's aggressive marketing of baby food
undermined breastfeeding, especially in developing world
countries, argued consumers. Many of the corporations mentioned in this chapter, including L'Oréal, Procter & Gamble,

and Unilever, have been embarrassed by consumer groups, which have exposed and, indeed, forced them to change animal testing practices. Chunks of their advertising budgets – nearly $10 billion combined – go toward repairing damage done by active consumers. As a supplement to this point: we can only imagine what the animal rights organization Peta thought when Naomi Campbell, who had in 1994 appeared in one of its ads proclaiming that she would "rather go naked than wear fur," declared three years later "I do like wearing fur and I still do" and proceeded to festoon herself with sable, mink, and other animal skins.

The same changes leading to global media and the proliferation of entertainment were responsible for diffusing information to new consumers. This information equipped and enabled them to exert their influence over the marketplace. This kind of approach is consistent with the image of the consumer at the center of this book: aware, discerning, and judicious. Corporations have been catalyzed into restoring a new order in which they have needed to respond in kind – treating consumers as well-briefed subjects who knew that corporations and their ad agencies were always trying to anticipate their next move, rather than "inert functionaries of consumerism" (to snatch a phrase from Paul Ohler 2010: 36). They were, said a corporate head to fellow executives, "watching you watching them in order to figure out how they act" (quoted in Schor 2004: 50).

Competing for their "soul" has brought corporations and their advertising agents to their mettle. Using celebrities as today's equivalent of sandwich men is integral to the response. The challenge to advertisers and the corporations they served, according to Lewis and Bridger, was that, unlike traditional customers, new consumers tended "to reject mass-produced and mass-marketed commodities in favor of products and services that can claim to be in some way authentic" (2001: 4).

The "quest for authenticity" drives new consumers to pay $10,000 for a Leica lens that lacks many of the features of most

Japanese equivalents, such as autofocus and power winder. Leica products have the "aura of authenticity" that derives from their founder, who was a German mountaineer in the early twentieth century. While Lewis and Bridger don't cite them, we might also include Nike's Air Jordan IV, produced in 1989 and regarded by many as the quintessential piece of footwear. Pairs fetch $1,000 or more on today's market. It's the same quest that motivates consumers to spend inordinate amounts of money on some designer handbags, even though there are knockoffs that look almost the same at a thirtieth of the price. Even then, only *some* designer handbags; usually ones that have what Lewis and Bridger call "a subtle demonstration of uniqueness," such as a Chloé Silverado (at $1,900 (£1,086); Chloé took British retailer Kookaï to court for producing one that was too similar and retailed at £35 ($53)).

REAL AND IDEAL SELVES|

But is "authenticity" the quality most consumers are pursuing? Choi and Rifon raise an alternative: "Celebrities," they argue, "embody popular meanings in culture similar to those signified by products or brands" and consumers see them as "a representation of a variety of meanings that are drawn from the history of their careers" (2007: 317–18).

This complements a point made by Jan De Vos, who detects that celebrities "give commodities personalities by means of celebrity endorsements in advertising" (2009: 270). Meanings are, to use De Vos's term, bestowed on objects of merchandise by consumers, who are assisted in this endeavor by celebrities who give those objects "humanness and familiarity." So a consumer will see no special meaning in T-Mobile, but may be an admirer of Mariah Carey's five-octave range, her songs, her looks, the way she struggled out of a troubled background, even her moods, and attitude. Carey becomes what De Vos calls "an affective link" to the product.

> *The seemingly mundane act of shopping actually involves us in actively shaping a sense of self as well as acquiring possessions.*

When we buy products, we don't take to the store a rational, calculating mentality. We remain judicious, but appeal to emotion as well as logic when we make purchase decisions. Buying is affected behavior: it's influenced by feeling, sentiment, sensation, even passion. Cornel Sandvoss may not have buying phone providers in mind when he submits that popular celebrities "are appropriated by fans as meaningful resources in their everyday lives" (2005: 13). But it barely needs explication: when consumers buy, say, food or footwear endorsed by celebrities they admire, respect, or like, they are appropriating "meaningful resources" too.

In making the purchase, they give their pleasurable assent to both the celebrity and the product he or she is supporting. At this point, the motives that spurred the endorsers to lend their services seem less important than the appropriation that's made possible by the simple transaction. Consumption requires us to be discerning: we desire to buy certain products. Marketing generally and advertising in particular influence our choices, as do our status in society, income, and many other factors. Yet we still do the choosing; and we do it in a manner that is intended to communicate inward and outward.

Put another way: we buy products that are congruent with how we think and feel, who we think we are, our sense of self or identity; the way we use those same products expresses this to others. As Choi and Rifon observe of consumers: "They might view some of the images or meanings the celebrities represent to be relevant to their ideal self-image and purchase brands endorsed by the celebrities in hopes that they become similar to the celebrities by consuming these brands" (2007: 307).

Sandvoss adds: "The relationship between fans and their object of fandom goes beyond mere identification" (2005: 102). Being a fan often means appropriating the celebrity as "part of the publicly performed self" (2005: 111). Consumers are "shaping a sense of self through the object of fandom" (2005: 157).

The object of adoration, whether an individual celebrity, a team, a tv show, a track on a cd, or whatever, is seen as more than a possession. It can "become an integral part of their [the fans'] identity, vision of self, as much as their perception by others" (2005: 163). Sandvoss isn't referring only to the kind of people we discussed earlier, like Rebecca Schaeffer's killer, who taped the tv show in which she appeared, and the Steffi Graf fan who built a shrine to her. He means anyone who enters into a transaction in which they form an emotionally significant relationship with a celebrity or something he or she represents, appears in, or produces. Buying shampoo might not implicate a consumer in such a relationship with whoever is endorsing the product; but, like it or not, it means they are involved in the same social practice, albeit at a different level.

My earlier remark about having echoes of an ad man's pitch bears repeating here. On Sandvoss' account, the emotional relationship often dismissed as marketing verbiage is actually the crucial nexus that helps explain why most of us, not just those marginalized as devotees, are awed – and I mean impressed rather than frightened – by celebrities. It's because they have become resources when we think about ourselves, position ourselves, and reflect on how we would like others to see us. The seemingly mundane act of shopping actually involves us in "actively shaping a sense of self" as well as acquiring possessions.

Schudson's position is comparable: he views the buying of goods as an attempt to build what the anthropologist Mary Douglas once called "an intelligible universe" (quoted in 1993: 160). An empirical study by Steven Kates provides evidence of what he calls "identity projects": "Consumption is reflexive," he concludes, meaning that products are used to achieve status and "consumer practices are read and displayed with interpretive frameworks that incorporate explicit concerns about inclusion, exclusion, social meaning, classification of people and objects, and the privileged status of this knowledge" (2002: 399).

Robin Andersen suggests that some advertising styles acknowledge this, promoting a kind of social organization for like-minded shoppers: "Lifestyle messages promise a sense of group membership, but membership earned through commodity consumption" (1995: 120). Once in the hands of consumers, the commodity becomes a resource, perhaps a valuable one in constructing group identity and even "a sense of belonging," as Andersen puts it.

Andersen despairs at this, as she does about the entire cultural shift that started in the 1980s. "A narrow view that telescopes all problems into personal faults" is the way she captures the prevailing outlook and the one that informs contemporary advertising. Celebrities are brought in simultaneously to highlight those faults and to signal a relatively easy way to fix them. Hence the term "retail therapy."

Advertising coaxes consumers into vainly pursuing a lifestyle that's tantalizingly within reach yet forever beyond their grasp. The merchandise it offers might supply consumers with the raw material to shape personal and group identities, but there's still only merchandise on the counter. Or is there? David Luna and Susan Forquer Gupta are two among many scholars who believe that the merchandise is loaded: "Culturally-constituted meaning first moves into the persona of the celebrity. Then, the meaning moves from the celebrity into the product. Finally, it moves from the product into the consumer" (2001: 48).

We need to modify this in the light of the arguments presented in this chapter: the meaning doesn't just "move" into the consumer. The consumer originates the meaning. All the corporate power in the world can't put meaning into merchandise.

Affixing to it the signature of a Kidman or a will.i.am plays if there is a receptive population of consumers who read the celebrities in a way that makes them attractive and credible; or invests those celebs with the right kinds of meaning. Meaning isn't just transferred: it's created.

Whether wearing, driving, drinking, or just filling space in the fridge with products, we are using them. Anything at all we do with the products we buy suggests something about ourselves. This sounds uncomfortably like an ad man's pitch, though Madison Avenue execs are unlikely to want to acknowledge whether they see their products as being appropriated by the consumer or the consumers being appropriated by them. After all, and as Deborah Root reminds us in her *Cannibal Culture*: "Appropriation occurs because cultural difference can be bought and sold in the marketplace" (1996: 68).

While Root is writing about the manner in which the artifacts and images of different cultures have been turned into commodities, her point is resonant: aspirational consumers are actually striving to be different when they make their purchases. Lewis and Bridger make the point that new consumers "devote more time, effort and energy to closing the gap between their real and ideal selves" (2001: 29). They might be just buying merchandise, but they're buying into the prospect of making a difference to their lives.

Lewis and Bridger suggest that a "striving for self-actualization" fuels the quest for authenticity. Even this is for sale. Root again has a salient remark: "The apparent seamlessness between culture and the marketplace means that anything can come under the purview of capital" (1996: 86). So, while self-actualization, or the process of becoming all that one is capable of being, might be a long, laborious, painstaking, and possibly tortuous process, buying products is not. Commodities make the entire project more manageable. Everything is for sale. Where once we defined our ambitions and selves by the work we performed and what we produced, we now consume to be who we are and who we want to be. In buying something that has it, or at least its aura – a quality that emanates subtly – a consumer steps closer to being the person they want to be. That's what makes them aspirational consumers.

In the 1980s, analyses of market segmentation revealed the exploitable potential of the African American market. Ethnicity, like age, gender, income, occupation, and location, was a variable that enabled advertisers to target populations according to their demographic profiles. Celebrity culture, or, to be more precise, the conditions under which it developed, changed the ways in which markets segmented, forcing advertisers to find new ways of reaching potential consumers. The same technology that brought us unlimited entertainment also brought us boundless information. The same curiosity that made us privy to the private lives of celebs made us inquisitive about the products we were expected to buy.

Consumers checked on the ethics of the manufacturer, studied labels, read guarantees, compared prices, and weighed up options. The market segment, a concept that had been a functional servant of the advertising industry practically since the advent of mass society in the 1920s, looked suspect. Segments were still there, but groups moved between them, defying a consistent, stable categorization.

The boundaries between segments are now continually broken as we move between positions. In this sense, the market reflects the way in which we understand ourselves. Identity was once seen as the essence or core that remains with us through the life course: nowadays, it's conceived as an assembly or moving configuration of different, often temporary, ways of imagining and presenting ourselves – what Ohler calls "*labile personae.*" We might move through several dozen different identities during a day, changing with changing contexts. Identities exist only in relation to everything else in the surrounding environment.

Picture the consumer at the center of a spider's web, each filament around him or her representing tastes in products: one for music, clothes, food and drink, gadgets, and so on. Each strand takes the consumer to different groups of like-minded consumers in whose company he or she thinks about the self differently. As the consumer slithers across the slender, thread-like fibers, he or she encounters new groups and adopts new identities, without ever needing to stop and think about any fixed foundation of qualities or properties that constitute a unique identity. Instead, the consumer has several, coexisting identities, all based on consumption.

While they don't discuss it in exactly these terms, Lewis and Bridger depict their new consumer in a broadly compatible way. "The mass market is disintegrating," they argue, offering the "taste web" as an alternative. This allows for a more flexible conception of consumers as capricious, inconsistent, erratic, and unsettled – though not entirely unpredictable. After all, if they believe some figures, identify with others, like still others, and find some attractive, then they can be persuaded to follow those figures.

There aren't many Pied Pipers who can command obedience as well as respect and due deference, though Nike's sales figures suggest that Jordan came close. And, in any case, there's no such thing as obedience in celebrity culture, though, in previous eras, advertisers had an easier time in persuading consumers to submit to their directions, mandates, prescriptions, or other kinds of injunctions.

> *Celebrities have made it harder than ever to spot where the advertising stops and everything else starts.*

Among the many criticisms of celebrity culture is that it's turned us all into zealous idolaters, who not only follow the exploits of irrelevant characters, but clamor to buy the products we suspect they use, or at least like. The imperative to acquire is never far away from celebrities. Yet, in this chapter, I've presented various arguments that resuscitate the consumer from what many writers imagine is a comatose state. Consumers are engaged in what might pass as a creative process: the endorsed products, even the menial items you pick up in a supermarket, are resources and, as such, usable. I can anticipate the incredulous response: so when I grab a bottle of shower gel that's endorsed by Kristen Stewart or somebody, I'm actually shaping my identity? It sounds a heady and implausible proposition. But think of the manifold ways in which celebrities surreptitiously affect us.

Every morning, newspapers, even the most sober broadsheets, hum with news on celebrities. Radio and television programs don't so much feature celebrities as provide virtual showcases for them. Many of the internet sites we visit exist because of them. This is before we even consider the advertising that has been the focus of this chapter. Whether buying groceries, a new car, house, vacation, pharmaceuticals, stocks, or almost anything, we are forced to accept that, if it can be exchanged for money, it can bear the mark of a celebrity, sometimes several. Politics is fast becoming a favored territory of celebrities eager to exploit their profile for higher purposes (as I will discuss later). Our speech is affected by what we hear celebs say and even how they say it. Our children unwittingly copy them. Our colleagues gossip about them. We sense their presence.

There is a kind of celebrity pulse beating through society. No matter how we try, we can't fail to feel it. It's either specious or illogical, or both, to suggest that the way we think about ourselves and present ourselves to others is *not* influenced by celebrity culture. Consumption has replaced work as the heart that regulates this pulse. So much of who we are and what we do depends on it. The proliferating appearances of celebrities have made it harder than ever to spot where the advertising stops and everything else starts.

BLACKNESS

PROOF OF A COLORBLIND SOCIETY

When she emerged on her own tv show on September 8, 1986, she was an improbable emblem for a new society: a slightly podgy African American woman in a raspberry-colored outfit, her hair coiffed into one of those big eighties dos. Over 4,000 episodes later, Oprah Winfrey, at 57, quit the daily grind of the talk show, with billions in the bank and an annual income estimated by *Forbes* at $300 million. Oprah's influence was unmissable and inescapable: her support for Barack Obama's presidential bid was the most valuable political endorsement in history. She changed countless people's lives with her simple yet persuasive philosophy. Her incessant stress on individual aspiration and self-reliance endeared her to vast audiences. It's as if she prodded her followers and asked: "Why wait for society to help you when you can help yourself?" Or: "Why waste effort trying to move mountains when you can move your own butt?" Oprah didn't ask these exact questions, but the inquiry is implicit in everything she did as a public figure.

Oprah seemed to deliver the final corroboration. If this wasn't the end of racism, then, at least, an end was in sight.

This is part of the reason why recent history is unimaginable without Oprah – because she helped change that history. She offered a new image of black Americans, intelligent, ambitious, questioning, and individualistic. She didn't align herself with great causes, at least not in a way that compromised her individuality. She didn't rail against racism. And she didn't blame history for the injustices of today. In fact, she insisted that history was just that: past events. Yet, every time we saw or heard Oprah, we were reminded that this was an African American and a woman who had confronted cathartic challenges and had overcome them to become probably one of, if not *the* best-known, most influential, and certainly one of the richest women in the world.

Most of us enjoy being entertained by musicians, actors, and sports stars. We might begrudge them the often staggering amounts of money they earn, but this doesn't stop us buying downloads, going to the movies, or paying our tv subscriptions. Watching Oprah or Denzel Washington doesn't prompt us to think about how, today, there are many, many more African American entertainers or movie stars in lead roles than there were 20 years ago. And it probably doesn't make us wonder whether Oprah or Washington are representatives of a new generation of high-achieving African Americans. But, in a sense, they are. Like many other celebrities, they have visibility, influence, and money and, as such, they advertise a conception of the good life. But black celebrities advertise other conceptions: about racism and the arrival of a colorblind society. Occasionally, they'll speak explicitly about these matters. Very occasionally: for the most part, they remain silent, as if subdued by the overpowering demands of behaving with good grace so as not to incite controversy or resentment.

In 1998, before Beyoncé had gone solo, when Michael Jackson was still alive, and the same year writer Toni Morrison hailed Bill Clinton as "our first black president," historian Jacqueline Jones wrote: "We find nothing incongruous in appreciating the talents of African-American entertainers and professional athletes (male and female), who are paid millions of dollars each year, while accepting the apparent fact that millions of black men, women, and children are doomed to languish in impoverished communities, without the educational credentials and work opportunities that provide access to the blessings of a high-tech society" (1998: 234).

Jones was right: we don't find incongruity. There is none: being entertained by black celebrities is perfectly in harmony with accepting what Jones called the "apparent fact" that the overwhelming majority of African Americans fail to make progress or achieve success of any substantial kind. The fact is actual rather than apparent. However unwittingly, black celebrities have sold the idea that America is no longer manacled to its history. It is a history pitted by racism, segregation, and victimization. Undeniable progress since civil rights has promoted the ideal of a place where racism and other forms of bigotry have no purchase. The election of Obama, himself a political celebrity, seemed to validate if not the arrival, then the imminence, of a colorblind society.

Black celebrities are definitely creating an impression. But in what sense are we using "impression"? An effect, an imitation, an idea, feeling, or opinion formed without conscious thought or with little evidence? This is one of the questions we might ask about black celebrities.

Prominent African Americans now populate politics, as well as entertainment and sports – the two spheres where they have traditionally excelled. In practically every area of today's society, there are black people who are not just successful, but also visibly, sometimes ostentatiously successful. Earl Ofari Hutchinson discerned that Tiger Woods' success in particular had been interpreted as "final proof that America is a colorblind society, and discrimination mostly a figment of the warped imaginations of many African-Americans" (1998).Obama's political success presumably added to the weight of evidence. Actually, Woods is no more proof of a colorblind society than the movie *John Carter* is proof of life on Mars. But that's not Ofari Hutchinson's point: he means that Woods delighted practically everyone. A near-perfect black man with none of the multiple pathologies typically associated with blacks, he conquered a sport that had historically excluded all but affluent whites and became one of the most celebrated men in the world. African Americans hailed him as a paragon. Whites hailed him as a game-changer. The game wasn't golf.

Ofari Hutchinson was writing in 1998, but the potency of his argument is enhanced, not diminished, by Woods' serial acts of moral turpitude, which left consumers ravening for more as they expressed their disapproval. Woods was once what Helán E. Page calls an "embraceable black male" (1997). He became another African American man who used his sporting gift to earn millions, enjoyed a lifestyle to envy, then regressed to a more primal state in which his base instincts exerted themselves. He resembled the likes of Mike Tyson and Michael Vick more than Michael Jordan.

For decades, even centuries, people have rhapsodized over black athletes, as they have black singers, dancers, and other kinds of entertainers. In recent years, blacks have moved into politics, commerce, and the professions. Their progress has been accepted as evidence of the arrival of the much-heralded but seldom-substantiated color-blind society. The appearance in the late 1980s of Oprah and other literate, intelligent, and perceptive figures seemed to deliver the final corroboration. If this wasn't the end of racism, then, at least, an end was in sight.

LIKE ANIMALS IN A ZOO |

Entertainment is never *just* the provision of amusement or enjoyment: it's an opportunity to learn, if we know what questions to ask. For example: why were white audiences entertained by white performers pretending to be black who toured America and England in burlesque shows that ridiculed blacks? Blacks and their culture fascinated whites in the nineteenth century; they still do, it seems.

In early nineteenth-century America, troupes of minstrels toured eastern regions, performing songs, dances, recitations, and comedy. The minstrel shows consisted of white singers and dancers in "blackface," meaning that their faces were covered in theatrical makeup, or burnt cork. They would sing, dance, play banjo, and clown around, creating crude caricatures of inoffensive "plantation niggers," or "coons," the popular name of southern blacks. Daddy Rice (1808–60) was the most famous of these minstrels.

White audiences loved them, probably because they affirmed what they wanted to know: that there was no need to feel guilty or afraid. This appeasement was especially comforting against a background of slave rebellions, many of which were inspired by Christian beliefs – the Virginia insurrection of 1831 organized by Nat Turner being the most celebrated. These uprisings suggested a different image of African Americans to the ones suggested in both the minstrel shows and popular literature of the day. "Responsive to kindness, loyal, affectionate, and co-operative," is how the typical slave was depicted in many of the popular novels, according to George M. Frederickson, who reports on what he calls a "romantic racialist image" that circulated through literature and popular thought (1987).

The historian Robert Toll points out that African American beliefs, songs, dances, and folklore were taken by the white minstrels. "The presence of these distinctively Afro-American themes supports the view that minstrels borrowed from black culture," writes Toll (1974: 50). He sees significance in this "because it was the first indication of the powerful influence Afro-American culture would have on the performing arts in America," but is careful to point out: "It does not mean that early minstrels accurately portrayed Negro life or even the cultural elements that they used. They did neither" (1974: 51).

Two years after the Emancipation Proclamation of 1862, slavery was abolished and four million African Americans were freed. Some of them found employment in minstrel troupes, offering a new form of entertainment: unlike white artists who mimicked blacks, they were authentic representatives of the black population, or perhaps the black species, "like animals in a zoo," as Toll puts it (1974: 206).

> *Was it better for black actors to achieve success in roles as loyal maids and fawning darkies, or to risk not working at all?*

Black performers themselves profited from the minstrel shows. Some, like Billy Kersands, grew prosperous by playing up to widely held and oversimplified images of blacks. Others, such as James Bland, enjoyed popularity in Europe as well as the US. Horace Weston (1825–90) "was the first African American banjoist to achieve a significant reputation," according to Robert B. Winans and Elias J. Kaufman (1994: 10).

Flanked by white owners and producers in the wings, the minstrels laid on a costumed performance for the delectation of whites. "Coon songs" were popular compositions. A respectful acknowledgement of blacks' musical gifts, their untutored sense of rhythm, and their instinctual ability to amuse others might have been offered as compliments. But they were conditional. Blacks were granted access to some, though not all, cultural areas, entertainment being the main one, sports the other. And they were expected to embellish not compromise stereotypes; "darkie," "nigger," and "coon" were popularized in their music.

The keenness of whites to learn more about black life, not through study but through entertainment, was a feature of this period that endured through the twentieth century and, arguably, to the present day. While they may once have been satisfied with other whites' interpretations, they later warmed to the authenticity supposedly conveyed by black artists and performers. This opened up opportunities for African Americans to explore their own capabilities as entertainers of whites.

For most of the twentieth century, blacks distinguished themselves in entertainment, on stage, then in radio, film, and, from the late 1940s, television. Many were prepared to shuffle into the narrow range of roles created for them by whites, roles summarized in the title of Donald Bogle's book *Toms, Coons, Mulattoes, Mammies, and Bucks* (2001). Others, like Matilda Sissieretta Jones (1869–1933) and Paul Robeson (1898–1976), clung to their artistic integrity and established international reputations. Robeson was the preeminent black performer of his generation, though he became a deeply divisive figure: he found the pressures of being a serious and, in his case, a politically involved artist too much to bear and was ostracized. A football player turned singer and actor, he memorably sang "Ol' Man River" in the second film adaptation of Edna Ferber's paean to the traveling Mississippi theaters, *Show Boat*, and distinguished himself in the title role of *Othello*. He used his prominence to argue for civil rights in a period when the USA was racially segregated and made known his communist sympathies. His demise effectively issued a caution to other black entertainers.

Domestic servants, bumptious chumps, and brainless strongmen were among the one-dimensional parts reserved for black entertainers in the salad days of radio (1920s–1940s). During this time, Hollywood stars began to burst from silent movies into talkies, as films with speech were known. Lena Horne (1917–2010) was the first African American, man or woman, to secure a long-term contract with MGM, then the most powerful Hollywood studio, and by the mid-1940s was reputedly the highest-paid black actor. But she too paid a price; as she famously said: "I didn't get much of a chance to act." She usually appeared – looking vivacious – and sang, but became frustrated at her lack of opportunities to act seriously.

Ethel Waters (1896–1977) brought herself up from destitution, working for a time in domestic service. So, when, in her fifties, she was offered a job in the title role of the tv series *Beulah*, she presumably thought acting as a maid was preferable to being one. The television series was based on a successful radio show that had started in the 1930s, and that had originally featured a white actor as the eponymous housekeeper-cum-cook. Hattie McDaniel (1895–1952) took over. She'd been playing Beulah in the radio show after finding film roles scarce. McDaniel had endured protests in front of cinemas in 1939 when civil rights groups, including the NAACP, objected to her depiction of Scarlett O'Hara's devoted slave, Mammy, in *Gone With the Wind*. The role was her specialty: she had virtually made a living out of it since the 1920s, when she toured on the vaudeville circuit, usually spoofing the plantation mammy caricature. Her biographer Jill Watts reckons, though typecast, McDaniel tried to subvert stereotypes of black docility and simplemindedness; though this never persuaded her critics that her career was anything but a disservice to African Americans.

In 1934, five years before the release of *Gone With the Wind*, Clarence E. Muse (1889–1979), himself an African American who had managed to make a living as a Hollywood actor, self-published a pamphlet entitled *The Dilemma of the Negro Actor*. In it, he reasoned that the black actor has the choice of being responsible to black audiences in his or her screen portrayals, or being a successful black stereotype for "the white audience with a definite desire for buffoonery and song." Was it better, Muse asked, for black actors to achieve success in mainstream roles as loyal maids and fawning darkies, or to risk not working at all by insisting on better parts and more equitable representation?

BILL COSBY: PLAYING BY WHOSE RULES? |

After the first slaves arrived in Virginia in 1619, slavery became the single most important component of the American economy and thus the source of its prosperity. After nearly 250 years, the cultural patterns carved by slavery were deep and, in the eyes of many, ineradicable. Yet somehow, the nation had to make what must have seemed an accommodation of gargantuan proportions. Popular entertainment offered a gratification: it showed black people in the way whites wanted to see them – as fools, minions, or primitives governed by sexual impulses rather than rational thoughts. Casting black actors and other kinds of entertainers in these roles was not an accident, but nor was it the result of the pernicious scheming of racist producers: audiences sought amusement rather than provocation or confrontation. Amusement often derives from comfort. The entertainment industry was responsive.

Sydney Poitier (b. 1927) was a singular actor. Educated in the Bahamas, he traveled to the USA as a teenager and triumphed by winning an Oscar for his supporting role in 1963's *Lilies of the Field*. Poitier refused to succumb to the kind of parts typically reserved for black males and, instead, portrayed unusual characters. Unusual, that is, for black actors: for example,

Poitier played a teacher at a London school, a doctor engaged to the daughter of an affluent white San Franciscan couple, and, in perhaps his most famous film role, a Philadelphia detective helping a murder investigation in Mississippi. *In the Heat of the Night* was a challenging film role for a black actor and Poitier reprised it in a sequel *They Call Me Mister Tibbs!*. The film was released in 1970, and Poitier completed a trilogy with *The Organization* in 1971.

Poitier was an urbane, cosmopolitan figure, gracious of manner and refined of taste. He seemed freed of provincial attitudes. There was no trace of ghetto in him. It was probably this apparent contradiction that halted his progress: after 1971, his parts were either peripheral or predictable, or else in television movies. He could have been a mirror held to America, with its developing black bourgeoisie and a generation of aspiring entrepreneurs, professionals, and politicians.

Performers who deliberately avoided stereotypes had to be resourceful if they were to survive. William Henry Cosby Jr. (b. 1937) was, and did. A standup comic in his early post-military career, he brought a sardonic edge to his tv roles and, in 1984, appeared in a sitcom that might have been an allegory. *The Cosby Show* centered on a well-to-do family living in an affluent area of New York. Bill Cosby played Cliff Huxtable, an obstetrician, and his wife was a lawyer; their children were at college. Cosby never claimed its characters were representative of black people, though, actually, he could have: in the 1980s, America's black population was variegated, so the fictional family was representative of a relatively small but growing affluent and upwardly mobile class.

Clint Wilson and Félix Gutiérrez's analysis of why the media's portrayal of ethnic groups changed in the 1980s is enlightening. There had been "dramatic changes in the relationship between advertising and racial minorities" since the 1960s, they wrote. The occupants of the ghettos and barrios were waiting to be exploited. "Advertisers promote consumption of their products as a shortcut to the good life, a quick fix for low-income consumers" (1985: 128).

Wilson and Gutiérrez documented how, when the civil rights legislation of 1964 and 1965 finally began to take effect, African Americans attracted the interests of advertisers, whose business was, of course, aspirations. "You may not be able to live in the best neighborhoods, wear the best clothes, or have the best job, but you can drink the same liquor, smoke the same cigarettes, and drive the same car as those who do" was the message advertisers were delivering to black people (1985: 128). Minorities were urged to remain mindful that they lived in "a system of inequality that keeps them below national norms in education, housing, income, health and other social indicators," cautioned the researchers (1985: 130).

Cosby and his tv family were exemplars: excellent models of African Americans who suffered from none of the usual dysfunctional traits typically equated with blacks and enjoyed all the fruits of consumer happiness. Just like a well-adjusted white family in fact. This is the first sense in which the show was an allegory, revealing a different picture of black life to the one often shown on tv or film. Both media had barely deviated from time-honored types previously.

"*The Cosby Show* offered viewers the comfort of seeing characters with whom they identified enjoy the spoils of Western capitalism," observed Timothy Havens in 2000. He meant *most* viewers: many were made to feel deeply uncomfortable by the show's depiction of black life in the 1980s and early 1990s. For example, Sut Jhally and Justin Lewis agreed, "The Huxtables proved that black people can succeed" (1992: 97). But they pointed out that one of the effects of the show was to "encourage white people, looking around them at the comparative prosperity of white over blacks, to believe in an imagined cultural superiority" (1992: 97).

Leslie B. Inniss and Joe R. Feagin concurred with the first part of this: "The overall impression is that the American dream is real for anyone who is willing to play by the rules" (1995: 709). Inniss and Feagin never explicate those "rules," but let's guess they involve not grumbling about discrimination, or getting involved in radical politics, and certainly not getting mixed up in the kind of misdemeanors associated with rap artists in 2000s. Rules change. Inniss and Feagin also add, "We are left with the impression that they will not face any barriers or obstacles in their quest for the good life. They are decidedly upper middle class and can only go up – no discrimination or downward mobility for the Huxtables or by extension for Blacks as a group" (1995: 709).

While many praised Cosby for challenging stereotypes and advancing a fresh and unusual image of black life, others decided his influence on white America was *too* persuasive: if the Huxtable family could make it amid the enterprise culture promoted by President Ronald Reagan (1911–2004), why couldn't the other 15 million or so blacks? "*The Cosby Show*, by demonstrating the opportunity for African Americans to be successful, implicates the majority of black people who have, by the Huxtable criterion, failed," maintained Jhally and Lewis. "They [the Huxtables] also prove the inferiority of black people in general" (1992: 94–5).

As the show became an advertisement for how blacks could and perhaps should live, so Cosby himself became a living ad, not just for the good life portrayed in the show, but for, among others, Coca-Cola, DelMonte, Ford, Kodak, and, most famously, Jell-O pudding. Staying in character, he smirked his way through one of the USA's most popular, long-running campaigns. The Jell-O commercials played no small part in his ingratiation: he became a kind of symbol, not so much of how middle America saw black men, but of how they would like them to be – manifestly trustworthy and not the least bitter.

By the time of *The Cosby Show*'s disappearance in 1992, other ethnic minority entertainers had emerged, partly in emulation of Cosby, partly in response to the shifting market, and perhaps partly in satisfaction of a deal. The deal was this: we'll invite you to see the world through the eyes of a black family, which will not only amuse but reassure you. The droll Cosby and his hilarious family painlessly removed any uncomfortable thoughts about the failure of civil rights to reduce racism to an irrelevance. Viewers became guilt-free peeping toms watching the private goings-on of a typical black family. *Typical?* Maybe the Huxtables were actually representative of a tiny fraction of the African American population. This was easily forgotten amid the laughter.

AN ALTERNATIVE NARRATIVE: RODNEY KING |

In many respects, Cosby was like Oprah: an advertisement for himself, someone who used his own life as a means of recommending something – in this case, ambition. Cosby aimed high and wished other African Americans would follow his example. Like Oprah, he had a relatively humble background, in his case in Philadelphia (where he was born in 1937), and joined the navy, completing his high school studies through a correspondence course. He won an athletics scholarship at Temple University, Philadelphia, and supported himself through part-time work behind a bar.

Rodney King was a discomfiting celebrity: prone to alcohol and drug abuse, victimized by racist police officers, he became the catalyst for riots across the United States.

In the late 1980s, Cosby and Oprah were like two pillars: strong, reliable, and supportive of a generation of African Americans that was becoming familiar with success. Michael Jackson was at the height of his popularity. Denzel Washington won the Oscar for best supporting actor in 1989's *Glory*. Also in 1989: Britain's Naomi Campbell became the first black model to appear on the front cover of *Vogue*'s September issue; Colin Powell was appointed Chairman of the Joint Chiefs of Staff, becoming the first African American to achieve the highest military ranking in the US Armed Forces; Douglas Wilder became the US's first elected black governor. And, in 1990, an unknown Barack Obama became the first African American president of the *Harvard Law Review*. Yet, of all the black people who rose to prominence during that period, the one who made the deepest impression on history was not an entertainer or politician, nor even a public figure until March 3, 1991.

In the early morning hours of that day, the 25-year-old black man was subjected to a vicious assault at the hands of four white police officers at the side of a highway in Los Angeles. Rodney King (1965–2012), on parole for a robbery conviction at the time, said he heard one of the cops threaten: "We are going to kill you, nigger!" Almost three decades after the final vestiges of segregation had been dismantled, King's beating issued a reminder that racism had a resistant quality. King himself became an accidental and reluctant celebrity. When riots broke out following the 1992 trial at which the police officers were acquitted, King appealed for calm. He pleaded on television: "People, I just want to say, you know, can we all get along? Can we get along?," the question becoming a slogan for the 1990s.

Twenty years after the riots, he told the *Los Angeles Times*: "People look at me like I should have been like Malcolm X or Martin Luther King or Rosa Parks . . . But it's hard to live up to some people's expectations, which [I] wasn't cut out to be."

King was a discomfiting celebrity: his personal drama as a black man, prone to alcohol and drug abuse, victimized by racist police officers, who became an unwitting catalyst for riots across the United States, made the nation feel uneasy. It posed an unsettling and embarrassing alternative to the narrative played out by Cosby, Oprah, and other black models of success and fulfillment. In a sense, King was not just playing out a narrative: he *was* the narrative. Neal Gabler proposes: "Celebrity is narrative, even though we understandably conflate the protagonist of the narrative with the narrative itself and use the terms interchangeably" (2009). I interpret this to mean that some figures don't just play a role in a real-life drama, but embody an entire story, often a parable-like story that illustrates a moral point or delivers a kind of lesson. Celebrities' lives provide us with entertainment, but often there is something to be learned from their experiences. Certainly, this was the case with King. His narrative communicated a disunity that might have been neglected amid the rise of conspicuously high-achieving African Americans.

King's was the kind of retrograde narrative that would have probably passed without too much media attention in the 1960s, or even the 1970s, when racial profiling, police brutality, and racial violence were commonplace. But in the enlightened 1990s, it was a high-voltage shock to the system. It provided, to use another of Gabler's phrases, "human entertainment"; but, remember, entertainment is not the same as amusement.

King sued the LAPD and was awarded $3.8 million in damages, plus another $1.6 million toward legal costs. It was retribution of sorts, though it annulled much of the goodwill he garnered in the aftermath of the incident. He used his money to launch a hip-hop music label, but the project foundered and, by the early 2000s, King was fading slightly into the collective memory. The election of Barack Obama as president in 2008 seemed to dispatch the King case to history, though King himself suggested: "He [Obama] wouldn't have been in office without what happened to me," adding, "So I am glad for what I went through. It opened the doors for a lot of people."

King briefly pushed back into public view in the election year, when he joined the reality show *Celebrity Rehab with Dr. Drew*, but, by this point, he and the riots were remnants of an age that was at once proximate yet distant. The beating took place seventeen years before Obama's election.

In 2002, ten years after the so-called "Rodney King riots," and with King himself receding slightly in the public memory, Donovan Jackson, an African-American teenager, and his father, Coby Chavis, stopped for fuel at a gas station in Inglewood, California. White police officers questioned Jackson about his car's expired license plate and proceeded to handcuff him face down. The police then slammed Jackson into the police car. Like the King beating, it was captured on video. The Jackson incident also brought to mind more recent incidents in Los Angeles, such as that of a homeless black woman who was shot to death by an officer because, he said, she was holding a screwdriver in a threatening manner, and that of an African American actor who was shot nine times at a Halloween party after he pointed a fake gun at a police officer. In Riverside, east of Los Angeles, a young black woman sleeping in her car with a gun in her lap was shot to death by officers who had been unable to wake her. The officers were cleared in all three cases. King remains the hauntingly significant victim of racially motivated police brutality, but he is far from the only one.

In June 2012, King, then 47, was found dead at the home he shared with his fiancée in California.

|THE FAÇADE OF RACE TRANSCENDENCE

By 1994, the convulsions of the riots touched off by the King case were subsiding. So, when Whoopi Goldberg declared, "I am not an African American, I am an American," it sounded like a wooden stick being rattled around inside the hollow of a tree where a number of large stinging wasps had taken up residence. Goldberg had risen to prominence in 1985 when she memorably played the "poor, female, ugly and black" Celie in the film of Alice Walker's Pulitzer Prize-winning novel *The Color*

Purple. The remark brought a stinging rebuke from Ron Walters, who used his column in the *Washington Informer* to launch an attack, not only on Goldberg, who, he argued "spent considerable effort to distance herself from her African-origin identity," but also on Morgan Freeman, O.J. Simpson, Pelé, and Michael Jackson (1994: 17).

Walters' critique had two prongs. "They are the stock in trade of the neutered black" in that they either occupied or chose roles that were the "stuff of deep racial stereotypes." Goldberg was "a modern day Aunt Jemima," while Freeman often played a servile "step-and-fetchit" character. The sports heroes were loved for their thrilling athleticism, but for nothing more, and, as such, carried the stigma of the "Black jock." Since the mid-1990s, both Goldberg and Freeman have broadened their character tableaux, and Simpson and Jackson were involved in unforgettable scandals. But, even if Walter's first prong appears blunter than it did in 1994, his second remains sharp.

The celebrities in question had all reached the level of the "cultural pantheon where race is irrelevant, or where although race may at times be relevant, it carried an altogether different meaning for them" (1994: 17). Walters argued that the "denial of black identity" is a common operation among people who have gained an acceptance to the elite, whether of movies or sports. Were Walters able to anticipate the rise of Colin Powell, he would have to include him in his criticism: Powell famously refused to prefix his status with "black."

"Attempting to transcend race and become something they can only be at the sufferance of someone else . . . is the classic condition of a slave," wrote Walters, notifying readers that, stripped of celebrity status, his subjects would be urgently reminded of what it means to be black. As they have risen, they have given the impression of transcending race. What's more, as Walters puts it: "Whites would be willing to join with them in the façade that they had all transcended race, as long as Whoopi, Morgan, O.J., and others did not threaten their status and as long they continued to make them feel good, make them laugh" (1994: 17).

Perhaps surprisingly, Bill Cosby evaded the salvo. Walters took issue with "Black conservatives," who played not the race card but the "race neutrality" card in a way that "brings them the acclaim of whites." By this, he means that many celebrities from ethnic minority backgrounds, in their efforts to stay audience-friendly, downplay the significance of racism in contemporary culture. In 2004, Cosby appeared on CNN and berated and blamed black parents for allowing themselves to remain victims and suffering in poverty. While the ideology was consistent with that of Huxtable, it was delivered with a rumbling gravitas that was quite at odds with the more familiar Cosby of the 1980s.

Do all ethnic minority celebrities become blissfully unaware of their compatriots as they rise to fame? Or do they deliberately stifle their comments to avoid the kind of controversy that could ruin their careers? Do they become conservative and "race neutral" as they draw the "acclaim of whites"? Or do they draw the acclaim because they are conservative and race neutral? These are not exactly options, of course. The reality is that all these are, in some measure, true, some celebrities succumbing more easily than others to the inevitable pressure toward race neutrality.

Barack Obama never actually said, "I never felt entitled to anything because I was black," but it was implicit. He mapped his way to the presidency by avoiding the option of racial politics, but without detouring into the kind of conservatism Walters despised. During his electoral campaign and under pressure, Obama, on March 18, 2008, delivered arguably his most powerful address to date. He opened with words extracted from the Preamble to the United States Constitution, "We the people, in order to make a more perfect union," and went on to chronicle his own interconnected ethnic heritage: "I am the son of a black man from Kenya and a white woman from

Kansas." Then he moved to his personal progress: "I've gone to some of the best schools in America and lived in one of the world's poorest nations." In an inspired and redolent passage, with a sure nod to his African American doubters, Obama reminded his audience: "I am married to a black American who carries within her the blood of slaves and slaveowners – an inheritance we pass on to our two precious daughters."

HALLE BERRY AND THE ONE-DROP THEORY |

What are black celebrities supposed to do? Should they claim their authority to promulgate views on every issue that affects black people? Or should they go about their business like any other entertainer, politician, or reality tv star of whatever ethnic background? The question was cued by Muse in the 1930s, answered by Robeson in the 1950s, posed differently in the 1990s by Walters, and returned to by Halle Berry in 2011.

Halle Berry's point was that blackness is not a thing, a category, a group, and probably not even a designation any more.

Born in Cleveland, daughter of an African American father and a white Liverpool-born mother, Berry raised a daughter fathered by a white French-Canadian, Gabriel Aubry. When Aubry challenged her for custody, Berry raised doubts about his ability to care for the daughter: "I'm black and I'm her mother, and I believe in the one-drop theory," she told *Ebony* magazine, invoking a statute passed in Tennessee in 1910, when Jim Crow laws compelled strict segregation of blacks and whites in every sphere of society. Anti-miscegenation laws of the time prohibited unions of people considered to be of different racial types, and these remained until 1967, when the Supreme Court repealed them completely.

"I feel she's black," Berry said of her daughter. It was a curious announcement from the first African American woman to win the best actress Oscar (for her role in 2001's *Monster's Ball*). Did she seriously believe that anyone with any trace of sub-Saharan ancestry, however minute ("one drop"), can't be considered white and, in the absence of an alternative lineage – for example, Native American, Asian, Arab, Australian Aboriginal – must be considered black?

Berry had shown an awareness of history when she dedicated her Oscar thus: "This moment is so much bigger than me. This moment is for Dorothy Dandridge, Lena Horne, Diahann Carroll. This is for every faceless woman of color who now has a chance tonight because this door has been opened."

This was hardly controversial and Berry had occasionally talked about the particular predicament of people of mixed ethnic parentage, but had never made an issue of it. At various points, she had also used black, African American, biracial, and woman of color to describe herself. She had also talked, in measured terms, of how she never felt accepted as white, despite her white mother. But her appeal to the one-drop rule seemed a bit like an economist trying to explain the trade deficit by casting the runes. Or perhaps, like Storm, the mutant she played in *X-Men: The last stand*, watching the Weather Channel before deciding what to wear – the character can create lightning, avalanches, heat waves, rain, and tornadoes at will. Actually, while it seemed irrational, Berry's explanation of her actions was far removed from any kind of divinatory stones or pseudoscience: "I do identify with my white heritage. I was raised by my white mother and every day of my life I have always been aware of the fact that I am biracial."

This didn't suggest she *accepted* such a conventional census category, or labels such as biracial or even multiracial; but nor was she returning to black as if it were a default setting. Black, in her argument, is no longer a label: it is a *response* to a label – a response, that is, to not being white. Blackness, on this account, doesn't describe a color, a physical condition, a lifestyle, or even an ethnic status in the conventional sense: it is a reaction to being regarded as different or distinct. For Berry, it seems black no longer describes a designated group of people: it is the way in which those who have been identified as distinct from and opposite to whites have reacted; their answer. When Berry allowed, "that's what she's going to have to decide," she meant that her daughter has some measure of discretion in the way she responds. Blackness is now a flexible and negotiable action; not the fixed status it once was.

Black people were and probably are "those to be spoken for or about rather than with," to use a suggestive phrase from Juliana Mansvelt (2010: 147). Cultural practices, images, and artifacts are still predicated on black people as continuously and unchangeably different. But Berry's point was that blackness is not a thing, a category, a group, and probably not even a designation any more. The one-drop rule was an incongruous imposition on an otherwise sophisticated argument, an argument that carried added force, coming from someone not known for her outspokenness or her humor. On Berry's account, ethnicity becomes a matter of choice, people electing their ethnic identities. Note the use of plural identities: Berry's child may change hers as she grows, perhaps opting for several at one time, changing to suit different situations. It will be – probably already is – possible to have multiple ethnicities, all interchangeable and all utterly fluid. We live a "liquid life," as Zygmunt Bauman calls it (2010).

> *Black celebrities occupy a place in the popular imagination analogous to that of showroom mannequins in a storefront.*

So, does this take us anywhere nearer the question presented at the start of this section? One implication of Berry's argument is that it's a question that can only be asked if you presume there are categories of blackness and whiteness: one doesn't make sense without the other. Whites in bygone time "came to define themselves by what they were not," says Peter Kolchin (2002). There is nothing natural about being white. Not in the sense we understand it today. Whiteness has origins in the second half of the seventeenth century when English, Irish, Scottish, and other European settlers in America began to see themselves not as individuals or members of national groups, but as parts of a race. Slaves, or bondsmen, were conveniently grouped as another race. Whiteness had connotations of purity, goodness, and moral excellence, and, even after 1954, when segregation was ruled unconstitutional, the connotation persisted. So much so that black entertainers were obliged to masquerade. Entertainers as diverse as Nat King Cole (1919–65), who incidentally was the first African American to have his own radio and tv series, Little Richard (b. 1932), and Tina Turner (b. 1939) wore heavily tinted makeup in their successful attempts to appeal to mainstream audiences. Even so, it came as a surprise when, in 2011, Beyoncé appeared in Los Angeles at the Grammys looking almost as pale as Gwyneth Paltrow. The buzz started: could the extravagantly glamorous wife of the world's leading hip-hop artist, known for her opulent lifestyle, ranked by *Forbes* as the ninth most powerful woman in the world, with annual earnings of $35 million, actually be lightening her skin? I can't hazard an answer and, in any case, it's not crucial to our argument: what's certain is that whiteness has held its power. It's a power described by Jennifer Esposito: "Because whiteness is normalized, anyone who falls outside of whiteness . . . becomes different or other" (2009: 525). By Other (it usually takes a capital O), she means something that's distinct from, different to, or the opposite of something else.

Whiteness is germane to everything I've written about in this chapter. Think about it: would anyone write a chapter on *white* celebrities? Do we ever talk about white sports stars, or white actors, or white anything? The very fact that we use the adjective *black* in these and other contexts alerts us not to its uncommonness, and certainly not to its irrelevance, but to its abiding significance. No argument that purports to analyze the cultural relevance of black celebrities can dispense with the property that makes them *black* celebrities.

"The blackness that marks us off for permanent subordination and various forms of abuse is also what gives us a sense of identity, community, and history," writes David Lionel Smith, detecting an apparent incongruity (1997: 182). Blackness and the resolution of racism are not just incompatible but irreconcilable: remove the subjection and exploitation by whites and the reasons for black identity or even blackness disappear. Blackness, no less than whiteness, is an invention: they have both been fabricated from the same historical materials.

WHITENESS AS INVISIBLE NORMALITY |

No person alive is a racist. Everyone lives in fear of being described as such. Yet the paradox is, as we know from the summaries of previous pages, that race continues to matter and its effects are felt. This is John Hartigan's argument (2009). He believes race has for long been an organizing principle in American culture: a method of what he calls "determining belonging," by which I presume he means identifying the right personal or social qualities to be a member of a particular group. In order to do this, there must be a way of contrasting the right qualities with the wrong ones. Blacks have, historically, not belonged; their function was to remind whites what they were not. Whites could not have regarded themselves as a "white race" without another group with which to contrast themselves.

The people who were, in the seventeenth century, excluded from the white race have entertained, amused, charmed, engrossed, inspired admiration, and earned extravagant praise. They have served up all manner of dazzling performances, primarily for the delectation of whites. Should we expect the latest generation of entertainers, sports stars and all-round celebrities to do or be anything more? Meghan S. Sanders and James M. Sullivan's research steers us toward an answer. They predicate their findings thus: "Racism has transformed into a new form of racism called symbolic racism" (2010: 202).

This involves the belief that blacks no longer face discrimination; their lack of progress is due to their unwillingness to work hard enough; they demand too much, too soon; they get more than they deserve. A study by Mark Peffley and Jon Hurwitz complements this preference for individual makeup over social circumstances: "Whites . . . are much more likely to view black criminality as being dispositionally caused, believing the reason blacks are more likely to be arrested and imprisoned than whites is that blacks commit more crimes" (2007: 1007). ("Dispositionally caused," I dare say, means brought about by people's inherent qualities of mind and character.)

None of this seems new or surprising. But the sources of symbolic racism, say Sanders and Sullivan, are the media: whites respond not to black people, but to *representations* of black people. Sanders and Sullivan's research shows: "There is a difference of perception for African American groups and African American individuals." They mean that whites see black individuals differently to blacks as a group; they might like, admire, and respect certain individuals – actors, athletes, musicians, for example – but fail to generalize the qualities of which they approve to black people as a whole.

When individuals whom whites may admire are represented in the media negatively, as, for example, Mike Tyson, Michael Vick, and Wesley Snipes were, whites regard their cases as "more similar and representative of the group." On the other hand "positive individuals," as Sanders and Sullivan call them, are considered untypical and unrepresentative of African Americans as a group. Figures such as Halle Berry, Jamie Foxx, and Will Smith are identified as African Americans who are viewed positively and liked but are not understood as representative of blacks. Stereotypes from history continue to infect contemporary thinking.

The researchers may well have explored the influence of *ressentiment*, this being a mental state first introduced by Friedrich Nietzsche (1844–1900) to describe suppressed feelings of envy and hatred that can't be acted on. While their study didn't reveal this, it would be consistent to assume that whites have a grudging rather than unconditional admiration for someone such as music and film producer, rapper and all-round impresario P. Diddy, who has a net worth of $475 million, or Serena Williams, who limped by on $12 million per year in the dog days of a tennis career festooned with titles.

If Sanders and Sullivan's experiment is as secure as it sounds, perhaps the presence of so many African American celebrities has had a far less positive impact among the white population than it appears. Black celebrities probably occupy a place in the popular imagination analogous to that of showroom mannequins in a storefront: used for display purposes and not necessarily an accurate reflection of what's inside the store.

The belief that black people's "lack of progress is due to their unwillingness to work hard enough" complements a point made by George Lipsitz: "What was once done to them by white racists, this line of argument contends, Blacks are now doing to themselves" (2011: 1). So, successful black people are exceptional and reap the bounties of a meritocracy that rewards ability. But they are hardly representative of the majority of African Americans who remain in charge of their own destinies and contrive to hinder their own progress even when all the obstructions of racism have been removed.

Esposito's inference broadens the picture. There is, she conjectures, an "image of black people in the white mind" and "This black image is often informed by prominent 'exceptions' to the rule" (2009: 532). While she doesn't include this corollary, I presume she wouldn't object if I add: white self-consciousness is informed by images of blacks, as a painter's subjects are brought into relief by the use of contrasts.

Esposito discerns how the idea of whiteness-as-normal "makes it convenient to blame people of color, as individuals, for problems that are inherently based on the group's social location" (2009: 524). This chimes with Sanders and Sullivan's findings.

In 1997, the historian Paul Spickard reflected that, since the 1960s, America had experienced a "modest softening of the lines between the races." Apart from the word "race" to describe cultural groups, it seemed an unexceptional statement: more than three decades after civil rights, some abatement of the strife and divisions that marked America's prehistory would have been expected. Spickard then added: "This is not to suggest that race is becoming less important in American public life – on the contrary, it continues to shape people's life chances far more drastically than white conservative rhetoric would have us believe" (1997: 153).

Dirk Philipsen elaborates: "The entire spectrum of life experiences by Americans not only are perceived, but also processed and acted upon in a way that is pervasively racialized" (2003: 190). By racialized, I take it that Philipsen means treated in a way made comprehensible in terms of race. If this doesn't surprise us quite as it should, why is that? Perhaps because it resembles commonsense: the patterns of inequality I've outlined can be rendered intelligible in terms of a mutant racism that has adapted to changing environments and continues to exert a maleficent influence, or as an expression of blacks' inability or perhaps unwillingness to improve their material positions. The latter seems a more popular option.

Perhaps this has pushed many African Americans into a mood of resignation, if not fatalism. Earl Sheridan sums up their stance: "Racism is irrelevant not because it no longer exists, as the conservatives argue, but because it is unbeatable" (2006: 190). At times, it certainly appears so: its obduracy has apparently convinced black celebrities that the most productive way ahead is around it. This has prompted Julie Novkov to enquire: "Could a postracial state be something other than a state in which racial subordination was rendered politically unspeakable though still structurally present?" (2008: 658).

The reader must decide whether this is preposterous or profound. Initially, I thought the former, but, on reflection, I veer toward the latter: the situation Novkov conjectures is actually a decent summary of today; her speculation about whether it can ever be anything different makes us wonder whether, in a truly postracial society, we could conceptualize black people at all.

What about whites? Matthew W. Hughey reckons whiteness is now "less of a synonym for invisible normality" than it was just a few years ago (2011: 1291). When Toni Bruce argues, "the instability of dominant discourses means that the boundaries of the 'normal' must be constantly marked," she implies there is more transience than we typically assume (2004: 862). Hundreds of years of conceiving people as black slaves an impression of permanence. A genuine postracial culture would change this. The term black celebrity would be meaningless: postracial would mean dispatching blackness and whiteness to oblivion.

It's against this background that we should assess Halle Berry, or, more specifically, the narrative she expresses. On the one hand, she reminds us that history leaves stains, one of which becomes visible only under close scrutiny. The stain is whiteness. Anyone who isn't unambiguously white is, on Berry's account, black. On the other hand, she advocates a world in which ethnicity becomes a matter of choice, people – like her daughter – electing their ethnic identities. Note the use of plural identities: Berry's child may change hers as she grows, perhaps opting for several at one time, changing to suit different situations. It should be – probably already is – possible to have multiple ethnicities, all interchangeable and all utterly fluid. Her narrative is a combination of what is and what might be.

I opened this chapter with Ofari Hutchinson's argument that Tiger Woods and, by implication, other conspicuously successful black celebrities are interpreted by wider society as evidence that the colorblind society has arrived and the condition many describe as postracial is within reach. Prominent black figures, whether in entertainment or politics, are abundantly available. And when they are presented with the opportunity to make pronouncements on racial or ethnic matters, they are likely to encourage black people to stop griping and start thinking and acting for themselves. Oprah typifies this tendency to offer themselves as models to be emulated and avoid engaging in debates that could affect their own popularity. Perhaps the specter of Paul Robeson remains. Or, perhaps, all black celebrities graduate from what Rasheed Z. Baaith calls the Michael Jordan School: "The theme of which is get the money, don't say anything substantial and for heaven's sake, never offend white people" (2002: 8).

It's a piercing appraisal and one that assumes that black celebrities carry the responsibility to use their status as a kind of political and social lever. It also assumes that people like Berry are intimidated by the prospect of losing their popularity; this doesn't appear to be the case. It's possible that more celebrities who define themselves as black will, perhaps inadvertently, challenge overworked, worn-out racial categories. In the process, they will render the very term black celebrities intellectually bereft and practically useless.

TALENT

MONGREL GENRE|

talent Special aptitude, faculty, gift (for music etc.; for doing); high mental ability. *Oxford English Dictionary*

talent Innate ability, aptitude, or faculty, esp. when unspecified; above average ability. *Collins English Dictionary*

If ever a word was in need of redefinition, it's talent. Celebrity culture has practically turned into an archaism – so old-fashioned that it's almost laughable. At least, the way it's defined formally by the English language's foremost dictionaries. Up till the year 2001, this appeared to be clear and uncontested. Then came *Big Brother*.

In the early twenty-first century, just as in any other period of its history, television attracted critics. "One new category of entertainment programme was particularly under attack," write Asa Briggs and Peter Burke in their book *A Social History of the Media*. "So-called 'reality TV' shows such as *Castaway 2000*, *Big Brother* and *I'm a Celebrity . . . Get Me Out of Here!*, which exploited melodramatic settings, and which critics considered morally repugnant" (2005: 262).

While Briggs and Burke don't specify why critics thought reality tv was morally repugnant, as opposed to aesthetically, informatively, educationally, or just plain repugnant, one such critic, Brian Johnson, of *Maclean's* shed a little light when he described it as "a mongrel genre that lets us pass judgment while indulging in some safe, Disneyfied voyeurism" (2001: 56).

Voyeurism, certainly. But Disneyfied? This implies that the entertainment was safe and family-oriented. Not, if Jonathan Bignell is to be believed: "Reality TV emphasizes intimacy, it mirrors aspects of the lives of some of its viewers and it not only represents but also debates the meaning of domestic space and the interrelationships of people who inhabit the same space" (2005: 176). This was, and still is, adults-only entertainment. Some of the figures viewers could view and perhaps identify with were contemptible, manipulative liars, if not downright scumbags.

Reality television tended to turn its characters' vices into virtues, so that people who displayed ignorance, dishonesty, or some kind of depravity became praiseworthy. Many of those who appeared in reality tv shows were well rewarded with endorsements, record contracts, and other kinds of profitable assignments. Several of them became celebrities for no other reason than they were recognizable. Reality tv made it possible for someone working at a supermarket checkout one week to be nationally famous the next. Or someone serenading commuters with a guitar on street corners at Christmas to be a best-selling recording artist by Easter. Reality shows changed television and its viewers.

The criticisms of reality tv are comprehensive, though most of them are easily discounted. Boring: then why do so many viewers watch them? Passive: then why do millions vote? Demeaning to participants: then why do so many clamor for a chance to appear on television? Patronizing to viewers: then why don't they switch channels? Scarcely believing critics have been astonished by the popular appeal of reality tv.

Blake Brooker believes: "The reasons for being interested in celebrities are luminously obvious," and then goes on to identify: "Looks, talent, power, luck, wealth, appetite, intelligence, drive" and a few other attributes worthy of our admiration (quoted in McCutcheon *et al*. 2010: 9). But reality tv stars often make a point of reminding us they have only one of the above (the fourth attribute) and still stake a claim on our admiration – perhaps attention would be more accurate.

Today, we are aware of the legion of undeserving souls who are lucky enough to stumble into a reality tv show and emerge celebrities. We are always reminded these fortunate people have no talent. Yet we consumers spend money on magazines and other printed media that feature them, we might even buy products they endorse or license, and we definitely watch them on our tv sets. Actually we don't just watch them: we involve and enmesh ourselves in reality tv. As "The cross-articulations between media and audience have become more complicated," Sara L. Knox detects. "The audience is already implicated in the show" (2000: para 37).

While she was writing in 2000 and not specifically about the then embryonic reality genre, Knox's argument armed readers for what was to come. She wrote of "the fragility of the line between 'realtime' and 'showtime'" and "the collapsed space" between audiences and tv shows. She also anticipated that reality tv "has the power to rethread the fabric of culture" (2000). Did it? Jan De Vos doesn't give an answer to this, but he does provide a start.

De Vos discerns a similarity between today's reality tv and a series of psychological experiments designed to explore how people react when subjected to challenges, tests, or trials. There is, he argues, a resemblance "not only in the settings it uses, but also the underlying logic . . . creating the illusion of an 'equipment-free' reality" (2009: 267). This is a promising lead.

De Vos cites experiments by Stanley Milgram (1933–84) and Philip Zimbardo (b. 1933), both of whom were interested in the malleability of individuals' wills and the power of human groups to affect the individual. Actually, even before their studies, there had been several psychological experiments that showed how relatively unproblematic it was to create conditions under which people could be made to do things, even when they didn't want to.

> **Did they act the way they did because of free will or were they determined or influenced by something else?**

In 1936, for instance, Muzafir Sherif took subjects into a darkened room individually and asked them to make judgments about how far and in what direction a beam of light was moving. The evaluations were wildly diverse. When the subjects were taken back in, this time in a group, the judgments converged, indicating that individuals tended to conform to the judgments of the group regardless of their personal perceptions. Later, in 1955, Solomon Asch asked subjects to decide which of a number of lines was longer. Although the correct answer was obvious, Asch planted subjects who'd been instructed deliberately to guess way off the mark. When the genuine subjects agreed with the phony estimates, Asch concluded that forces to conform to others overpowered a person's ability to make simple sensory judgments.

These studies highlighted the influence of collectivities in affecting both the thought and behavior of individuals, even in the face of often bizarre, conflicting evidence. Individuals were more comfortable conforming than they were challenging majority views. The study adduced by De Vos is Milgram's 1974 *Obedience to Authority*, in which subjects were told they were participating in learning experiments: "learners" were fastened into an electrically wired chair and had electrodes attached to their bodies. The subjects were told to test the learners and, if they got an answer wrong, zap them with electric shocks. Actually, the learners were in on the experiment and didn't receive the shocks; they just reacted dramatically to convince the subjects.

The results were disturbing: subjects were prepared to keep upping the electric jolts, even when they believed the learners were in excruciating pain. Each time the subject would object, a researcher would snap back: "Please continue" or "You *must* go on." Milgram found that 65 percent of the subjects obeyed, progressing all the way to the maximum voltage of 450 volts. Subjects surrendered their autonomy to the experiment, believing it to be conducted in the spirit of science. The unsettling research disclosed plasticity in the human makeup and a high tolerance for administering harm on others.

If there was a single academic study that presaged reality tv in intent, format, and shared an "underlying logic," it was Zimbardo's prison simulation in 1971. Twenty-four subjects were randomly split into two groups, "prisoners" and "guards," and instructed to act out role-appropriate behavior in a specially constructed prison at Stanford University. Those playing guards were given suitable uniforms and accessories, while the prisoners were assigned numbers and made to wear muslin smocks. The experiment soon edged toward catastrophe as guards tormented the captives, imposing punishments cruelly and arbitrarily. They took away basic rights, such as mattresses, food, and washing facilities from the prisoners, one of whom went on hunger strike in protest at the callous treatment. Zimbardo aborted the experiment, though this in itself was a more interesting conclusion than he might have hoped for (Haney *et al.* 1973; see also Insight Media 1990).

Expectations of normal behavior went awry: closeted away and commissioned with the authority to behave in unfamiliar ways, some guards swiftly adopted conduct that bordered on the sadistic. Even in its incomplete state, the experiment disclosed how human behavior is susceptible to quite dramatic change by adjustments to situational contingencies. The lesson: put people in unfamiliar environments and assign them unusual power and instructions and their behavior changes, often in a way that seems "out-of-character." Questions about the ethics of this type of research effectively prevented a replication – at least, in an academic setting.

The two shows responsible for the rapid spread of the reality format seemed like the televisual offspring of Zimbardo's experiment. *Big Brother* and *Survivor* were both based on European ideas, the former's name inspired by George Orwell's all-seeing sentinel in *1984*. They took the observational format of shows such as *COPS* and MTV's *The Real World* and added the contrivance of enclosed environments and new tasks. If the results had been as dramatic as the experiments, viewers would probably have looked only through their parted fingers. In the event, they proved fascinating rather than repellent.

| ORDINARINESS*

Writing in 2000, shortly before *Big Brother*, the psychologist David Giles wrote about Maureen Rees, a Welsh woman, who appeared in a BBC documentary called *Driving School*, a kind of visual diary of Rees's learning to drive. In 1997, it didn't seem an auspicious premise for a documentary series, but it became popular and Rees became something of a well-known figure, not because of her abilities; more likely because of her lack of them. Or possibly because of her lack of any special or distinctive features. "Maybe she represents the next-door neighbour, or the woman you see regularly in the bus queue or at the supermarket checkout," pondered Giles as he tried to unravel the

*noun, the condition of having no special or distinctive features; from Latin *ordinarius*

reasons for her sudden popularity: "Someone *so* ordinary that a real relationship might be a distinct possibility" (2000: 70).

It was an interesting insight and one that led Giles to suggest: "The television viewing world is a bottomless pit of potential celebrities . . . Perhaps the democratization of fame is still not complete" (2000: 71).

If by democratization, Giles meant accessible to everyone, he was right: since 2000, when he was writing, any number of media outlets have provided entry portals for "potential celebrities," as Giles called them. But it's the other seemingly innocuous phrase "someone *so* ordinary" that's simultaneously complex and fundamental.

People with no particular distinguishing features or capabilities, and who would, in most circumstances, be uninteresting, became irresistible – like forces of nature. Rational viewers didn't offer logical reasons for following reality tv characters: they just related to them; they *got* them. Ordinariness, that uncomplicated, straightforward, unornamented, and authentic quality shared by, well, practically everyone became captivating.

The medium helped: where film deliberately staked out an immense distance between its stars and audiences, television closed up the space, making its figures more recognizably authentic. Television "allows its personalities to function as figures of identification and 'reachable' ideals of wealth, extravagance and glamour," observe James Bennett and Su Holmes (2010: 71). Even so, script-less, non-professionals without personae or profiles had to have a decent justification for their existence. Or did they?

> *Notions of privacy and intimacy were undergoing radical revision.*

Actually, there were several shows before the British series that made ordinariness interesting. Two shows in particular, *An American Family* and *The Family*, carried the nucleus for contemporary reality tv. Airing on PBS in 1973, the former chronicled the everyday life of a family in the throes of a divorce (the backstory of the documentary was dramatized in an HBO film in 2011). In the following year, a British series focused on another family, this one happily united. The dialogue between family members in both cases resembled bad acting with dialogue that could be either spirited or lifeless. There was no commentary or intrusive interviews: just a naturalistic recording of family life. At a time when cop shows such as *Cagney and Lacey* and *The Sweeney* and epic documentaries such as BBC's *The Ascent of Man* were in vogue, a faithful register of family life should have worked like a sedative on any viewer without boundless patience.

Remember, though: this was a time when psychological studies by Milgram and others were probing the reasons behind our seemingly rule-following behavior and there was a general interest in the plasticity of people. Did they act the way they did because of free will or were they determined or influenced by something else? And, if they were determined, could we identify the determinants and change them? These were big questions and they were not about to be answered by a couple of tv shows. Yet there was a sense in which an invisible observer's perspective on the everyday goings-on in most people's idea of an ordinary home complemented the overall line of inquiry. After all, the shows provided a lens through which viewers could gaze at ordinary human beings interacting with equally ordinary human beings in settings and situations that were ordinary. If they were to be seen as experiments – and, in a sense, they were – they were naturalistic ones, deriving from real life.

Several television documentaries followed the cinéma-vérité model, avoiding artificiality or artistic effect. "An early popular form of reality TV programming in the US began with the introduction of *COPS* in the early 1980s," observes Mark P. Orbe. "This show allowed viewers to follow police officers in major US cities as they go about their day-to-day interactions with the general public" (2008: 347).

Susan Murray and Laurie Ouellette add: "Yet, it wasn't until the premiere of *The Real World* on MTV in 1991 that we began to witness the emergence of many of the textual characteristics that would come to define the genre's current form" (2008: 4).

Of all the characteristics, the one that appeared to matter most was: making the unseen seen. To put it another way: turning private lives inside out, so they were visible to everyone. Both *Family* documentaries had done this, but, in the 1970s, privacy was a valued freedom. Later, at a time when notions of privacy and intimacy were undergoing radical revision, the condition of being free from being observed by others seemed ripe for adaptation. *The Real World*'s congruence with other aspects of culture is obvious.

In 1991, NBC introduced *The Jerry Springer Show* to American television: this was a standard-fare, daytime talk show for a few years, before it was revamped into a sort of group confessional session, guests invited to share their dirty little secrets with a studio audience and millions of tv viewers. It became a wildly successful format with the British-born host Jerry Springer inviting guests to reveal and explore unimaginably intimate details. Unimaginably, that is, in the early 1990s. Nowadays, people share without inhibition, suggesting how elastic the concept of privacy has become.

Over 4,000 miles away from the Chicago studio where Springer's show was filmed, a Dutch tv producer, John de Mols, must have been watching and learning. People were becoming unselfconscious and utterly relaxed about talking frankly, even about aspects of their lives that made audiences blush. What if you could make them not just talk but behave in a way that would register the same reaction? De Mol, a partner of Netherlands-based tv production company Endemol, seems to have had an MTV moment: an idea that must have seemed doomed from its inception, but which developed so successfully that it changed culture.

Big Brother first aired in the Netherlands in 1997. Ostensibly, the show was a competition. This was a crucial innovation: it invited viewers to vote which of the contestants, or housemates, in the confined living space were to stay and which ones were to be evicted. To return briefly to Knox's point about implicating viewers in a program, *Big Brother* turned the audience from passive viewers to guilt-free peeping Toms with power over the destinies of those they were peeping at. Viewers dictated the *dramatis personae* of the show and so mapped the course it took over its series, which lasted three months in many editions.

Since *BB*, a great many unscripted programs labeled reality tv have incorporated interactivity, encouraging viewers to vote out (and, by implication, vote in) contestants, none more spectacularly than those purportedly striving to discover singing talent. "The key persuasive strategy of the show is that the public decides who will win by voting with their telephone or through cell phone text messages," write Irving Rein and Ben Shields about *American Idol* (2007: 71). Similar shows such as *The X Factor* and *America's Got Talent* strayed a long way from the closed environment of the *Big Brother* house or the rain forests of *I'm a Celebrity . . . Get Me Out of Here!* and *Survivor*, but they shared the same interactive connection.

Rein and Shields are right in divining the attraction of reality show: having the capacity to influence not just a show but other people's destinies is an intoxicating prospect. But interactivity allows a two-way flow of influence. Television responds to viewers' inputs, but also affects viewers, not just in drawing them to their tv sets, computers, or smartphones, but in all manner of ways.

Television talent shows had been interactive practically since the dawn of the medium: in the USA, *Arthur Godfrey's Talent Scouts*, where struggling singers were brought to New York to perform before a studio audience and then be judged by way of an applause meter, was, like many early American tv shows, an adaptation of a radio program. CBS canceled the tv show in 1958, but many variations followed. These included *The Gong Show* in the 1970s and *Star Search*, which ran from 1983 to 1995. British television's *Carroll Levis Discoveries* started in 1957, though *Opportunity Knocks,* which ran from 1956 to 1978, was its most successful and enduring contribution to the talent show genre. Viewers cast votes by sending in postcards. The innovation of *New Faces*, which started in 1973, was its panel consisting of established singers, producers, and agents.

In a sense, the talent contest was a staple of television: relatively inexpensive to produce and reliable in its power to draw viewers. But, by the end of the twentieth century, it seemed exhausted. Then came a kind of hybrid, incorporating elements of the fly-on-the-wall documentary with a talent search. *Popstars* was originally a New Zealand tv show with a format that was later licensed to over 50 countries. It aired in 1999. A British version was produced by Syco, a production company headed by Simon Cowell. The show mutated into several forms, including *Pop Idol*, which launched in 2001. *American Idol* started in the USA the following year. Britain's *The X Factor* began transmission in 2004 and, in 2011, spawned an American version of the show. The . . . *Got Talent* shows were on both sides of the Atlantic. In all cases, an interactive element ensured viewers were, to use Knox's term yet again, implicated.

The gratification comes from being able to understand and share the feelings of those who are being humiliated.

Shows employing similar formats with interactive involvement appear almost every month. The search for new talent, whether singing, modeling, cooking, and so on, is almost by definition never-ending. "We live in a fame epidemic now, don't we?" Cowell asked Ann Oldenburg, of *USA Today*, in 2006. Cowell alluded to the kind of optimism that motivated the raw material of his shows. "Everyone wants to be famous, and to me that's part of the charm of these shows." Even allowing for the moderately amusing misuse of the word "charm," Cowell has a point: the infectious impulse to be famous probably inspires both his participants and a good part of his audience. Like viewers of confessional shows, audiences simultaneously gloat and envy. William Egginton captures the pleasure of *The X Factor*-type contests as follows: "We usually watch reality TV not to witness those who win the contests, but to watch the human dramas that emerge around those who lose" (2009: 179). We are thrilled, says Egginton, by "their humiliation."

On this account, reality shows are less like stages, more like stocks – those medieval wooden contraptions with holes for securing someone's hands and feet, in which criminals were locked and exposed to public ridicule or assault with rotten eggs or fruit. As Egginton puts it, the hapless wannabes lend us, the viewers, "a false sense of superiority," even if we would gladly exchange places. There is gratification in watching others humiliate themselves, then mocking their inadequacies. And yet there is never a shortage of participants willing to submit themselves to the grand mortification.

Even the variants of reality shows secrete this appeal. Dramality (drama+reality) shows, such as the USA's *Jersey Shore* and Britain's *The Only Way is Essex*, were semi-naturalistic, feigning a window on the lives of young people, but in contrived situations and occasionally scripted lines. As in many straight-up reality shows, there was a conceit – an artistic device. Running side by side with the main narrative is a subsidiary story. "Just think of the personal and social breakdowns," prompts De Vos, reminding us how every show in which people are boxed in, or invited to pour out their hearts, makes us witnesses to some kind of emotional meltdown "aesthetized for our pleasure" (2009: 277).

De Vos and, for that matter, Egginton are not referring to *Schadenfreude*, the pleasure derived from someone else's misfortune: the gratification comes from being able to understand and share the feelings of those who are being humiliated. The longing for visibility is, as Cowell pointed out, infectious.

The democratization of fame, as Giles called it, made fame accessible to all manner of ethnic, gender, and national minority groups and, in this sense, "contributed a decisive impulsion to identity politics worldwide," as Jèrôme Bourdon puts it. Bourdon continues: "They [reality shows] have given the highest form of social visibility, prime-time television, to groups altogether neglected beforehand" (2008: 78).

In this respect, reality tv remains a democratizing force. But Bourdon sees a paradox: he calls reality tv "self-despotism," meaning that, in their desire for visibility, participants submit themselves to an oppressive and frequently cruel form of control – "a concomitant regression of democracy" (2008: 77).

Other writers are concerned about the democratizing appeal of reality shows. Christopher E. Bell, for example, in his book on *Idol*-type shows, claims, "the version of participatory democracy presented by *Idol* is only illusory" (2010: 189).

Let me pause to consider what exactly democracy means. Sheldon S. Wolin clarifies: "The traditional understanding of democracy is that it is a system by which the citizenry delegates power to the government" (2008: 43). Viewers of reality tv (the citizenry) effectively delegate power to the show to reject or include the people chosen to entertain them. Is Bell's critique misplaced?

Bell discerns three ideological messages in *American Idol*, in particular, and, presumably, all other reality talent shows. "The central illusion," he states, is "the ideological fallacy that 'anyone can make it' if only s/he can be 'discovered'" (2010: 49). The deception Bell sees through is not of democracy but of *meritocracy*, a system of government by people selected solely because of their ability and nothing else. The second message is that "we, the people" are steering the vehicle; our votes determine the outcome of shows. Third: "By erasing the distinction between citizen and consumer . . . *Idol* couples democratic process with purchasing power" (2010: 189).

Bell is right on all three counts.

|THE TALENT OF KIM KARDASHIAN

The implication of Bell's argument is that watching reality tv – and I am referring to the genre in its widest sense to include any unscripted show involving non-professional actors or broadcasters as its centerpiece – can be like staring uninterestedly at the wallpaper of a house you're renovating in Holland, then peeling it off to discover a sketched self-portrait of Van Gogh daubed beneath it. One layer holds more fascination than the other.

The top layer might appear tedious: human beings, unknown or moderately famous, interacting with each other in an artificial environment and compelled to perform prestructured tasks. Judged on their ability to perform the tasks, the players, if we might call them that, are involved in a survival of the fittest, fitness in this instance being based on their appeal to the viewers. If their singing or their appearance or just the way they conduct themselves in their daily interactions entertains the viewers, they vote for them.

The democratic element of reality tv extended to many of the participants too. Those who came to the fore via *Big Brother*, for example, were not even famous in the first instance. Many of the contestants, especially those who were voted off early in the shows, never actually became famous. And several more enjoyed the most evanescent type of fame before returning to obscurity. For instance, the winter 2004 season of British television's *I'm a Celebrity . . . Get Me Out of Here!* featured Fran Cosgrave, whose main qualification for inclusion was that he had been out with a member of the girl band Atomic Kitten.

As a result of his tv appearance, he was invited onto a series of other reality shows, though none with the audience of *I'm a Celebrity . . . Get Me Out of Here!* He later appeared in some advertisements before completing his elliptical route back to ordinary life and was last reported as working for a recruitment agency in the south of England.

Others like Jade Goody remained popular after her fourth-place exit from Britain's third season of *Big Brother* in 2002. She was all but executed by the press for being loud, fat, and dim. Death threats were taken seriously enough to warrant police protection. Goody was almost an object lesson in contrariness: critics panned her mercilessly, while viewers found her irresistible. Bizarrely, the media antipathy ensured her a kind of afterlife, so that she came out of the house to a plethora of lucrative assignments that kept her busy for years and lent permanence to what might otherwise have been ephemeral renown. Over the next few years, she featured in over 20 reality shows, licensed her own fragrance, released dvds, published an autobiography, and wrote her own magazine column. In 2008, she collapsed on the set of a reality television show in India and was later diagnosed with cancer. She died in 2009, the last few weeks of her life, perhaps fittingly, filmed as a documentary.

Unquestionably, the longest-lasting celebrity to emerge from a reality show is Kim Kardashian, who amassed a multimillion-dollar fortune after capitalizing on her appearance in E!'s *Keeping Up with the Kardashians* in 2007. Like Paris Hilton, she had featured in a sex video uploaded onto the internet – never a bad move for an aspiring celebrity. She also filed for divorce after only 72 days of marriage to basketball player Kris Humphries. Like most reality tv stars, Kardashian was slighted for her lack of any obvious talent, though Maseena Ziegler, of *Forbeswoman*, proposed she was neither without talent nor a capacity for work: "While she may be gifted in the art of self-promotion, her success is further solidified by hard graft" (2012). Both parts of the proposition have substance: furthering one's own progress by attracting publicity and increasing general awareness is a gift of sorts, and hard graft is always applauded.

KK herself has weighed in with her own thoughts on the subject: "I work really hard – I have seven appointments tomorrow before 10am. I'm constantly on the go. I have a successful clothing line. A fragrance. I mean, acting and singing aren't the only ways to be talented. It's a skill to get people to really like you for *you*, instead of a character written for you by somebody else" (quoted by Emma Brockes 2012).

This loops us back to the question I used to open this chapter: do we need to revise our definition of talent?

|GAGA'S GIFT

Susan Boyle became famous after appearing on *Britain's Got Talent* in 2009. Much of her narrative was biographical: a middle-aged woman from a remote part of Scotland, gauche of manner and inelegantly dressed, she sang "I dreamed a dream" from *Les Misérables*. The video was uploaded to YouTube and, within days, Susan Boyle was globally acknowledged as a clunky-looking but unquestionably gifted singer. She was, according to Su Holmes, "invoked as culturally reassuring evidence of the fact that 'talent' – in itself an ideological construct that is never clearly defined – still exists (and is waiting to be discovered)" (2010: 74).

Both of Holmes' points are of interest and deserve closer inspection. Talent, she reckons is an ideological construct, presumably meaning that it forms part of the thinking characteristic of a group, social class, or political belief system, and lacks a clear definition. Susan Boyle provided proof that reality shows do harbor people who have it – however it's defined.

It could be argued that many showbusiness celebrities and the Hollywood stars who preceded them have a stake in perpetuating the idea that talent is a scarce aptitude. Even so, the interest in their private lives that we accept so matter-of-factly today is arguably greater than interest in whatever passes for talent. The big attraction of celebrities is not what they have, but what they do. As Neal Gabler contends: "Most of the people we call celebrities have accomplished something" (2001: 3).

Sometimes their accomplishments are remarkable, though mostly they are humdrum: they appear and do banal things; either way, they are still accomplishments; even seizing people's attention with your presence is an accomplishment of sorts: The preeminent exponent of the twenty-first century was Lady Gaga. "Every public appearance – even, absurdly, at airports, where most celebrities want to pass incognito – has been lavishly scripted in advance with a flamboyant outfit and bizarre hairdo," observed Camille Paglia (2010: 4).

Paglia points out that: "Gaga showed early talent as a pianist but was never a prodigy." She intends this as a barb, but Paglia labors with a too-conventional concept of talent: if Lady Gaga had a gift, it was in commanding interest, not in her music – in her conspicuously artificial persona.

Is there any intrinsic reason why people should be more concerned with Lady Gaga than Kim Kardashian? Are they both equally talented, or talentless? And are these relevant questions today? Love her or hate her, Lady Gaga's artistry is in her ability to communicate to her millions of devotees, affectionately known as "little monsters," and countless others besides. She may, as Paglia scornfully points out, "communicate mutely via a constant stream of atomized, telegraphic text messages," but this is powerful language. When she appears, she is still communicating, this time through her ostentatiously decorated body. She's only properly appreciated through her dramatic performances, while Kardashian's worth is only grasped by observing her everyday routines.

Lady Gaga might be more than a match for Kardashian when it comes to singing, but she is easily outscored in the ordinariness contest. Perhaps Gaga was one of several interchangeable blonde wig-wearing singers. She would appear in one of several guises, such as a silent-screen siren, an Arabian princess, or a BDSM freak; she was, also, as Paglia describes her, "calculated and artificial, so clinical and strangely antiseptic." On the other hand, there was something indisputably unique, something authentically workaday, something ingenuously commonplace, something innocently green about Kardashian that charmed audiences. She never pretended to be able to sing, dance, act, write, or have any quality beyond her natural good looks. She just appeared and behaved normally.

Kardashian, and the other celebrities who emerged from reality tv shows, knew they had no talent, at least not in the conventional sense. Like artless children who stumble on a stash of new Xboxes, they made the most of their good fortune. They usually busied themselves endorsing products, attending openings, making cds, appearing on talk shows; cashing in on their instant and, for most, transitory fame. Kardashian earned $18 million from endorsements and licensing in 2012 alone.

Consumers did not seem to mind, though. In his *Understanding Celebrity*, Graeme Turner states that different types of celebrity engender different types of responses: "Audiences place individual celebrities somewhere along a continuum that ranges from seeing them as objects of desire or emulation to regarding them as spectacular freaks worthy of derision" (2004: 55).

Turner compares responses to Nicole Kidman (b. 1967) and Anna Nicole Smith (1967–2007), the former attracting "more admiration" than the latter, even though Kidman's admirers may be mindful of the media apparatus and publicity machinery she has at her disposal. In other words, Turner suggests that audiences recognize something in Kidman that they do not in Smith and place her on a different part of the emulation/derision continuum.

Celebrity culture rewards presence rather than anything as uncertain as talent or its correlates.

Turner might have a point, but his example is an awkward one. Kidman in the early twenty-first century was Hollywood royalty. Emerging from the acclaimed low-budget Australian film *Dead Calm* in 1988, Hawaii-born, Australia-raised Kidman was offered a part opposite Tom Cruise in *Days of Thunder*. Late in 1990, she married Cruise, a deed that earned her more international recognition than any of her previous roles. Hollywood parts – such as "Dr Meridian" in *Batman Forever* – followed, though her performances in independent films such as *To Die For* and *Portrait of a Lady* protected her from charges that her status owed more to her husband than to her own merit. Still, her marriage to Cruise, which ended in 2001, coincided with her becoming a featured actor and her elevation to celebrity status.

The other Nicole also married well: in her case to billionaire oil tycoon J. Howard Marshall, who died aged 90 in August 1995, 13 months after the wedding. Smith was 26 when they married. The *Playboy* "Playmate of the Year" in 1992, Smith appeared in *Naked Gun 33⅓: The final insult* and *The Hudsucker Proxy,* both in 1994. Yet it was her misalliance that aroused public interest, especially after it became known that she stood to inherit nearly $0.25 billion. Marshall's family contested the bestowal and a court battle ensued. Smith was awarded $88 million.

Just as she seemed destined to return to anonymity, albeit a plush anonymity, E! The Entertainment Channel capitalized on the rising popularity of the then novel reality tv form by featuring Smith in a show that involved shooting her and her entourage as they navigated their way through, shops, clubs, hotels, and anywhere else. *The Anna Nicole Show* débuted in 2002 and followed the earlier MTV show *The Osbournes* in straightforwardly recording the directionless activities of a bunch of people with lots of money and even more free time.

Highlights included their having breakfast and playing video games. Somehow, the inertia conjured the interest of viewers and Smith returned to the spotlight. She died as a result of an overdose of prescription drugs in 2007. A biopic *Anna Nicole* was released within months of her death.

Maybe, as Turner suggests, Smith elicits a different response from consumers to Kidman. But are they more likely to look down on Smith and be in awe of Kidman? Cynics might spot parallels amid the divergent career paths. Others might suspect that celebrity culture rewards, as we have noted before, presence rather than anything as uncertain as talent or its correlates. Still others might regard both as products of an overpowering media that lends specious importance to anyone who can draw viewers to a screen and readers to a tabloid.

> *The democratizing tendency of celebrity culture encourages viewers to decide what is and isn't talent.*

There is, as Turner reflects, a "paradoxical relationship between the celebrity and their public." Smith had no pretensions: she didn't say she could act (she had just one acting lesson) or sing; nor did she try to disguise her early lap-dancing job as a career interlude. She didn't even try very hard to contest the copious charges that she was a gold-digger. Yet clearly consumers took pleasure in watching her. This is what Turner regards as the "arbitrariness" of celebrity: "Sometimes no amount of publicity can generate public interest; at other times, the public reveals a mind of its own in its reactions to a specific individual" (2004: 55).

That "mind," to stick with Turner's words, creates and uncreates celebrities. We can acknowledge the powerful roles of the media and corporate interest groups, without losing the force of Turner's punch: we, the consumers, ultimately determine who or what interests us. And perhaps that same mind declares what is and isn't talent.

Talent, as traditionally defined, refers to abilities that are immanent, that is, they exist in someone. The abilities are exceptional rather than ordinary, inborn rather than learned. Wolfgang Amadeus Mozart (1765–91), epitomized talent: a child prodigy, he was composing from the age of five. His music was and indeed still is recognized for its purity of form and melody, and his influence was pervasive. We need not deny his prowess to understand how the reception of his music defined its status. While some of Mozart's work carried the qualities of the earlier Baroque, the harmony, restraint, structure, and adherence to recognized standards of form were associated with the Classical period, beginning about 1730. Romanticism, which embraced much of the nineteenth century, was a reaction against the orderliness of classicism. Mozart's music was received by a culture steeped in the aesthetic qualities of ancient Greece and Rome, qualities that permeated architecture, literature, and other art forms. Others recognized Mozart's talent: it was a quality attributed, or ascribed, to him.

Had Bob Dylan (b. 1941) delivered one of his songs of apocalyptic foreboding, such as "The times they are a-changin'," in 1764, rather than 1964 (its actual year of release), would there have been a response of rapture and veneration, as there was in the late twentieth century? No one would doubt Dylan, like Mozart, had a singular, creative talent; the noun *genius* does not sit uncomfortably with either musician. But context, I have little need to remind readers, is everything: talent, like any other attributable characteristic, should be understood in the circumstances in which it makes sense. Most people see talent as a natural, invariant property that springs up spontaneously in select individuals across the ages. But try thinking of it in a similar way to fashion: there isn't anything *intrinsically* fashionable – things, places, people, and trends only become fashionable or unfashionable by common agreement; by decree of the public mind to repeat Turner's phrase. If talent is seen as the manner in which a culture responds rather than an individual trait, it is like the times – a-changin'.

I can hear the objections: talent is immortal; it is changeless, visible across space and time. Perhaps. But, if so, talent has become both less and more visible in recent years. The democratizing tendency of celebrity culture encourages viewers to decide what is and isn't talent, not by reference to esoteric conceptual definitions, but by simply asking themselves a question: am I agreeably engaged? Is this so different from the questions asked by the audience that attended Prague's Teatro di Praga for the premiere of *Don Giovanni* in 1787? Were they wondering profoundly whether they were hearing the most thrilling, heart-stoppingly beautiful music ever created, and whether the composer had been blessed by the gods with gifts of unique brilliance? More likely they, like viewers of reality tv, were just enjoying themselves.

> **talent** the collective action of regarding *qualities or features that are recognized as* having great value in a population as belonging to someone

POLITICS

CHAPTER HIGHLIGHTS

- Some entertainers, such as Bono and Tim Robbins, are politically engaged, but never run for political office
- Involvement in political causes has unpredictable consequences for celebrities
- Celebrities who become politicians arrive like white knights ready for battle
- Bill Clinton emerged undamaged from a scandal that would have ruined other politicians
- Since the 1990s, the media's focus has switched from hard to soft news
- Many politicians emerge as fully fledged celebrities, Barack Obama being a prime example
- Celebrity culture has done to politics what Starbucks has done to coffee

A well-publicized bout of illicit sex never did any celebrity's reputation harm; often, a lot of good. But moving bank accounts can be quite damaging; especially if the account-holder is known as a champion of egalitarianism, enemy of injustice, and stalwart supporter of human rights around the world.

The U2 frontman had toured Africa, established the pressure group Debt AIDS Trade Africa (DATA), and become one of the most vocal supporters of the Make Poverty History campaign. The columnist Joshua Green had Bono in mind when he wrote: "certain celebrities have established themselves as powerful presences to be consulted and wooed" (2004: 34).

In 2005, Bono helped persuade world leaders to double aid for Africa to $50 billion a year by 2010 and erase the debt of the

18 poorest countries on the continent. Political scientist Andrew Kamons reflected: "Bono has been arguably the most decisive factor in reframing the global debate on third world debt reform" (2007: 146). Whatever people thought of his music – and, at that time, U2 had sold at least 130 million albums – they couldn't fault Bono's politics: he was unerringly on the side of the angels.

> **Bono has never held, or even sought political office. And probably for good reason.**

So, when the Irish government announced it intended to scrap a break that lets musicians and artists avoid paying taxes on royalties, Dublin-born Bono and other members of U2 moved their music publishing company to the Netherlands, where the government then charged about 5 percent tax on royalties, less than half the Irish rate. *Forbes* estimated the band earned $110 million in 2005. The transfer could have been justified in the interests of tax-efficiency, were it not for the fact that, a year before, Bono had appealed to the Irish Prime Minister to raise overseas aid to 0.7 percent of gross national product by 2007 from the 0.5 percent level at which it then stood. By withdrawing the band's tax payments, he was reducing the very revenue that funded that aid.

It was a contretemps soon overlooked and had little impact on Bono's credentials as a crusader against poverty. But it served to underline how carefully celebrities need to tread when they wander away from the tributaries of entertainment or sports and into the mainstream of politics and world events. Bono has splashed energetically, but never taken a plunge into deep water. Since he marked his arrival as the social conscience of rock music in 1985, when he, with former rocker Bob Geldof, organized the LiveAid concert from London's Wembley Stadium, Bono has remained resolutely a musician. He has never held, or even sought political office. And probably for good reason.

Some celebrities seem mindful of 2 Corinthians 11: 14: "Even Satan disguises himself as an angel of light." Consider Tim Robbins' declaration: "I don't like politicians. I think they lie all the time," he told Mark Ganem, of *W* magazine. "I don't support candidates. I resent having to vote for the lesser of two evils" (1999: 337). Robbins has put the screws on politicians for years; not literally, of course, but through his plays and movies, such as 1992's *Bob Roberts* and 1995's *Dead Man Walking.* A defender of free speech, Robbins was a frequent critic of America's overseas entanglements.

So was Mia Farrow, who, in the 1970s, protested against the US military involvement in Vietnam and, with her then husband, became one of the first actors to adopt a Vietnamese war orphan. It was what Kerry Bystrom sarcastically describes as "adoption as an alternative mode of politics, an affective and intimate political act that will somehow right the wrongs of aggressive American imperialism" (2011: 216).

Bystrom argues this "mode of politics" (i.e. the manner in which politics is expressed) is based on a conservative vision ("non-Western people portrayed as unable to attend to their own basic needs"). It is one shared by Madonna, who adopted children born in Malawi, the landlocked country in southern central Africa, where there is high infant mortality and a prevalence of HIV-Aids, and by Angelina Jolie, who has adopted children from Cambodia, Ethiopia, and Vietnam. Jolie became a goodwill ambassador for the United Nations, a role that led her, as Chris Connelly points out, "to some 20 countries on fact-finding trips; to donate thousands of dollars and help raise millions more; and to speak out, albeit cautiously, on behalf of the world's dispossessed" (2005: 70–1).

Darrell M. West and John M. Orman have a name for prominent figures who immerse themselves in the issues of the day and express political ideas through words or deeds, but without seeking office: "famed nonpolitico spokespersons" (2003). A "politico" is an informal name for a politician, which, of course, none of the above has been. Nor has Jane Fonda (b. 1937), who has been involved in several political causes since 1970s, when she first expressed her opposition to the USA's involvement in the Vietnam War. Charlton Heston (1923–2008) was much further to the right of the political spectrum: an active member of the US gun lobby until ill health forced him to withdraw in 2003. George Clooney testified before the United Nations (UN) Security Council about ending the genocide in Darfur. Cameron Diaz campaigns for environmental causes. Russell Simmons speaks out about war and HIV-Aids. Paul Weller was part of the broad leftwing alliance known as Red Wedge. Patrick Stewart worked with Amnesty International. There are many other entertainers who have aligned themselves with political movements or causes. Clint Eastwood used to, though he actually did enter formal politics, serving as nonpartisan mayor of Carmel-by-the-Sea, California, 1986–88; he also addressed the crowd at the 2012 Republican National Convention in Tampa.

When celebrities advocate, they publicly support, recommend, or fight for a particular cause or policy. There is still drama in their appearance at rallies, on marches, or signing petitions; but it appears unmediated. No one coerces them into making their politics known; in most cases, their management probably advises against it. So there is a sense in which everyone agrees they are not acting, or performing for the gallery. They are just doing something out of conviction. Their actions register truth. Take Sean Penn for example.

|THE DIXIE CHICKS' DIGRESSION

Penn (b. 1960) wore his politics on his sleeve when he visited Baghdad in 2002, shortly before the war on Iraq (i.e. the second Gulf War). He visited hospitals, schools, poor neighborhoods, and the Iraqi Foreign Minister's office, before returning to the USA to report on his findings via a paid-for page in the *Washington*

Times and an open letter to the then president George W. Bush. Since then, Penn has risked collateral damage by politicking as and when his conscience demands, often rendering himself unpopular with the media. He was called "an embarrassment to his profession and his country" after visiting Venezuela and appearing at a rally with socialist leader Hugo Chavez in 2012. He was also lauded for founding his J/P HRO nonprofit aid group in the aftermath of Haiti's deadly 2010 earthquake.

The sheer unpredictability of reaction must inhibit many celebrities' involvement in political causes, apart from those that elicit universal approval. Of course, it could be argued that Penn's status was already so well established by 2002 that he had little to lose. He'd already got movies such as *Carlito's Way* (1993), *Dead Man Walking* (1995), and *The Thin Red Line* (1998) under his belt. His father, Leo Penn (1921–98), was blacklisted after supporting the Hollywood 10, a group of screenwriters, directors, and producers who were ultimately imprisoned for their refusal to answer the House Un-American Activities Committee's questions concerning Communist sympathies during the McCarthy era.

The investigations into alleged communist infiltration in American public life between 1950 and 1954 created an exceptional atmosphere, and a great many members of the film industry who suffered during that time would have prospered in a different era. Frank Sinatra (1915–98) contributed financially and gave his name to various causes and organizations up till 1948. "Sinatra's connections with the left ended abruptly, when he became the target of a red-baiting campaign that contributed to an astounding downward spiral in his career," reveals Gerald Meyer (2002: 312).

Given Sinatra's popularity, particularly after his appearance in 1953's *From Here to Eternity*, it is interesting to think how his political exploits could have hurt his career. But think about Muhammad Ali, for many the most popular athlete in history. In 1966, he expressed his disapproval of America's military conflict in Vietnam: "No Viet Cong ever called me nigger." Refusing the draft pushed his popularity to its nadir. "No wonder that 24 years later [1990], Michael Jordan refused to support a Black candidate for the US Senate in his home state against a known segregationist because 'Republicans buy sneakers too,'" writes Robert Lipsyte (2011: 8D).

There were moments in history when espousing political views could be – and was for some – ruinous. Now, passionately committed celebrities who stray away from the safe confines of entertainment and declare their loyalty to a cause or issue of political importance appear believable and, if anything, add gravitas to their reputation. There are occasional exceptions.

In March 2003, Natalie Maines, the Lubbock, Texas-born singer with the Dixie Chicks, announced during a concert in London that she was "ashamed the president of the United States is from Texas." It was ten days before the invasion of Iraq. President George W. Bush was born in New Haven, Connecticut, but served as Governor of Texas from 1995 to 2000. The three-woman band was at the height of its popularity: the Grammy-winning *Home* had been the best-selling country album in the United States for the previous seven months, and "Travelin' soldier," about an American soldier returning from the war in Vietnam, was at number one in the singles chart.

The comments were received enthusiastically in London, but, in the USA, radio stations pulled Dixie Chicks tracks from playlists after complaints from listeners. One station in Kansas City invited listeners to a ritualistic dumping of the band's cds and tapes into garbage cans. The band received death threats and its hitherto successful career stalled. Maines' attempt at limiting the damage was an apology for being "disrespectful," which she retracted in *Time*, though not for three years, by which time the furor had fizzled out.

The band continues to tour and release successful albums. Like Kanye West, the band will probably always be associated with its disparagement of George W. Bush. In the aftermath of

Hurricane Katrina in 2005, West weighed in with his famous "George Bush doesn't care about black people." The context of the assertion is often erased: West was talking without autocue to NBC cameras, making an appeal to raise money for the victims in New Orleans. He singled out the media for his initial broadside. "I hate the way they portray us in the media. If we see a black family, it says they're looting. See a white family, it says they're looking for food." An acerbic comment did the artist no harm. As we now know, the wave of anger that followed, if anything, enhanced West's career. But the Dixie Chicks probably rue the night they digressed from music into politics, however fleetingly.

Other celebrities believe there are obligations involved in being a public figure and enjoying the manifold benefits of celebrity status. "The influence of the artistic community is important," Warren Beatty told Steve Chagollan and Ted Johnson. Beatty (b. 1937) is an actor whose associations with matters of public policy go back to the 1960s, when he opposed the Vietnam War. He subsequently campaigned for universal healthcare, gun control, and other issues, broadly aligning himself with the Democratic Party. In fact, he campaigned with Robert Kennedy during his bid for the Democratic nomination in 1968.

Visibly committed to expressing his political views, Beatty remained mindful of the pitfalls of political engagement: "A lot of the public can, quite understandably, resent attention being drawn to political matters by what is invariably called a 'celebrity'" (2008: A5).

Beatty's suspicions are backed up by a poll conducted for the *Hollywood Reporter* in 2002, which concluded 76.5 percent of Americans disapproved of movie actors "injecting politics" into their work. "Would a moviegoer shy away from paying to see a film that starred an outspoken actor they disagree with?" asked Paul Bond. A significant 44.3 percent of those polled said they would (2002: 61). But the others were in a majority, however small. The poll may not be reliable, but it seems a believable distribution and it makes parlaying one's status into politics a risky maneuver.

Apart from alienating fans and drawing their resentment, celebrities risk the ire of critics such as George Monbiot, who detected that Bono and other politically motivated celebrities had become, as the title of his article indicates, "Bards of the powerful" (June 21, 2005). A bard is an honored poet. Monbiot censured celebrities who become so cozy with political leaders that they lose the capacity to express a criticism.

Diane Negra pokes a related criticism at the likes of Jolie and the other transnational adopters: "The celebrity-driven 'family values' representational regime suggests that forms of social, racial, class, and even international inequality can be resolved through the assembling of families" (2010: 60). Instead, as Monbiot puts it, "They are lending legitimacy to power."

Most celebrities aren't interested in undermining the legitimacy of the political system. In fact, some commit themselves wholeheartedly to the system, preferring to work inside it. Arnold Schwarzenegger, for instance, gave up showbusiness to become Governor of California in 2003 (he later resumed his film career). Imran Khan, after a distinguished cricket career, founded his own political party and, in 2002, was elected to the National Assembly of Pakistan. There are many more figures who migrate from spheres ordinarily associated with amusement or agreeable distraction to the serious world of politics, tempted, we assume, by the prospect of using their celebrity status to practical effect. Unlike Bono and other celebrities who avoid formal politics, they must convince everyone, not just political leaders. A rock star with his heart in the right place, a seriousness of purpose, a sense of mission, and a crusading approach to grand issues typically has the respect of millions. But can he represent them? As Ted Johnson writes: "Entertainment figures who run for office not only have to persuade the public that they are serious, but that they should be taken seriously" (2011: 4).

Several have pulled off the feat, the most conspicuously successful being Ronald Reagan (1911–2004), who was a middling Hollywood actor before entering politics, serving as governor of California, 1967–74. He was elected president of the USA and occupied that office 1981–89. His early career obviously assisted his initial foray into politics, though Reagan could hardly be accused of capitalizing on his status: he ran for presidential election 15 years after his last picture, which was released in 1964. While he appeared in a 1965 tv series, any impetus he gained from his celebrity status soon dissipated.

> *Politics has become indistinguishable from ordinary entertainment.*

Sonny Bono (1935–98), former partner of Cher, gave up singing to become a Republican mayor of Palm Springs, California; he served in the US House of Representatives till his death in 1998. Jesse Ventura (b. 1951), once known in professional wrestling as "The Body," was governor of Minnesota, 1999–2002. Britain's Glenda Jackson (b. 1936) appeared opposite George Segal in 1973's *A Touch of Class* and Walter Matthau in 1978's *House Calls* before becoming a Labour Member of Parliament (MP). Sebastian Coe went into politics after a glittering track career: from 1992, he was a full-time MP, but failed to win re-election in 1997; he remained in the Conservative Party.

The evidence offered by these and other popular figures seems to be that being known as an entertainer is an advantage in politics. At least for the most part: a reality tv star or someone best known for being funny or for their superficiality would meet with resistance. The above-mentioned Ventura was a popular, flamboyant wrestler on television. Yet he was able to convince voters that he didn't just flex his muscles and bounce opponents around, or out of, the ring; he could think too. He was what Ann Conley and David Schultz call a "politainer" – "simultaneously an entertainer and a politician" – and this helped him bridge a credibility gap. "The public is willing to leave its critical facilities at the door," write Conley and Schultz. "The politainer becomes a commodity like Coke or Snicker's [sic] bars" (2000: 49).

Conley and Schultz argue that politics has incorporated revisions to both style and substance to the point where it has become indistinguishable from ordinary entertainment: "One result of the merger of politics and entertainment is that the impression people now have of public officials is framed more by jokes and less by their stances on the issues" (2000: 57).

"Politics is now thought of as entertainment," confirm Conley and Schultz. Politicians have to entertain as well as lead and govern. Celebrities who are accustomed to amusing audiences have a distinct advantage, boosted even more by the willingness of citizens to tolerate a lack of substance that would be too much to bear in other politicians. Matt Bai and David Brauer have also used Ventura's venture into politics (he was elected mayor of Brooklyn Park, Minnesota in 1991, then Governor of Minnesota in 1999) as an occasion to analyze the changes in the political climate of the 1990s: "When voters everywhere seemed weary of politics-as-usual, the wrestler turned radio personality became the ultimate symbol of revolt" (1998: 38).

The implication of their argument is that politicians of all stripes seemed to be replicating themselves: what might once have been major party divisions were being seen by voters as minor differences of opinion. We could add to this a growing perception that politicians are unscrupulous, dishonorable, unprincipled, immoral, frequently corrupt, usually debauched, and always ready to prioritize their own welfare and interests over those of the people they are meant to represent.

Then a white knight arrives on horseback, clad in a suit of shining armor, boasting a devotion to the service of people, and displaying a chivalrous spirit of adventure – all useful credentials in a world where politicians are typically regarded as self-serving hypocrites At least, that's how West and Orman make sense of the of politically inexperienced celebrities who ride into politics. Like knights, celebrities have rank or honor conferred on them as a reward for personal merit or services outside politics. In this sense, they haven't been smeared. Often, they have enough means to be above the corrupting influences that pervade politics. And, importantly, they have credibility: why would someone want to trade in a glamorous and lucrative lifestyle for something as prosaic as public duty if not out of a sense of service? But, perhaps even more importantly than this, they have recognizability: their image is known prior to their entry into politics. This saves a good deal of painstaking work and money, trying to establish a politician in the public consciousness.

BILL CLINTON AND THAT WOMAN

"The camera never lies." It's a well-known saying, though not a very reliable one. Since the famous televised John F. Kennedy–Richard M. Nixon presidential debates of 1960, there has been little doubt that the camera can overwhelm truth. Nixon held his own in the discussions and the majority of those who listened to the debates on radio believed he came out on top. But, on tv, his ghostly pallor and jowly cheeks made him appear a less attractive candidate than his fresh-faced opponent, who emerged triumphant in the election. At the time of the Kennedy–Nixon debates, the printed medium was the most credible source of news. Despite its domestic growth over the previous decade, television was still something of a novelty and lacked the punch of newspapers and journals. We have since grown evermore reliant on television for our political information, as we have for all kinds of information.

Kennedy was the first modern politician to realize the potential of television in politics. Gil Troy argues that he showed that the supposed polarity between commander-in-chief and celebrity-in-chief is a false one. Presidents are policy-makers, she argues; but, since JFK, they have to be "popular figures" too (1998).

By the early 1990s, all remnants of solemnity and somberness had been obliterated as if by the touch of a remote control button. Television's mandate to entertain, divert, and amuse and its accent on the image over the word contrived to turn televised politics into a form of pleasure. "Our politics becomes synonymous with advertising," propounded Lewis H. Lapham in 1993. "The inanity of the American political debate follows from the reduction of the words to wands with which to perform the rituals of omnipotence" (1993: 21). He meant that politicians were releasing less and less information and assuming more and more power to effect changes in a way a fairy godmother waves her wand and grants a mortal's wishes. Lapham probably had a conjuror's wand in mind: it adds a theatrical flourish to the sleight of hand. On Lapham's account, television's notional truthfulness can give credence to the impossible and unbelievable; and that's what politics is about.

Since Lapham's diatribe, politics has become, if anything, more like advertising. And advertising has become more like other forms of entertainment: slick, diverting, often amusing and sometimes even gratifying. Television could be blamed; but, as Kamons points out: "A politician's ability to take advantage of innovations in media has long been central to his or her electoral success" (2007: 145). So only the ones we have forgotten about are likely to have ignored the potential of the media. The politicians who have made most impression have, like JFK in 1960, made use of the media.

Kamons then raises the interesting question: "Why settle for politicians who attempt to emulate celebrities when one can have the celebrities themselves?" (2007: 145). The answer has two parts. First, only a handful of nonpolitico entertainers risk a full-tilt Schwarzeneggerian move into politics, most preferring sniping from long range, Bono-style. Second, politicians may once, as Kamons notes, have emulated celebrities; but, since the ascendancy of Bill Clinton in 1992, politicians don't emulate, imitate, or reproduce the style and manner of celebrities: they are celebrities in their own right.

Clinton (b. 1946) is a liminal figure, occupying a position on both sides of the celebrity divide: he had a successful political career as governor of Arkansas, 1979–81 and 1983–93, before becoming president. Clinton cut a beguiling figure en route to the presidency: telegenic and good-looking, he also had the sheen of authenticity, appearing natural and relaxed on television. "Clinton drew upon forms of self-presentation developed in the entertainment industries," maintains David Hesmondhalgh. "He studied the way in which television performers established a rapport with their audiences" (2005: 131).

Hesmondhalgh cites in particular the way in which music videos on cable and satellite tv channels had enabled performers to establish a new kind of rapport with viewing audiences. Perhaps more significantly, we should add the changes in presentational style occasioned by the 24-hour news stations with their fast-paced audio-visual economy that rarely tested the patience of viewers.

Clinton arrived at the White House in 1993 in the middle of a media revolution, with cable television providing a 24-hour news cycle. His arrival also coincided with a voyeurism diffusing through the population: consumers' interest in private lives practically commissioned the media's intrusive approach and obliged even presidents to expose themselves. On one memorable occasion in 1992, Clinton donned Ray-Bans and played saxophone on a late-night talk show. Yet there was more celebrity to Clinton than anyone dared to imagine and, in 1998, he became the central figure of a scandal bigger than anything dreamed up by Madonna.

There was a stunning moment shortly after the scandal broke when Clinton appeared on national television and affirmed: "I did not have sexual relations with that woman." That woman was Monica Lewinsky, White House aide, and her account of her relationship with the president was somewhat different. The US president is always a figure of great interest by virtue of his position (there's never been a female president), and this and the several other allegations of sexual peccadilloes that followed marked Clinton out as someone worthy of even greater interest.

Clinton was the US president for two terms of office and, for a while, under threat of impeachment. So the scandal could have had wider-reaching repercussions than it actually did. And the fact that Lewinsky actually worked in politics gave it added relevance. As the concupiscent details of the case unfurled – the semen-stained dress, the cigar, the secretly recorded phone conversations – interest built and, for the final two years of the twentieth century, Lewinsky was one of the most famous women in the world. Her celebrity status manifested in several books about her, an assortment of well-paid endorsement deals, her own line of accessories, and a reality tv program in which she featured. She then faded from view.

Did the affair hurt Clinton? He had narrowly avoided a controversy about his wilder years as a student, when he issued his famous "I did not inhale" statement about his supposed marijuana smoking. The Lewinsky denial could have undermined his credibility. "Both comments damaged Clinton's presidency, because they suggested an untrustworthy, slippery leader," reasons Chris Rojek (2012: 81).

In December 1998, within months of the denial, Clinton achieved his career-highest approval rating of 73. His average approval rating during his term of office was 55.1, below JFK, but above Reagan, Jimmy Carter, and George W. Bush, among others. He enjoyed a consistently high approval rating among the "baby boomer" generation (those born in the immediate post-Second World War period). An experts' poll in 2011 placed Clinton at 19 in the all-time list of presidents. So either Rojek is wide of the mark, or honesty was no longer part of the presidential job description.

> *Clinton brought a sense of showmanship and his occasional peccadillos only intensified the drama of his presidency.*

Clinton remained as president till 2001, when he left office after serving his complete second term. He also acquired a status distinct from that of other politicians who leave legacies. Clinton could have been remembered for bringing together Israel's Yitzhak Rabin and Yasser Arafat of the Palestine Liberation Front on the White House lawn in 1993, or signing the 1994 Kremlin Accords that stopped the preprogrammed nuclear missiles, or organizing peace talks for Bosnia and Herzegovina in 1995, or ordering cruise missile strikes on Afghanistan in 1998. He could also be remembered as the first president to have solicited the public's favor in spite of deeds that would have damned politicians from earlier eras.

Clinton, though, was a politician for the celebrity era. Squeaky-clean politicians whose worst vice was an extra-marital fling were, by the 1990s, remnants of another age. Compare his experience with that of former civil-rights leader and Washington, DC mayor Marion Barry, who, in 1990, was convicted of cocaine possession. A female friend had lured him into a police sting: at their assignation, hidden cameras captured him smoking crack. During his six-week trial, accounts of his sex and drug binges, backed by evidence from pimps and pushers, were relayed to homes via television. He served six months in jail, but, two months after his release, he returned to the city council and, within three years, was reelected mayor. In another sex-related case, New York governor Eliot Spitzer resigned after being implicated in a federal investigation into inter-state prostitution in 2008. He barely broke stride, returning in his own television show, his credibility intact.

John Edwards, a 2004 vice presidential candidate, had an affair with a woman while his wife was dying of cancer. This was scandal enough to blow him off course in his bid for president in 2007, but he would probably have navigated his way back had it not been for allegations that he masterminded a $1 million cover-up of his affair, misusing funds from two wealthy campaign donors. Substance abuse, carnal activities, and sundry other deviant behaviors are, it seems, forgivable; in a way, they humanize a politician, exposing a few of the kinds of flaws all of us possess.

Clinton sailed close to the wind; but it blew in his favor. The political culture in which he prospered had lost the stiffness and propriety of earlier eras and his sexual misconduct was not thought unpardonable. Clinton brought a sense of showmanship and his occasional peccadillos only intensified the drama of his presidency. Even in the midst of the Lewinsky scandal, he battled on like a rock star in his fifties, determined to show his audience he had a few good songs in him. Clinton may not have been the greatest president, but he was surely the most consumable and, as if to prove this, he still tours the world, giving guest lectures, signing copies of his own books, receiving invitations to do spots on tv shows, and doing what celebrities do – appear.

|FROM CHALLENGE TO AMUSEMENT

The year before Clinton began his presidency, Carl Bernstein issued a stinging rebuke to the media and the political system. "The America rendered today in the American media is illusionary and delusionary – disfigured, unreal, disconnected from the true context of our lives," wrote Bernstein, who, 20 years earlier, with fellow journalist Bob Woodward, had initiated an investigation that culminated in the resignation of President Richard Nixon in 1974. Briefly: Nixon and his campaign staff had funded and approved break-ins and illegal surveillance of his political rivals, the Democrat Party, in the Watergate building in Washington, DC.

With Clinton smoothly negotiating his passage to the White House, Bernstein claimed the media had abandoned its critical approach to politics:

> The coverage is distorted by celebrity and the worship of celebrity; by the reduction of news to gossip, which is the lowest form of news; by sensationalism, which is always a turning away from a society's real condition; and by a political and social discourse that we – the press, the media, the politicians, and the people – are turning into a sewer.
>
> (1992: 22)

This was six years *before* the Lewinsky affair, remember.

Bernstein's prescription was simple: "It is the role of journalists to challenge people, not merely to amuse them." Maybe it *was*. But the media has played a crucial role not simply in reporting political events, but in structuring how those events appear and interpreting what they mean for longer than Bernstein assumed. Gail Collins, for example, documents how the media's appetite for prurient political gossip has been around since the 1800s (2007). And Lauren Langman reveals that, in the 1930s, both Hitler and Roosevelt had sensed the potential of radio and film to disseminate not only political information, but also images, especially images of great spectacles, such as rallies and marches, all faithfully covered by the media (2002).

Langman adds: "With the growth of consumerism after WWII, aided and abetted by television, it would not be long until 'telepolitics' as a marketing strategy would join with consumerism as a means of 'selling' dreams, desires, and self-hood" (2002: 517).

The title of Neil Postman's book, *Amusing Ourselves to Death,* captures the self-destructive process he believes the medium, or rather our fixation with it, brought about (1985). Whereas, once, populations would have flocked to meetings to watch, listen, and ask questions of politicians for anything up to four hours, they now grow impatient after a couple of minutes of watching tv. Even if Bernstein would not have accepted Postman's overall theory, he would have acknowledged that television had pushed politics toward entertainment. And that the rest of the media then responded in kind. One implication of this is that the credibility once reserved for printed media had dissipated by the early 1990s. On these accounts, the softening of political news is a process with an ancestry, rather than something that sprang out of the post-Watergate period; though there is evidence of significant gear change in that period.

Kathy Koch asked, in the title of her article, "Can the media regain the public's trust?" (1998). As part of her answer, she uncovered "the roots of newspapers' obsession with soft news," which, she argued, lay in two research projects of the late 1970s. One concluded that people read newspapers primarily for hard news, while the other, led by focus group researcher Ruth Clark, found that readers favored lifestyle stories. This was the 1970s, remember.

Clark's conclusions were tempered by the study's subjects' realization that the media had responsibilities to inform and educate as well as to entertain, though this tended to be overlooked. "Predictably, perhaps, newspaper editors across the country embraced Clark's study," Koch reported. Politics started to give way to lifestyle. If any medium epitomized this move, it was *USA Today*, a national (and later international) newspaper launched in 1982, incorporating colorful graphics and relatively short (500-word) stories with lots of entertainment news and little reporting on government or world politics. In a decade in which economic downturn affected most of the corporate sectors, including the media, the paper consistently turned a profit. It convinced its proprietors, Gannett Publishing, that it had hit on a successful formula.

Citizens are increasingly treated as fans.
TIMOTHY C. WEISKEL

The tabloids specializing in scandal were adversely affected around this time. Koch reckons that, during the 1980s, when independent and family-owned publications were taken over by large corporations, managers and proprietors started to take note of *USA Today*'s commercial success. Hard political news was either reduced or written in a personalized way. Politicians, their partners, or even their extramarital lovers became the foci of political news, which was why, as Leo Braudy put it: "Everybody from the *New York Times* down starts a story – even one about ideas or policies – with an anecdote of some sorts" (quoted in Neimark 1995. I suspect Braudy might disapprove of this book too).

A parallel tendency has been for political systems to supply politicians who are ideologically indistinguishable and who are projected as much as entertainers as political leaders. How often have we heard politicians described as "boring," as if this was a heinous sin? The effort to produce aesthetically acceptable candidates whose ideas are subordinated to other, cosmetic considerations has brought what W. Russell Neuman calls "excessive sameness" in all politicians served up by television (2002). As we are only "partially attentive" when viewing and listening to them, eye-catching characteristics or memorable catchphrases linger in the mind of an audience that has become accustomed to passivity. Such characteristics and catchphrases come easily to some politicians, especially those versed in working the media. "The economy, stupid," for example, is from Bill Clinton's 1992 presidential campaign.

You don't have to be a historical revisionist to suspect some sort of political pandering – by which I mean indulging the electorate – has been going on since the start of what used to be called the mass media, the *mass* in this instance meaning a large number of ordinary people who could afford a few pennies for a newspaper. No newspaper or, for that matter, radio or tv station, let alone website, ever gave the masses neutral, factual, undiluted political reportage; journalistic style has always intruded in some way. But it would be heedless not to recognize a change-up in the 1990s. "A politically obsequious press and a movie-loving public," as Timothy C. Weiskel calls the coupling, introduced a "politics of distraction" (2005: 393).

Weiskel shares much the same view as Bernstein, Langman, and the other critics who see the replacement of serious politics by a part-amusement, part-therapy, part-soporific activity enthusiastically covered by a samey, anodyne media. He argues that the corporate media convergence facilitated by the Reagan administration, 1981–89, changed "the news profession of journalism" into an industry: "This industry has been purchased by and is now operated as a fully owned subsidiary of the entertainment business" (2005: 403).

Global corporations, such as Disney, Viacom, and Time Warner, wield control over the entertainment as well as news media, and, according to Weiskel, represented what used to be hard news (politics, foreign affairs, finance, and other serious topics) as a "sideshow" that distracts rather than concentrates attention. "Citizens are increasingly treated as fans," writes Weiskel.

Tim Barney agrees: "What the trend toward celebrity and spectacle has done is level the news to the style and interest of the market-driven media in search of audience share" (2001: 2336). Barney concludes: "It has contributed to our distrust of politics." Maybe feeling we can't rely on politicians or even the institution of politics complements feeling that they are meant to entertain, not just govern.

OBAMA: NOT *LIKE* A CELEBRITY |

> The things that matter to people: jobs and gas prices and how we
> bring down the deficit, how do we deal with the changes going on
> in the world? We can't be distracted by sideshows and, as I said at
> my press conference, carnival barkers, who are going around trying
> to get attention.

Barack Obama was talking to Oprah Winfrey, in May 2011. Oprah seemed to agree, inviting him to widen his argument: "Do you think that there's a disconnection in general in terms of sideshows and carnival barkers?" she asked, extending his analogy for the gossip media. (A carnival barker is someone who stood at the entrance of the traveling entertainment shows that were popular in the nineteenth century, loudly announcing the offerings to the crowds.) Obama replied: "The line between entertainment and politics has blurred and so reality tv is seeping into how we think about our politics."

> *To call Oprah's approval an endorsement is like calling*
> *the Sistine Chapel a church.*

It was meant as a criticism, or at least a sardonic reflection. Yet the president of the United States was speaking not at a press briefing or in the context of a presidential address, but on *Oprah*, the highest-rated television talk show in history, a show that at its peak pulled in 42 million viewers and, even in its final stages, drew six million. It was syndicated to over 140 countries around the world. Obama may have understood the irony of his pronouncement, but it didn't seem that way. All the same, it was a breathtakingly impudent remark to make on one of the world's foremost citadels of mass entertainment.

The absorption of politics into celebrity culture was well advanced by the time of Obama's ascent, though no politician had assimilated the obligations and prerogatives as decisively as Obama. When, in 2010, Jeffrey C. Alexander wrote, "Obama is not like a celebrity, he is one," he was reiterating what everyone had known for at least three years (2010: 414). That was when Oprah Winfrey, a friend of the then emerging Illinois senator, affirmed her support for his presidential candidacy. It was the first time that Oprah had endorsed – not to mention thrown her brand behind – a political candidate. By fall 2007, she had helped raise $3 million for the campaign. Endorsements didn't guarantee votes, of course: at the time *USA Today* reported: "More than six in 10 adults say endorsements aren't that important in deciding whom they'll support for president" (October 22, 2007).

We might supplement this with the results of research by an English research team. "Celebrity endorsements can be effective in driving voter intention if politics is not salient for the eligible voter," concluded Ekant Veer *et al*. "If the voter is . . . actively thinking of politics and political issues the effect of the celebrity endorsement is negated" (2008: 445).

Even so, to call Oprah's approval an endorsement is like calling the Sistine Chapel a church – true, but hardly evocative. Few celebrities had as much authority as Oprah: she could turn a book into a bestseller just by mentioning it, or send stocks plunging by changing her diet (in 1996, she said she'd stopped eating burgers and the cattle-feeding industry lost an estimated $87.6 million in days). Oprah's was probably the most valuable political endorsement in history. It effectively validated Obama's celebrity status.

Obama's presence in social media enhanced that status. A 19 million Twitter following ensured daily contact, and demonstrated his understanding that the days when politicians gave only limited accessibility to the media and the electorate were gone. Like other celebrities, they were available for public consumption.

Obama was probably not so different from other twenty-first-century politicians: they all sell wares, by which I mean goods, articles, services, and commodities, even if they are designed and packaged as ideas, policies, programs, and the other staples in which they trade. Often, their most valuable wares are their personae, those aspects of their character that are presented and perceived by others. In 2008, Obama was selling a new configuration, an arrangement of familiar elements in an unfamiliar form: a black politician who defied the usual color-coding; who had interests in housing, education, crime, transportation, and the economy as they affect everybody; who refused to address the African American population as a homogeneous entity with unchanging interests; who hadn't risen from the pulpit, earned his stripes in the struggles of the 1960s, and purported to speak for all black people.

It was a novel and, in the event, appealing persona, though one that earned him critics. Of them, Christopher Hedges was one of most scathing. Writing not so much a critique as a dismissal in the Jewish magazine *Tikkun*, Hedges proclaimed: "Brand Obama is about being happy consumers. We are entertained. We feel hopeful" (2010: 33).

Considered against the background of the merging spheres of politics and entertainment, this doesn't sound so severe. But there is more. "Like all branded products spun out from the manipulative world of corporate advertising," writes Hedges. A brand is, of course, a type of product, manufactured for a market under a specific name. "This product is duping us into doing and supporting a lot of things that are not in our interest." Leaving aside for the moment what Hedges assumes is in "our" (though I presume he means either all his readers', or, more probably, everyone's) interest, there is a rational argument underlying the bluster. It is: "Brand Obama offers us an image that appears radically individualistic and new. It inoculates us from seeing that the old engines of corporate power and the vast military-industrial complex continue to plunder the country" (2010: 33).

There are, of course, other critiques, though the one advanced by Hedges is pertinent to the present discussion: he realizes that Obama was a by-the-numbers politician who produced a masterwork. As Ruth Conniff wrote in 2008: "Obama's opponents have used charges of identity politics and celebrity worship to tar him. But no one is really immune" (2008: 22). Identity politics refers to the tendency of people of a particular ethnicity, religion, social class, and so on to form political alliances, moving away from traditional party politics. You know what celebrity worship means. Conniff thinks every politician is liable to be infected (if we use her biological metaphor), suggesting that the whole environment is now contaminated by the values of entertainment.

| IN THE REALM OF ENTERTAINMENT

The logic shared by all politicians dictates that they entertain as well as inform electorates. If they don't, they perish – or are slaughtered by a media that subscribes to a compatible logic. But is the association between entertainment with distraction and passivity valid? In the context of his discussion of contemporary political interviewers, Michael Higgins observes how television programs with a political focus "resituate political style within the realm of entertainment rather than refashion conventional entertainment to cover issues of politics" (2010: 104). Television has not changed format or style to accommodate political discourses; for example, by screening open hall meetings, speeches, or other traditional forms of public address. Instead, political discourse has been fitted into the context of television, with one-to-one interviews, debates, and forums taking place in floor-managed studios and within specific times.

Celebrity culture has done to politics what Starbucks has done to coffee.

Obvious? Of course; that's the point. Consumers are habituated to certain presentational styles, and politicians who either can't or won't adjust to the exigencies of the media will simply appear anachronistic or unaccommodating. One of the implications of Higgins' point is that entertainment values do not necessarily threaten the integrity or rectitude of politicians; only the naive would assume there was a plenitude of these qualities among politicians at any time in history. Nor do they interfere with consumers' access. Higgins provides an example of British Prime Minister Tony Blair (b. 1953) who, during his tenure as Prime Minister, 1997–2007, resisted formal interviews wherever possible and opted for "softer chat-show formats."

The manner of his disclosures was certainly congruent with the times; whether consumers learned anything more, or seriously less, about Blair as a result is open to conjecture. And it is destined to remain open to conjecture.

Choreographed interviews and stage-managed debates are now familiar features of the political landscape; presentations are sometimes bravura, other times bungling. But they are usually entertaining. Celebrity culture has done to politics what Starbucks has done to coffee. It lacks variety, but is quickly prepared and easy to consume. And it is branded.

I opened this chapter by reminding readers about the intrusions of celebrities into areas that might be considered none of their business. And I'm closing it with a reminder about the reverse effect: the penetration of showbiz values into politics. As we've seen in previous chapters, we can no more understand celebrity culture without the media than make omelets without eggs. Politics is, by definition, a public sphere. Yet perhaps never quite as public as it is today. As well as being able to relay news instantly from every part of the world to every part of the world, the media enables viewers to scrutinize their political leaders to an extent unheard of as recently as the 1990s. The surveillance carried out by new media is more invasive and perhaps more meddling than ever. Celebrity culture itself is, in some senses, an accommodation of this, celebrities surrendering any trace of a private life in exchange for publicity. Politicians too have had to strike that bargain. They play by the same rules as all other celebrities.

SPORTS

THE NEW SEX|

Maria Sharapova, Katy Perry, LeBron James, George Clooney, David Beckham, Jay-Z. Today, we tend to think of top athletes in the same way as singers, actors, and other popular entertainers. Certainly, their earnings and status are on a par with fellow celebrities. They are among the most visible people in the world. Forty years ago, it would have been an insult to call a boxer or a football player a celebrity. Athletes were not trying to entertain spectators: they were trying to win contests in competitive environments. What entertainment ensued was a byproduct in the sense that fans enjoyed watching. But to compare athletes with singers, actors, or – perish the thought – supermodels would have been borderline defamatory.

Rubbing shoulders with Hollywood stars or pop singers was strictly for athletes whose aspirations extended beyond sport.

When he was still known as Cassius Clay, Muhammad Ali famously met the Beatles in 1964. Ali, probably more than any other athlete in history, was conscious of his persona: "The Beatles wanted *my* autograph," he once declared. Ali was a singular athlete; in his (and possibly any other) time, unique.

A couple of Ali's contemporaries, Joe Namath (b. 1943), of the New York Jets, and George Best (1946–2005), of Manchester United and other clubs, were playboy athletes in the 1960s. Indistinguishable from popstars in appearance, Namath and Best led uncannily parallel, indulgent lives of excessive drinking and prodigious womanizing. They were square pegs in round holes. Today, their exploits would be expected from well-paid celebrity athletes with hedonistic inclinations. The 1960s contrived a different environment, one in which sportsmen played sport and reporters reported how they performed on the field, rather than in bars and clubs.

It was a half-century ago, though it seems as far away as Charles Dickens' London. Now it seems any athlete with a recognized level of proficiency is competing on and off the sports field: for spots on tv shows, a newspaper column, and, of course, lucrative endorsement contracts, which may be a crude but serviceable index of celebrity status. Endorsements also offer a recording device for the changes in rank, standing, or stature of prominent athletes. Another index is a signature eau de cologne.

Anyone with a degree of visibility in or out of sports is sure to be offered the opportunity to lend their name and image to a product or two. What was once a supplementary stipend is now the main source of the highest-earning athletes' income. Salaries, prize monies, and match fees are now the bonus payments: advertising brings in the serious money. The top six earners in sports derive, on average, 80 percent of their money from advertising, or related marketing activities, such as licensing their names. Nine of out every ten dollars Tiger Woods earned during his peak years came from endorsements (including a few cents from his fragrance, of course). Same with Phil Mickelson, the golfer. Roger Federer also had a remunerative endorsement portfolio, with nine companies, including Nike, Rolex, Mercedes-Benz, and Credit Suisse, collectively paying him more than $30 million (£22m) annually. Federer also has his own fragrance.

Like other familiar celebrities known for something other than contemptibly shameful conduct, the sportsmen had advertisers chasing them. When Woods was disgraced, some advertisers with which he had contracts invoked an escape clause, while others, including Nike, stuck with him. But, before the 1980s, conformity to conventionally accepted standards of behavior or morals was a necessary condition for anyone in the public view with an interest in earning a little extra from advertising. In the mid-twentieth century, homosexuality was regarded as transgressive and any form of impropriety was given a wide berth. Being gay would have nullified any chance Rock Hudson (1925–85) had of securing endorsements and, for that matter, any leading film part. In fact, Hudson's sexual orientation was a tightly held secret for most of his career, permitting him to advertise cigarettes. He died of an Aids-related illness. Gregory Peck and Claudette Colbert were among the many other Hollywood stars who advertised products. Soft and alcoholic drinks were also keen on actors providing their advertising with a personal focus. Unlike the rock stars of the mid-twentieth century, they were less liable to cross moral boundaries by getting into drugs or groupies. When they did, only the cognoscenti knew of their errant behavior: the Hollywood machine made sure of that.

Hollywood stars were perfect for advertising: in addition to their conspicuousness, they had glamour. This made them models for aspirational consumers. As Nigel Thrift states: "The glamorous persona is often associated with high-end fashion. It involves a combination of sex appeal, luxury, celebrity, and wealth" (2008: 18).

Lack of glamour wouldn't have deterred advertisers of beer, razors, and certain brands of cigarettes with blue-collar sensibility – in other words, the kinds of products used by sports fans. A product like General Mills' breakfast cereal Wheaties had a potential market that spanned many demographics. Over the years, its advertising agency contracted all manner of sportsmen and, actually, women – Babe Didrikson (1914–56) and Mary Lou Retton, for example – for its publicity and marketing. Sam Snead (1912–2002), Jack Dempsey (1895–1983), and Johnny Weissmuller (1904–84) all had Wheaties contracts, as did Joe DiMaggio (1914–99), who almost became glamorous by association when he married Marilyn Monroe in 1954 (the marriage lasted 274 days, probably making him seem even more glamorous).

Timex watches discovered a market among sports fans: the company ran ads featuring, among others, heavyweight boxing champion Rocky Marciano (1923–69) and Mickey Mantle (1931–95), the New York Yankees player. Wristwatches have a kind of sports aesthetic. British cricketer and football player Denis Compton (1918–97) fronted a campaign for Brylcreem hair products, also endorsed in the 1990s by David Beckham. While it sounds odd today, golfer Ben Hogan (1912–97) was a pitchman for cigarettes as well as golf equipment.

But notice what all the notable sports stars mentioned so far have in common: they were, or are, white. African American heavyweight champion Joe Louis (1914–81) featured in cigarette ads and promoted Buick cars: in defeating the German boxer Max Schmeling in 1938, Louis prefigured the Allies' victory over Nazism and hence became a nationalistic symbol. Jackie Robinson (1919–72) endorsed a soft drink called Cremo in the 1940s. Robinson was the first black player in the major leagues. They were exceptional athletes, but figures of social significance too, which is probably why they were able to attract advertisers. But few African American entertainers and athletes had advertising deals. Black people were overrepresented among the lowest socio-economic classes and, as such, had limited disposable income. It was not until the 1980s that advertisers woke up to the prospect of a newly affluent black bourgeoisie that could be turned into a promising market for consumer goods.

"The essence of an endorsement strategy consists of creating an emotional tie between the consumer and the athletes, thus increasing both brand and product awareness and improving the image of the company," write George Stone *et al.* (2003: 95–100). It's a naive way of interpreting endorsements: the "essence" is not so much to create a so-called "emotional tie" as to induce consumers to buy products. But the second point about "improving the image of the company" is worth considering: the very nature of sports made it prohibitive. Titles were lost as well as won, competitors turned from heroes to villains, the vicissitudes of competition made athletes unreliable endorsers.

And then something happened: sports replaced sex. At least according to Donald Katz, who reflects that, in the early 1990s: "Sports had arguably surpassed popular music as the captivating medium most essential to being perceived as 'young and alive.'" Katz goes further: "Sports, as never before, had so completely permeated the logic of the marketplace in consumer goods that by 1992 the psychological content of selling was often more sports-oriented than it was sexual" (1994: 25–6).

I presume Katz means that the set of principles underlying and guiding sports began to inform advertising and marketing: clean, wholesome, rule-governed competition; healthy, young, likeminded individuals dedicated to the pursuit of excellence through hard work, honest endeavor, and an insatiable appetite for success; a lifestyle conducive to the promotion of good health and moral wellbeing. Sports appeared a positive force. About that, everyone was agreed. So why not use the consensus to sell stuff? The products need not have any genuine connection with sports; that's where the creativity of advertising enters: linking products as diverse as deodorants, alcoholic beverages, and cars with sports. Advertisers can forge these kinds of links in their sleep. Remind yourself of this when you next notice a sports figure advertising a product. Ask: what has this product got to do with sports?

> **Would a major car company want its commercials voiced over by an actor who had been imprisoned for drugs violations?**

Katz may be right, though he doesn't explain why sports figures and the connotations they brought to advertising became so popular at the turn of the 1990s. One reason was that the tried-and-tested Hollywood stars were becoming less reliable. Elizabeth Taylor had serenely navigated a passage through the waters roiled by her *affaire de coeur* in the early 1960s. She endorsed chocolates, shampoo, soap, and a range of Elizabeth Arden fragrances. Her contemporary Jane Fonda (b. 1937, Taylor was born 1932) had a different kind of scandal when, in 1972, she visited Hanoi, Vietnam, during the midst of the Vietnam War. In addition to being photographed on a North Vietnamese anti-aircraft battery, she later called returning prisoners of war liars for claiming they had been starved, tortured, and brainwashed. Advertisers steered clear, though, in the 1980s, she became the symbol of fitness culture and, in the 2000s, endorsed L'Oréal products, suggesting a total rehabilitation of image.

Scandals were never alluring to advertisers, especially if they involved sex or politics. Drugs scandals were not prevalent enough to make much difference. Robert Mitchum's minor scrape in 1948 was hushed up. But, by the 1980s, there were warning signs. John Belushi died in 1982 at the age of 33 after shooting up a speedball of cocaine and heroin. Dennis Quaid made his addiction to cocaine in the 1980s known, revealing that the drug was widely used in the film industry. Robert Downey Jr. was another actor with drug dependency: he was arrested on several occasions in the 1990s. In 1989, Rob Lowe, then 25, was at the center of a sex tape scandal involving two teenage women, one of whom was 16 and so underage. There were other cases that escaped the formerly reliable machine, suggesting that either more stars were engaging in deviant behavior, or, more likely, that Hollywood could no longer suppress stories of such behavior reaching the light of day. Either way, advertisers were wary: would a major car company want its commercials voiced over by a recognizable actor who had been imprisoned for drugs violations? (Actually, a rehabilitated Downey, in 2010, signed with Nissan to voice its Leaf commercials.)

With Hollywood actors losing their previously unquestioned dependability, advertisers were obliged to exercise more caution in their choice of endorsers. They could have turned to narrative-driven ads, but publicly known figures were especially effective in a market that was rapidly segmenting and difficult to target. Hollywood stars were well known to all, particularly the most desirable 18–49-year-old white demographic. Think back to Chapter 8, in which I picked out the qualities that make some figures effective endorsers: consumers need to identify with them, in the sense that they can recognize and associate closely with the person, and believe they share characteristics with that person, or at least what they know of the person. But they also have to attribute credibility to that person. In other words, the endorser has to be capable of persuading consumers that something is a good thing. So advertisers searched for people consumers would trust.

Sports figures were not perfectly trustworthy. In 1988, Ben Johnson was sent home from the Seoul Olympic Games after winning the 100 meters in record time, but then failing a dope test. It was, at the time, the greatest scandal in sports history and cast a shadow across not simply track, but the entire sports landscape. Six years later, the figure skater Nancy Kerrigan was physically attacked by the ex-husband and bodyguard of one of her Olympic rivals, Tonia Harding. Between the two cases, there was the Tyson rape trial. No one could have believed sport was inhabited by doe-eyed innocents capable only of acts of heroism. But Johnson and the other miscreants were dramatically anomalous characters who made headlines around the world. In sports terms, they were Other: figures who were distinct from, or opposite to, sports competitors. Their distinctness served as a reminder of what sports *was not*. Johnson, in particular, was depicted as a model of everything iniquitous, depraved, and degenerate in sports. So who was the model of everything admirable, praiseworthy, virtuous, and excellent?

|MICHAEL JORDAN IN "A DRUG-INFESTED, TOO-BLACK LEAGUE"

Nike has, for decades, been a purveyor of easy-on-the-conscience representations of the black urban experience to the middle-brow masses. In 1985, after eight years of steady growth and increasing profits, the sports goods company reported two consecutive losing quarters. Competitors, such as adidas, Puma, and, especially, Reebok, were taking advantage of the enthusiasm for aerobics, which Nike had missed. Nike's marketing strategy was to use established sports figures to endorse its products. So, when it signed Michael Jordan, there was a risk: he was, like the majority of other NBA players, black and, at that stage, unproven in the pro ranks. The NBA itself had an image problem: it was widely regarded as, to quote the *Los Angeles Times Magazine* writer Edward Kiersh, "a drug-infested, too-black league." Its players were, to use Tyrone R. Simpson's arresting phrase, "excessively libidinal, terminally criminal, and socially infernal" (1992: 7).

This had commercial implications summed up by Kiersh: "Sponsors felt the NBA and its black stars had little value in pitching colas and cornflakes to Middle America."

Nike used Jordan primarily as a sales instrument: his role was to move branded footwear and apparel.

David Halberstam points out that, in 1984, Nike had revenues of $919 million and a net income of about $40 million, and, by the end of 1997, the company's revenues were $9 billion, with a net income of around $800 million (1999: 412–13). Jordan had made about $130 million from Nike at that stage. In a 1998 issue of *Fortune* magazine, Roy Johnson analyzed what he called "The Jordan effect," meaning Jordan's impact on the overall US economy. The Air Jordan line was worth, in sales, $5.2 billion (about £3.2 billion). For that, you could buy Manchester United, the Dallas Cowboys, the New York Yankees, and still have enough change to snap up Jordan's own club from 1984 to 1998, the Chicago Bulls. But the overall value of Jordan-related sales over a 14-year period from 1984 was even more: $10 billion (£6.16bn). Johnson, almost inevitably, has his own fragrance.

The sales figures alone are impressive, but, in the marketing process, something more impressive happened: Jordan was presented as an "atypical Black figure," as David L. Andrews and Michael L. Silk call him, "distanced, from the discourses of irresponsibility, hypersexuality, deviance, unruliness, and brutish physicality routinely associated with African American males in general, and NBA players in particular" (2010: 1629).

Prominent black athletes had a reputation for being unpredictable. Magic Johnson (b. 1959), who played for the Lakers from 1979, was diagnosed HIV-positive shortly before being selected to play for the US basketball team that won a gold medal at the 1992 Olympic Games. Mike Tyson (b. 1966) won the first of his world titles in 1986; in 1992, he was convicted of rape. So, when Nike first signed up Jordan in 1984, there were questions. Would an African American with little profile beyond the NCAA (National Collegiate Athletic Association) and no experience in the pro ranks become popular enough to move sports shoes? Would he self-combust and wind up involved in some kind of shame-inducing episode? The answers were, of course: yes and no.

The NBA in the 1990s became a one-man show that other players were allowed to crash. Jordan was like air, or, I should say, Air: he was everywhere, all the time. There was no escape from his image, whether on tv, in movies, on cereal boxes, on posters, you name it. It was as if he was a palpable presence. All most people saw was a representation, usually in the context of advertising. Yet, there was a sense in which people not only liked him, but also felt they knew this crisply wholesome, indubitably clean-living, and utterly harmless dark-skinned, but not dark man.

Nowadays, commercial companies seem to be able to create salable celebrities by pushing buttons. But, in the late 1980s, there was no surefire way, and, given the historical suspicions about black sportsmen in general and the NBA in particular, Nike's contract was less an investment, more a gamble. But one that paid off, of course. "It was Nike's commercials that made Jordan a global superstar," Naomi Klein suspects (2001: 52). There had been other gifted athletes before Jordan, though none reached what Klein calls "Jordan's other-worldly level of fame."

> *Get the money, don't say anything substantial and, for heaven's sake, never offend white people.*
>
> *RASHEED Z. BAAITH*

Klein isn't questioning Jordan's basketball prowess. But, pre-Jordan, sports stars, no matter how good or great, were athletes who happened to do advertising. They weren't synonymous with a brand, as Jordan was. Nike changed all that: the company embarked on what Klein calls "mythmaking," creating an aura around Jordan. "Who said man wasn't meant to fly?" asked one of the early ads, showing the apparently gravity-defying Jordan. The other-worldliness translated smoothly into sales. So, while other figures, such as Jesus, Che Guevara, Marilyn Monroe, and Muhammad Ali were icons, none was manufactured as such. Jordan was. His iconic status was designed to sell Nike goods. But, somewhere in the manufacturing process, Jordan came to symbolize a new version of blackness, what Helán E. Page, in 1997, called "embraceable male blackness," something with which whites would feel safe.

"When we view black men in our media, their representations generally fall into two reductive, disparate categories," revealed Ed Guerrero in 1995 (by reductive, he means presented in a simplified form). "On the one hand, we are treated to the grand celebrity spectacle of black male athletes, movie stars, and pop entertainers . . . conspicuously enjoying the wealth and privilege that fuel the ordinary citizen's material fantasies." On the other, "we are also subjected to the real-time devastation, slaughter, and body count of a steady stream of faceless black males on the 6 and 11 o'clock news" (1995: 183).

Guerrero named Jordan, along with Michael Jackson and Bill Cosby, as personifications of the former category. Jackson had, in 1993, been accused of making "sexual offensive contacts" with a 13-year-old boy. Cosby was 58 when Guerrero wrote. Jordan, at 32, was a more apposite reflection of the "grand celebrity spectacle" category.

When Thomas Oates and Judy Polumbaum conclude, "Jordan was able to escape both the patronizing and demonizing extremes often associated with black athletes," they miss the point (2004: 196). He didn't "escape" them: he rendered them irrelevant. Here was a black man with none of the usual faults habitually associated with black men, in fact no faults at all. He didn't talk politics and his comments about the condition of black people were anodyne. Rasheed Z. Baaith condensed Jordan's philosophy thus: "Get the money, don't say anything substantial and, for heaven's sake, never offend white people" (2002: 8).

Nike didn't want Jordan to upset anybody. That was the whole point: his embraceable quality was intended to be good for all groups, male and female, black and white, old and young.

For Dylan A.T. Miner, Jordan, or rather the brand he personified, "represented the commodification of blackness to a globalizing marketplace" (2009: 92). At a time when black athletes predominated not just in basketball, but also in many other major sports, most of the recognizable faces were white. Black athletes were not typically inundated with endorsement offers; more usually they were regarded with suspicion. Jordan was a different type of black athlete.

No figure in history had moved so much merchandise as Jordan. While often described as an icon, it's worth remembering that icons are usually regarded as representative symbols of something: manhood, for example, or freedom, or a new era, and so on. What did Jordan symbolize?

Jordan was a living human being, a flawed mortal who played basketball for the Lakers, and, according to a 1992 book by Sam Smith, demanded special treatment at the expense of his teammates and had an unseemly gambling habit (Jordan admitted he'd written a check for $57,000 in settlement of a gambling debt). Jordan was also a fantasy: he lived in the minds of the countless acolytes who believed they knew him. This was the Jordan of the imagination. It was the Jordan Nike made and sold – just like a commodity. Jordan was not just the cynosure of 1990s sports, but the first truly modern sports celebrity.

| BRAND BECKHAM: LIKE SOAP POWDER

The idea of affixing the name of an athlete to a product seems ridiculously obvious nowadays. It's hardly possible to get through a day without seeing some football or baseball player citing the benefits of something or other (Pelé's approval for Viagra was noteworthy, if only because he insisted he didn't need to take the product). Yet, as we've seen, prior to the 1980s, sports stars were recruited only sporadically to lend their support to products: they had almost oddity value. Why did athletes suddenly become ubiquitous after Jordan?

Jordan himself is a big part of the answer. He introduced the quality that was missing from earlier athletes – glamour. Jordan possessed, to repeat Thrift, "a combination of sex appeal, luxury, celebrity, and wealth." Correction: consumers attributed these qualities to Jordan. It's what we ascribe to figures, not what they actually have, that influences how we respond to them. After Nike's sales of Air Jordan surged, advertisers took note: prominent athletes were known largely for their competitive prowess. In itself, this might pique interest; it may even convince consumers that a certain athlete's choice of razors or wristwatch was a reliable guide for future purchases. But what if an athlete could be turned into a thing of wonder? An exquisitely decorated body with gilded ornamentation that could perform daring feats on the field of play, strut at fashion shows, and pout at cameras.

The February 14, 2000 edition of *Sports Illustrated* bore a cover picture of Jordan wearing a tee-shirt (Nike, naturally) with the legend WIZARDS. Strapped across the image was BOSS JORDAN: HOW GOOD WILL HE BE? Jordan, then 37, had just bought the Washington Wizards basketball club and was about to start the final phase of his active playing career; he played for the Wizards until 2003. By this time, many outstanding basketball players had established themselves, not just on court but as all-purpose celebrities. Shaquille O'Neal had made records and appeared in movies as well as playing ball. Kobe Bryant was also emerging. Tiger Woods was in the fourth year of a five-year deal with Nike. Neither Bryant nor Woods had, at this stage, been involved in the scandals that would, in a perverse way, define their careers. It could be argued that none of these had Jordan's aura, that is, the distinct atmosphere that surrounded him. There is some truth in this. Jordan surfaced at a particular moment in history and was the first figure of his kind; there could never be an exact equivalent. The latter-day celebrity athletes weren't lesser beings or epigones; they just weren't the first.

Meanwhile, in Manchester, England, David Beckham was ruffling the feathers of his club manager, Alex Ferguson. Married in 1999 to the then Victoria Adams, alias Posh Spice, Beckham combined his spectacularly successful sports career with an even more spectacular career in modeling, advertising, and sundry other activities, including attending premieres and accompanying his popstar wife to fashion shows where he consorted with her designer friends. Ferguson, an old-school manager, made it clear he regarded Beckham's extracurricular activities as unnecessary distractions. Those activities resulted largely from a bulging portfolio of contracts with global brands such as adidas, PepsiCo, and Police eyewear.

By the time Beckham met his future wife in 1997, the Spice Girls had already released four global hit singles and an album, *Spice*, that had by then sold 10 million copies (and would eventually sell 28 million). Yet the band hadn't even been on a concert tour. Victoria had also announced her career intentions: "Right from the beginning I said I wanted to be as famous as Persil Automatic" (Britain's best-selling detergent). Some – including this writer – suspected Victoria, well versed in the art of celebrity-making, stealthily put Beckham together with her own manager Simon Fuller, whose 19 agency was focused at the time on showbiz rather than sports figures (Lewis Hamilton and Andy Murray were among the athletes who signed with 19 later).

The fee Real Madrid paid for his services reflected his brand value more than his athletic proficiency.

Acclaimed in Europe and Asia, in 2000, Beckham was still relatively unknown in the USA. The movie *Bend It Like Beckham*, in which he didn't appear, but which had the effect of promulgating his name, wasn't released until 2002. When he transferred from Manchester to Real Madrid in 2003, however, the name Beckham had global resonance. Whether swigging Pepsi or preening behind shades, his seemingly self-replicating image was, it appeared, inescapable. It was around this time that the term Brand Beckham was insinuated into the popular vocabulary. The object of Brand Beckham was – we can only presume, because this was never publicly stated – to create a multipurpose word and accompanying image capable of adding market value to any conceivable product that was available for purchase. And the market was wide: right from felt-tip markers selling for less than the price of a copy of *Vogue* to the kind of clothes that would grace the front cover of that magazine's September issue. Cologne (of course), underwear, motor engine oil, and a miscellany of other items were all marketed under the name of Beckham.

In terms of calculation, ambition, and brazenness, Brand Beckham was equal to anything dreamt up by Phil Knight when he first signed Jordan to Nike. The contrasts are revealing: Jordan was marketed as a sports genius, a freak – and I mean a very unusual figure, rather than someone with a striking physical abnormality, though Nike pushed his gravity-defying superpowers. It was commonly considered that his inspiration arrived easily and his perfect execution on court casually slipped into place. By contrast, Beckham was promoted like an uncommunicative pop artist: before he moved to Madrid, he barely gave interviews, and was never seen in public, apart from on game days or at red carpet events. His detractors too often overlooked this attention to detail, but it helped create and perpetuate a Beckham mystique, a fascinating and glamorous aura of mystery. There's that quality again: aura. The air of secrecy surrounding Beckham wouldn't have been of any consequence if no one were interested. But millions were enticed by the inaccessible and unapproachable yet dashing figure whose every move, it seemed, was carefully planned and monitored.

The comparisons between Beckham and Jordan were underlined by Beckham himself when he insisted on the same number 23 Jordan wore at the Bulls for his own Real Madrid shirt (and later on his LA Galaxy shirt). But Jordan was undeniably the best basketball player of his – and, for many,

any other – generation. No one ever rated even peak-form Beckham in the world's top 20, perhaps not even top 50 players. The transfer fee Real Madrid paid for his services, €35 million (£28m/$45m) reflected his brand value more than his athletic proficiency (American readers: in soccer, players are traded for money rather than exchanged for other players or draft picks). "Real Madrid's commercial revenue from club merchandise sales, such as replica shirts, increased 67% in Beckham's first season alone," observe John Vincent *et al*. "The acquisition of Beckham also helped open up new markets in Asia and the United States [and] helped propel Real Madrid past Beckham's former club Manchester United as the world's richest club in 2004" (2009: 175).

No one could accuse Brand Beckham of selling itself cheaply: in 2004, Gillette offered David Beckham an estimated £40 million ($65m) to front a worldwide campaign for a new razor. There was a backstory to the deal: shortly before, the clean-living family man, who radiated health and wellbeing, was reported to have been having an affair with Rebecca Loos, who worked for his former agency. Beckham himself said nothing, though Loos was generous in confessing all to the media. For a while, she became a celebrity in her own right, as befits a woman who claims to have had sex with one of the world's most lusted-after men. Doomsayers who predicted the end of Brand Beckham clearly misunderstood the chemistry of celebrity culture. Far from ruining the brand, the scandal heightened interest in it: no longer the too-good-to-be-true model of piety, David Beckham was just another guy after all. He would succumb to temptation just like anybody else. The hitherto angelic image now had a dash of devilry. As we know, consumers like celebrities to be less godlike, more human.

Sales of the M3 Power razor Beckham endorsed spiked by 13 percent in the year following the start of his contract, suggesting the efficacy of the brand. Further deals with global brands Armani and Vodafone followed, leading even skeptics to assume

Beckham could sell anything. That included association football, a game played all over the world, including the USA, where
it is a very poor relation to baseball, basketball, American football, and hockey, and is known as soccer (the word was once
used in England and is derived from the abbreviation "assoc,"
i.e. short for "association").

Presumably, this was Philip Anschutz's reasoning when he
offered Beckham what seemed a catastrophic amount of money
to move from Madrid to Los Angeles to play for LA Galaxy, a
club owned by Anschutz's company AEG. Anschutz (net worth:
$7 billion) was a founding investor of Major League Soccer
(MLS), the league in which the Galaxy competed. AEG also
owns the Houston Dynamo club and at various times during
the history of MLS has held ownership in the Chicago Fire,
San Jose Earthquakes, New York/New Jersey MetroStars, and
D.C. United. Hence, Anschutz had a heavily vested interest in
promoting soccer in America. Beckham's five-year deal, starting
2007, was thought to be worth $207 million (£128 million).

By the end of his first contract with the Galaxy, Major League
Soccer was feeling the effects of Brand Beckham: the league, which
once had to pay broadcasters to air its games, had signed a $30-mil-
lion, three-year deal with NBC, supplementing agreements it already had with ESPN, Fox, and Univision; and the Galaxy agreed
to a deal with Time Warner Cable worth $55 million over ten years.
Attendances grew, year-on-year. Even so, the outlay on Beckham
and other marquee players from outside the USA made it impossible for MLS to turn a profit, and, in 2012, Beckham's departure
left the league only marginally better off than when he'd arrived.

AUTHENTIC SHARAPOVA |

The cases of Jordan and Beckham should prod us into wondering: are athletes different to popular entertainers – including reality tv stars –who, most of us assume, are reacting spontaneously

to forces all around them, cashing in on their ability to monitor their times? Athletes are not Johnny-come-lately arrivals: they've been doing the same things for decades: kicking or throwing balls, hitting each other, running around tracks, and so on. We can't help but imagine today's celebrity athletes closely resemble yesterday's sports stars; in fact, we don't have to imagine when we see so much archival footage on tv.

Where there were once "colorful characters" or superstars, there are now celebrity athletes, or icons – images created by corporate interests for the purpose of selling in a market that respects no national boundaries. In this vital respect, they are closer to showbusiness entertainers than athletes. Corporations like adidas and Armani waste no time in co-opting young men and women into their grand projects, determining their value separately from their competitive accomplishments. Celebrity athletes are given the same kind of treatment as any other kind of celebrity: they're turned into commodities and made to function as marketing vehicles. They rarely, if ever, resist. Is it so demeaning to display your D-Star automatic chronograph if Rado are paying you a seven-figure sum to be their "brand ambassador" (to use the preferred euphemism for endorser)? Nicole Kidman's dignity didn't suffer by wearing an Omega, nor did Daniel Craig's. Athletes have been absorbed into celebrity culture just like entertainers. Or have they?

Barry Smart thinks not: it is impossible to "subordinate the ethos of sport to values of entertainment and commerce." By ethos, Smart means the characteristic spirit of sports, as manifested in its principles and the aspirations of its competitors. Athletes are not just performers who work to amuse audiences: their task is primarily to win and this is not necessarily related to entertaining at all. Unlike other celebrities, especially those whose transitory fame comes via reality tv, sports stars have "authenticity." This is a term Smart uses to stake out the difference between athletes and all other celebrities. He means that, in order, to become known, they must first demonstrate competence, if not excellence, in their sport. There are occasionally lamentably inept athletes at major tournaments who are widely publicized for their gameness. But their time in the sun is usually short and, for the most part, athletes who rise to global fame "confirm the authenticity of their exceptional status, their significant difference, if not their uniqueness" (2005: 195).

> *Athletes are not so different from other entertainers: what they do, or how they perform is of only superficial importance.*

Smart isn't so dazzled by this that he doesn't recognize that: "Since the 1960s a series of economic and cultural processes have transformed the world of sport" (2005: 18). The "threat" posed to authenticity – "a vulnerable quality," he reckons – by commercial interests is apparent everywhere. And yet: "The authenticity of sporting figures like Michael Jordan, Tiger Woods and David Beckham ultimately derives from the quality of their playing performance, from their records of success in competition" (2005: 195).

Authenticity is one of those words that create an illusion: it looks like a synonym for genuineness or legitimacy, whereas it hides a transaction, as we revealed in Chapter 10. "Authenticity is a tricky concept," concluded Deborah Root in a different context. "The term can be manipulated and used to convince people they are getting something profound when they are just getting merchandise" (1996: 78).

Root wasn't writing about sport, though her argument travels well. When she refers to a "commodification of authenticity," she could be referring to the way in which various areas of the culture industry work to turn playing skills into "pure artistry," "natural talent," or even "genius." These are terms to which sports fans have become accustomed. Undeniably, there are athletes who have convinced everyone they possess them: Wayne Gretzky, Michael Schumacher, and Roger Federer are among an elite group of sportsmen who utterly dominated their particular sports for unfeasibly long periods. Their achievements are a matter of record and defy contrary arguments.

Every branch of entertainment boasts incomparable artists with incomparable talent. It forces us to confront a question we have raised before: is talent inherent or is it ascribed? The conventional view is that talent is a natural aptitude or skill, something people are gifted with at birth. I suggested a more elliptic conception, understanding talent from contextual clues: talent is whatever we agree to call talent. It's a matter of convention that we agree the capacity to hit tennis balls with a racket at great force and with great accuracy constitutes a talent; or an adeptness at playing scripted roles with persuasive conviction; or a skill in playing musical instruments or singing in a way that others enjoy. Time changes contexts, of course: we don't find many talented lute players nowadays. Talent, from this perspective, is something audiences credit; an acknowledgement of uncommon ability, rather than the ability itself. Athletes are not so different from other entertainers: what they do, or how they perform is of only superficial importance. More significant is how consumers respond to them.

Let's take Maria Sharapova, of whom Steffi Graf once said: "She is so talented, so there was always a chance that she would come back to this level." Graf's opinion is widely shared: Sharapova had talent and used it to stage a comeback when her career seemed doomed. In 2009, Sharapova, then 22 going on 23, slumped to 126th in the world women's tennis rankings, her all-time lowest position. She hadn't won a major tournament for over a year, and struggled with an incessant shoulder injury. After a promising start to her career, the Russian-born, US-based player faded and was hardly a factor in Grand Slam events. Then, in 2012, she bounced back to peak form and won the French Open Championships.

Her desultory tennis form up to this point didn't have much, if any, effect on her celebrity status. Sharapova (b. 1987) had been the most conspicuous and highest-earning female athlete in the world since 2004. And has remained that way since. In the 12 months after she hit rock bottom, she earned $25 million (£15.7m), twice as much as any other female in sport.

Even while her prize money dried up, she prospered from an endorsement portfolio that included Nike, Head, Evian, Clear Shampoo, Sony Ericsson, Tiffany, TAGHeuer, and Parlux, which made MARIA SHARAPOVA FOR WOMEN eau de parfum. Even while she suffered on court, Sharapova extended her Nike agreement in 2010 for eight years in a deal worth potentially as much as $70 million. Sales of her Nike line of tennis apparel shot up 26 percent in 2010 and her ballet flat was the top-selling shoe at Cole Haan.

By the time she rediscovered her early career touch, her earnings were up to $27.1 million, over $10 million more than Serena Williams, who is often acknowledged as the best woman tennis player ever (and whose fragrance is called Serena Glam Slam). Sharapova's earnings were about half that of Rihanna and Lady Gaga, and about $7 million less than Kristen Stewart, but more than Sofia Vergara or any other female tv star. Sharapova has over eight million Facebook friends.

Circumstances, not looks, ethnicity, or playing prowess influence who becomes a celebrity.

Even if we accept Graf's point that Sharapova had talent, her prodigiousness in securing the lucrative endorsement deals and maintaining visibility appears disproportionate to what Smart would regard as her authentic achievements on court. Sharapova may not have singlehandedly subordinated the ethos of sports to entertainment and commerce, but she showed how perfectly each complemented the others. She was consistently the best-known, most frequently googled, most avidly followed female athlete in the world during the early twenty-first century. Serena Williams and other Grand Slam-winning contemporaries, such as Sam Stosur and Victoria Azarenka, could beat her on court, but nowhere else. And as if to underline her unmatched supremacy as a commodity, she announced her intention to change her name to *Sugarpova* for the duration of the 2013 US Open. *Sugarpova* was the name of a product she endorsed. She dropped the idea, but only after the media had covered the story.

Historically, there are athletes whose dominance in their respective sports would seem to justify crediting them with talent, yet who register little recognition beyond those sports. In the 1970s and 1980s, David Bryant (b. 1931) was supreme in lawn bowls, as was Geet Sethi (b. 1961) in billiards in the 1990s, and Phil Taylor (b. 1960) in darts. Netball's Vicki Wilson (b. 1965) and squash's Heather McKay (b. 1941) were leaders of their respective sports. Much garlanded as Bryant and the others were, they were never offered big endorsement contracts, nor afforded the kind of celebrity status enjoyed by the athletes mentioned earlier in this chapter. Being in the right sport – one that receives media attention – matters; but there are other factors. Sharapova was white, over six feet tall, and had the kind of looks we often associate with supermodels. Beckham also had good looks. Woods didn't. Jordan was decent looking, but not drop-dead; and, of course, he was an African American. There are no rules: context, as ever, is vital to understanding why some athletes have been, and still are, acknowledged as authentically great and others remain largely unknown.

Circumstances, not looks, ethnicity, or playing prowess influence who becomes a celebrity. We don't have to deny Smart's claim that some athletes are better than others: we simply have to point out that this may, in some contexts, have a bearing on their status, while, in others, it may not.

| TO THE CENTRE

In answering the question "Why has sport moved from the periphery to the centre of popular culture?" John Horne writes, "The media, sponsors and marketing agencies are merely exploiting a growing interest in sport, which has been created by increasing media coverage of sport" (2006: 80). Yet surely they weren't "merely exploiting": they were actively propelling sports to their central position. Advertisers made the athletes featured in campaigns more visible, recognizable, and, in a self-fulfilling way, more attractive to other advertisers.

Horne believes that there were other factors at work, the interest in health, fitness and the overall wellbeing of the body being another. In Chapter 7, we saw how the culture of narcissism nourished an awareness of the body. Sports provided an arena in which hale and hearty bodies were displayed. A more decisive change was, as we saw in Chapter 4, the proliferation of television channels and their obvious requirement: content. Sports provided relatively cheap content: production costs were low compared to drama and, for commercial tv companies, the advertising income more than offset them. ESPN's venture in 1980 was every bit as audacious as that of MTV (which, as we noted earlier, launched in 1981). While the latter filled its airtime with music, ESPN showed nothing but sports. By 1998, the channel was received by 70 percent of all US households and broadcast 23 percent of all televised sports. The network's reach extended to 160 different countries and it provided services in 19 languages.

Surely, you can have too much of a good thing. Not when it comes to sports, it seems. Between 1991, when the National Basketball Association clinched a $600 million four-year deal with NBC television, and 2011, when the NFL signed tv deals worth $27 billion (£16.65bn) over nine years, sports underwent an astonishing transformation, not just in the USA but elsewhere in the world. In the same period, England's Premier League's tv deal rose from £304 million ($460.4m) over five years to £3 billion ($4.54bn) over three years. This reflects the value of the product sports delivers, but also the status of competitors, who not only earn as much as, and in many, many cases, more than, entertainers, but who also have comparable status.

Where once tv viewers watched competition, now they consume spectacle, as Horne puts it (2006: 89). Sports are presented in much the same way as other forms of entertainment, whether music, drama, or news. And, as they are also consumed in the same way, why shouldn't we call sports entertainment? This might not sound such a defamatory question today, but it would once have been a slight against the competitive endeavors that separated heroes from other mortals and provided events that were regarded by many with spiritual reverence.

At the same time, the rogue elements of sports have been domesticated. Once, there was no place for rebels or political protestors. Resistance was turned into stylistic affectation, making people like Andre Agassi, Eric Cantona, and Dennis Rodman seem like insurgent forces instead of the housetrained poseurs they really were. Nike, more than any other advertiser, expertly honed their images to represent youthful insolence. More likely they were agents of containment working on behalf of an organization that "positioned itself as a rebellious, maverick, and anti-authoritarian company," as Jim McKay describes Nike (1999: 418).

One wonders how Nike might have managed Muhammad Ali, who spoke out in favor of the separation of blacks and whites, and who opposed the social integration championed in the 1960s and till the present day? Or Diego Maradona, a fervent admirer of Cuban leader Fidel Castro, whose hand he kissed in deference. Or Tommie Smith and John Carlos, who were expelled in shame after their Black Power salute at the 1966 Olympic Games and never allowed to compete in sports again. Or even Billie Jean King whose sexuality became the source of scandal in 1981 when her secretary took legal action against her and outed her as a lesbian. In their own ways, these and many other athletes resisted conformity, whether protesting against war, consorting with Communist leaders, or transgressing sexual norms. As such, they were internationally known, admired by some, abhorred by others. But they were not celebrities. Their private lives weren't pored over, they weren't hunted by paparazzi, and their reputations were built from athletic accomplishments, not advertisements. None had their own signature cologne.

Deeds that were once regarded as violations cost all these figures dearly: today, they would be the equivalent of rhodium. Stigmatized, or, in Smith and Carlos's case, ostracized in their day, they might be notorious now. And that isn't necessarily a bad thing for a celebrity.

As sports morphed into popular entertainment, their main characters were subject to the same treatment as other celebrities. The rewards were great: $60 million+ is no longer such an extraordinary yearly income for many elite performers. For such earnings, the surrender of any residual private life, a promise not to misbehave, and an outward commitment to the values of sports must seem a fair exchange.

THEORY

September 2012. The Duchess of Cambridge is "a young lady, not an object." Kate Middleton's lawyer seemed to be stating the obvious, as she and her husband began unprecedented legal action over topless photos in *Closer*, a French magazine. The pictures revealed "particularly simple and deeply intimate moments in the life of this couple that have no reason to be on a magazine cover," according to the lawyer. They were taken without the royal couple's consent on September 5, while the Duke and Duchess were on vacation in the southeast of France. St. James's Palace issued a statement containing the sentence: "The incident is reminiscent of the worst excesses of the press and paparazzi during the life of Diana, Princess of Wales."

Diana died 15 years earlier. The wedding of William and Kate in 2011 drew 26 million viewers around the world to their

CHAPTER HIGHLIGHTS

- Celebrities embody a story or several stories: they are living narratives
- Have we *always needed* celebrities as reminders of what's right and wrong?
- The media is responsible for the rapid reproduction of celebrities
- Public relations, or pr, is the central agency in the production of fame today
- Some theorists compare celebrity culture to religion and celebrities to gods
- Celebrities keep us doing what we do best – buying stuff that makes us feel good

televisions. The editor of *Closer* was unrepentant, defending her decision to publish the pictures by insisting there was "nothing degrading" about the photographs and claiming she could not understand the couple's reaction. "These photos are not in the least shocking. They show a young woman sunbathing topless, like the millions of women you see on beaches."

The same kind of defense could have been offered – were it necessary – in 1962, when pictures of Elizabeth Taylor in a passionate embrace with Richard Burton were taken without either person's knowledge and relayed around the world. The pictures, as we now know, catalyzed interest in the private lives of famous figures and, effectively, started a process that forms the subject of this book. Taylor died a year before the royal scandal.

Life on our planet has become a set of random narratives watched by all via closed-circuit surveillance, reality tv cameras, or smartphones. Almost every second of our day is monitored by some sort of device, often for the purpose of selling us products. Celebrities symbolize this existence: they've voluntarily surrendered their lives to 360° surveillance, not to government agencies, but to the news media. They are everywhere and so, in a way, are we.

"Celebrity culture is a ubiquitous and spreading phenomenon. It has infiltrated most if not all aspects of life," avers Pete Ward. "From sports and politics to entertainment and economics, the celebrity has become a key building block in the way that the media present and interpret life" (2011: 131). This isn't a satisfying pronouncement on contemporary life; but it isn't a condemnation either: Ward is simply making an observation of the way we live. We create figures who we sense do something, or have and show qualities worthy of our attention, and follow them. Follow can mean admire, appreciate, imitate, care about, or adopt the style of someone. The exact way we follow is of less importance than the reasons why we have become so engrossed in the lives of others, whether the Duchess of Cambridge or an inept contestant on *The X Factor*. Some blame the media: they practically confer celebrity status on all manner of people regardless of what they have actually done, or not done, then expose us perpetually to images and stories of those people. But that's hardly an explanation: the media act as our proxy – we authorize them to act on our behalf. The media doesn't manipulate us. If it presented us with material we found intolerable, disagreeable, or just plain boring, we'd withdraw our commission; in other words, we wouldn't read, watch, or listen.

> *Entertainment is not just the provision of amusement or diverting performances. It is an opportunity to learn.*

Neal Gabler argues that, while the media has been crucial, it has not foisted celebrities on unwitting consumers or imposed unwelcome stories about them on audiences. Following celebrities "is actually a new art form that competes with – and often supersedes – more traditional entertainments like movies, books, plays, and TV shows," according to Gabler" (2009: 1).

In contrast to many critics who trivialize celebrity culture as superficial, frivolous, and meretricious, Gabler believes it can provide us with life lessons. Certain celebrities resonate with us because they capture a cultural moment. Gabler accepts that the widespread interest in people we may never meet is initiated by the media. This much is obvious: consumers' first brush with figures who are destined for celebritydom is through the media, though not necessarily the traditional media Gabler has in mind – social media have become increasingly vital since 2009. But there is a reason why those figures were publicized in the first place: they provide narratives for us. A narrative is an account of connected events, such as a story, a history, a record, or a chronicle. It can convey a moral or a lesson in what is right or prudent, or bad or foolish. And it is always open to interpretation: interpreters who search narratives usually reveal hidden meanings. In fairness, Gabler doesn't develop its meaning as I have, but I doubt if he'd object to my explication: it's consistent with his overall perspective.

Gabler illustrates his approach with the life of Michael Jackson, which he characterizes as

> a long, fascinating soap opera that included not only his success but also his tiffs with his family, his erratic behavior, his plastic surgeries, his bizarre marriages, his masked children, his brushes with the law, his alleged drug use, and finally his mysterious death.

The name Michael Jackson fills some people with loathing, while others literally worship him as they would a deity; there are countless others whose feelings fall somewhere between the extremes and whose reactions have doubtless changed over the years. But everyone is aware of Jackson and – I believe this is implicit in Gabler's argument – everyone has learned something from his life.

Entertainment, as I have pointed out before, is not just the provision of amusement or diverting performances. It is an opportunity to learn: just because we enjoy a play, a book, or a movie doesn't mean we don't assimilate and digest new information, become aware of issues, or commit to memory lines or scenes that we find valuable. At the very minimum, we are challenged to think. If we are not, we're not stimulated, and it probably isn't entertainment at all. Jackson's life was a spectacular event, a multiplot story with a glamorous *dramatis personae* and a barely believable conclusion that may yet prove not to be a conclusion at all. As far as Gabler is concerned, Jackson himself, the human individual, was not a celebrity: the narrative in which he was a central figure was the object of our fascination: "That is why one can be famous, as Queen Elizabeth is, without necessarily being a celebrity, as Princess Di was. One has name recognition, the other a narrative."

Fame is, of course, an ancient phenomenon and, as I will show shortly, several theories use it synonymously with celebrity. Gabler's point, however, is subtle: celebrities have to be "living out an interesting narrative," or else we and, by implication, the media cease to take notice. Occupying a position that traditionally confers fame on an individual isn't the same as being a celebrity. The Pope is famous, as are the Secretary-General of the United Nations and the Majority Leader of the House of Congress. Their fame is a function of their office. Any of them could become a celebrity if they do or say something that excites us. Then why have celebrities only recently sprung up? According to this account, they should have been around for centuries. This is where the media rises in importance.

Gabler cites Walter Winchell (1897–1972), the American newspaper and radio gossip columnist, who, in the gloom of the 1930s, kept his followers rapt with distracting tales. "Winchell turned us into a nation of yentas" (a yenta is a gossip or busybody). The preoccupation with others' lives created a sense of cohesion amid the fragmentation occasioned by the Great Depression. Western societies grew less unified. In Chapter 5, I described how *The Lonely Crowd* described a society composed of atomized individuals who interacted with each other, but who had had no meaningful ties or obligations other than those arising from self-interests. The typical American of the 1950s had become "other-directed." Disunited over politics and values, and sharing fewer and fewer common experiences, consumers found an odd comfort in the common denominator of music, film, and, increasingly and perhaps most importantly, television.

In recent decades, movies and television programs and, to a lesser extent, plays and novels "have subsisted on providing us with verisimilitude so that we feel what we are watching or reading is real," reasons Gabler. We've learned to identify with characters. While Gabler doesn't refer explicitly to parasocial interactions (as we have in earlier chapters), his theory leads us to presume he has something similar in mind when he states, "we imagine what happens to them [the characters] really matters."

Celebrities are real enough; there are real consequences to their actions and there is always something at stake. So we don't have to suspend disbelief as we often do when reading or viewing works of fiction. And there's always the bonus: "Celebrity narratives have no final chapter." Consumers are always waiting for a new installment. In effect, celebrities are not people, but entire stories that enrapture us, at the same time imparting lessons, however minor. Celebrities elicit intense engagement, not mindless escapism. Like film, novels, and other art forms, they stimulate the imagination. "Just as the most complex films, novels, and plays have layers of meaning and even profound truths, so do the best and longest-lasting celebrity narratives," writes Gabler, whose earlier work in 2001 outlined his theory of narratives.

Effectively, *we* – not the media, advertisers, or global corporations – have created celebrities, because celebrity culture provides what traditional art and entertainments once offered. Actually, Gabler doesn't notice that they still do offer stimulation, but we have either become jaded, blasé, or impossible to surprise – probably all three.

Gabler likens celebrity to *kudzu*, the quick-growing Asian climbing plant. The plant has become a pest in the southeastern USA, but I sense that's not what he means – a pestilent growth that attacks more useful forms of life. Certainly, Gabler believes celebrity culture has subordinated the media to its demands. Since celebrities are narratives, they require magazines, newspapers, television shows, and the internet to promote and disseminate them. We should also add social media, which has arguably become more important than the other media in transmitting and perpetuating celebrity culture. All media are filled with celebrity narratives; all culture is permeated with celebrity. As Gabler puts it: "We practically breathe it."

Tom Payne is one of the authors who regard celebrity as the same as fame. "To be famous is to be different, and even if you're famous for something quite ordinary, you're still distinguished by the property of fame itself," he claims (2009: 6). "We need famous people to operate outside the realms of what we consider normal or decent" (2009: 29). They issue reminders of where the boundaries of acceptability lie. Payne likens those boundaries to a red rope with a bouncer in front of it. "The important thing is that they [famous figures] are unlike us . . . if they weren't different, they wouldn't be famous" (2009: 33).

Payne's approach to celebrity culture shares with Gabler's the idea that celebrity culture fortifies the mind by blending the dramatic with the didactic. Celebrities personify or embody meaningful stories, or narratives. "The world of celebrities is not real. It is like the world of movies," Payne maintains (2009: 142). Later, he observes: "That distant world has become ours" (2009: 152).

Like Gabler, Payne contends that celebrities come to our notice when they are involved in some intriguing plot. While he doesn't use the metaphor, he seems to suggest celebrities' lives are like coloring books, in the sense that they leave us to fill in the actual colors however we like. "We end up with our own stories, rather than the real ones."

Payne dates the evolution of celebrity culture to the late fourth millennium BC, or the Bronze Age, which, incidentally, followed the Stone Age and preceded the Iron Age. It's associated with the first European civilizations and the beginning of urban life in China. Payne's prehistoric investigations lead him to conclude that, in the Stone Age, "modern ideas of fame don't apply at all." When we are analyzing cultures so ancient, we should remain wary of the dangers of comparing historically distinct culture epistemically: what counts as knowledge and the criteria for validating knowledge can and does change, often radically, through history, making evaluations unreliable. Payne pays no heed to the eternally protean nature of knowledge when he plots the history of celebrity.

In Chapter 1, I revealed how many writers, especially historians, agree that celebrity culture is not new; though none traces its *fons et origo* as far back as the Bronze Age. So, when Payne asserts that fame "is present throughout most of human history," it prompts us to wonder if it's one of those "needs" the humanistic psychologist Abraham Maslow (1908–70) wrote of in the 1950s in his attempt to explain human motivation: an essential human requirement that is an ever-present in all populations. The primary needs are biological (hunger, thirst, and so on) and there are levels of ever-more cultivated needs, including the need for affiliation with others, aesthetic needs, and the need to find fulfillment in realizing our potential. While Payne doesn't cite Maslow (whose theory was published in 1954), he might have done: the need for famous people who can operate in a world where the rules that govern the conduct of the rest of us don't apply.

Payne's is less a unified theory, more a sampler menu of celebrity possibilities through the ages and across cultures. The writer sees celebrity culture less as a new phenomenon, more the latest incarnation of the characters who featured in myths, legends, and tales of yore. Whether actual or fictitious, the figures were, and are, usually exaggerated and idealized by an audience who read meanings into their exploits. Those exploits offered simple stories as *exempla*, tales that illustrated some truth or wisdom. Payne thinks today's celebrities have similar functions: "We struggle to make sense of them. We make patterns out of them and make tales of the famous fit the structures of fables" (2009: 239). Payne liquefies time, place, and ontology in his attempt to make celebrity culture intelligible as a kind of moral education.

Dr Faustus, the sixteenth-century German necromancer, who is reputed to have sold his soul to the devil, evokes similarities with reality tv show contestants. Rock stars become Homeric heroes. Madame de Pompadour (1721–64), the mistress of Louis XV, is on the same continuum as Cinderella and Jennifer Aniston. Deities, demigods, and mere mortals collide. Myths, legends, and real-life events all give out moral messages for our edification. We can practically see Payne's think-bubble: "This is a great idea. No evidence, but what intuition!"

> *In their search for comparisons, historians have turned up powerful similarities with cultures of the past, though they also neglect contrasts.*

It is indeed an intuitively clever idea, though one so daring that it slips the shackles of theory entirely and becomes an imaginative rumination rather than an explanation. Payne is in no doubt that our fascination with celebrities did not start with Madonna, or even Elizabeth Taylor, and precedes the rise of what we now consider the entertainment industry. He's slightly more doubtful about whether or not our "obsession," as he calls it, is detrimental. In view of his argument that it has been with us for so long, we assume not. While he never invokes Maslow's theory, my comparison invites the conclusion that the passion for celebrities, real or fictitious, has the same kind of status as our need for love, friendship, and intimacy – what Maslow called "social needs." According to your take, Payne's argument is either sagaciously predicated on, or terminally compromised by, this.

Payne is one of a number of writers who *historicize* celebrity culture, i.e. treat it as an historical phenomenon. Leo Braudy is another. Like Payne, he uses fame and celebrity synonymously. His thesis is that fame, as we know it, arrived after the seventeenth century. While Johannes Gutenberg (c. 1400–68) had produced a printing press in the mid-fifteenth century, the widespread use of movable type followed, evolving into a print culture in the seventeenth century. The printing of bibles hastened the spread of Protestantism, and international trade, together with urban life, contributed to the rise of literacy. Fame, according to Braudy, was democratized in the sense that it was accessible to a variety of figures who were able to distinguish themselves through achievements and have those achievements acknowledged by anyone who could read, or listen to those who could read – audiences (1997).

Fame, for Braudy, is a modern phenomenon, though not an especially recent one, and certainly not one that depends on the kind of mass media that emerged in the late nineteenth and early twentieth centuries. Printing from a flat surface, or lithography, and steel-plate engraving were available from the 1830s. Louis-Jacques-Mandé Daguerre's influential form of photography (daguerreotype) was used in print media in the mid-nineteenth century and, eventually, allowed print media to accompany text with halftone photographic images. Radio didn't become available until the 1920s. Braudy is mindful of the impact of these technologies, but, for him, print, not broadcast media, was the prime mover of fame, at least fame as we know it.

When did mediated relationships begin? In other words, when did people begin connecting indirectly via intermediate agencies? Many historians believe that linking up in this way ended our dependence on face-to-face interactions for our information and opened the way for knowing-at-distance. We could learn about figures about whom we knew nothing firsthand. Some historians believe that the circulation of knowledge facilitated by even rudimentary printing presses from the eighteenth century was sufficient for mediated relationships: "While arguably still not a mass society in the twentieth-century sense, it was certainly possible for knowledge of the deeds and images of the famous to percolate further down the social scale than ever before," argues Simon Morgan (2001: 106).

Morgan contends that there is evidence of cultures of celebrity from the late eighteenth century. The spread of print culture and the reproduction of images of the famous promoted literacy and hence a progressively large population of literate consumers; in other words, an audience. Consumers engaged with ideas rather than people and events. Stella Tillyard locates this slightly earlier than Morgan: "In the first half of the eighteenth century a process occurred by which a nascent culture of celebrity began to form side by side with an existing culture of fame" (2005: 22).

Tillyard specifies three specific sets of circumstances: a weak English monarchy with limited moral authority, the lapsing of legislation controlling the numbers of printing presses and to some extent printing itself, "and a public interested in new ways of thinking about other people and themselves." The new thinking involved "speculation and gossip far freer, more direct, personal and scurrilous than we have today" (2005: 22)

This is an appealing but limited claim: appealing because it suggests an enthusiasm for the kind of casual, unconstrained conversation or reports about other people that has become current; limited because of the difficulties in comparing modes of thinking three centuries apart. The same problem limits the theories of all those who want to historicize celebrity culture.

The features that historians pick out as hallmarks of celebrity culture do appear to have existed before the 1980s, perhaps way before if Payne is to be believed. Even the taste for tittle-tattle, as Tillyard reminds us, has a long history. And, while we often think of the media as an innovation, this is because new methods and products are developed and introduced constantly, giving the appearance of freshness. It's easy to forget that the first piece of kit was invented around 1455.

Gossip is not mere talk about other people's private lives; it is the cognitive architecture of celebrity culture.

In their search for comparisons, historians have turned up powerful similarities with cultures of the past, though they also neglect contrasts. There are many facets of today's culture that are distinct, unprecedented, and seemingly exclusive. They are, in other words, context-specific and unique. As readers will now be aware, the argument that runs through this book suggests celebrity culture is the product of the particular circumstances in which it originated and developed. This invites questions for historians.

Were consumers with a taste for gossip in the eighteenth century like today's capricious fantasists who acclaim odious and sometimes criminal behavior just because they like the misbehaving figures? Were they able to commission the rise, fall, and, sometimes, annihilation of characters with a mere shift of interest, as they do today, courtesy of social media? Were their impulses stimulated by figures they thought epitomized the good life, envisioned as a cornucopia of consumer goods, endless novelty, and designer lifestyles? Did they communicate with the famous and the not-so-famous, without ever knowing if anyone was reading, or listening, or even if there was anyone there at all? For contemporary consumers, gossip is not mere talk about other people's private lives; it is the cognitive architecture of celebrity culture.

Precursors? Of course, there have been antecedents or forerunners of celebrity culture. Print culture, mass society, perhaps even the Bronze Age are parts of celebrity culture's lineage, but only in the way that Einstein's theory of relativity is part of the nuclear fusion reactor's lineage. One is made possible by the prior existence of the other, but it isn't an extension of it.

THE WORLD THROUGH A LENS

In the 1960s, when Daniel Boorstin was completing the first edition of his *The Image: A guide to pseudo-events in America,* he wondered about the effects of living in an "illusory" world of created characters. Mediated, two-dimensional images were becoming as important to us as real people: we only needed to flick a switch or open a magazine and we were in the alternative world. Compared to this, our own world must have seemed colorless and uninteresting. In Boorstin's world, people exchanged ideas and gossiped about stars and tv characters rather than learning about each other and, by implication, about themselves.

The early 1960s: the Beatles, Martin Luther King, Motown, Joe Namath, *Cleopatra*. The names seem to be from a different age. They are. Yet we know them all. And they're all comprehensible and not just as historical entities. The media supports a vivid imagination. We might be detached observers, but we feel we know, perhaps do actually know, all about the Beatles and the story of Motown without having to delve into the history books. The media is just *there,* like a Greek chorus, different voices singing different things simultaneously and continuously.

This is where our story of celebrity began, of course. The early 1960s witnessed the beginning of our new enchantment. Our senses were massaged or manipulated by a newly tenacious media that fed on the real people behind the image. Of course, what they were doing is delivering new images to replace the old.

There were potent images that lingered in the mind long after the early sixties: the first live transatlantic television broadcast via the Telstar satellite in 1962; the assassination of John F. Kennedy in 1963; the first spacewalk in 1964; England's World Cup win in 1966 (watched by about 400 million tv viewers). These were delivered by television. The "illusory" world grew both bigger and smaller to viewers watching "live" transmissions of events 250,000 miles away.

Essentially, the same media that delivered the first moon landing delivered celebrities. To be precise, images of celebrities. In the first edition of *Celebrity/Culture*, I described David Giles' make-believe invitation to his readers to put themselves in the shoes of a famous female recording artist. After a harrowing experience with the paparazzi, she is summoned to the studios by her record company to make a second album, a single from which is going to be released ahead of the album. When the single becomes available for download, the press office arranges over a hundred interviews and the singer is whisked around the country to make tv and radio appearances. "You are replicated furiously," Giles assures the hypothetical singer/reader. "Dozens of newspapers and glossy, full-colour magazines carry photographs of you . . . The video, for a start, receives heavy 'rotation' on specialist TV channels and several plays on terrestrial TV" (2000: 52).

For this edition, we need to update Giles' example, perhaps by adding the Facebook hate campaign that starts when perezhilton.com reports how she once gave away a Chihuahua someone had given her as a birthday present; and the 500,000-strong Twitter following to whom she issues six daily tweets; and the YouTube video that gets 85,413,500 views in its first six months, more than Nicki Minaj's "Starship" (Nicki was furious). Buoyed by the initial success, she accepts an invitation to sit on *The X Factor*'s judges' panel but, after discovering Nicki Minaj is also on the panel, on the condition that she gets extra security. (This is what Mariah Carey did when she thought Minaj had threatened her during the 2012 *American Idol* series.)

The single sells well, prompting another few weeks of "saturation media coverage," and every time the song is played whether on radio, tv, iPod, or whatever, "You are *there*," says Giles (2000: 52). And "there" in 2000 was on a stationary medium; now it means literally anywhere the consumer decides to take his or her portable device.

The singer obviously isn't physically there: Giles means that her presence is summoned by a visual or audile representation that registers in the imagination. Jessica Evans tenders a phrase to capture this: "Mediated persona is a useful term in that it reminds us how celebrity as a category *is absolutely dependent on the media* to create and disseminate a persona to an audience" (2005: 19).

Evans' emphasis reveals the colossal importance she places on the role of the media in the creation and perpetuation of celebrity. Giles is equally convinced of the media's efficacy in bringing celebrity culture into being, though his emphasis is on the way in which technology has taken matters to a new level.

Braudy's history of fame alerts readers to the manner in which primitive media were used not only to circulate news but also to glorify and lionize rulers, whether kings, generals, priests, or saints. "So it can be argued that there is much continuity between the representations of the famous in the past and the present," writes Evans (2005: 20).

> *The media drives celebrity production but the texts that circulate have a life of their own.*

Citing examples from history, Evans argues that even the "pseudo-events" Boorstin believed were stage-managed episodes specific to the twentieth century have much older precedents. Louis XIV (the seventeenth-century French king, not the San Diego band) was adept at making carefully designed public rejoicings appear spontaneous. The point is: public relations is not as new as we think, and the media, even before the age of print, were used as promotional vehicles (I'll return to this shortly). Fame then has always involved some mediating agency that represents and disseminates news and images.

While her approach accentuates historical continuity, Evans identifies the period 1890–1930 as "crucial," when "the mass media invented a particular kind of 'star' persona" (2005: 23). This is slightly later than the take-off phase identified in Chapter 2, though Evans' argument is in broad agreement: in making the private lives of entertainers a part of their overall public persona, the emerging media, in concert with the film industry, nurtured a new kind of relationship between the famous and their audiences. Between them, there were texts, defined by Evans' collaborator Frances Bonner as "socially constructed assemblages of items such as spoken or written words, or pictures" (2005: 59). (An "assemblage" is something made of unrelated things joined together, so the text is basically anything that's intelligible to the consumer, or the person doing the "reading".)

In Evans' model, then, there are three conceptual elements: the production, text, and reception. While each contributes to making celebrity a meaningful social entity, the relationship between them is variable. Culture industries might produce a particular set of images or personae of celebrities, but there is no guarantee that audiences will interpret them in the way intended: the texts may be quite different. "Reception" is perhaps a poor choice of words in that it implies passivity, whereas consumers are seen as discriminatingly selecting and decoding media messages in a way that resists manipulation.

The media and the elaborate organizations that augment them might drive celebrity production and, as such, remain the engine of the model, but the texts that circulate in a way have a life of their own once in the public discourse (actually "in" the public discourse isn't quite appropriate as the discourse is actually constituted or made by the public).

Giles sees less historical continuity. New media technologies rupture developments, opening up unanticipated opportunities for aspiring celebrities. They did so in the fourteenth century, when the modern theater became popular, providing a "vehicle . . . for creating fame." Then again in the fifteenth century with the invention of the printing press; engravings were a popular way of portraying the human face before photography. "Celebrity is essentially a media production, rather than the worthy recognition of greatness," Giles says, echoing Evans, naming hype as its "purest form."

Hype has no object of any value: it just implies "that a phenomenon can be made to appear valuable, even when its value is non-existent" (2000: 20). While he doesn't go into the etymology of the term, we might mention that its root is *huperbolē*,

The Greek for "excess," from which we get hyperbole, an exaggerated statement. Giles cites P.T. Barnum as the pioneer of hyping: the techniques he used for publicizing the exhibits of his shows were much the same as those used today. The Hollywood film industry's publicity machine refined and perfected what was an art for Barnum into something resembling a science. After the 1950s, domestic television became a new medium for creating celebrities *par excellence*. There had been nothing to compare with tv: it served to shrink the distance between viewers and events and the people who featured in the events; but it also began to create events of its own – shows, performances, competitions, and even news items specifically made by and for television. The video recorder pushed things further, allowing viewers to play events over and over again. As with Evans, Giles' stress is on the media as the engine that drives celebrity culture. The actual celebrities are almost incidental to the theory.

Giles believes that there is a longstanding and even desperate desire for fame among human populations. Changing forms of media have effectively made it possible for more and more people to gain the kind of mass exposure that brings fame. Myriad media around the globe rapidly and exponentially reproduce images of people. "The proliferation of media for publicizing the individual has been reflected in a proliferation of celebrated individuals," writes Giles. "As the mass media has expanded, so individuals have had to do less in order to be celebrated" (2000: 32).

The process copies itself like replicating DNA. Technological developments in the media have enabled humans to reproduce images of themselves "on a phenomenal scale, thus providing an evolutionary rationale for the obsessive pursuit of fame." (2000: 53).

While both Evans and Giles acknowledge that other writers (and I need to include myself in this group) see something qualitatively distinctive and exceptional about contemporary celebrity culture, they highlight the continuity in the role of the media. Admittedly, Giles pinpoints the bewilderingly fast reproductive properties of today's media as crucial to the fleeting celebrities that flit across our screens today and disappear next week. But celebrity culture is continuance masquerading as uniqueness. The media were always pivotal: their forms have changed; their effects haven't.

THE SCIENCE OF FAME|

Mark Borkowski accepts the indispensability of the media to celebrity culture and advances the argument one step by offering a set of rules that formally enunciates how people become celebrities. He even expresses it scientifically: $F(T) = B+P(1/10T+1/2T^2)$. F is the level of fame. T is time, measured in three-monthly intervals. B is the base level of fame, such as an unknown reality tv entrant. And P is the increment of fame above the base level "that establishes the individual firmly at the front of public consciousness" (2008: 372). Borkowski calls this "the fame formula."

It sounds formalistic, but makes more sense when we consider Borkowski's overall approach. "Celebrity, as we understand it now, was invented the moment D.W. Griffith moved his camera to take a close-up of one of his stars in the early years of silent film," Borkowski proposes (2008: 379). I should explain Griffith (1875–1948) was an American film director, whose most famous work was *The Birth of a Nation*, released in 1915. Filmgoers watched actors' "pearlescent faces filling screens in the same way one might imagine a god's face." Five years earlier, the disappearance of actor Florence Lawrence alerted the film industry to the exploitability of actors.

Unlike Gabler, but in common with the other theorists mentioned in this chapter, Borkowski unites fame and celebrity, but he assumes film brought a new kind of fame, not just mediated but mediated in a certain way. Borkowski contends that this type of fame could be expanded and practiced: it didn't just happen. An entire industry of publicists was charged with the responsibility of "transforming the base metal of the actor into the gold of celebrity" (2008: 379).

> **A new thermodynamic reaction must be set off under the famous thing or person, most likely by a publicist.**
> *MARK BORKOWSKI*

Borkowski's stress on the industrial apparatus that promotes fame indicates that celebrity culture owes more to the suppliers than to consumers' demands. Fans, it seems, can always be manipulated. But not completely: they still have to be convinced that something or someone is worthy. "Fame still, on the whole, relies on someone being possessed of an extraordinary talent, even if that talent is as simple as owning an extraordinarily photogenic face" (2008: 373).

This appears to contradict his thesis, but Borkowski isn't naive enough to assume extraordinarily talent stands still: it is always being reevaluated and, while he doesn't spell this out, he allows that extraordinary talent can include just being loud, vulgar, and "faintly ridiculous," indicating that talent is basically whatever consumers decide it is. Ridiculousness would not constitute a talent in the conventional sense. How about having an affair with a celebrity athlete? Or performing a heinous act that incurs widespread revulsion or profound disapproval? Being named as the paparazzo who took the photograph of the topless princess?

Borkowski is less interested in the behavior that propels people to the fore of public consciousness – which could be potentially anything; more in the mechanisms that come into play after the spike – and, by spike, Borkowski means the sudden, short-lived surge in media coverage. This is where P (increment of fame above base level) comes into play: repetition is a weak claim on consumers' interests. "However fame can be sustained and refreshed, just as long as there is something new to give it the necessary impetus," writes Borkowski (2008: 373).

Fame, on this account, is contagious. But it needs to be professionally transmitted: "After that initial rush of fame, a new thermodynamic reaction must be set off under the famous thing or person, most likely by a publicist" (2008: 371). The choice of adjective is skillful: thermodynamics deals with the relations between heat and other forms of energy, and Borkowski presumably believes traditional or social media coverage converts into other types of coverage, including gossip and networking, and then back into further media coverage, which then precipitates increased consumer attention.

Borkowski's central point is that there is little if anything spontaneous, intrinsic, impulsive, or random about this process: it's premeditated and sustained by the external stimulus of businesses. The professional maintenance of a favorable public image is known, of course, as public relations, or just pr. Borkowski, himself a pr professional, believes this business has become a central agent in a consumer society.

James Monaco's 1978 book *Celebrity: The media as image makers* and Lisa Lewis' 1992 book *The Adoring Audience: Fan culture and popular media*, as their titles suggest, concentrated on the power of pr in both governing the depiction of celebrities and influencing the experience of consumers through the manipulation of the media earlier in the twentieth century. Borkowski's argument, while consistent with these earlier accounts, suggests the industry became more refined and exact from the 1990s.

There are too many gaps in Borkowski's argument to call it a theory, but there are too many insights to ignore it. It is a kind of insider's perspective, the view of someone who has been involved in the alchemical transformation he writes of. The pr apparatus can, he argues, turn anybody into a celebrity, almost regardless of anything they say or do. That's the easy part. Perpetuating it beyond three months and converting that status into a fungible commodity that has exchange value in a market is the harder part. This is why pr companies are central to the maintenance of fame, and, by implication, to celebrity culture as a whole.

Borkowski doesn't look specifically for narratives in celebrities: his principal interest is in how celebrities are manufactured and for what purpose. The content or the story embodied by a celebrity is less important than the machinery of pr: practically anyone can become famous, no matter how dull and uninteresting they may be. Giles and those stressing the colossal power of the media would probably concur. Gabler and Payne, by contrast, are interested in mood, motivation, and emotion: the reasons why consumers are drawn to celebrities. At the risk of simplifying the distinction: the former are analysts of the objective features, while the latter examine the subjective meanings of celebrities.

| WORSHIPING THE CELEBRITY

Who says God is dead? Chris Rojek, for one, believes humanity has become a godless culture. "Incontrovertibly, for some time, in the West, organized Christian religion has been in transparent decline," he writes, the use of "transparent" seeming to preclude dispute or denial (2012: 119). Priests, rabbis, and imams shouldn't start looking for new jobs just yet, though. Rojek's "incontrovertible" evidence documents a decline in affiliated believers, people who claim to adhere to organized religions, not people who no longer consider themselves followers of any particular faith. Christian denominations collectively make up the numerically biggest organized religion in the world: nearly a third of the world's formal adherents are Christians. Islam is the world's second-largest religion, but, unlike Christianity, its following is growing (currently commanding 21 percent). Judaism, Hinduism, Sikhism, and Buddhism remain stable.

So, the decline in Christianity does not necessarily reflect a global decline in religion. Nor, as Rojek explains, does it indicate, "the cognitive and spiritual framework constructed around the belief in the Deity is now irrelevant" (2012: 119–20). I presume this means that human understanding through thought, experience, and the senses (i.e. cognition) continues to proceed on the assumption that there is a creator and Supreme Being, and that non-material (i.e. spiritual) pursuits remain of importance, even in an increasingly material world.

Religion has been under threat since before the eighteenth-century Enlightenment, which used reason and individualism to challenge traditions of prejudice and superstition. Science and technology addressed many of the questions asked and answered by religion and poured them into a different mold. It reshaped them in a way that invited answers, without any recourse to faith. Science offered proof. This occasioned a gradual decline, not so much in religious belief, but in the significance religion had in society, especially western European societies. Secularization spread, though perhaps not as universally as enthusiasts of science would like. Religion has held fast and still dominates the politics and culture in some parts of the world. In others, it's retreated temporarily, only to return with renewed influence. But science meant that religion's power to bewitch had been weakened. The overall project started by the Enlightenment brought with it disenchantment. This has led some writers to conclude that celebrities have served to re-enchant a world in which deities have either been abandoned or emptied of their power, leaving what Rojek calls a "post-God world."

"Celebrities are our myth bearers; carriers of the divine forces of good, evil, lust and redemption," declared Jill Neimark (1995: 56). Rojek agrees: "Without a religious compass to inform them, and still carrying fervour for a higher, dynamic direction, men and women have cast their nets around for various substitutes. Celebrity culture has filled the vacuum" (2012: 120). In spite of the confusing metaphors (nets and vacuums), we get the point: humans' search for an intelligible set of ideas to explain existence has for long focused on a transcendent form of being or form of intelligence and, as that focus has become less credible, so a space devoid of identifiable figures (a vacuum?) has been left.

"Post-God celebrity is now one of the mainstays of organizing recognition and belonging in secular society," writes Chris Rojek (2001: 58). Celebrities appear as gods in human form or simulacra of departed deities. Celebrity culture, in this view, becomes a functional equivalent of religion, with beliefs and practices associated with religion "converging" with those of celebrity culture.

> *For Ward, the celebrity is the existential being in us all, appearing to live out our fantasies and fears.*

Ostensibly, Pete Ward agrees with this, but with a crucial revision: the like-for-like exchange of old gods for new doesn't take account of changes in both patterns and experiences of worship. He identifies a shift away from the focus on a Supreme Being and toward "a religion of the self" and an emphasis on the subjective meaning worship has for the believer. "Celebrity culture in many ways is part of this new religious terrain," reasons Ward (2011: 69). Religions don't exist separately from contemporary culture: they constitute a great part of it; in other words, they combine with other institutions to form culture. So it's meaningless to isolate religion from celebrity culture: neither is freestanding; they're intermixed.

Ward senses that religion today is characterized by expressive individualism, expressive in this instance meaning effectively conveying thoughts or feelings – the way we worship expresses how we think and feel. Ward invokes Paul Heelas's idea of dedifferentiation (1998). Actually, it's not Heelas's term, but a biological concept meaning a reversal of the process of growth in which cells or tissues become different – they lose their special characteristics. Ward follows Heelas's adaptation to the social sphere. "The collapse of the distinction between secular and religious discourses" has left individuals freely choosing their own beliefs "unconstrained by the boundaries of tradition," as Ward puts it (2011: 70). Traditions survive, though many change, while others collapse. Individuals draw on some traditions and discard others. Ward's overall point is that the conventional divisions of religious and secular or sacred and profane have dissolved, leaving a smorgasbord of beliefs from which everyone and anyone can select their own, according to taste. Whether these qualify as religious is of no consequence: only the meaning they have for the believer matters. Religion is no longer a separate sphere concerned with matters beyond or above the range of normal or merely physical experience. It is *lived*.

The inner life, or the self, has become "the focus of attention and energy," Ward propounds. Religion was once seen as an answer to the question "How can I be saved?" But the more pressing question now is: "How can I feel good about myself?" We've all been turned into "spiritual carnivores," hungry for new answers.

Self-absorption, that is, the preoccupation with one's own emotions and interests, is nothing new. Christopher Lasch documented how this shaped the character of Western society in the 1970s, and we covered his argument in Chapter 7. Tom Wolfe also wrote on this in *New York* magazine: his "The 'me' decade and the third great awakening" actually welcomes the coming of narcissism as "the greatest age of individualism in American history," as he put it (1976). Ward's observations on the twenty-first century appear familiar, though he notices how market forces have both encouraged narcissism and offered solutions to the discontents it fosters: "The advertising industry has offered a steady stream of promises for a better life and constant improvement" (2011: 71).

For Ward, the celebrity is the existential being in us all, appearing to live out our fantasies and fears, as if under our control, but not complete control: "The worship of celebrity is the worship of the self writ large" (2011: 71).

We find ourselves in this spiritual marketplace where religion is personalized and our search for inner peace, happiness, contentment, fulfillment, or some other kind of blessedness bears comparison with our search for a smartphone. Religion, says Ward, is just as susceptible to commodification as more tangible products. And, while he doesn't name them, some religions even have endorsers, albeit unpaid: Buddhism/Richard Gere; Scientology/Tom Cruise; Kabbalah/Madonna; Islam/Akon; there are many other celebrities who make their religious beliefs known. Ward also offers the thought that religions are now as accessible to believers or potential believers as consumer goods. Count how many religious symbols you see people wearing, whether as jewelry, or on a tee-shirt, or in a car, or practically anywhere.

Religion doesn't define a segmental experience in which people reserve a day or days of the week for worship, then forget it: its impact is more total, yet less constraining. Ward's view is that we find spiritual experience in an expanding spectrum of beliefs, many of which wouldn't necessarily come under the heading religion: yoga, for example. The self, rather than the congregation, assembly, or church, is of paramount importance. Religion, for Ward, doesn't stand in opposition to popular culture: it adapts and survives, indeed flourishes through it.

Celebrity culture is not an ersatz religion: the topography of today's cultural landscape simply doesn't permit the demarcation of the sacred and the profane, certainly not in the way it did 20 years ago. But, in a way, celebrities are new gods: they may not be divine, but their images and sounds guarantee a kind of immortality.

| LEGITIMATING CAPITALISM

The Roman satirist Juvenal (c. 60–c. 140) might have been reflecting on the way his countrymen in the first century of the Common Era assigned celebrity status to gladiators when he coined the phrase *panem et circenses*. Translated as "bread and circuses," it describes the way in which ancient Roman leaders would provide food and entertainment to the underprivileged plebeians, allowing them access to the spectacular gladiatorial contests and chariot races at the Colosseum and other vast stadiums. Without the agreeable distractions and a full stomach, the masses might have grown discontented and started to wonder why they had little money, lived in inadequate accommodation, and, unlike their rulers, could never afford life's luxuries. Immersing themselves in the excitement of the contests and cheering on their champions diverted their attention away from more mundane matters.

Juvenal was alluding to power, specifically the uneven distribution of it and how this imbalance was maintained. The sections of the population that had little power and no real chance of gaining the advantages that go with it had to be placated somehow. If not, they might have grown restless and begun to ask searching questions that could destabilize power arrangements. Keeping them satisfied maximized the chances that they wouldn't notice. The entertainment might have been good, wholesome fun – well, as wholesome as pitching humans against lions can be – but it also served an ideological purpose. It fostered a style of popular thinking that was compatible with a particular type of political and economic system.

Critics of sports, such as Paul Hoch (1972) and Jean-Marie Brohm (1978), wrote challenging polemics in the 1970s, identifying sports events as amusements that kept the working class preoccupied. Too preoccupied, it turned out, to oppose capitalist systems that were designed to exploit them. Drawing on Marx's opiate thesis, in which he likened religion to a drug that dulls the senses and provides a temporary sensation of well-being, critics saw sports as a kind of functional equivalent of religion, commanding the attention of millions of fans without delivering any tangible improvements to their lives. Sports and, by implication, other types of popular entertainment have ideological utility: they solidify the status quo.

This invites the kind of images of heads of mega-corporations gathered around a table, hatching plots designed to keep the working classes from noticing how the system works against them. Neither Hoch nor Brohm, nor any of the other theorists who followed their leads pictured the scene so melodramatically. Sports and entertainment today might be overpraised and soak up too much of our time and money; but they haven't been designed to assist society's ruling power holders. They are best viewed as convenience rather than connivance.

Celebrity athletes aren't the only ones doing ideological work: *all* celebrities do. This is hardly a profound statement: more a statement of the obvious. They massage our senses in a way not totally dissimilar to the gladiators. Like the citizens of ancient Rome, we are captivated, enthused, and thrilled by people we don't know and who probably don't care about us (despite what Lady Gaga said). Maybe we don't have the same deprivations from which we have to be distracted, but there are serious issues that impact on everybody: climate change, globalization, war, for instance. These and other issues already provoke widespread dissent and, often, outright protest. The prospects for even more forceful protests might be great, were it not for the diverting power of celebrities. At least, that's what theorists of the bread and circuses school would argue. Even those who are not persuaded by the basic version have converted its premise into a more sophisticated model, the engine of which is still ideology.

Charles L. Ponce de Leon argues that celebrity culture is the "direct outgrowth of developments that most of us regard as progressive: the spread of a market economy and the rise of democratic, individualistic values" (2002: 4). P. David Marshall agrees and extends this line of argument to the present day: celebrity culture fits the requirements of consumer capitalism, which needs a self-replenishing demand for disposable products and a liberal democracy that upholds the sanctity of individualism. Celebrities are not just people; they are influential representatives. They represent "subject positions that audiences can adopt or adapt in the formation of social identities" (1997: 65). There is a "celebrity-function," which is to "organize the legitimate and illegitimate domains of the personal and the individual within the social" (1997: 57).

Matt Hills interprets this: "The celebrity or star appears to give rise to, and anchor their very own authenticity and individuality. But what appears as a natural property of the charismatic celebrity is actually produced by discourses of celebrity" (2005: 151). Giles pares this down to basics: "The capitalist system uses celebrities to promote individualism and illusions of democracy (the 'anyone can do it' myth) . . . capitalism retains its hold on society, by reducing all human activity to private 'personalities' and the inner life of the individual" (2000: 19, 72).

Capitalism's growing dependence on hyper-consumerism has led to an ethic of hedonism and health, excess and extravagance.

A culture fixated on the exploits of inconsequential people, who may be hugely entertaining but offer few tangible benefits to society and make no appreciable impact on the lives of people, apart from helping them spend money, is unlikely to be a crucible of political discontent. At least, according to this analysis. An alternative might emphasize the role of prominent figures in fomenting opposition to, for example, globalization and foreign policy. But Marshall suggests the citizens of a society in which celebrities are valued are likely to be docile and manageable. They're also likely to be aspirational: they have hopes and yearnings to be celebrities themselves. This is, of course, an individualistic ambition. The whole effect is a stable society in which people identify with celebrities, buy products that bear their imprimatur, structure their goals around being famous, and rarely pause to reflect critically on the political order.

Graeme Turner believes that Marshall's "proposition that the celebrity-commodity provides a very powerful form of legitimation for capitalism's models of exchange and value by demonstrating that the individual has a commercial as well as a cultural value" (2004: 25).

Like the proto-celebrity gladiators, today's celebs serve political ends in providing pleasure. They participate, however unwittingly, in a process that entices – some might say inveigles – us into thinking about ourselves and Them in a particular way: as freestanding individuals living in a merit-rewarding society; and one, we might add, in which the good life advertised by celebrities is open to anyone with enough money. This is, for Turner, the primary function: "Celebrities are developed to make money" (2004: 34). In the kind of competitive market system fostered by capitalism, only ever-increasing consumption can keep the system running. Despite the title of this book, celebrity is business first, culture second.

Turner insists that any account of celebrities must be predicated on the recognition that "the interests served are first of all those of capital." Capitalism's growing dependence on what some call hyper-consumerism has led to an ethic of hedonism and health, excess and extravagance. Prudence, self-denial, deferred gratification, and all manner of frugality have been rendered old-fashioned by a culture that continually tries to develop discontents that can be salved only by buying commodities. Celebrities have to be understood in this context: they operate with the advertising industry – almost *as* an advertising industry – to persuade, cajole, and convince consumers that dependence is nothing to be ashamed of. If we depend on commodities, so what? As long as we have money enough to assuage the urge to consume, there is no problem.

None of the contemporary theorists on celebrity culture subscribes to the crude bread and circuses explanation. If that were so, celebrities would be no more than eye-catching diversions that prevent us noticing more pressing issues. Yet, there is a sense in which both Marshall and Turner understand the utility of celebrities to the capitalist enterprise and believe that this is their *raison d'être* – the purpose that accounts for their very existence.

LOGIC OF CONSUMERISM |

Perhaps the celebrity is, as Gabler detects, a living narrative secreting a moral that we find both intriguing and instructive; or possibly an age-old symbol that's constantly revised and updated in a way that makes him or her appear fresh. Maybe the modern form of celebrity is an outgrowth of a media that replicates itself faster than a virus. Borkowski's fame formula may offer a preposterous method, but his overall argument about the manufacture of fame gains traction, not with every new celebrity, but with every one-time celebrity who is returned to the cultural wilderness bereft of pr. And there will be plenty of them in the years ahead.

At a different level, some make sense of celebrity culture by comparing it to a new religious movement; perhaps it *is* a new religious movement. The similarities in patterns of worship, expressions of veneration, and even in gratifications are compelling. The sometimes-fanatical devotion we show has tempted some writers into seeing celebrity culture as a kind of secular religion; impulse seems to dictate the behavior of some consumers more certainly than calculation.

Yet, for others, celebrities, though often godlike, are actually mere instruments of a capitalist system geared only to realizing a profit, but adapting elegantly to changing markets. If this is so, then the concept of an entire industry calibrated to its requirements is not so far-fetched.

There's support for all of these theories, or models of celebrity culture, though none of them provides a complete answer to the question: Why?

Celebrity culture is guided by the logic of consumerism and the celebrities are guided by this basic message: enjoy novelty, change, excitement, and every possible stimulant that can be bought over a shop counter or via a website. The message falls on receptive ears. Consumers thrill to the sight and sound of celebrities, not because they're dupes, suckers, airheads, or simpletons, but because they have become willing accomplices in the enterprise. They too are guided by the logic of consumerism.

Appetites that were once damned as the cause of unhappiness and instability are extolled. An expansion of demand for commodities and a continuous redefining cycle of what's luxury and what's necessity have led to the elevation of new groups into the sphere of consumption we know as celebrity culture.

As the first wave of theories of celebrity culture arrived, much of the critical impulse concerned its democratizing effect. The pronouncement of death for the old-style stars and egalitarian promises of fame for all seemed to herald a new continuous communion in which celebrity status was available to everyone, regardless of talent, if only for short periods. Reality television, as we learned earlier, seemed to confirm the promise.

Accompanying this and integral to it was what we might call a democratization of taste. Consumer items that might once have been associated with the rich and famous became widely available. Everyone could participate in a version of the good life. The once-unbreachable wall between Them and Us was replaced by gossamer thin gauze that was thin enough to be seen through and occasionally torn. Consumers defined themselves by the commodities they bought. Derek Layder alludes to this when he observes: "The pervasive effects of consumerism link identity and social status to the market for commodities" (2006: 53). "The compulsive buying of new fashions and new products" is one manifestation of this.

In 1991, Christopher Lasch wrote of the kind of society he dreaded, one in which abundance would appear to be available to everyone, while in reality being restricted to the wealthy: "The progressive conception of history implied a society of supremely cultivated consumers" (1991: 531). We now have them. In this sense, celebrity culture has been successful: the seamless unity occasioned by the end of the traditional Them and Us has brought delirious pleasure to billions the world over. Consumers devour magazines, movies, downloads, and practically everything else bearing the image, signature, or just aura of celebrities. And celebrity culture has been even more successful than Lasch could have imagined. It thrives in painlessly easing money away from people who, in a genuine sense, feel themselves part of the communion, which is less about spiritual unity, more about market harmony.

Celebrity culture does not, of course, come with a free pull-out panacea for all the problems that afflict us in the early twenty-first century. For all the well-intentioned efforts of the campaigning celebrities we discussed in Chapter 11, we have to conclude that they have prompted big questions, though without answering them. But there may still be opportunities: after all, there has probably never been a comparable time in history when so many people have held the ability to influence, inspire, and perhaps incite others to action. We've seen glimpses of this when celebrities confront particular issues, such as global warming, globalization, or debt relief. But, so far, there has been no wide-ranging vision that might shape the way in which people view the world.

This is probably asking too much: what celebrity is prepared to risk rearranging the thoughts of his or her fans in a way that will undermine their devotion? "Stop buying my downloads, don't rent from Netflix, or go to the movies. And don't buy cologne, clothes, or the jewelry just 'cause you see celebs wearing something similar. But, above all, become interested in people who say things that enlighten or do things that matter!" This would be like trying to stop a car with no brakes while driving it.

Celebrity culture has offered us a distinctive vision, a beguiling one too: one in which there are few limits, an expanding range of opportunities and inexhaustible hope. Celebrities themselves are, as I've stressed throughout, the living proof of this. Ideas like restraint, prudence and modesty have either been discredited or just forgotten. Celebrity culture has replaced them with impetuosity, frivolity, prodigality. Human impulses like these were once seen as vices; now they are almost virtuous.

Universal consumption, the promise of luxury for all, and an endless cycle of insatiable desire have been introduced, not through political discourse, but through the creation of a new cultural group. Celebrities have energized our material expectations, helping shape a culture in which demand is now a basic human experience. What were once luxuries are now regarded as necessities. What was once improvement is now replaced by upgrading. For all the fantasy and escapist tendencies it radiates, celebrity culture's most basic imperative is material: it encourages consumption at every level of society.

Celebrity culture's paradoxical feat is not in advancing a worldview in which social discontents have their causes in the scarcity of material commodities so much as in promoting an idea that we shouldn't think about this long enough to distract ourselves from what we do best – consume even more of those very commodities.

Perhaps the archetypal celebrity is, as Ward and some of the other theorists seem to suggest, the existential being in us all; but maybe there is a much more superficial explanation: the celebrity just represents the way life on our planet has become a set of random narratives watched by all via closed-circuit surveillance, reality tv cameras, or smartphones.

TIMELINE

18th Century

- The Age of Reason advances scientific discoveries that undermine religious ideas and hasten secularization. Energized by the Enlightenment, the Industrial Revolution, which begins late in the century, creates new wealth and eventually gives the West political and economic hegemony. Education and political power are diffused through the class structure. The revolution is given impetus by the inventions of the steam engine and the spinning machine, their respective creators, Watt and Arkwright, earning international acclaim in the 1760s. Military leaders such as Nelson and Napoleon are held in reverence. Kant and Rousseau are renowned intellectuals, the latter being an influence behind the French Revolution of 1789. Goya, Voltaire, and Beethoven are prominent artistic, literary, and musical figures. Newspapers have been in evidence since 1665 when the *London Gazette* began publishing; the *Boston News-Letter*, which began publishing in 1704, is America's first recorded newspaper; only the educated minority read newspapers.

19th Century

1829
- George Stevenson builds his steam train "The Rocket," which becomes crucial to the industrial process.

1831
- Michael Faraday's experiments with electromagnetism stimulate work on broadcasting, leading to radio.
- The term "fancy" – a possible forerunner of "fan" – is in popular use to describe aficionados of prize fighting.

1832
- A rotary device called a phenakistoscope demonstrates motion pictures; the zoetrope is a similar experimental machine.

1837
- Samuel Morse pioneers telegraph signaling; news and information can be transmitted almost instantaneously.

1842
- Charles Dickens crosses the Atlantic to tour America and further his renown.
- The rotary press is introduced; this becomes crucial to publishing.

1852
- William Fox Talbot's experiments suggest that tones can be reproduced by means of photographic screens.

1859

- Blondin (aka Jean-François Gravelet) first crosses Niagara, a feat that adds to his growing international renown.
- Darwin's *The Origin of Species* is published, introducing a theory of natural selection that adds to secularization; Darwin becomes, according to Janet Browne (writing in 2003), "a nineteenth-century scientific celebrity."

1861

- Blondin appears at London's Crystal Palace, turning somersaults on stilts on a rope stretched across the central transept, 170 feet (52 meters) off the ground.

1871

- P.T. Barnum launches what becomes known as "The Greatest Show on Earth," using contrived stories to publicize his show in a manner that foreshadows what is later known as hyping.

1876

- Alexander Graham Bell exhibits his telephone at the World's Fair in Philadelphia.

1879

- A primitive form of radio is introduced.

1880

- The multiple reproduction of photographs and illustrations in halftone – that is, composed of minute dots – by newspapers and journals heralds the beginning of a "graphic revolution" in which the ability to reproduce images mechanically improves and images become central to popular culture, at first through photography and, later, television. **CONDITION**

1882

- Already a major literary and theatrical figure, Oscar Wilde tours America.

1883

- Buffalo Bill Cody's Wild West Show starts touring; it becomes one of the most popular forms of entertainment in the Western world.

1887

- German sociologist Ferdinand Tönnies writes about the replacement of *Gemeinschaft*, or community, with *Gesellschaft*, which describes modern society.

1894

- Thomas Edison's kinetoscope, a device that makes the exhibition of motion pictures possible, is demonstrated in New York; this is one of precursors of cinema, another being the Lumière brothers' *cinématographe*, which is unveiled the following year.
- The term "fan" is in popular use to describe baseball enthusiasts.

1895

- Marconi perfects the radio, or wireless.

1896

- Blondin gives his final performance in Belfast.

1899

- "Conspicuous consumption" is a phrase used by economic theorist Thorstein Veblen to describe the emerging pattern of signifying membership of a social group through consumable items. **CAUSE**

20th Century

1900

- Prominent figures are renowned for their achievements in the previous century, and include explorers (for example, Stanley and, later, Peary), inventors (Edison, Marconi), military leaders (Lee, Kitchener), political leaders (Theodore Roosevelt, Disraeli), scientists (Pasteur, Lister), literary figures (Dickens, Melville), and financial and industrial leaders (Rockefeller, Ford, who starts his motor company in 1903). Florence Nightingale, the nurse, is famous for her heroic work caring for soldiers in the Crimean War. Prominent artistic and literary figures, such as Tchaikovsky (who died in 1893) and Renoir (d.1919), are noted for the body of work they produce. Incumbents of senior religious positions, such as Popes and Archbishops, are revered. Entertainers and athletes are regarded as less worthy of attention.

1901

- Queen Victoria, a monarch of international prominence, dies, ending her 64-year reign as Queen of Great Britain and Ireland and closing a period characterized by temperance and prudishness.

1904

- Sir J.A. Fleming invents the radio valve, which is designed to detect radio waves in the air, and improves the quality of wireless transmission.

1905

- Neon signs are introduced; these are used for advertising and become literally a sign of fame ("your name in lights").

1907

- *Scientific American* is the first journal to use the word "television."

1910

- The faked death of Florence Lawrence to create publicity for "The Biograph Girl" presages the start of the "star system."
- Film magazines, such as *American Magazine*, go into print, reflecting the growing interest in film gossip.
- King Edward VII, of Great Britain and Ireland, son of Queen Victoria and Prince Albert, appears in a print advertisement endorsing Angelus piano-players.

1913

- US President Theodore Roosevelt lends his name to a new toy called the Teddy Bear.
- Harry Houdini performs his most famous feat, escaping from a straitjacket while suspended upside down in a glass and steel tank filled with water.
- Between now and 1928, the average amount of fabric needed to dress a woman declines 36 percent from 19.25 yards (17.6m) to 7 yards (6.4m), suggesting a sharp move away from Victorian traditions.

1915

- Release of D.W. Griffith's influential film *The Birth of a Nation*. Mark Borkowski believes, "Celebrity, as we understand it now," was invented when Griffith first used his innovative close-up shots in his films.

1921

- Roscoe "Fatty" Arbuckle is arrested for the sexual assault and manslaughter of a female actor at a party in San Francisco; although he is cleared, his films are withdrawn and his film contract canceled; he dies destitute in 1933.

1922

- RCA begin selling "radio music boxes," effectively heralding popular broadcasting; by the mid-1930s, about 60 percent of homes in the USA and Britain have radios, even though the broadcasts they receive are limited.

1925

- Greta Garbo, of Sweden, signs a contract with MGM, becoming Hollywood's leading female actor, first in silent films and then in talkies; her taciturn, often cold attitude and refusal to talk to journalists creates a mysterious aura that fortifies her iconic status.

- The telephotographic ("telephoto") lens is invented by C. Francis Jenkins; this makes it possible for photographers to gain images of distant objects.

1927

- Five radio listeners die, supposedly from heart attacks, during the Gene Tunney–Jack Dempsey world heavyweight title fight.
- Charles Lindbergh earns international recognition for the first transatlantic flight; his renown is enlarged later by tragedy when his son is kidnapped and murdered.
- Warner Brothers release *The Jazz Singer*, the first motion picture to include dialogue; the first all-talking film *Lights of New York* is released the following year.

1929

- There are 23 million cars in the USA, a steep rise from 8 million ten years earlier; greater mobility assists both physical and social liberation.

1931

- *The Public Enemy* is the first of a series of films in which James Cagney adopts the tough, gangster image that will become emblematic of his Hollywood career.

1932

- The film of Ernest Hemingway's *A Farewell to Arms* is released; by this time, a public "Hemingway" image has emerged.

1935

- In *Captain Blood*, Errol Flynn introduces the swashbuckling hero-adventurer screen persona that he emulates in his private life.
- Howard Hughes, the industrialist and film producer, is acknowledged as a hero for breaking the air speed record, though he achieves even greater renown from the mid-1950s when he mysteriously refuses to be seen in public. He dies a recluse in 1976.

1938

- Sociologist Robert Merton's study "Social structure and anomie" is published, highlighting the influence of consumer aspirations and the power of the market economy on individuals. **CAUSE**

1939

- John Wayne's role in *Stagecoach* creates an enduring persona that Wayne retains throughout during his career: strong, heroic, patriotic and traditionally masculine.

1941

- 1st tv commercial is screened.

1945

- Second World War ends and its military heroes, such as Eisenhower and Montgomery, are held in reverence, as are statesmen like F.D. Roosevelt and Churchill. In the immediate postwar period, they, together with scientists and discoverers, such as Baird, Curie, Einstein, Goodyear, and Whittle, and explorers, such as Amundsen, Fuchs, and Hillary, are exemplary figures with the quality of moral leadership. The authority of such heroic figures from the first half of the century slowly erodes over subsequent decades, confidence discharging more rapidly in the 1980s. **CONDITION**

1946

- Television is exhibited at the World's Fair in New York; sets for domestic use become available. **CONDITION**

1948

- Lucille Ball is cast as "Liz Cugat" in *My Favorite Husband*, a CBS radio show that develops into *I Love Lucy*.

- *TV Guide* begins publication; by the 1970s, it is one of the best-selling magazines in the USA.
- Community Access Television begins in Pennsylvania; this later develops into cable tv.
- Gandhi is assassinated; his efforts in the Indian struggle for independence from British rule distinguished him as a charismatic leader.

1949

- Baseball player Eddie Waitkus is shot by a fan in Chicago, becoming the first victim of what later became known as stalkers.
- Bill Bernbach (1911–1982) co-founds Doyle Dane Bernbach; he becomes one of the most influential people in advertising history, challenging the accepted wisdom that advertising is an emergent science.

1950

- *The Lonely Crowd: A study of the changing American character* by David Riesman and his colleagues is published; it documents the fragmentation of social life anticipated by Tönnies 63 years earlier.
- James Stewart negotiates a contract allowing him a share of the profits for the movie *Winchester '73*, which is released this year. (The eponymous lever-action rifle was itself a popular icon, being used by a variety of western entertainment figures, including Buffalo Bill and John Wayne.)

1951

- *I Love Lucy* begins; it becomes the most commercially successful television show of the 1950s, turning Lucille Ball into one of the best-known women in the world.

1954

- The Senator Joseph McCarthy hearings are televised.
- Marilyn Monroe appears in the nude on the centerfold of the first issue of *Playboy*. Her next nude photoshoot was in 1962, shortly before her death.

1955

- Solomon Asch's psychological studies disclose the importance of peer groups in influencing judgment and opinions.
- Commercial television starts in Britain, ending the BBC's monopoly; the development opens new opportunities for advertisers, including American advertisers. First commercial is for Gibbs SR toothpaste.

1956

- Psychologists D. Horton and R.R. Wohl publish their article "Mass communication and parasocial interaction" in the journal *Psychiatry*; it suggests how tv viewers can form one-sided relationships with figures they have never met.

1957

- The Soviet Union sends the first satellite, Sputnik 1, into orbit.
- Vance Packard's *The Hidden Persuaders*, a book that reveals the extensive influence of advertising, is published; it is complemented in 1959 with the author's *The Status Seekers*, an analysis of how people crave consumer goods not for their use, but for the prestige they confer on the owner. **CAUSE**
- Suzy Parker (1932–2003), the face of Coco Chanel and forerunner of supermodels, earns an unprecedented $100,000 per year.

1958

- In his *The Affluent Society*, economist J.K. Galbraith argues that basic material needs have been satisfied by mass affluence and that advertising has become crucial in creating excessive consumption and a corresponding consumer debt. **CAUSE**
- Tazio Secchiaroli, a freelance newspaper photographer, sparks pandemonium in Rome by taking shots of King Farouk, Ava Gardner, Anita Ekberg, and others without their permission. Pictures of the events appear in various publications.
- Telephoto lenses for use on 35mm cameras are now in regular production.
- US National Association of Broadcasters bans subliminal advertising, i.e. below the threshold of consciousness and so affecting viewers without their being aware of it.

1960

- Federico Fellini's film *La Dolce Vita* features a Secchiaroli-like "Signor Paparazzo" (described by his mistress as a "vulture") and introduces a new generic noun to the popular vocabulary.
- The televised John F. Kennedy–Richard M. Nixon presidential election debates highlight the power of television in shaping perception.
- About 90 percent of homes have a television set.

1961

- In his book *The Image*, Daniel Boorstin offers what seems at the time an amusing tautology, suggesting there is an emergent class of people who are well known for their "well-knownness".

1962

- Marcello Geppetti takes his influential photograph of Elizabeth Taylor and Richard Burton. **TRIGGER**
- Telstar 1 provides an eight-minute transmission; Telstar 1 is the first of several communications satellites capable of sending signals to earth that go into orbit over the next several years; they provide the stimulus for the development of a global media. **CONDITION**

1963

- Charismatic US President John F. Kennedy is assassinated by Lee Harvey Oswald in Dallas, Texas; the killing is captured on film by private citizen Abraham Zapruder.

1964

- Taylor marries Burton in Montreal; Burton is Taylor's fifth husband; after 10 years, the world's most renowned couple divorce, only to have a secret wedding ceremony in Africa in 1975, followed by a second honeymoon 16 months after splitting up. In 2012, the movie *Liz and Dick* dramatizes the romance, with Lindsay Lohan in the role of Taylor.
- The summer Olympics in Tokyo are broadcast internationally "live".

1965

- Foster Grant start an ad campaign featuring the likes of Raquel Welch, Woody Allen, Peter Sellers, and other Hollywood stars of the period wearing sunglasses, in its "Who's that behind the Foster Grants?" advertising campaign.

1966

- Former Hollywood actor Ronald Reagan is elected governor of California; he is re-elected in 1970.

1967

- George Best's fame broadens as he features in Manchester United's win over Benfica in the European Cup Final.

1968

- The *National Enquirer* moves headquarters and changes policy; circulation increases.
- Athletes Tommie Smith and John Carlos expose the power of global television to highlight social and political issues when they make Black Power gestures on the Olympic victory rostrum in Mexico City.

1969

- Apollo 11 beams images from the moon's surface back to earth.
- Britain's *Affluent Worker* study discloses a materialistic working class with bourgeois aspirations. **CAUSE**
- Joe Namath leads the New York Jets to an upset victory in the Super Bowl.
- Andy Warhol launches his magazine *Inter/View*, in which he famously predicts: "In the future, everyone will be world-famous for fifteen minutes."
- McDonald's (founded 1948) updates its logo to feature the now-iconic "golden arches" that feature on its franchises.

1971

- Philip Zimbardo's prison simulation experiments disclose interest in human interaction, which later manifests in reality television.

1972

- Photographer Ron Galella receives a federal court order barring him from approaching within 50 yards of Jacqueline Kennedy Onassis or her children.
- The *Star* magazine launches, prefiguring an increase in publications specializing in gossip.
- Jane Fonda visits Hanoi, Vietnam, during the midst of the Vietnam War.
- Computer scientists show an early version of what is later to become the internet.

1973

- *An American Family*, a fly-on-the-wall documentary is shown; it anticipates the format of reality tv; a similar British show, *The Family,* features the same approach.

1974

- Cher and Sonny Bono begin divorce proceedings; the *National Enquirer* builds popularity by carrying full details of the breakup.
- Psychologist Stanley Milgram's study *Obedience to Authority* shows how effectively human behavior can be manipulated given the appropriate circumstances.
- *People* magazine launches.

1975

- Cher and Sonny Bono divorce.

1976

- HBO begins full transmission, showing the Muhammad Ali–Joe Frazier fight from Manila; it uses a transponder on a commercial satellite, which relays signals to cable systems; the technology allows the global exchange of television (or telephone) signals by means of microwaves directly to the home, without the need for relay stations; within two years, HBO, which specializes in movies and sports, is the most popular cable channel with 1.5 million subscribers. **CONDITION**

1977

- The *National Enquirer* sells 7 million copies of the issue featuring pictures of Elvis Presley in his coffin.

1978

- The British Conservative Party led by Margaret Thatcher appoints Saatchi & Saatchi (founded in 1970) as its advertising agency and wins three successive elections. The agency's campaigns changed the course of British politics. One iconic poster shows a dole queue snaking out from an employment office and disappearing into the distance. The strap is: "Labour isn't working," and beneath, in smaller type, "Britain's better off with the Tories."

1979

- *The Culture of Narcissism by* Christopher Lasch is published; it describes a culture increasingly reliant on the media to define its "needs." **CONDITION**

1980

- Reagan is elected president of the USA; he is re-elected in 1984.
- ESPN starts transmission; by 1998, it broadcasts to 160 countries.
- CNN starts operations; within 20 years, it reaches 212 countries, with a combined audience of 1 billion.

1981

- Diana marries Prince Charles. The Royal Wedding attracts 28 million British television viewers and 750 million worldwide.
- MTV starts transmission; in 1987, the first of several analogous stations around the world is launched.
- Assassination attempt on Reagan by a fan fixated on Jodie Foster.
- *Us* adds to the growing number of celebrity magazines.

1982

- *USA Today* is launched by Gannett Publishing.

1983

- Madonna releases her first self-titled album.
- Michael Jackson's "Billie Jean" is entered onto MTV's playlist after a dispute with CBS.
- The Reagan administration announces a program of deregulating (decreasing government control of) business and broadcasting, and facilitates more competition among American media companies.
- 50 major media corporations dominate the global industry.

1984

- Burton dies of a cerebral hemorrhage; Taylor's apprehension about the media deters her from attending the funeral.
- *The Cosby Show* begins airing; by the early 1990s, the African American consumer market is estimated to be worth $200 billion.
- Michael Jordan leads the US national team to Olympic gold medal; he later turns professional and signs a landmark deal with Nike; the Olympic Games are broadcast in stereo.

1985

- LiveAid concerts in aid of a famine in sub-Saharan Africa signify the power of popular entertainers to raise awareness of social issues through the media.

1986

- Oprah Winfrey's Chicago talk show goes on national television.

1987

- There are now only 29 corporations that dominate the global media.

1988

- Rob Lowe's career is in the ascendance after a series of successful films. He is 22.

1989

- Madonna's *Like a Prayer* album is released; Pepsi pulls out of a $5 million endorsement deal with her.
  TRIGGER
- Sky satellite tv channel is launched.
- Rob Lowe's career is threatened when a sex tape featuring him and two girls, one of whom is under 16, is released; ten years later, he reappears triumphantly in the tv show *The West Wing*.

1990

- Warner Communications and Time Inc. merge in a $14.1 billion deal to create the world's largest media corporation; together with other media corporation takeovers and realignments, it combines to reduce the number of dominant media corporations to 23.
- Madonna's "Justify my love" is excluded from MTV's playlists.

1991

- CNN reports on Persian Gulf War "live."
- The film *Truth or Dare*, or *In Bed With Madonna*, as it is entitled in Britain, goes on general release.
- *The Jerry Springer Show* begins broadcasting.
- William Kennedy Smith is acquitted of rape after a highly publicized trial.

1992

- Mike Tyson's rape trial is a global *cause célèbre*; Tyson is sentenced to three years' imprisonment
- Diana and Charles announce their separation.
- Madonna's book *Sex* goes on sale at $50 (£30).
- MTV starts *The Real World*, a precursor of reality television.
- Two serious books on fans, Henry Jenkins' *Textual Poachers* and *The Adoring Audience* edited by Lisa A. Lewis, challenge popular conceptions by viewing fandom as a form of empowerment.
- Bill Clinton accentuates the importance of image management during his successful US presidential election campaign.

1993

- Critics berate *Body of Evidence*, featuring Madonna.

1994

- The O.J. Simpson trial commands the attention of the world's media.
- A fan of tennis player Steffi Graf stabs her rival Monica Seles during a game in Germany.
- Michael Jackson marries Lisa Marie Presley, daughter of Elvis, in a secret ceremony in the Dominican Republic that evades the purview of the paparazzi; the couple deny they are married for two months; eighteen months later, Presley files for divorce.

1995

- Hugh Grant is fined and put on two years' probation after pleading no contest to charges of lewd behavior with prostitute Divine Brown on Hollywood's Sunset Strip; in the following years, he makes several successful films, including *Four Weddings and a Funeral*.

1996

- The Spice Girls' "Wannabe" is released and launches a band that is later listed by *Forbes* as one of the top global "brands"; the band portends the rise of other "manufactured" performers.
- Tiger Woods makes his professional début and signs a five-year deal with Nike valued at $40 million.
- Disney takes over Capital Cities/ABC for $19 billion, creating a movie, tv and publishing giant with capacity for vertical integration; it is the biggest media deal to date and reduces the number of dominant media corporations to 12.
- Madonna earns plaudits for her lead role in the film *Evita*.
- The US Telecommunications Act deregulates the media industry, giving corporate Hollywood a near-monopoly of cinema ownership and cable tv (permitting more vertical integration); President Bill Clinton negotiates first rights for US companies in Latin American broadcasting and gives himself "fast track" approval on trade deals for media companies.
- Ricardo Lopez mails a package containing sulfuric acid to Björk's London home and then kills himself in front of a video camera.

1997

- The *Daily Mirror* pays a reported £265,000 ($450,000) for British rights to publish shots of Diana and Dodi Al-Fayed on their vacation off Sardinia. The photographer Mario Brenna earns an estimated $7 million from global sales of the pictures.
- Diana dies in a car accident in Paris; the photographers who chase her prior to the crash are later cleared of wrongdoing. **TRIGGER**

1998

- Clinton's affair with Monica Lewinsky dominates the media and sparks impeachment proceedings; Clinton remains in office until 2001.
- George Michael is fined and ordered to do community service after being found guilty of lewd behavior in a public lavatory in Los Angeles.
- Robert Downey Jr. tells a Los Angeles County judge his addictions are like "a loaded gun in my mouth . . . and I like the taste of gun-metal." Downey is in the middle of a series of numerous arrests, rehab visits, and incarcerations.
- Madonna is subpoenaed and appears to give evidence against a stalker.
- 66 percent of US homes have cable tv.

1999

- Viacom purchases CBS for $34.5 billion, the biggest media acquisition at this point; there are now only 11 dominant media corporations.
- Hollywood actors join antiglobalization protesters challenging the World Trade Organization conference in Seattle.
- *Heat* launches in Britain as a general entertainment magazine; after a year of disappointing sales, it adopts a celebrity-centric approach and its sales soar.

- John de Mol launches a new show he has designed on Dutch television; within six years, 70 versions of *Big Brother* are shown in countries around the world.
- *PopStars*, a documentary series following the creation of an all-girl group, True Bliss, from 500 contestants, is shown on New Zealand television; it is a seminal program with many variations being produced globally over the following years.

21st Century

2000

- British and American versions of *Big Brother* start; in the USA, *Survivor* begins.
- AOL acquires Time Warner in a deal valued at $166 billion (£100bn) to create the biggest of the ten dominant media corporations in the world.
- French tennis player Natalie Tauziat criticizes the priority the media afford "aesthetics and charisma" in sport; it is a veiled reference to Anna Kournikova, 12th-ranked women's tennis player, but the world's highest-paid female athlete with an income of over $10 million, only 6.4 percent of which is prize money, the rest from endorsements and photoshoots for, among others, *Esquire*, *GQ*, and *Maxim*.
- Venus Williams signs a $40 million promotional deal with Reebok; this is thought to be the most lucrative endorsement contract held by a female.
- *OK!* magazine secures the exclusive contract with Michael Douglas and Catherine Zeta-Jones to cover their New York wedding; archrival *Hello!* publishes unauthorized photographs.
- A British version of *PopStars* begins, its eventual winners emerging the following year.

2001

- Hear'Say, the band formed from the British *PopStars*, becomes the first group to top the British single and album charts simultaneously with début releases; the band begins to break up within a year; Liberty X, a band formed out of losing contestants, has more commercial success than the winners.
- The Spice Girls break up.
- *Pop Idol* starts in Britain.
- Wynona Ryder is arrested for shoplifting in Beverly Hills.

2002

- Angelina Jolie adopts a child from Cambodia. She later adopts a further two children and has three biological children.
- Bono establishes foundation called Debt, AIDS, Trade, Africa (DATA).
- Beyoncé features in her first film, *Austin Powers in Goldmember*.
- *American Idol*, the US counterpart to Britain's *Pop Idol*, starts; by 2006, it averages 27 million viewers and becomes the USA's most expensive program for advertising after the Super Bowl, with 30-second spots costing $700,000 (£420,000).
- There are just nine dominant media corporations: AOL Time Warner, Disney, Bertelsmann, Viacom, TCI, General Electric, Rupert Murdoch's News Corp., Sony, and Seagram, all with vertical integration capacities.
- A team of British and US psychologists introduces the "celebrity worship scale" to measure individuals' intensity of interest.

2003

- Michael Jackson is interviewed on television and indicates that he has shared his bed with children.
- Arnold Schwarzenegger is elected governor of California; he serves until 2011, then returns to film.
- Excerpts of a sex tape featuring Paris Hilton are uploaded; 13 million viewers watch the tv show *The Simple Life* in which she features; over the next three years, she is contracted to appear in eight films.
- Jennifer Aniston appears on the cover of *Vogue*'s best-selling issue of the year (and again in 2004). *InStyle* also features her in its best-selling edition.
- Madonna kisses both Britney Spears and Christina Aguilera at MTV Music Awards.
- Beyoncé's first solo album, *Dangerously in Love*, sells 6 million copies.
- Douglas and Zeta-Jones are awarded £14,500 ($22,000) damages from *Hello!* magazine for breach of privacy and rights "of confidence"; Zeta-Jones famously says in her evidence that £1 million ($1.5m) is

not very much money to her and to spend three times that amount [in legal costs] to recover less than £15,000 ($22,715) defies all logic.
- Oprah Winfrey is valued at over $1 billion by *Forbes*.
- Kobe Bryant is tried for sexual assault; he is subsequently cleared.
- LeBron James turns professional and signs a reported $90 million contract with Nike.
- David Beckham moves from Manchester United to Real Madrid after globally reported transfer negotiations.

2004
- Facebook incorporates and moves its operating base to Palo Alto, California. Less than a year later, it buys the domain name facebook.com. By 2010, it has 900 million users.
- *The X Factor* starts in Britain.
- Beckham is involved in an internationally publicized scandal after reports of an extra-marital affair.
- Martha Stewart begins a five-month prison sentence; she is released in 2005 to find her companies prospering.
- Princess Caroline of Monaco wins a key ruling from the European Court of Human Rights, which confirms that the publishing of paparazzi photographs of the Princess in a public place was a violation of her right to privacy.
- Cosmetic surgeries increase at a yearly rate of 17 percent in the USA (now 214,200 procedures; or 1 person in every 1,168) and 35 per cent in Britain (16,350; or 1 in 3,670). When nonsurgical cosmetic procedures, such as Botox, laser hair removal, and chemical peels, are added, the totals are: USA: 8 million; UK: 500,000.
- The US publication the *Star* is revamped as a glossy magazine; it started as a tabloid in 1972.

2005
- Michael Jackson is cleared of child molestation charges after one of the most publicized trials in history; over 1,000 journalists are sent to Santa Maria, California, to cover the event.
- A Los Angeles court jails for three years a stalker who threatened to cut Catherine Zeta-Jones into pieces.
- *Hello!* magazine wins a legal battle to overturn a ruling, which would have forced it to pay £2 million ($3.5m) to *OK!* for publishing unauthorized shots of the Douglas/Zeta-Jones wedding; the previous ruling on damages (from 2003) stood.
- *OK!* launches an American edition.
- *Vanity Fair* has its all-time best-selling issue, featuring a tell-all cover story on Jennifer Aniston whose break-up with Brad Pitt was given extensive global media coverage, including a record five successive weeks on the cover of *Us*.
- Kanye West is reproached for his criticism of George Bush following the devastation of New Orleans by Hurricane Katrina.
- There are 22,000 cosmetic surgery operations in Britain (1 person in 2,727); this is a third more than in 2004.
- Golfer Michelle Wie turns professional, aged 16, with $10 million worth of endorsement contracts.
- Kate Moss loses several modeling contracts, worth an estimated £6 million ($10m) after being pictured by a British newspaper using cocaine.

2006
- Kate Moss attracts several new modeling contracts, worth an estimated £12 million ($20m), months after being exposed by a British newspaper for using cocaine.
- Governor Arnold Schwarzenegger signs a California law that increases penalties against overly aggressive paparazzi.
- Twitter is founded; within 6 years, it has 500 million users.
- *People* magazine records sales of 3.6 million copies.
- Madonna takes her adopted son David to London; the adoption is finalized the following year. She later adopts another child from Malawi.
- Victoria Beckham launches her own denim line, dVb Style, as well as an eyewear range and a fragrance, Intimately Beckham.

2007

- David Beckham transfers to Los Angeles Galaxy for a reputed $128 million.
- *Keeping Up with the Kardashians* premieres on E!. Five years later, *Forbes* assesses Kim Kardashian's earnings at $16 million, largely from reality tv, endorsements, and product licensing.

2008

- *Fame,* Lady Gaga's first album, is released and goes on to sell 15 million copies (and counting). Lady Gaga (b. 1986) is the first artist in history to claim four US number one hits from a debut album ("Just dance," "Poker face," "LoveGame," and "Paparazzi").
- Victoria Beckham introduces a secondary label, Victoria by Victoria Beckham, at New York Fashion Week.

2009

- Tiger Woods' scandal results in his withdrawal from competition. Accenture, AT&T, and Pepsi drop him, but he remains the highest-paid athlete in the world thanks to huge deals with Nike, Electronic Arts, and Upper Deck.
- Michael Jackson dies; two years later, his personal physician Dr Conrad Murray is convicted of involuntary manslaughter.
- Oprah announces the end of *The Oprah Winfrey Show.* Her earnings for the year are $315 million.
- *The X Factor* attracts its peak viewing audience of 17.2 million, i.e. 27.6 percent of the total British population.
- Madonna, now 52, has the fourth-highest-grossing tour of the year, bringing in $6 million a night and $138 million overall.
- Britney Spears's comeback gathers momentum: her 98-date tour draws $130 million in gross box-office receipts, and she signs endorsement deals with Elizabeth Arden and Candie's to bring her yearly earnings to $64 million.
- Beyoncé continues to expand her business empire beyond music: endorsement deals with companies ranging from Nintendo to L'Oréal and her own House of Dereon fashion line add to the $86 million she grosses from a 93-stop world tour.
- Lady Gaga's 106-date tour draws $95 million. She teams up with Polaroid, Virgin Mobile, Monster Cable, and Viva Glam in marketing deals.

2010

- Lady Gaga's appears at the MTV Video Music Awards in a dress apparently made of raw meat.
- Simon Cowell ends his *American Idol* run in favor of producing a US version of his own show, *The X Factor.*

2011

- Elizabeth Taylor dies, aged 79.
- Amy Winehouse dies, aged 27.
- Royal Wedding of Kate Middleton and Prince William draws 26 million British viewers and 2 billion worldwide.
- Kim Kardashian's wedding draws 10 million viewers to E! on October 9. Three weeks later, Kardashian files for divorce.
- Welsh football player Ryan Giggs is named on Twitter as having taken out an injunction over an alleged affair with a reality tv star. The case reveals that several other football celebrities have taken out injunctions to prevent the publication of information about their private lives.
- *The X Factor* begins in the USA.
- Lady Gaga gives interview in which she reveals that she "adheres to a strict diet plan."

2012

- Lady Gaga reveals that her weight gain (of about 25 lbs, 11.34 kgs) is attributable to her father's Italian cooking, and advises via Twitter: "The dieting wars have got to stop."
- Katie Holmes files for divorce from her husband of five years, Tom Cruise. The reason is believed to be concerns over the effect of Cruise's beliefs in Scientology on their daughter.
- Tom Cruise is named by *Forbes* as the highest-paid actor in the world, with $75 million earned between May 2011 and May 2012.

- Kristen Stewart is the highest-paid female in Hollywood with earnings of $34.5 million.
- Kmart pay Sofia Vergara a $7 million advance for a new product line.
- Madonna is threatened with legal action after a concert in Paris where a swastika-embellished image of National Front leader Marine Le Pen is shown.
- British singer and *The X Factor* judge Tulisa Contostavlos wins a legal apology from her former boyfriend Justin Edwards, aka Ultra, after intimate footage of her is leaked online.
- French magazine *Closer* publishes pictures of the Duchess of Cambridge, Kate Middleton, sunbathing topless with Prince William in the south of France. The couple take legal action against the publication.
- Stalking is made a criminal offense in Britain, with a maximum sentence of five years' imprisonment.

2013

- Lance Armstrong appears on Oprah Winfrey's OWN tv channel and admits he took performance enhancing drugs during his competitive career.
- Prince Harry reveals: "I don't believe there is such a thing as a private life any more."
- David Beckham announces his retirement from sports.
- An estimated 300 photographers plus tv news crews from around the world camp for up the three weeks outside a West London hospital, where the Duchess of Cambridge gives birth to her first baby, George. In media terms, it is the most eagerly awaited birth in history.
- News of the break-up of Michael Douglas and Catherine Zeta-Jones' 13-year marriage circulates: both Douglas and Zeta-Jones had been objects of unwelcome attention from worshipful fans.
- In the tenth anniversary year of Britain's *The X Factor*, its creator Simon Cowell approves of a musical based on the show and becomes the center of a scandal when it's revealed that he's to become a father; the mother is a married woman.
- One Direction, a band that emerged from *The X Factor*, break the record for most views on Vevo in 24 hours with *Best Song Ever*. Miley Cyrus' video for *We Can't Stop* held the previous record with 10.7 million views in its first day online. The One Direction movie *This is Us* makes $17 million in its debut weekend in the USA – a huge take for a concert film.
- Cheryl Cole, one-time judge on *The X Factor* who came to prominence with the group Girls Aloud, which emerged in 2002 from the British tv show *Popstars: The Rivals*, template for *The X Factor*, has a photograph of her newly tattooed backside distributed internationally.
- Maria Sharapova announces and then abandons plans to change her name to *Sugarpova*, a product she endorses; widely criticized, the plans create global news from the Middle East to the South Pacific.
- Miley Cyrus appears at MTV Music Video Awards (VMAs) dressed in flesh-colored latex underwear. Despite the scorn of the global media earned by her performance, she sells 90,000 digital downloads of her new track, which debuts the day of the VMAs. The impact is also felt in social media: the former Hannah Montana has a 112 percent rise in activity, adding 226,273 new Facebook fans and 213,104 new Twitter followers. Cyrus' manager reportedly sums up her VMA performance: "It could not have gone better."
- Kanye West performs for Kazakhstan president Nursultan Nazarbayev's grandson for a $3 million fee. Other celebrities who have performed for world leaders with questionable human rights records include Mariah Carey, Beyoncé, Usher, and 50 Cent—all of whom have performed for Libyan dictator Muammar Gaddafi or members of his family; Seal, who performed for Ramzan Kadyrov, head of the Chechen Republic under whose rule torture was commonplace; and Sting, who performed for Islam Karimov, president of Uzbekistan.

BIBLIOGRAPHY

Alexander, Jeffrey C. (2010) "Barack Obama meets celebrity metaphor," *Society*, vol. 47, no. 5, pp. 410–18.

Alperstein, Neil M. (1991) "Imaginary social relationships with celebrities appearing in television commercials," *Journal of Broadcasting and Electronic Media*, vol. 35, no. 1 (winter), unnumbered.

Altman, Howard (2005) "Celebrity culture," *CQ Researcher*, vol. 15, no. 11 (March 18), pp. 1–32.

Andersen, Robin (1995) *Consumer Culture and TV Programming*, Boulder CO: Westview.

Andrews, David L. and Jackson, Steven J. (2001) "Introduction: sport celebrities, public culture, and private experience," pp. 1–19 in David L. Andrews and Steven J. Jackson (eds) *Sport Stars: The cultural politics of sporting celebrity*, London: Routledge.

Andrews, David L. and Silk, Michael L. (2010) "Basketball's ghettocentric logic," *American Behavioral Scientist*, vol. 53, no. 11, pp. 1626–44.

Anonymous (2004) "Face value: star power," *The Economist,* vol. 372, no. 8387 (July 8).

Asch, Solomon (1955) "Opinions and social pressures," *Scientific American*, vol. 193, pp. 31–5.

Baaith, Rasheed Z. (2002) "Tiger Woods and Michael Jackson," *Broward Times*, vol. 51, no. 5, p. 8.

Bai, Matt and Brauer, David (1998) "Jesse Ventura's 'body' politics," *Newsweek*, vol. 132, no. 20, p. 38.

Barbas, Samantha (2004) "Weighty issues," *American Quarterly*, vol. 56, no. 4, pp. 1115–24.

Barney, Tim (2001) "Celebrity, spectacle, and the conspiracy culture of Election 2000," *American Behavioral Scientist,* vol. 44, no. 12, pp. 2331–7.

Basil, Michael D. (1996) "Identification as a mediator of celebrity effects," *Journal of Broadcasting and Electronic Media*, vol. 40, number 4 (fall), pp. 478–96.

Bastin, Giselle (2009) "Filming the ineffable: Biopics of the British royal family," *a/b: Auto/Biography Studies*, vol. 24, no. 1, pp. 34–52.

Bauman, Zygmunt (2001) "Consuming life," *Journal of Consumer Culture*, vol. 1, no. 1, pp. 5–29.

Bauman, Zygmunt (2010) *Liquid Life*, Cambridge: Polity.

Beer, David and Penfold-Mounce, Ruth (2009) "Celebrity gossip and the new melodramatic imagination," *Sociological Research Online*, vol. 14, no. 2. Available at: http://bit.ly/-BeerCelebGossip.

Bell, Christopher E. (2010) *American Idolatry: Celebrity, commodity and reality television*, Jefferson NC: McFarland & Co.

Bennett, James and Holmes, Su (2010) "The 'place' of television in celebrity studies," *Celebrity Studies*, vol. 1, no. 1, pp. 65–80.

Berlanstein, Lenard R. (2004) "Historicizing and gendering celebrity culture: Famous women in nineteenth-century France," *Journal of Women's History*, vol. 16, no. 4, pp. 65–91.

Bernstein, Carl (1992) "The idiot culture: Reflections of post-Watergate journalism," *The New Republic*, vol. 206, no. 23, pp. 22–8. Available at: http://bit.ly/-BernsteinIdiotCulture.

Bethke Elshtain, Jean (1997) "Mourning in America," *The New Republic*, vol. 217, no. 13, p. 25.

Bignell, Jonathan (2005) *Big Brother: Reality TV in the twenty-first century*, London: Palgrave Macmillan.

Biography Resource Center (2004) "Errol Flynn" *Biography Resource Center*. Farmington Hills MI: Thomson Gale. Available at: http://galenet.galegroup.com/servlet/BioRC.

Bishop, Ronald (2011) "The transcendent metrosexual: Affirmations of hegemonic masculinity in press coverage of the birth of Tom Brady's son," *Journal of Sports Media*, vol. 6, no. 2, pp. 89–125.

Bloomfield, Steve (2005) "Fresh-faced and 16. So why are girls like her buying anti-wrinkle cream?" *Independent on Sunday*, February 20. Available at: http://bit.ly/-BloomfieldFreshFaced.

Blum, Virginia L. (2003) *Flesh Wounds: The culture of cosmetic surgery*, Berkeley, CA: University of California Press.

Blum, Virginia L. (2007) "Objects of love: *I Want a Famous Face* and the illusions of star culture," *Configurations*, vol. 15, no. 1, pp. 33–53.

Bogle, Donald (2001) *Toms, Coons, Mulattoes, Mammies, and Bucks: An interpretive history of blacks in American films*, 4th edition, New York: Continuum.

Bond, Paul (2002) "Poll: Most tune out celeb politics," *Hollywood Reporter*, May 31, p. 61.

Bonner, Frances (2005) "The celebrity in the text," pp. 57–95 in Jessica Evans and David Hesmondhalgh (eds) *Understanding Media: Inside celebrity*, Maidenhead, England: Open University Press.

Boon, Susan D., and Lomore, Christine D. (2001) "Admirer–celebrity relationships among young adults: Explaining perceptions of celebrity influence on identity," *Human Communication Research*, vol. 3, pp. 432–65.

Boorstin, Daniel (1992) *The Image: A guide to pseudo-events in America*, New York: Random House.

Borkowski, Mark (2008) *The Fame Formula: How Hollywood's fixers, fakers and star makers created the celebrity industry*, London: Sidgwick & Jackson.

Bourdon, Jérôme (2008) "Self-despotism: Reality television and the new subject of politics," *Framework*, vol. 49, no. 1, pp. 66–82.

Braudy, Leo (1997) *The Frenzy of Renown: Fame and its history*, 2nd edition, New York: Vintage.

Briggs, Asa and Burke, Peter (2005) *A Social History of the Media: From Gutenberg to the internet*, 2nd edition, Cambridge: Polity.

Brockes, Emma (2012) "Kim Kardashian: My life as a brand," *Guardian*, September 7. Available at: http://bit.ly/-BrockesKK.

Brohm, Jean-Marie (1978) *Sport: A prison of measured time*, London: Ink Links.

Bronfen, Elisabeth (2002) "Celebrating catastrophe," *Angelaki: Journal of the Theoretical Humanities*, vol. 7, no. 2 (August), pp. 175–86.

Brooks, Carol (2004) "What celebrity worship says about us: Gossip can serve a purpose," *USA Today*, News section (September 14), p. 21a. Available at: http://bit.ly/-BrooksCelebWorship.

Browne, Janet (2003) "Charles Darwin as a celebrity," *Science in Context*, vol. 16, pp. 175–94.

Bruce, Toni (2004) "Making the boundaries of the 'normal' in televised sports: The play-by-play of race," *Media, Culture, Society*, vol. 26, no. 6, pp. 861–79.

Bystrom, Kerry (2011) "On 'humanitarian' adoption (Madonna in Malawi)," *Humanity*, vol. 2, no. 2, pp. 213–31.

Campbell, James T. (2000) "'Print the legend': John Wayne and post-war American culture," *Reviews in American History*, vol. 28, no. 3, pp. 465–77.

Caputi, Jane (1999) "The second coming of Diana," *NWSA Journal*, vol. 11, no. 2, pp. 103–23.

Carlson, Margaret (1997) "Blood on their hands?" *Time*, vol. 150 (September 8), p. 46.

Chagollan, Steve and Johnson, Ted (2008) "Passionate politico's policies," *Variety*, vol. 299, no. 48, p. A5.

Chia, Stella C. and Ling Poo, Yip (2009) "Media, celebrities, and fans: An examination of adolescents' media usage and involvement with entertainment celebrities," *Journalism and Mass Communication Quarterly*, vol. 86, no. 1, pp. 23–44.

Choi, Sejung Marina and Rifon, Nora J. (2007) "Who is the celebrity in advertising? Understanding dimensions of celebrity images," *Journal of Popular Culture*, vol. 40, no. 2, pp. 304–24.

Collins, Gail (2007) *Scorpion Tongues: Gossip, celebrity and American politics*, 2nd edition, New York: Harper Perennial.

Conan Doyle, Sir Arthur (1981) 'The adventure of the Three Gables', pp. 1023–32 in *The Penguin Sherlock Holmes*, London: Penguin.

Conley, Ann and Schultz, David (2000) "Jesse Ventura™ and the brave new world of politainer politics," *Journal of American and Comparative Cultures*, vol. 23, no. 3, pp. 49–59.

Connelly, Chris (2005) "Angelina Jolie sets the record straight," *Marie Claire*, vol. 12, no. 7, pp. 69–74.

Conniff, Ruth (2008) "Obama's task," *The Progressive*, October 22, pp. 22–3.

Coombe, Rosemary J. and Herman, Andrew (2001) "Culture wars on the net: Intellectual property and corporate propriety in digital environments," *South Atlantic Quarterly*, vol. 100, no. 4, pp. 919–47.

Corona, Victor P. (2011) "Memory, monsters, and Lady Gaga," *Journal of Popular Culture*, vol. 44, no. 2, pp. 1–19.

Cotts, Cynthia (2003) "Fame by numbers," *The Village Voice*, vol. 48, no. 49 (December 3–9), p. 32.

Cox, Donna (1999) "*Diana: Her true story*: Post-modern transgressions in identity," *Journal of Gender Studies*, vol. 8, no. 3, pp. 323–38.

Curnutt, Kirk (1999) "Inside and outside: Gertrude Stein on identity, celebrity and authenticity," *Journal of Modern Literature*, vol. 23, no. 2, pp. 291–308.

Dalton, Stephen (2005) "Heroes of their degeneration," *The Times,* times2 section (September 30), p. 22.

De Tocqueville, Alexis (2003) *Democracy in America* (translated by Gerald Bevan, edited by Isaac Kramnick), London: Penguin.

De Vos, Jan (2009) "On cerebral celebrity and reality TV: Subjectivity in times of brain scans and psychotainment," *Configurations*, vol. 17, no. 3, pp. 259–83.

deCordova, Richard (1990) *Picture Personalities: The emergence of the star system in America*, Urbana IL: University of Illinois Press.

Del Gizzo, Suzanne (2010) " 'Glow-in-the-dark authors': Hemingway's celebrity and legacy in Under Kilimanjaro," *The Hemingway Review*, vol. 29, no. 2, pp. 7–27.

Deutsch, Helene (1986) "Some forms of emotional disturbance and their relationship to schizophrenia," pp. 74–91 in Michael H. Stone (ed.) *Essential Papers on Borderline Disorders: One hundred years at the border*, New York: New York University Press.

Dixon, Wheeler Winston (1999) *Disaster and Memory: Celebrity culture and the crisis of Hollywood cinema*, New York: Columbia University Press.

Duerden, Nick (2005) "Beyond doubt," *Independent Magazine*, August 28, pp. 12–14.

Egginton, William (2009) "The best or the worst of our nature: Reality tv and the desire for limitless change," *Configurations*, vol. 15, no. 2, pp. 177–91.

Ellroy, James (1990) *LA Confidential*, New York: Warner Books.

Esposito, Jennifer (2009) "What does race have to do with *Ugly Betty*? An analysis of privilege and postracial(?) representations on a television sitcom," *Television and New Media*, vol. 10, no. 6, pp. 521–35.

Evans, Jessica (2005) "Celebrity, media and history," pp. 11–56 in Jessica Evans and David Hesmondhalgh (eds) *Understanding Media: Inside celebrity*, Maidenhead, England: Open University Press.

Evans, Jessica and Hesmondhalgh, David (eds) (2005) *Understanding Media: Inside celebrity*, Maidenhead, England: Open University Press.

Fairfield, Charles (1997) "Race, rage, and denial: The media and the O.J. trials," *The Humanist*, vol. 57, no. 4, pp. 24–6.

Ferri, Anthony J. (2010) "Emergence of the entertainment age?" *Social Science and Modern Society*, vol. 47, no. 5, pp. 403–9.

Fonda, Jane (1981) *Jane Fonda's Workout Book*, New York: Simon & Schuster.

Foucault, Michel (1979) *The History of Sexuality*, vol. 1, London: Allen Lane.

Fowles, Jib (1992) *Why Viewers Watch: A reappraisal of television's effects*, Newbury Park, CA: Sage.

Fowles, Jib (1996) *Advertising and Popular Culture*, Newbury Park, CA: Sage.

Fraser, Benson P. and Brown, William J. (2002) "Media, celebrities, and social influence: Identification with Elvis Presley," *Mass Communication and Society*, vol. 1, no. 2 (May), pp. 183–207.

Frederickson, George M. (1987) *The Black Image in the White Mind: The debate on Afro-American character and destiny, 1817–1914*, New York: Oxford University Press.

Gabler, Neal (1989) *An Empire of Their Own: How the Jews invented Hollywood*, New York: Anchor Books.

Gabler, Neal (2001) "Toward a new definition of celebrity," Norman Lear Center: University of Southern California, Annenberg. Available at: http://bit.ly/-GablerTowardNewDef.

Gabler, Neal (2009) "The greatest show on earth," *Newsweek*, December 11. Available at: http://bit.ly/-GablerGreatestShow.

Galbraith, John Kenneth (1958) *The Affluent Society*, New York: Houghton Mifflin.

Gamson, Joshua (1992) "The assembly line of greatness: Celebrity in twentieth-century America," *Critical Studies in Mass Communication*, vol. 9 (March), pp. 1–24.

Gamson, Joshua (1994) *Claims to Fame: Celebrity in contemporary America*, Berkeley CA: University of California Press.

Ganem, Mark (1999) "Rockin' Robbins," *W*, vol. 28, no. 12, p. 337.

Garland, Robert (2010) "Celebrity ancient and modern," *Society*, vol. 47, no. 6, pp. 484–8.

George, Nelson (1988) *The Death of Rhythm and Blues*, New York: Pantheon.

Giles, David (2000) *Illusions of Immortality: A psychology of fame and celebrity*, London: Macmillan.

Goldthorpe, John, Lockwood, David, Bechhofer, Frank, and Platt, Jennifer (1968) *The Affluent Worker: Industrial attitudes and behaviour*, Cambridge: Cambridge University Press.

Gomery, Douglas (2005) *The Hollywood Studio System: A history*, London: British Film Institute.

Green, Joshua (2004) "Madonna wants me," *Atlantic Monthly*, vol. 293, no. 2, pp. 32–4. Available at: http://bit.ly/-GreenMadonna.

Green, Michelle (2002) "Those lips, that face. . ." *People*, vol. 61, no. 15 (April 19), pp. 127–8.

Guerrero, Ed (1995) "The black man on our screens and the empty space in representation," pp. 181–9 in Thelma Golden (ed.) *Black Male: Representations of masculinity in contemporary American art*, New York: Abrams.

Guest, Katy (2005) "Show over! Are we finally sick of celebs?" *Independent on Sunday*, February 20. Available at: http://bit.ly/-GuestShowOver.

Halberstam, David (1999) *Playing for Keeps: Michael Jordan and the world he made*, New York: Random House.

Hall, Steve, Winlow, Simon, and Ancrum, Craig (2008) *Criminal Identities and Consumer Culture*, Cullompton, Devon: Willan.

Haney, C., Banks, W.C., and Zimbardo, P.G. (1973) "Interpersonal dynamics in a simulated prison," *International Journal of Criminology and Penology*, vol. 1, pp. 69–97.

Harris, Cheryl (1998) "A sociology of television fandom," pp. 41–54 in Cheryl Harris and Alison Alexander (eds) *Theorizing Fandom: Fans, subculture and identity*, Cresskill, NJ: Hampton Press.

Harris, Cheryl and Alexander, Alison (eds) (1998) *Theorizing Fandom: Fans, subculture and identity*, Cresskill, NJ: Hampton Press.

Harris, Daniel (2008a) "Celebrity bodies," *Southwest Review*, vol. 93, no. 1, pp. 135–44.

Harris, Daniel (2008b) "Celebrity deaths," *Antioch Review*, vol. 66, no. 4, pp. 616–24.

Hartigan Jr., John (2009) "What are you laughing at? Assessing the 'racial' in US public discourse," *Transforming Anthropology*, vol. 7, no. 1, pp. 4–19.

Havens, Timothy (2000) "'The biggest show in the world': Race and the global popularity of *The Cosby Show*," *Media, Culture and Society*, vol. 22, no. 4, pp. 371–91.

Hedges, Christopher (2010) "Celebrity culture and the Obama brand," *Tikkun*, vol. 25, no. 1, pp. 33–72.

Heelas, Paul (1998) "Introduction: On differentiation and dedifferentiation," pp. 1–18 in Paul Heelas, David Martin, and Paul Morris (eds) *Religion, Modernity and Postmodernity*, Oxford: Wiley.

Hellmueller, Lea C. and Aeschbacher, Nina (2010) "Media and celebrity: Production and consumption of 'well-knownness'," *Communication Research Trends*, vol. 29, nos. 4–3, pp. 3–35.

Helton, Tena L. (2010) "What the white 'squaws' want from Black Hawk: Gendering the fan–celebrity relationship," *American Indian Quarterly*, vol. 34, no. 4, pp. 498–520.

Henderson, Amy (1992) "Media and the rise of celebrity culture," *Organization of American Historians Magazine of History*, vol. 6 (spring), pp. 1–6.

Hesmondhalgh, David (2005) "Producing celebrity," pp. 97–134 in Jessica Evans and David Hesmondhalgh (eds) *Understanding Media: Inside celebrity*, Maidenhead, England: Open University Press.

Higgins, Michael (2010) "The 'public inquisitor' as media celebrity," *Cultural Politics*, vol. 6, no. 1, pp. 93–110.

Higham, Charles (1980) *Errol Flynn: The untold story*, New York: Doubleday.

Hills, Matt (2005) *How To Do Things With Cultural Theory*, London: Hodder Arnold.

Hilton, Paris and Ginsberg, Merle (2005) *Confessions of an Heiress: A tongue-in-chic peek behind by pose*, New York: Simon & Schuster.

Hoch, Paul (1972) *Rip Off the Big Game: The exploitation of sports by the power elite*, New York: Anchor Doubleday.

Hodgkinson, Mark (2012) "Steffi Graf: Sharapova is a complete tennis player," *The Tennis Space*, June 9. Available at: http://bit.ly/-Hodg kinsonSteffi.

Holden, Anthony (1993) *Behind the Oscar: The secret history of the Academy Awards*, New York: Simon & Schuster.

Holmes, Su (2010) "Dreaming a dream: Susan Boyle and celebrity culture," *Velvet Light Trap*, no. 65, pp. 74–6.

Home Office (2003) *Statistics on Women and the Criminal Justice System: A Home Office publication under Section 95 of the Criminal Justice Act 1991*, London: HMSO.

Hooper, Nancy (1995) "Celebrities at risk," *Risk Management*, vol. 42, number 5 (May), pp. 18–34.

Hoopes, David and Heverin, Drew (2009) "Celebrity culture and the rise of the ordinary: Interview with Dr. Joshua Gamson," *disClosure*, no. 19, pp. 38–43.

Horne, John (2006) *Sport in Consumer Culture*, Houndmills, England: Palgrave Macmillan.

Horton, D. and Wohl, R.R. (1956) "Mass communication and parasocial interaction," *Psychiatry*, vol. 19, pp. 215–29.

Houston, Andrew (2010) "Views and reviews: Celebrity as fantasy screen," *Canadian Theatre Review*, no. 141, pp. 94–6.

Hubert, Susan J. (1999) "Two women, two songs: The subversive iconography of 'Candle in the wind'," *National Women's Studies Association Journal*, vol. 111, no. 2, pp. 124–37.

Hughey, Matthew W. (2011) "The (dis)similarities of white racial identities: The conceptual framework of 'hegemonic whiteness'," *Ethnic and Racial Studies*, vol. 33, no. 8, pp. 1289–309.

Hutchinson, Earl Ofari (1998) "The price of fame for Tiger Woods," *New Pittsburgh Courier* (national edition), vol. 89, no. 32 (April 22), p. A7.

Ingram, Billy (nd) "A short history of the *National Enquirer*" (two parts). Available at: http://bit.ly/-IngramTabloids.

Inniss, Leslie B. and Feagin, Joe R. (1995) "*The Cosby Show*: The view from the black middle class," *Journal of Black Studies*, vol. 25, no. 6, pp. 692–711.

Insight Media (1990) *Quiet Rage: The Stanford prison experiment*, DVD/VHS, New York: Insight Media.

Jenkins, Henry (1992) *Textual Poachers: Television fans and participatory culture*, New York: Routledge.

Jhally, Sut and Lewis, Justin (1992) *Enlightened Racism:* The Cosby Show, *audiences, and the myth of the American dream*, Boulder, CO: Westview.

John, Juliet (2007) "'A body without a head': The idea of mass culture in Dickens's *American Notes* (1842)," *Journal of Victorian Culture*, vol. 12, no. 2, pp. 173–202.

Johnson, Brian D. (2001) "We like to watch: 'Reality TV' is the new pornography, mainstream voyeurism," *Maclean's*, vol. 114, no. 5 (January 29), p. 56.

Johnson, Roy S. (with additional reporting by Ann Harrington) (1998) "The Jordan Effect: The world's greatest basketball player is also one of its great brands," *Fortune*, vol. 137, no. 12 (June 22). Available at: http://bit.ly/-JohnsonJordan.

Johnson, Ted (2011) "Fallen stars: Celebs, politics an uneasy mix," *Variety*, vol. 423, no. 2, p. 4.

Jones, Jacqueline (1998) "Race and gender in modern America," *Reviews in American History*, vol. 26, no. 1, pp. 220–38.

Jones, Meredith (2008) *Skintight: An anatomy of cosmetic surgery*, New York: Berg.

Kaminer, Wendy (2008) "The corrosion of the American mind," *Wilson Quarterly*, vol. 32, no. 2, pp. 91–4.

Kamons, Andrew (2007) "Of note: Celebrity and politics," *School of Advanced International Studies (SAIS) Review*, vol. 27, no. 1, pp. 145–6.

Kates, Steven M. (2002) "The protean quality of subcultural consumption: An ethnographic account of gay consumers," *Journal of Consumer Research*, vol. 29, no. 3 (December), pp. 383–400.

Katz, Donald (1994) *Just Do It: The Nike spirit in the corporate world*, Holbrook MA; Adams Media.

Kiersh, Edward (1992) "Mr. Robinson vs. Air Jordan: The marketing battle for Olympic gold," *Los Angeles Times*, March 22, p. 7. Available at: http://bit.ly/-KiershMrRobinson.

King, Barry (2010) "Stardom, celebrity, and the money form," *Velvet Light Trap*, no. 65, pp. 7–19.

King, Natalie, Touyz, Stephen, and Charles, Margaret (2000) "The effect of body dissatisfaction on women's perception of female celebrities," *Journal of Eating Disorders*, vol. 27, pp. 341–47.

Kirby, David (2001) "Will the real out celebrities please stand up?" *The Advocate*, nos. 828/9 (January 16), pp. 56–58.

Klara, Robert (2011) "I see dead people," *Brandweek*, vol. 52, no. 10 (March 14), p. 10.

Klein, Naomi (2001) *No Logo*, London: Flamingo.

Kleinberg, Aviad (2011) "Are saints celebrities? Some medieval Christian examples," *Cultural and Social History*, vol. 8, no. 3, pp. 393–7.

Knight, Jennifer L., Giuliano, Traci A., and Sanchez-Ross, Monica G. (2001) "Famous or infamous? The influence of celebrity status and race on perceptions of responsibility for rape," *Basic and Applied Social Psychology*, vol. 23, no. 3, pp. 183–90.

Knox, Sarah L. (2000) "A world made of glass: Crime, culture and community in an age of hyper-media," *Theory and Event*, vol. 4, no. 4. Available at: http://bit.ly/-KnoxWorldMadeofGlass.

Koch, Kathy (1998) "Can the media regain the public's trust?" *The CQ Researcher*, vol. 8, no. 48 (December 25), pp. 1–25.

Kolchin, Peter (2002) "Whiteness studies: The new history of race in America," *Journal of American History*, vol. 89, no. 1, pp. 154–73.

Lange, Rense and Houran, James (1999) "The role of fear in delusions of the paranormal," *Journal of Nervous and Mental Disease*, vol. 187, no. 3, pp. 159–66.

Langman, Lauren (2002) "Suppose they gave a culture war and no one came: Zippergate and the carnivalization of politics," *The American Behavioral Scientist*, vol. 46, no. 4 (December), pp. 501–37.

Lapham, Lewis H. (1993) "The theatre of celebrity," *The Progressive*, vol. 57, no. 8, p. 21.

Lapham, Lewis H. (1997) "Fatted calf," *Harper's*, vol. 295 (November), pp. 11–14.

Lasch, Christopher (1980) *The Culture of Narcissism: American life in an age of diminishing expectations*, London: Abacus.

Lasch, Christopher (1991) T*he True and Only Heaven: Progress and its critics*, New York: W.W. Norton.

Layder, Derek (2006) *Understanding Social Theory*, second edition, London: Sage.

Leff, Leonard (1997) *Hemingway and his Conspirators: Hollywood, Scribners and the making of American celebrity culture*, Lanham MD: Rowman & Littlefield.

Lerner, Barron H. (2006) *When Illness Goes Public: Celebrity patients and how we look at medicine*, Baltimore MA: Johns Hopkins University.

Lewis, David and Bridger, Darren (2001) *The Soul of the New Consumer*, London: Nicholas Brealey.

Lewis, Lisa A. (ed.) (1992) *The Adoring Audience: Fan culture and popular media*, London: Routledge.

Lipsitz, George (2011) *How Racism Takes Place*, Philadelphia PA: Temple University Press.

Lipsyte, Robert (2011) "Why can't athletes have opinions?" *Miami Times*, May 25, p. 8D. Available at: http://bit.ly/-LipsyteWhyAthletes.

Luckett, Moya (2010) "Toxic: The implosion of Britney Spears's star image," *Velvet Light Trap*, no. 65, pp. 39–41.

Luna, David and Forquer Gupta, Susan (2001) "An integrative framework for cross-cultural consumer behavior," *International Marketing Review*, vol. 18, no. 1, pp. 45–69.

Maddox, Alton H. (2003) "Oh no! Kobe joins Tawana as racial victim," *New York Amsterdam News*, vol. 94, no. 30 (July 24), p. 12.

Madonna, Meisel, Steve (photographer) and O'Brien, Glenn (ed.) (1992) *Sex*, New York: Vintage/Ebury.

Maltby, John, Day, Liza, McCutcheon, Lynn E., Gillett, Raphael, Houran, James, and Ashe, Diane D. (2004) "Personality and coping: A context for examining celebrity worship and mental health," *British Journal of Psychology*, vol. 95, pp. 411–28.

Mansvelt, Juliana (2010) *Geographies of Consumption*, London: Sage.

Margolis, Stacey (2009) "The rise and fall of public opinion," *ELH: English Literary History*, vol. 76, no. 3, pp. 713–37.

Marshall, P. David (1997) *Celebrity and Power: Fame in contemporary culture*, Minneapolis MN: University of Minnesota Press.

Maslow, Abraham (1987, first published 1954) *Motivation and Personality*, New York: HarperCollins.

McCutcheon, Lynn E., Ashe, Diane D., Houran, James, and Maltby, John (2003) "A cognitive profile of individuals who tend to worship celebrities," *Journal of Psychology*, vol. 137, no. 4 (July), pp. 309–14.

McCutcheon, Lynn E., Lange, Rense, and Houran, James (2002) "Conceptualization and measurement of celebrity worship," *British Journal of Psychology*, vol. 93, no. 1, pp. 67–87.

McCutcheon, Mark A., Leduc, Gilles, Mady Kelly, Diana, Martin, Sue Ann, and Brooker, Blake (2010) "Celebrity musings: Brushes with fame and other thoughts on celebrity," *Canadian Theatre Review*, no. 141, pp. 7–9.

McKay, Jim (1999) "Book review: Robert Goldman and Stephen Papson, *Nike Culture: The sign of the swoosh*," *International Journal of Cultural Studies*, vol. 2, no. 3, pp. 418–21.

McPherson, Heather (2000) "Searching for Sarah Siddons: Portraiture and the historiography of fame," *Eighteenth-Century Studies*, vol. 33, no. 2, pp. 281–4.

Meloy, J. Reid (1997) "The clinical management of stalking: 'Someone is watching over me. . .'," *American Journal of Psychotherapy*, vol. 51 (spring), pp. 174–84.

Merschman, Joseph C. (2001) "The dark side of the web: Cyberstalking and the need for contemporary legislation," *Harvard Women's Law Journal*, vol. 24 (spring), pp. 255–92.

Merton, Robert K. (1969) "Social structure and anomie," in D.R. Cressey and D.A. Ward (eds) *Delinquency, Crime and Social Process*, New York: Harper & Row.

Meyer, Gerald (2002) "Frank Sinatra: The Popular Front and an American icon," *Science and Society*, vol. 66, no. 3, pp. 311–35.

Meyers, Erin (2009) " 'Can you handle my truth?' Authenticity and the celebrity star image," *Journal of Popular Culture*, vol. 42, no. 5, pp. 890–907.

Milgram, Stanley (1974) *Obedience to Authority: An experimental view*, New York: Harper & Row.

Miner, Dylan A.T. (2009) "Provocations on sneakers: The multiple significations of athletic shoes, sport, race, and masculinity," *CR: The New Centennial Review*, vol. 9, no. 2, pp. 73–107.

Monaco, James (ed.) (1978) *Celebrity: The media as image makers*, New York: Delta.

Monbiot, George (2005) "Bards of the powerful," *Guardian*, June 21. Available at: http://bit.ly/-MonbiotBardsPowerful.

Morgan, Simon (2011) "Celebrity: Academic 'pseudo-event' or a useful concept for historians?" *Cultural and Social History*, vol. 8, no. 1, pp. 95–114.

Murray, Susan and Ouellette, Laurie (2008) "Introduction," pp. 1–20 in Susan Murray and Laurie Ouellette (eds) *Reality TV: Remaking Television Culture*, 2nd edition, New York: New York University Press.

Nataraajan, Rajan and Chawla, Sudhir K. (1997) " 'Fitness' marketing: Celebrity or non-celebrity endorsement?" *Journal of Professional Services Marketing*, vol. 15, no. 2, pp. 119–30.

Nederveen Pieterse, Jan (1992) *White on Black: Images of Africa and blacks in Western popular culture*, London: Yale University Press.

Negra, Diane (2010) "Brangelina: The fertile valley of celebrity," *Velvet Light Trap*, no. 65, pp. 60–1.

Neimark, Jill (1995) "The culture of celebrity," *Psychology Today*, May/June, pp. 54–7; 87–90.

Neuman, W. Russell (2002) *The Future of the Mass Audience*, Cambridge: Cambridge University Press.

Newbury, Michael (2000) "Celebrity watching," *American Literary History*, vol. 12, nos. 1 & 2, pp. 272–83.

Newbury, Michael (2011) "Celebrity and glamour: Modernism for the masses," *American Literary History*, vol. 23, no. 1, pp. 128–34.

Newman, Roberta (2003) "It pays to be personal: Baseball and product endorsements," *NINE: A Journal of Baseball History and Culture*, vol. 12, no. 1, pp. 25–42.

Novkov, Julie (2008) "Rethinking race in American politics," *Political Research Quarterly*, vol. 61, no. 4, pp. 649–59.

Oates, Thomas and Polumbaum, Judy (2004) "Agile big man: The flexible marketing of Yao Ming," *Pacific Affairs*, vol. 77, no. 2 (summer), pp. 187–211.

Ohler, Paul (2010) "Forms of ambivalence to 'tabloid culture' in Edith Wharton's *The Custom of the Country*," *ESC*, vol. 36, nos. 2–3, pp. 33–62.

Oldenburg, Ann (2006) "Talent show fever," *USA Today*, June 16. Available at: http://bit.ly/-OldenburgTalentShowFever.

Orbe, Mark P. (2008) "Representations of race in reality TV: Watch and discuss," *Critical Studies in Media Communication*, vol. 25, no. 4, pp. 345–52.

Packard, Vance (1957) *The Hidden Persuaders*, New York: Random House.

Packard, Vance (1959) *The Status Seekers*, Chapel Hill NC: University of North Carolina Press.

Packard, Vance (1960) *The Waste Makers*, New York: McKay & Co.

Page, Helán E. (1997) " 'Black male' imagery and media containment of African American men," *American Anthropologist*, vol. 99, no. 1, pp. 99–111.

Paglia, Camille (2010) "What's sex got to do with it?" *Sunday Times* (London), September 12, p. 14.

Payne, Tom (2009) *Fame: From the Bronze Age to Britney*, London: Vintage.

Peffley, Mark and Hurwitz, Jon (2007) "Persuasion and resistance: Race and the death penalty in America," *American Journal of Political Science*, vol. 51, no. 4, pp. 996–1012.

Petty, Ross D. and D'Rozario, Denver (2009) "The use of dead celebrities in advertising and marketing: Balancing interests in the right of publicity," *Journal of Advertising*, vol. 38, no. 4, pp. 37–49.

Philipsen, Dirk (2003) " '. . . One of those evils that will be very difficult to correct': The permanence of race in North America," *Journal of Negro Education*, vol. 72, no. 2, pp. 190–207.

Ponce de Leon, Charles (2002) *Self-Exposure: Human-interest journalism and the emergence of celebrity in America, 1890–1940*, Chapel Hill NC: University of North Carolina Press.

Poster, Mark (2008) "Global media and culture," *New Literary History*, vol. 39, no. 3, pp. 685–703.

Postman, Neil (1985) *Amusing Ourselves to Death*, New York: Penguin.

Rein, Irving and Shields, Ben (2007) "Reconnecting the baseball star," *Nine: A Journal of Baseball History and Culture*, vol. 16, no. 1, pp. 62–77.

Rich, Joshua (2002) "Leave it to diva," *Entertainment Weekly*, no. 654 (May), p. 84.

Richards, David (1997) "Paparazzi's flashes of fame: In NY, a photohistory of the celebrity-chasers," *Washington Post*, September 9, p. E01.

Riesman, David, with Glazer, Nathan and Denney, Reuel (1950) *The Lonely Crowd: A study of the changing American character*, New Haven, CT: Yale University Press.

Rojek, Chris (2001) *Celebrity*, London: Reaktion.

Rojek, Chris (2012) *Fame Attack: The inflation of celebrity and its consequences*, London: Bloomsbury Academic.

Root, Deborah (1996) *Cannibal Culture: Art, appropriation, and the commodification of difference*, Boulder CO: Westview Press.

Rubenstein, Diane (1997) " 'That's the way the Mercedes Benz': Di, wound culture and fatal fetishism," *Theory and Event*, vol. 1, no. 4, pp. 1–8. Available at: http://bit.ly/-RubensteinThats.

Sacks, Danielle (2003) "Who's that girl?" *Fast Company*, no. 76 (November), p. 32.

Sanders, Meghan S. and Sullivan, James M. (2010) "Category inclusion and exclusion in perceptions of African Americans: Using the stereotype content model to examine perceptions of groups and individuals," *Race, Gender and Class*, vol. 17, no. 3/4, pp. 201–32.

Sandvoss, Cornel (2005) *Fans: The mirror of consumption*, Cambridge: Polity.

Schiller, Lawrence (2012) *Marilyn & Me: A memoir in words and photographs*, Cologne, Germany: Taschen.

Schor, Juliet B. (2004) *Born to Buy: The commercialized child and the new consumer culture*, New York: Scribner.

Schudson, Michael (1993) *Advertising, the Uneasy Persuasion: Its dubious impact on American society*, New York: Routledge.

Server, Lee (2002) *Robert Mitchum: "Baby I Don't Care"*, New York: St. Martin's Griffin.

Sharkey, Jacqueline (1997) "The Diana aftermath," *American Journalism Review*, vol. 19, no. 9, pp. 18–25.

Sheridan, Earl (2006) "Conservative implications of the irrelevance of racism in contemporary African American cinema," *Journal of Black Studies*, vol. 37, no. 2, pp. 177–92.

Sherif, Muzafir (1936) *The Psychology of Social Norms*, New York: Harper & Row.

Sherman, Len (1992) *Big League, Big Time: The birth of the Arizona Dia-mondbacks, the billion-dollar business of sports, and the power of the media in America*, New York: Pocket Books.

Sinwell, Sarah E.S. (2010) "Sex, bugs, and Isabella Rossellini: The making and marketing of Green Porno," *WSQ: Women's Studies Quarterly*, vol. 38, nos. 3 & 4, pp. 118–37.

Smalley, K. Bryant and McIntosh, William D. (2011) "The loss of fame: Psychological implications", *Journal of Popular Culture*, vol. 44, no. 2, pp. 385–397.

Smart, Barry (2005) *The Sport Star: Modern sport and the cultural economy of the sporting celebrity*, London: Sage.

Smith, David Lionel (1997) "What is black culture?" pp. 178–194 in Wahneema Lubiano (ed.), *The House that Race Built: Original essays by Toni Morrison, Angela Y. Davis, Cornel West, and others on black Americans and politics in America today*, New York: Vintage Books.

Smith, Robert and Seltzer, Richard (2000) *Contemporary Controversies and the American Divide: The O.J. Simpson case and other controversies*, Lanham MD: Rowman & Littlefield.

Smith, Sam (1992) *The Jordan Rules*, New York: Simon & Schuster.

Snyder, Robert W. (2003) "American journalism and the culture of celebrity," *Reviews in American History*, vol. 31, no. 3, pp. 440–8.

Spears, Britney (2004) "Madonna," *Rolling Stone*, no. 946, pp. 124–5.

Spickard, Paul (1997) "Review of *Neither Black Nor White: Thematic explorations of interracial literature* and *The New Colored People: The mixed-race movement in America*," *Journal of American Ethnic History*, vol. 18, no. 2, pp. 153–6.

Stone, George, Joseph, Matthew, and Jones, Michael (2003) "An exploratory study on the use of sports celebrities in advertising: A content analysis," *Sport Marketing Quarterly*, vol. 12, no. 2, pp. 94–102.

Strozier, Charles B. (2002) "Youth violence and the apocalyptic," *American Journal of Psychoanalysis*, vol. 62, no. 3 (September), pp. 285–99.

Susman, Warren I. (1984) *Culture as History: The transformation of American society in the twentieth century*, New York: Pantheon.

Sweet, Matthew (2005) *Shepperton Babylon*, London: Faber & Faber.

Tennant, Mike and O'Reilly, Terry (2009) *The Age of Persuasion: How marketing ate our culture*, Toronto: Knopf Canada

Thrift, Nigel (2008) "The material practices of glamour," *Journal of Cultural Economy*, vol. 1, no. 1, pp. 9–23

Tillyard, Stella (2005) "Celebrity in 18th-century London," *History Today*, vol. 55, no. 6, pp. 20–7.

Toll, Robert (1974) *Blacking Up: The minstrel show in nineteenth-century America*, New York: Oxford University Press.

Tönnies, Ferdinand (1957) *Gemeinschaft and Gessellschaft* (translated by Charles Loomis), Ann Arbor MI: Michigan State University Press.

Troy, Gil (1998) "JFK: Celebrity-in-Chief or Commander-in-Chief?" *Reviews in American History*, vol. 26, no. 3, pp. 630–6.

Turner, Frederick (2011) "Lady Gaga and civil religion," *Society*, vol. 48, pp. 495–7. Available at: http://bit.ly/-TurnerGaga.

Turner, Graeme (2004) *Understanding Celebrity*, London: Sage.

Underwood, Nora (2000) "Body envy," *Maclean's*, vol. 113, no. 33 (August 14), pp. 36–40.

Veer, Ekant, Becirovic, Ilda, and Martin, Brett A.S. (2008) "If Kate voted Conservative, would you? The role of celebrity endorsements in political party advertising," *European Journal of Marketing*, vol. 44, nos. 3/4, pp. 436–50.

Vincent, John, Hill, John S., and Lee, Jason W. (2009) "The multiple brand personalities of David Beckham: A case study of the Beckham brand," *Sport Marketing Quarterly*, vol. 18, no. 3, pp. 173–80.

Walters, Ron (1994) "Celebrity and racial neutrality," *Washington Informer*, vol. 30, no. 51, p. 17.

Ward, Pete (2011) *Gods Behaving Badly: Media, religion, and celebrity culture*, Norwich, UK: SCM Press.

Watts, Jill (2005) *Hattie Mcdaniel: Black ambition, white Hollywood*, New York: Amistad.

Weber, Brenda R. (2009a) "Review of *Skintight: An anatomy of cosmetic surgery, Self-Transformations: Foucault, ethics, and normalized bodies*, and *Surgery Junkies: Wellness and pathology in cosmetic culture*," *WSQ: Women's Studies Quarterly*, vol. 37, nos. 1–2, pp. 289–99.

Weber, Brenda R. (2009b) *Makeover TV: Selfhood, citizenship, and celebrity*, Durham NC: Duke University Press.

Weiskel, Timothy C. (2005) "From sidekick to sideshow—celebrity, entertainment, and the politics of distraction: Why Americans are 'sleepwalking toward the end of the earth'," *American Behavioral Scientist*, vol. 49, no. 3, pp. 393–409.

West, Darrell M. and Orman, John M. (2003) *Celebrity Politics*, Englewood Cliffs NJ: Prentice Hall.

West, Shearer (2004) "Roles of authority: Thespian biography and celebrity in eighteenth-century Britain," *Biography*, vol. 27, no. 3, pp. 609–11.

White, T.H. (1958) *The Candle in the Wind*, London: Collins.

Wilson III, Clint C. and Gutiérrez, Félix (1985) *Minorities and Media: Diversity and the end of mass communication*, Newbury Park CA: Sage.

Wilson, Julie A. (2010) "Star testing: The emerging politics of celebrity gossip," *Velvet Light Trap,* no. 65, pp. 25–38.

Wilson, Scott (1997) "The indestructible beauty of suffering: Diana and the metaphor of global consumption," *Theory and Event*, vol. 1, no. 4. Available at: http://bit.ly/-WilsonIndestructible.

Winans, Robert B. and Kaufman, Elias J. (1994) "Minstrel and classic banjo: American and English connections," *American Music*, vol. 12, no. 1, pp. 1–30.

Wolfe, Tom (1976) "The 'me' decade and the third great awakening," *New York*, August 23. Available at: http://bit.ly/-WolfeMe.

Wolin, Sheldon S. (2008) *Democracy Inc.: Managed democracy and the specter of inverted totalitarianism*, Princeton NJ: Princeton University Press.

Wood, Nona L. and Wood, Robert A. (2002) "Stalking the stalker: a profile of offenders," *FBI Law Enforcement Bulletin*, vol. 71, no. 12 (December), pp. 1–7.

Ziegler, Maseena (2012) "The Kim Kardashian effect—why being overly confident pays off," *Forbeswoman*, August 14. Available at: http://bit.ly/-ZieglerKimKardashianEffect.

FILMS

2001: A Space Odyssey, Stanley Kubrick, 1968.
About Last Night, Edward Zwick, 1986.
Adventures of Don Juan, The, Vincent Sherman, 1948.
Adventures of Robin Hood, The, Michael Curtiz and William Keighley, 1938.
Alamo, The, John Wayne, 1960.
Anna Nicole, Keoni Waxman, 2007.
Arthur, Steve Gordon, 1981.
Asphalt Jungle, The, John Huston, 1950.
Austin Powers in Goldmember, Jay Roach, 2002.
Aviator, The, Martin Scorsese, 2004.
Babe, The, Arthur Hiller, 1992.
Bad Influence, Curtis Hanson, 1990.
Barbarella, Roger Vadim, 1968.
Batman Forever, Joel Schumacher, 1995.
Bend It Like Beckham, Gurinder Chadha, 2002.
Birth of a Nation, The, D.W. Griffith, 1915.
Bob Roberts, Tim Robbins, 1992.
Body of Evidence, Uli Edel, 1993.
Boogie Nights, Paul Thomas Anderson, 1997.
Bridget Jones's Diary, Sharon Maguire, 2001.
Buffalo Bill, William Wellman, 1944.
Bus Stop, Joshua Logan, 1956.
Captain Blood, Michael Curtiz, 1935.
Carlito's Way, Brian De Palma, 1993.
Cleopatra, Joseph L. Mankiewicz, 1963.

Color Purple, The, Steven Spielberg, 1985.
Days of Thunder, Tony Scott, 1990.
Dead Calm, Phillip Noyce, 1988.
Dead Man Walking, Tim Robbins, 1995.
Deliverance, John Boorman, 1972.
Dempsey, Gus Trikonis, 1983.
Dirty Harry, Don Siegel, 1971.
Dolce Vita, La, Federico Fellini, 1960.
Evita, Alan Parker, 1996.
Fan, The, Tony Scott, 1996.
Farewell to Arms, A, Frank Borzage, 1932.
Fistful of Dollars, A, Sergio Leone, 1964.
Flashdance, Adrian Lyne, 1983.
For Whom the Bell Tolls, Sam Wood, 1943.
Four Weddings and a Funeral, Mike Newell, 1994.
From Here to Eternity, Fred Zinnemann, 1953.
Funny Girl, William Wyler, 1968.
Funny Lady, Herbert Ross, 1975.
Gentleman Jim, Raoul Walsh, 1942.
Gigli, Martin Brest, 2003.
Glenn Miller Story, The, Anthony Mann, 1953.
Glory, Edward Zwick, 1989.
Gone With the Wind, Victor Fleming, 1939.
Great Expectations, David Lean, 1946.
Green Berets, The, John Wayne/Ray Kellogg, 1968.
Hangover, The, Todd Phillips, 2009.
Herbie: Fully Loaded, Angela Robinson, 2005.
Houdini, George Marshall, 1953.
House Calls, Howard Zieff, 1978.
House of Wax, Paige Edwards, 2005.
Hudsucker Proxy, The, Joel Coen, 1994.
Hustler, The, Robert Rossen, 1961.
In the Heat of the Night, Norman Jewison, 1967.
Jazz Singer, The, Alan Crosland, 1927.
Jersey Girl, Kevin Smith, 2004.
John Carter, Andrew Stanton, 2012.
Julius Caesar, Joseph L. Mankiewicz, 1953

Killers, The, Don Siegel, 1964.
King of Comedy, The, Martin Scorsese, 1982.
Klute, Alan J. Pakula, 1971.
LA Confidential, Curtis Hanson, 1997.
Lights of New York, Bryan Foy, 1928.
Lilies of the Field, Ralph Nelson, 1963.
Lindbergh, Stephen Ives, 1990.
Liz and Dick, Lloyd Kramer, 2012.
Long Hot Summer, Martin Ritt, 1958.
Love Actually, Richard Curtis, 2003.
MacArthur: The Rebel General, Joseph Sargent, 1977.
Maltese Falcon, The, John Huston, 1941.
Monster's Ball, Marc Forster, 2001.
Moulin Rouge, Baz Luhrmann, 2004.
Mulholland Falls, Lee Tamahori, 1996.
My Cousin Rachel, Henry Koster, 1952.
Naked Gun 33⅓: The final insult, Peter Segal, 1994.
Natural, The, Barry Levinson, 1984.
Nine to Five, Colin Higgins, 1980.
Organization, The, Don Medford, 1971.
Perfect, James Bridges, 1985.
Pledge This, William Heins, 2005.
Portrait of a Lady, Jane Campion, 1996.
Pretty Baby, Louis Malle, 1977.
Prime Minister, The, Thorold Dickinson, 1941.
Psycho, Alfred Hitchcock, 1960.
Public Enemy, The, William Wellman, 1931.
Repo! The Genetic Opera, Darren Lynn Bousman, 2008.
Richard III, Laurence Olivier, 1955.
Sands of Iwo Jima, Allan Dwan, 1940.
Saturday Night Fever, John Badham, 1977.
Scary Movie 5, Malcolm D. Lee, 2013.
Scenes from the Class Struggle in Beverly Hills, Paul Bartel, 1989.
Seven Year Itch, The, Billy Wilder, 1955.
sex, lies and videotape, Steven Soderbergh, 1989.
Shallow Hal, Peter and Bobby Farrelly, 2001.
Show Boat, James Whale, 1936.

Smokey and the Bandit, Hal Needham, 1977.
Some Like It Hot, Billy Wilder, 1959.
Somebody Up There Likes Me, Robert Wise, 1956.
Something's Got to Give, George Cukor, 1962.
St. Elmo's Fire, Joel Schumacher, 1985.
Stagecoach, John Ford, 1929.
They Call Me Mister Tibbs!, Gordon Douglas, 1970.
They Shoot Horses, Don't They?, Sydney Pollack, 1969.
Thin Red Line, The, Terrence Malick, 1998.
This Is It, Kenny Ortega, 2009.
To Die For, Gus Van Sant, 1995.
To Have and Have Not, Howard Hawkes, 1945.
Touch of Class, A, Melvin Frank, 1973.
Truth or Dare/In Bed with Madonna, Alek Keshishian, 1991.
Wayne's World, Penelope Spheeris, 1992.
White Heat, Raoul Walsh, 1949.
Winchester '73, Anthony Mann, 1950.
X-Men: The Last Stand, Brett Ratner, 2006.

INDEX